ELLEN TERRY'S MEMOIRS

ELLEN TERRY AT 50
(Her Favorite Photograph)

ELLEN TERRY'S
MEMOIRS

WITH A PREFACE, NOTES
AND ADDITIONAL
BIOGRAPHICAL CHAPTERS BY
EDITH CRAIG AND
CHRISTOPHER ST. JOHN

GREENWOOD PRESS, PUBLISHERS
WESTPORT, CONNECTICUT

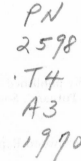

Originally published in 1932
by G.P. Putnam's Sons, New York

First Greenwood Reprinting 1970

Library of Congress Catalogue Card Number 77-100210

SBN 8371-4039-0

Printed in the United States of America

Preface

IN THIS new edition of Ellen Terry's autobiography, written during 1906 and 1907, and first published in its entirety under the title *The Story of My Life* in 1908, very few alterations have been made in the original text, beyond some cuts necessitated by the addition of the biographical chapters which complete the narrative. Corrections of slips, and other revisions calculated to increase the value of the book as an authoritative record, have been included in the editorial notes. We felt that if we began tinkering with Ellen Terry's work we might deprive it of its spontaneity, and decided to let well alone. The decision is all the more likely to be approved because people have recently been made aware of Ellen Terry's remarkable literary gifts. Since the publication of her correspondence with Bernard Shaw, revealing her as one of the most fascinating letter-writers that ever lived, and of her "Four Lectures on Shakespeare," permanently establishing her reputation as a great actress who studied character with penetrating insight, her genius for flashing down her thought on paper in a few vivid words has been widely proclaimed. Her old fame as a great actress and a great personality has been renewed after death by her fame as a writer, and possibly will be kept alive by it.

It may seem strange to those who discerned the fine quality of her autobiography when they first read it years ago that this literary fame should not have come to her until her letters to Bernard Shaw were published. Perhaps the explanation is that the memoirs of all celebrities who are not professional writers are approached with a certain prejudice. It is considered extremely unlikely that they will have any literary merit, and, such is the power of preconceived notions, when they possess it, it is often not perceived. Critical opinion of the memoirs of actors or actresses is further biased by an old tradition that the greatest of them are stupid outside their own art. It must be admitted that they have done little to discredit this tradition by their published writings. Their reminiscences usually consist of a series of egotistical anecdotes about their stage triumphs, and not realising that these would have a certain ingenuous charm if told by themselves without any literary pretence, they often delegate the telling to a professional writer. The few letters Irving really wrote himself are of far more interest than the many written for him by the journalists in his retinue at the Lyceum, and one often wishes when one reads the lectures they composed for him that he had expressed his own ideas in his own unaffected way. But he disliked writing, and was too much absorbed in his art to take the slightest interest in anything else. In this he differed from Ellen Terry, who, hard as she worked at the art for which she had an hereditary vocation as well as a natural genius, was never completely absorbed in it. Life interested her in other aspects than in its relation to the theatre; she found it easy and delightful to express this interest in writing. Letters were her medium, and she poured them out by the thousand. There is no better way of learning to do a thing than to do it. It was through the constant practice her correspondence gave her pen that Ellen Terry learned to write with a vividness, a grace, and above all with a directness, which make her autobiography a notable piece of literature.

Only a few people had the courage to rank it as high as that when it was first published. Max Beerbohm was one; the late George Wyndham another. Bernard Shaw, who, three years earlier, in an article on Ellen Terry, contributed to the Neue Freie Presse (Vienna), had alluded to the "real literary power of her direct and penetrating letters" may have been a third, but I have searched in vain for his tribute to her autobiography. There is plenty of documentary evidence on the other hand that the majority of the reviewers, to whom the timid reader looks for guidance before forming an opinion of a book, could not see, or would not proclaim, the greatness of The Story of My Life. They agreed that it was surprisingly good for an actress, but this was not very high praise, since, as we have already pointed out, the standard set by the reminiscences of actors and actresses is very low. Such a patronising tribute did not suffice to turn away the wrath of George Wyndham, as the letter printed below proves. We have quoted it in full because there is more in it of interest than the rebuke to the reviewers. It should help readers of the new generation to understand the position Ellen Terry occupied in the life of her time. Wyndham indirectly confirms a statement, made by Shaw, (also in the article in the Neue Freie Presse), that "every famous man of the last quarter of the 19th century, provided he were a theatre-goer, had been in love with Ellen Terry."

1 Lowndes Street S.W.
28 November 1908.

DEAR LADY,—

Once you were my hostess, and Henry Irving my host, at supper in the Beefsteak Room; and again, long before that, because you were Ophelia, Portia, Juliet, Beatrice, you were part of my youth.

But I make no excuse for writing. I have just finished The Story Of My Life. I shall begin it again tomorrow. Meanwhile I wish to thank you for having written the book with all my heart, and to tell you with all my head that it has its place with the very few autobiographies that will always be read. It angers me that reviewers should not have proclaimed this. What are they for?

The next time I am bullied into "responding for Literature," I shall tell them how great your work is, and how little they are not to have said so. Everybody who is alive enough to love life without fearing death is in love with your book. Your book is our youth, and it has in it more beauty than others show, more duty than other do.

You will never "have done with being beautiful" because by this book you have managed to play that part forever.

Yours gratefully,
GEORGE WYNDHAM

When Wyndham wrote the last sentence of his perfect tribute, it did not occur to him that as time went on that part of Ellen Terry's to which he alludes might be played in a theatre closed to the reading public. Yet this is what would have happened if this new edition of her book had not been published. For many years previously it had been out of print, and people whose interest in it had been roused by a quotation from its pages in an article, or by some public reference or other to its fascinations, found the quest of a copy required considerable pertinacity if it was to be successful. Wyndham's opinion that it has its place with the very few autobiographies "that will always be read" could be only very inadequately vindicated as long as it could not be read at all without an effort to which people are averse in these most labour-saving times. Now that the first step has been taken towards putting it among the classics, there is a hope that it will often be reprinted in the future, and the prophecy that it will always be read be fulfilled. At any rate the immediate danger of its going out of circulation and being forgotten has been averted.

Ellen Terry's record of her life covers a period of about sixty years. She had not quite finished it when in the autumn of 1906, the year of her stage jubilee, she went to America for a long tour under Charles Frohman's management. The two people responsible for this new edition of her book were members of the company she took with her. One of them, her daughter Edith Craig, was engaged as stage-manager, as she had been on Ellen Terry's tours of the English provinces in 1903 and 1904. She also played a part in "The Good Hope", which, with "Nance Oldfield", was alternated with "Captain Brassbound's Conversion" during the American tour. The other, Edith Craig's most intimate friend Christopher St. John, the author of the English version of "The Good Hope", who had for some time acted as a sort of literary henchman to Ellen Terry, had not such an obvious claim to be included in the company. In engaging her Ellen Terry was influenced by the fact that she was collaborating with her in her autobiography. They both hoped that they would be able to get on with it during the tour, but for a variety of reasons this proved impossible. The work had to be put on one side until Ellen Terry returned to England in the summer of 1907. It was resumed in circumstances which account for the undeniable scrappiness of the last chapters. During the American tour Ellen Terry had married again, and absorbed in the present, had lost interest in things past. Having other fish to fry, she left the task of finishing the book almost entirely to her collaborator. She, who had been in close touch with her chief in its earlier phases, now met her rarely. While Ellen Terry was touring the provinces with her husband in "Captain Brassbound's Conversion", there was nothing to do but make shift with her diaries and letters. It was only by resorting to copious quotations that the deserted collaborator was able to bring the autobiography up to the length required by contracts with editors and publishers.

Dr Johnson once expressed the opinion that the finest books in the world owe their existence to duns. This is an encouragement to admit that Ellen Terry's book might never have been written if she had not had the incentive of being eager to retrieve her fortunes. She had lost the greater part of her savings by her first venture into management at the Imperial Theatre in 1903, and any opportunity for making the loss good was welcome during the next few years. She regarded her autobiography as a potboiler, and never took any pride in it. Some of her most intimate friends did not even know she had written it until it was issued in instalments in American and English periodicals.

(McClure's Magazine and M.A.P.). There is no mention of it in her correspondence with Bernard Shaw, although she was writing to him frequently at the time she was engaged on it. This curious indifference was construed by some people as a proof that the book was not her own literary offspring. Its authorship was attributed to her collaborator, whose denials that she had done more than assist in the selection and arrangement of the material were for the most part ignored. It was not until the publication of the Shaw-Terry correspondence that the possibility that the collaborator had told the exact truth about her share in the autobiography was admitted. Then those who had asserted most confidently that it was no more genuine Ellen Terry than Mozart's Requiem genuine Mozart, began to waver. There was no doubt that the letters to Shaw were genuine, yet they were written in the self-same style as the autobiography, and brought as vividly before the reader the self-same woman, a woman who was like nobody else, physically, mentally or spiritually. In the course of a comparison between Ellen Terry and Henry Irving Shaw makes a point of this uniqueness. "They both had beautiful and interesting faces, but faces like Irving's have looked at the world for hundreds of years past from portraits of churchmen, statesmen, princes and saints, while Ellen Terry's face had never been seen in the world before. The much-abused word 'unique' is literally true of Ellen Terry. If Shakespeare had met Irving in the street, he would have recognized a distinguished but familiar type. Had he met Ellen Terry, he would have stared at a new and irresistibly attractive species of womankind."

Although *The Story Of My Life* was not a best-seller, it met with enough success in England and America to make publishers offer Ellen Terry generous terms for a sequel, but she could not be induced to write it. One reason for her disinclination may have been that it had distressed her to find that some candid remarks in the book had given offence. We remember her saying, apropos of a letter from the editor of an American journal on the subject of further reminiscences, that she was not going to put her foot in it again. Another time when the project of bringing her autobiography up to date was being discussed she raised the objection that although her memory of things long past was clear enough, she had but a vague and confused recollection of things less remote. "They would not be of the slightest interest to any one if I could remember them," she added, but she was talking in wartime when everything seemed of slight interest and importance

ix

compared with the daily massacre of innocents on the battlefield, and artists were particularly prone to pessimism about their value in the world. It is true however that Ellen Terry's public life was less eventful in age than in youth. Unlike her great contemporaries, Sarah Bernhardt, and Eleanora Duse, she was seen but rarely on the stage (although she did not definitely retire from it) for many years before her death. Her career as an actress ended soon after the date at which she ends her autobiography. But because, apart from her genius as an actress, she was a very remarkable woman, her saga is incomplete without the chronicle of her last years.

The obligation of those who possess the data for this chronicle to add it has been more fully realized by them since the publication of Gordon Craig's biographical study *Ellen Terry and Her Secret Self* (1932). Bernard Shaw has described the story, given in the appendix to Craig's book, of how the Shaw-Terry letters came to be published as a "string of flat whoppers", but this humorous aspersion on Craig's accuracy might not prevent his being accepted in the future as a reliable authority on his mother's last years if no comparison were possible between his record and another by some authority with equally impressive credentials. The claim of Ellen Terry's daughter to be such an authority is not likely to be disputed except by the few persons who are of the antiquated opinion that daughters count for less than sons. It is not so much for the instruction of readers to-day as for that of some future biographer of Ellen Terry who may consult both authorities, that the advantage one possessed over the other is emphasised. The daughter was constantly with her mother during the last twenty years of her life; the son saw her at rare intervals after the year 1904 when he went to live abroad. The correspondence between them slackened as Ellen Terry aged, and had ceased altogether for some time before she died. Consequently Gordon Craig had little direct knowledge on which to base the last chapters of his biography, and it is not surprising that as a record they should be inadequate, and at times inaccurate. It seems to us necessary that an accurate record of the last years and death of Ellen Terry should be published. In completing her memoirs we have tried to abstain from making statements which cannot be authenticated, and from presenting fanciful conjectures in the guise of ascertained truths. If we have failed in this we cannot offer the excuse that we knew no better—an excuse which can be offered for the little inaccuracies in Gordon Craig's book which some persons affected by them may have taken too seriously.

The biographical chapters, like this preface and the editorial notes, are the work of us both in council (although the actual writing is by one hand), but in them the cumbersome plural method of addressing the reader, adopted here to emphasise our joint responsibility, has been abandoned. The substitution of the singular personal pronoun was decided on not only on account of its greater simplicity; it was felt that it would allow the writer in the partnership, for whom it stands, more freedom to deal with some episodes in Ellen Terry's life than she could have if she spoke for Ellen Terry's daughter as well as for herself. What is true delicacy in a daughter may be false delicacy in a biographer.

We have found Ellen Terry the best authority on Ellen Terry. She knew herself, and could reveal herself, better than anyone else. From her letters, diaries and note-books we have derived by far the most valuable material for amplifying and completing her autobiography. We are none the less grateful for the permission given us by some of her correspondents, still living, and by the heirs of others who are dead, to quote passages from their letters to her. Thanks are also due to various authors and publishers who have sanctioned the quotation of passages from books containing references to Ellen Terry.

EDITH CRAIG

CHRISTOPHER ST. JOHN

Smallhythe, Tenterden, Kent.
June, 1932.

Contents

xiii

Illustrations

ELLEN TERRY'S

MEMOIRS

Ellen Terry's Introduction[1]

"When I read the book, the biography famous,
  And is this then (said I) what the author calls a man's life?
  And so will someone, when I am dead and gone, write my life?
  As if any man really knew aught of my life!
  Why even I myself, I often think, know little or nothing of my real life.
  Only a few hints—a few diffused faint clues and indirections—
    I seek . . . to trace out here."

                                                    WALT WHITMAN

FOR YEARS I have contemplated telling this story, and I wish now I
had not put off telling it so long. There is some truth in the jibe
that memoirs are usually written by people who are too old to remember
anything. I know my recollections of the past are more hazy and frag-
mentary to-day than at the time, about fifteen years ago, I wrote a few
of them down in *Stray Memories*. This would not be such a disadvantage
if I had kept a systematic record of my life. But although from my youth
I have been a diligent diarist, I have little to show for it. The diaries
I have preserved are queer miscellanies. I used paste-pot and scissors
more frequently than a pen. It was my custom to cut out anything in
my morning newspaper that interested me and stick it in my diary.
By the end of the year Mr. Letts might well have been ashamed to be
associated with it. It had been transformed from a neat little volume into
a sort of dustbin, overflowing with odds and ends of information. The
biggest elastic band made could hardly encircle its bulk, swollen by
newspaper cuttings, letters, dried flowers, recipes, telegrams, snapshots
and what not! Ransacking these medleys in the hope of finding something useful is like searching for a needle in a bottle of hay. I ought

---

[1] In Ellen Terry's annotated copy of the first English edition of *The Story of My Life*
there is evidence that she intended to revise some passages in the Introduction. They
have been omitted in this reprint. The reader has not been deprived of anything except
a few wholly unnecessary apologies from Ellen Terry for her literary shortcomings.

3

not to regret that about six years ago when I moved into a smaller house in London I burned a great many of my old diaries with other unmovable rubbish, yet I find myself yearning for them as I try to summon up remembrance of things past.

Well, it must be "now or never", I said in this year of my stage jubilee when I was urged to write my reminiscences. I consented, and then began to feel frightened. I knew much would be expected of me because I had had an eventful life, and known many of the most distinguished men and women of my time. My fifty years on the stage alone supplied enough material for fifty books, for each of those years had been full of incident. The difficulty was that as I looked back, I could not see my experiences spread out in bold relief. They stretched away from me in a dim perspective with my birth as the vanishing point.

How was I to begin? That was another difficulty! Fortunately it was eased by the remark of a friend who was helping me to arrange the material. "Begin at the beginning. What is the first thing you remember? Write that down as a start."

Once I had acted on this simple and practical suggestion, I felt happier about my task. The clearness and definiteness of that first memory encouraged me. If I could describe it, why not other memories less remote?

So I began the story of my life. I have told it faithfully according to my light, keeping in mind Othello's words: "Nothing extenuate, nor write down aught in malice." I have been helped in my researches by many kind people. I thank them all, and especially those who have allowed me to publish some of their letters to me.

ELLEN TERRY

4

PART ONE

AUTOBIOGRAPHY BY ELLEN TERRY

(1848–1906)

CHAPTER I

A CHILD OF THE STAGE

(1848–1858)

§ 1

THIS is the first thing I remember.

In the corner of a lean-to whitewashed attic stood a fine, plain, solid oak bureau. By climbing up on to this bureau I could see from the window the glories of the sunset. My attic was on a hill in a large and busy town, and the smoke of a thousand chimneys hung like a grey veil between me and the fires in the sky. When the sun had set, and the scarlet and gold, violet and primrose, and all those magic colours that have no names, had faded into the dark, there were other fires for me to see. The flaming forges came out and terrified while they fascinated my childish imagination.

What did it matter to me that I was locked in, and that my father and mother, with my elder sister Kate, were all at the theatre? I had the sunset, the forges, and the oak bureau.

I cannot say how old I was at this time, but I am sure that it wasn't long after my birth (which I cant remember, although I have often been asked to decide in which house at Coventry I was born!). At any rate, I had not then seen a theatre, and I took to the stage before many years had passed over my head.

Putting together what I remember, and such authentic history as there is of my parents' movements, I gather that this attic was in theatrical lodgings in Glasgow. My father was an actor, my mother an actress, and they were at this time on tour in Scotland. Perhaps this is the place to say that father was the son of an Irish builder, and that he eloped in a chaise with mother, who was the daughter of a Scottish minister. I am afraid I know no details of their romance. As for my less immediate ancestry it is "wropt in mystery." Were we all people of the stage? There was a Daniel Terry who was not only a famous actor in his day, but a friend of Sir Walter Scott's. There was an Eliza Terry, an actress, whose portrait appears in *The Dramatic Mirror* in

7

1847. But so far as I know I cannot claim kinship with either Eliza or Daniel.

I have a very dim recollection of anything that happened in the attic, beyond the fact that when my father and mother went to the theatre every night, they used to put me to bed and that directly their backs were turned and the door locked, I used to jump up and go to the window. My "bed" consisted of the mattress pulled off their bed and laid on the floor—on father's side. Both my father and my mother were very kind and devoted parents (though severe at times, as all good parents are), but while mother loved all her children too well to make favourites, I was, I believe, my father's particular pet. I used to sleep all night holding his hand.

One night I remember waking up to find a beautiful face bending over me. Father was holding a candle so that the visitor might see me better. It was my aunt—my mother's sister. I had never seen her before, and I thought for a while she was an angel. She had the softest, sweetest expression and deep-lidded golden eyes. She wore a brown silk pelisse and a bonnet, and a long gold watch-chain round her neck; it dangled on to my nose and woke me.

I hold very strongly that a child's earliest impressions mould its character perhaps more than either heredity or education. I am sure it is true in my case. What first impressed me? An attic, an oak bureau, a lovely face, a bed on the floor. Things have come and gone in my life since then, but they have been powerless to efface those early impressions. I adore pretty faces. I cant keep away from shops where they sell good old furniture like my bureau. I like plain rooms with low ceilings better than any other rooms; and for my afternoon siesta, which is one of my institutions, I often choose the floor in preference to bed or sofa.

What we remember in our childhood and what we are told afterwards often become inextricably confused in our minds, and after the bureau and Aunt Lizzie, my memory is a blank for some years. I cant even tell you when it was first decided that I was to go on the stage, but I expect it was when I was born, for in those days theatrical folk did not imagine that their children *could* do anything but follow their parents' profession.

I must depend now on hearsay for certain facts. The first fact is my birth, which should, perhaps, have been mentioned before anything else. To speak by the certificate, I was born on the 27th February, 1848, at Coventry. Many years afterwards, when people were kind enough to think that the house in which I was born deserved to be discovered, there was a dispute as to which house in Market Street could claim me.

8

handsome me — It was my Aunt — my mothers sister. I had never seen her before & I thought actually she was an Angel for she had the softest sweetest expression & deep little golden eyes. She wore a brown silk ~~flowered~~ Pelisse & a bonnet, & a long (old) watch chain round her neck. it dangled on to my nose & woke me.

A FRAGMENT OF ELLEN TERRY'S MANUSCRIPT

The dispute was left unsettled in rather a curious way. On one side of the narrow street a haberdasher's shop bore the inscription, "Birthplace of Ellen Terry." On the other, an eating-house declared itself to be "the original birthplace!" I have never been able to arbitrate in the matter, my statement that my mother had always said that the house was "on the right-hand side, coming from the market-place," being apparently of no use. I have heard lately that one of the birthplaces has retired from the competition, and that the haberdasher has the field to himself. I am glad, for the sake of those friends of mine who have bought his handkerchiefs and ties as souvenirs. There is, however, nothing very attractive about the house itself. It is better built than a house of the same size would be built now, and it has a certain old-fashioned respectability, but that is the end of its praises. Coventry itself makes up for the deficiency. It is a delightful town, and it was a happy chance that made me a native of Warwickshire, Shakespeare's own county. Sarah Kemble married Mr Siddons at Coventry too—another happy omen.

I have acted twice in my native town in old days, but never in recent years. In 1904 I planned to act there again, but unfortunately I was taken ill at Cambridge, and the doctors would not allow me to go to Coventry. The morning my company left Cambridge without me, I was very miserable. It is always hateful to disappoint the public, and on this occasion I was compelled to break faith where I most wished to keep it. I heard afterwards from my daughter (who played some of my parts instead of me) that many of the Coventry people thought I had never meant to come at all. If this should meet their eyes, I hope they will believe that this was not so. My ambition to play at Coventry again shall be realized yet.[1]

I can well imagine that the children of some strolling players used to have a hard time of it, but my mother was not one to shirk her duties. She worked hard at her profession and yet found it possible not to *drag* up her children, to live or die as it might happen, but to *bring* them up to be healthy, happy, and wise—theatre-wise, at any rate. When her babies were too small to be left at the lodgings (which she and my father took in each town they visited as near to the theatre as possible), she would bundle them up in a shawl and put them to sleep in her dressing-room. So it was, that long before I spoke in a theatre, I slept in one.

Later on, when we were older and mother could leave us at home,

---

[1] Since I wrote this, I have again visited my native town—this time to receive its civic congratulations on the occasion of my jubilee, and as recently as March of the present year I acted at the new Empire Theatre.

there was a fire one night at our lodgings, and she rushed out of the theatre and up the street in an agony of terror. She got us out of the house all right, took us to the theatre, and went on with the next act as if nothing had happened. Such fortitude is commoner in our profession, I think, than in any other. We "go on with the next act" whatever happens, and if we know our business, no one in the audience will ever guess that anything is wrong—that since the curtain last went down some dear friend has died, or our children in the theatrical lodgings up the street have run the risk of being burnt to death.

My mother had eleven children altogether, but only nine survived their infancy, and of these nine, my eldest brother, Ben, and my sister Florence have since died. My sister Kate, who left the stage at an age when most of the young women of the present day take to it for the first time, and made an enduring reputation in a few brilliant years, was the eldest of the family. Then came a sister, who died, and I was the third. After us came Ben, George, Marion, Flossie, Charles, Tom, and Fred. Six out of the nine have been on the stage, but only Marion, Fred, and I are there still.

Two or three members of this large family, at the most, were in existence when I first entered a theatre in a professional capacity, so I will leave them all alone for the present. I had better confess at once that I dont remember this great event, and my sister Kate is unkind enough to say that it never happened—to me! The story, she asserts, was told of her. But without damning proofs she is not going to make me believe it! Shall I be robbed of the only experience of my first eight years of life? Never!

During the rehearsals of a pantomime in a Scottish town (Glasgow, I think: Glasgow has always been an eventful place for me!), a child was wanted for the Spirit of the Mustard-pot. What more natural than that my father should offer my services? I had a shock of pale yellow hair, I was small enough to be put into the property mustard-pot, and the Glasgow stage manager would easily assume that I had inherited talent. My father had acted with Macready in the stock seasons both at Edinburgh and Glasgow, and bore a very high reputation with Scottish audiences. But the stage manager and father alike reckoned without their actress! When they tried to put me into the mustard-pot, I yelled lustily and showed more lung-power than aptitude for the stage.

"Pit your child into the mustard-pot, Mr Terry," said the stage manager.

"Damn you and your mustard-pot, sir!" said my mortified father. "I wont frighten my child for you or any one else!"

But all the same he was bitterly disappointed at my first dramatic

10

failure, and when we reached home he put me in the corner to chasten me. *"You'll* never make an actress!" he said, shaking a reproachful finger at me.

It is *my* mustard-pot, and why Kate should want it, I cant think! She hadnt yellow hair, and she couldnt possibly have behaved so badly. I have often heard my parents say significantly that they had no trouble with *Kate!* Before she was four, she was dancing a hornpipe in a sailor's jumper, a rakish little hat, and a diminutive pair of white ducks! Those ducks, marked "Kate Terry," were kept by mother for years as a precious relic, and are, I hope, still in the family archives!

I stick to the mustard-pot, but I entirely disclaim the little Duke of York in Richard III, which some one with a good memory stoutly insists he saw me play before I made my first appearance as Mamillius. Except for this abortive attempt at Glasgow, I was never on any stage even for a rehearsal until 1856, at the Princess's Theatre, when I appeared with Charles Kean in "A Winter's Tale."

The man with the memory may have seen Kate as one of the Princes in the Tower, but he never saw me with her. Kate was called up to London in 1852 to play Prince Arthur in Charles Kean's production of "King John," and after that she acted in all his plays, until he gave up management in 1859. She had played Arthur during a stock season at Edinburgh, and so well, that some one sang her praises to Kean and advised him to engage her. My mother took Kate to London, and I was left with my father in the provinces for two years. I cant recall much about those two years except sunsets and a great mass of shipping looming up against the sky. The sunsets followed me about everywhere; the shipping was in Liverpool, where father was engaged for a considerable time. He never ceased teaching me to be useful, alert, and quick. Sometimes he hastened my perceptive powers with a slipper, and always he corrected me if I pronounced any word in a slipshod fashion. He himself was a beautiful elocutionist, and if I now speak my language well it is in no small degree due to my early training.

It was to his elocution that father owed his engagement with Macready, of whom he always spoke in terms of the most affectionate admiration in after years, and probably it did him a good turn again with Charles Kean. An actor who had supported Macready with credit was just the actor likely to be useful to a manager who was producing a series of plays by Shakespeare. Kate had been a success at the Princess's, too, in child parts, and this may have reminded Mr Kean to send for Kate's father! At any rate he was sent for towards the end of the year 1853 and left Liverpool for London. I know I cooked his breakfasts for him in Liverpool, but I havent the slightest recollection of the next two years in London. As I am determined not to fill up the early blanks with stories of my own invention, I must go straight on to 1856, when rehearsals were called at the Princess's Theatre for Shakespeare's "Winter's Tale."

§ 2

THE Charles Keans, from whom I received my first engagement, were both remarkable people, and at the Princess's Theatre were doing very remarkable work. Kean the younger had not the fire and genius of his wonderful father, Edmund, and but for the inherited splendour of his name it is not likely that he would ever have attained great eminence as an actor. His Wolsey and his Richard (the Second, not the Third) were his best parts, perhaps because in them his beautiful elocution had full scope, and his limitations were not noticeable. But it is more as a stage reformer than as an actor that he will be remembered. The old happy-go-lucky way of staging plays, with its sublime indifference to correctness of detail and its utter disregard of archæology, had received its first blow from Kemble and Macready, but Charles Kean gave it much harder knocks and went further than either of them in the good work.

It is an old story and a true one that when Edmund Kean made his first great success as Shylock, after a long and miserable struggle as a strolling player, he came home to his wife and said: "You shall ride in your own carriage," and then, catching up his little son, added, "and Charley shall go to Eton!" Well, Charley did go to Eton, and if Eton did not make him a great actor, it opened his eyes to the absurd anachronisms in costumes and accessories which prevailed on the stage at that period, and when he undertook the management of the Princess's Theatre, he turned his classical education to account. In addition to scholarly knowledge, he had a naturally refined taste and the power of selecting the right man to help him. Planché, the great authority on historical costume, was one of his ablest coadjutors, and Mr Bradshaw designed all the properties. It has been said lately that I began my career on an unfurnished stage, when the play was the thing, and spectacle was considered of small importance. I take this opportunity of contradicting that statement most emphatically. Neither when I began, nor yet later in my career, have I ever played under a management where infinite pains were not given to every detail. I think that far from hampering the acting, a beautiful and congruous background and harmonious costumes, representing accurately the spirit of the time in which the play is supposed to move, ought to help and inspire the actor.

12

Such thoughts as these did not trouble my head when I acted with the Keans, but, child as I was, the beauty of the productions at the Princess's Theatre made a great impression on me, and my memory of them is quite clear enough, even if there were not plenty of other evidence, for me to assert that in some respects they were even more elaborate than those of the present day. I know that the buns of one's childhood always seem in memory much bigger and better than the buns sold nowadays, but even allowing for the natural glamour which the years throw over buns and rooms, places and plays alike, I am quite certain that Charles Kean's productions of Shakespeare would astonish the modern critic who regards the period of my first appearance as a sort of dark age in the scenic art of the theatre.

I have alluded to the beauty of Charles Kean's elocution. His voice was also of a wonderful quality—soft and low, yet distinct and clear as a bell. When he played Richard II the magical charm of this organ was alone enough to keep the house spell-bound. His vivid personality made a strong impression on me. Yet others only remember that he called his wife "Delly," though she was Nelly, and always spoke as if he had a cold in his head. How strange! If I did not understand what suggested impressions so different from my own, they would make me more indignant.

Now who shall arbitrate?
Ten men love what I hate,
Shun what I follow, slight what I receive.
Ten who in ears and eyes
Match me; they all surmise,
They this thing, and I that:
Whom shall my soul believe?

What he owed to Mrs Kean, he would have been the first to confess. In many ways she was the leading spirit in the theatre; at the least, a joint ruler, not a queen-consort. During the rehearsals Mr Kean used to sit in the stalls with a loud-voiced dinner-bell by his side, and when anything went wrong on the stage, he would ring it ferociously, and everything would come to a stop, until Mrs Kean, who always sat on the stage, had set right what was wrong. She was more formidable than beautiful to look at, but her wonderful fire and genius were none the less impressive because she wore a white handkerchief round her head and had a very beaky nose! How I admired and loved and feared her! Later on, the fear was replaced by gratitude, for no woman ever gave herself more trouble to train a young actress than did Mrs Kean. The love and admiration, I am glad to say, remained and grew. It is

13

rare that it falls to the lot of any one to have such an accomplished teacher. Her patience and industry were splendid.

It was Mrs Kean who chose me out of five or six other children to play my first part. We were all tried in it, and when we had finished, she said the same thing to us all: "That's very nice! Thank you, my dear. That will do."

We none of us knew at the time which of us had pleased her most.

At this time we were living in the upper part of a house in the Gower Street region. That first home in London I remember chiefly by its fine brass knocker, which mother kept beautifully bright, and by its being the place to which I was sent my first part! Bound in green American cloth, it looked to me more marvellous than the most priceless book has ever looked since! I was so proud and pleased and delighted that I danced a hornpipe for joy!

Why was I chosen, and not one of the other children, for the part of Mamillius, some one may ask. It was not mere luck, I think. Perhaps I was a born actress, but that would have served me little if I had not been able to *speak!* It must be remembered that both my sister Kate and I had been trained almost from our birth for the stage, and particularly in the important branch of clear articulation. Father, as I have already said, was a very charming elocutionist, and my mother read Shakespeare beautifully. They were both very fond of us and saw our faults with eyes of love, though they were unsparing in their corrections. In those early days they had need of all their patience, for I was a most troublesome, wayward pupil. However, "the labour we delight in physics pain," and I hope, too, that my more staid sister made it up to them!

The rehearsals for "A Winter's Tale" were a lesson in fortitude. They taught me once and for all that an actress's life (even when the actress is only eight) is not all beer and skittles, or cakes and ale, or fame and glory. I was cast for the part of Mamillius in the way I have described, and my heart swelled with pride when I was told what I had to do, when I realised that I had a real Shakespeare part—a possession that father had taught me to consider the pride of life!

But many weary hours were to pass before the first night. If a company has to rehearse four hours a day now, it is considered a great hardship, and players must lunch and dine like other folk. But this was not Kean's way! Rehearsals lasted all day, Sundays included, and when there was no play running at night, until four or five the next morning! I dont think any actor in those days dreamed of luncheon. How my poor little legs used to ache! Sometimes I could hardly keep my eyes open when I was on the stage, and often when my scene was over, I used to creep into the greenroom and forget my troubles and my art (if you can talk of art in connection with a child of eight) in a delicious sleep.

At the dress-rehearsals I did not want to sleep. All the members of the company were allowed to sit and watch the scenes in which they were not concerned, from the back of the dress-circle. This, by the way, is an excellent plan, and in theatres where it is followed the young actress has reason to be grateful. In these days of greater publicity when the press attend dress-rehearsals, there may be strong reasons against the company being "in front," but the perfect loyalty of all concerned would dispose of these reasons. Now, for the first time, the beginner is able to see the effect of the weeks of thought and labour which have been given to the production. She can watch from the front the fulfilment of what she has only seen as intention and promise during the other rehearsals. But I am afraid that beginners now are not so keen as they used to be. The first wicked thing I did in a theatre sprang from excess of keenness. I borrowed a knife from a carpenter and made a slit in the canvas to watch Mrs Kean as Hermione!

Devoted to her art, conscientious to a degree in mastering the spirit and details of her part, Mrs Kean also possessed the personality and force to chain the attention and indelibly imprint her rendering of a part on the imagination. When I think of the costume in which she played Hermione, it seems marvellous to me that she could have produced the impression that she did. This seems to contradict what I have said about the magnificence of the production. But not at all! The designs of the dresses were purely classic; but actors and actresses seemed unable to keep their own period and their own individuality out of the clothes directly they got them on their backs. In some cases the original design was quite swamped. No matter what character Mrs Kean was assuming, she always used to wear her hair drawn flat over her forehead and twisted tight round her ears in a kind of circular sweep—such as the old writing-masters used to make when they attempted an extra grand flourish. And then the amount of petticoats she wore! Even as Hermione she was always bunched out by layer upon layer of petticoats, in defiance of the fact that classical parts should not be dressed in a superfluity of raiment. But if the petticoats were full of starch, the voice was full of pathos, and the dignity, simplicity, and womanliness of Mrs Charles Kean's Hermione could not have been marred by a far more grotesque costume.

There is something, I suppose, in a woman's nature which always makes her remember how she was dressed at any specially eventful moment of her life, and I can see myself, as though it were yesterday,

15

in the little red-and-silver dress I wore as Mamillius. Mrs Grieve, the dresser—"Peter Grieve-us" as we children called her—had pulled me into my very pink tights (they were by no means *tight* but very baggy, according to the picture of me), and my mother had arranged my hair in sausage curls on each side of my head in even more perfect order and regularity than usual. Besides my clothes, I had a beautiful "property" to be proud of. This was a go-cart, which had been made in the theatre by Mr Bradshaw, and was an exact copy of a child's toy as depicted on a Greek vase. It was my duty to drag this little cart about the stage, and on the first night, when Mr Kean as Leontes told me to "go play," I obeyed his instructions with such vigour that I tripped over the handle and came down on my back! A titter ran through the house, and I felt that my career as an actress was ruined forever. Even now I remember how bitterly I wept, and how deeply humiliated I felt. But the little incident, so mortifying to me, did not spoil my first appearance altogether. *The Times* of May 1, 1856, was kind enough to call me "vivacious and precocious," and "a worthy relative of my sister Kate"; my parents were pleased (although they would not show it too much), and Mrs Kean gave me a pat on the back. Father and Kate were both in the cast, too, and the Queen, Prince Albert, and the Princess Royal were all in a box on the first night.

From April 28, 1856, I played Mamillius every night for one hundred and two nights. I was never ill, and my understudy, Clara Denvil, a very handsome, dark child with flaming eyes, though quite ready and longing to play my part, never had the chance.

I had now taken the first step, but I had taken it without any notion of what I was doing. I was innocent of all art, and while I loved the actual doing of my part, I hated the labour that led up to it. But the time was soon to come when I was to be fired by a passion for work. Meanwhile I was unconsciously learning a number of lessons which were to be most useful to me in my subsequent career.

§ 3

From April 1856 until 1859 I acted constantly at the Princess's Theatre with the Keans, spending the summer holidays in acting at Ryde. My whole life was the theatre, and naturally all my early memories are connected with it. At breakfast father would begin the day's "coaching." Often I had to lay down my fork and say my lines. He would conduct these extra rehearsals anywhere—in the street, in the 'bus—we were never safe! I remember vividly going into a chemist's shop and being stood upon a stool to say my part to the chemist! Such leisure as I had from my profession was spent in "minding" the younger children—an occupation in which I delighted. They all had very pretty hair, and I used to wash it and comb it out until it looked as fine and bright as floss silk.

It is argued now that stage life is bad for a young child, and children are not allowed by law to appear on the stage until they are ten years old—quite a mature age in my young days! I cannot discuss the whole question here, and must content myself with saying that during my three years at the Princess's I was a very strong, happy, and healthy child. I was never out of the bill except during the run of "A Midsummer Night's Dream," when, through an unfortunate accident, I broke my toe. I was playing Puck, my second part on any stage, and had come up through a trap at the end of the last act to give the final speech. My sister Kate was playing Titania that night as understudy to Carlotta Leclercq. Up I came—but not quite up, for the man shut the trap-door too soon and caught my toe. I screamed. Kate rushed to me and banged her foot on the stage, but the man only closed the trap tighter, mistaking the signal.

"Oh, Katie! Katie!" I cried. "Oh, Nelly! Nelly!" said poor Kate helplessly. Then Mrs Kean came rushing on and made them open the trap and release my poor foot.

"Finish the play, dear," she whispered excitedly, "and I'll double your salary!" There was Kate holding me up on one side and Mrs Kean on the other. Well, I did finish the play in a fashion. The text ran something like this:

> If we shadows have offended (Oh, Katie, Katie!)
> Think but this, and all is mended, (Oh, my toe!)
> That you have but slumbered here,
> While these visions did appear. (I cant, I cant!)
> And this weak and idle theme,
> No more yielding but a dream, (Oh, dear! oh, dear!)
> Gentles, do not reprehend; (A big sob)
> If you pardon, we will mend. (Oh, Mrs. Kean!)

How I got through it, I dont know! But my salary was doubled—it had been fifteen shillings, and it was raised to thirty—and Mr Skey, of Bartholomew's Hospital, who chanced to be in a stall that very evening, came round behind the scenes and put my toe right. He remained my friend for life.

I was not chosen for Puck because I had played Mamillius with some credit. The same examination was gone through, and again I came out first. During the rehearsals Mrs Kean taught me to draw my breath in through my nose and begin a laugh—a very valuable accomplishment! She was also indefatigable in her lessons in clear enunciation, and I can hear her now lecturing the ladies of the company on their vowels. "A, E, I, O, U, my dear," she used to say, "are five distinct vowels, so dont mix them all up together, as if you were making a pudding. If you want to say, 'I am going on the river,' say it plainly and dont tell us you are going on the 'riv*ah!*' You must say *her,* not *har;* it's *God,* not *Gud:* remo*n*strance, not rem*un*strance," and so forth. No one ever had a sharper tongue or a kinder heart than Mrs Kean. Beginning with her, I have always loved women with a somewhat hard manner! I have never believed in their hardness, and have proved them tender and generous in the extreme.

Actor-managers are very proud of their long runs nowadays, but in Shakespeare, at any rate, they do not often eclipse Charles Kean's two hundred and fifty nights of "A Midsummer Night's Dream" at the Princess's. It was certainly a very fascinating production, and many of the effects were beautiful. I, by the way, had my share in marring one of these during the run. When Puck is told to put a girdle round the earth in forty minutes, I had to fly off the stage as swiftly as I could, and a dummy Puck was whirled through the air from the point where I disappeared. One night the dummy, while in full flying action, fell on the stage, whereupon, in great concern for its safety, I ran on, picked it up in my arms, and ran off with it amid roars of laughter! Neither of the Keans was acting in this production, but there was some one in authority to give me a sound cuff. Yet I had such excellent intentions. 'Tis ever thus!

I revelled in Puck and his impish pranks, and unconsciously realised that it was a part in which the imagination can run riot. I believe I played it well, but I did not *look* well, and I must contradict emphatically the kind assumption that I must have been a "delightful little fairy." As Mamillius I was really a sweet little thing, but while I was playing Puck I grew very gawky—not to say ugly! My hair had been cut short, and my red cheeks stuck out too much. I was a sight!

The parts we play influence our characters to some extent, and Puck made me a bit of a romp. I grew vain and rather "cocky," and it was just as well that during the rehearsals for the Christmas pantomime in 1857 I was tried for the part of the Fairy Dragonetta and rejected. I believe that my failure was principally due to the fact that Nature had not given me flashing eyes and raven hair—without which, as every one knows, no bad fairy can hold up her head and respect herself. But at the time I felt distinctly rebuffed, and only the extreme beauty of my dress as the maudlin "good fairy" Goldenstar consoled me. Milly

18

Smith (afterwards Mrs Thorn) was Dragonetta, and one of her speeches ran like this:

"Ungrateful Simple Simon (darting forward) You thought no doubt to spite me!
That to this Royal Christening you did not invite me!
BUT—(Mrs Kean: *You must plaster that 'but' on the wall at the back of the gallery.*)—
But on this puling brat revenged I'll be!
My fiery dragon there shall have her broiled for tea!" (Rolling the "R" in broil *ad lib.!*)

At Ryde during the previous summer my father had taken the theatre, and Kate and I played in several farces which the Keeleys and the great comedian Robson had made famous in London. My performances as Waddilove and Jacob Earwig had provoked some one to describe me as "a perfect little heap of talent!" To fit my Goldenstar, I must alter that phrase and describe myself as a perfect little heap of vanity.

It was that dress! It was a long dress, though I was still a baby, and it was as pink and gold as it was trailing. I used to think I looked *beautiful* in it. I wore a trembling star on my forehead, too, which was enough to upset any girl!

One of the most wearisome, yet essential details of my education is connected with my first long dress. It introduces, too, Mr Oscar Byrn, the dancing-master and director of crowds at the Princess's. One of his lessons was in the art of walking with a flannel blanket pinned on in front and trailing six inches on the floor. My success in carrying out this manœuvre with dignity won high praise from Mr Byrn. The other children used to kick at the blanket and progress in jumps like young kangaroos, but somehow I never had any difficulty in moving gracefully. No wonder then that I impressed Mr Byrn, who had a theory that "an actress was no actress unless she learned to dance early." Whenever he was not actually putting me through my paces, I was busy watching him teach the others. There was the minuet, to which he used to attach great importance, and there was "walking the plank." Up and down one of the long planks, extending the length of the stage, we had to walk, first slowly, and then quicker and quicker until we were able at a considerable pace to walk the whole length of it without deviating an inch from the straight line. This exercise, Mr Byrn used to say, and quite truly, I think, taught us uprightness of carriage and certainty of step.

"Eyes right! Chest out! Chin tucked in!" I can hear the dear old man shouting at us as if it were yesterday; and I have learned to see of what value all his drilling was, not only to deportment, but to clear utterance. It would not be a bad thing if there were more "old fops" like Oscar Byrn in the theatres of today. That old-fashioned art of "deportment" is sadly neglected.

The pantomime in which I was the fairy Goldenstar was very frequently preceded by "A Midsummer Night's Dream," and the two parts on one night must have been fairly heavy work for a child, but I delighted in it.

In the same year (1858) I played Karl in "Faust and Marguerite," a jolly little part with plenty of points in it, but not nearly as good a part as Puck. Progress on the stage is often crab-like, and little parts, big parts, and no parts at all must be accepted as "all in the day's work." In these days I was cast for many a "dumb" part. I walked on in "The Merchant of Venice" carrying a basket of doves; in "Richard II" I climbed up a pole in the street scene; in "Henry VIII" I was "top angel" in the vision, and I remember that the heat of the gas at that dizzy height made me sick at the dress-rehearsal! I was a little boy "cheering" in several other productions. In "King Lear" my sister Kate played Cordelia. She was only fourteen, and the youngest Cordelia on record. Years after I played it at the Lyceum when I was over forty!

The production of "Henry VIII" at the Princess's was one of Charles Kean's best efforts. I always refrain from belittling the present at the expense of the past, but there were effects here which I have never seen surpassed, and about this my memory is not at all dim. At this time I seem to have been always at the side watching the acting. Mrs Kean's Katharine of Aragon was splendid, and Charles Kean's Wolsey, his best part after, perhaps, his Richard II. Still, the lady who used to stand ready with a tear-bottle to catch his tears as he came off after his last scene rather overdid her admiration. My mental criticism at the time was "What rubbish!" When I say in what parts Charles Kean was "best," I don't mean to be dogmatic. How should a mere child be able to decide? I "think back" and remember in what parts I liked him best, but I may be quite wide of the mark.

In those days audiences liked plenty for their money, and a Shakespeare play was not nearly long enough to fill the bill. English playgoers in the early 'fifties did not emulate the Japanese, who go to the theatre early in the morning and stay there until late at night, still less the Chinese, whose plays begin one week and end the next, but they thought nothing of sitting in the theatre from seven to twelve. In one of the extra pieces which these hours necessitated, I played a "tiger," one of those youthful grooms who are now a bygone fashion. The pride that I had taken in my trembling star in the pantomime was almost equalled

20

now by my pride in my top-boots! They were too small and caused me insupportable suffering, but I was so afraid that they would be taken away if I complained, that every evening I used to put up valorously with the torture. The piece was called "If the Cap Fits," but my boots were the fit with which I was most concerned!

Years later the author of the little play, Mr Edmund Yates, the editor of *The World*—wrote to me about my performance as the tiger:

"When on June 13, 1859 (to no one else in the world would I breathe the date!) I saw a very young lady play a tiger in a comedietta of mine called 'If the Cap Fits,' I had no idea that that precocious child had in her the germ of such an artist as she has since proved herself."

In "The Merchant of Venice," though I had no speaking part, I was firmly convinced that the basket of doves which I carried on my shoulder was the principal attraction of the scene in which it appeared. The other little boys and girls in the company regarded those doves with eyes of bitter envy. One little chorus boy, especially, though he professed a personal devotion of the tenderest kind for me, could never quite get over those doves, and his romantic sentiments cooled considerably when I gained my proud position as dove-bearer. Before, he had shared his sweets with me, but now he transferred both sweets and affections to some more fortunate little girl. Envy, after all, is the death of love!

Mr Harvey was the Launcelot Gobbo in "The Merchant of Venice"—an old gentleman, and almost as great a fop as Mr Byrn. He was always smiling; his two large rows of teeth were so *very* good! And he had pompous, grandiloquent manners, and wore white gaiters and a long hanging eye-glass. His appearance I should never have forgotten anyhow, but he is also connected in my mind with my first experience of terror.

It came to me in the greenroom, the window-seat of which was a favourite haunt of mine. Curled up in the deep recess I had been asleep one evening, when I was awakened by a strange noise, and, peeping out, saw Mr Harley stretched on the sofa. One side of his face was working convulsively, and he was gibbering and mowing the air with his hand. When he saw me, he called out: "Little Nelly! oh, little Nelly!" I stood transfixed with horror. He was still dressed as Launcelot Gobbo, and this made it all the more terrible. A doctor was sent for, and Mr Harley was looked after, but he never recovered from his seizure and died a few days afterwards.

Although so much of my early life is vague and indistinct, I can always see and hear Mr Harley as I saw and heard him that night, and

21

I can always recollect the view from the greenroom window. It looked out on a great square courtyard, in which the spare scenery, that was not in immediate use, was stacked. For some reason or other this courtyard was a favourite playground for a large company of rats. I dont know what the attraction was for them, except that they may have liked nibbling the paint off the canvas. Out they used to troop in swarms, and I, from my perch on the window-seat, would watch and wonder. Once a terrible storm came on, and years after, at the Lyceum, the Brocken Scene in "Faust" brought back the scene to my mind—the thunder and lightning and the creatures crawling on every side, the *greyness* of the whole thing.

All "calls" were made from the greenroom in those days, and its atmosphere was, I think, better than that of the dressing-room in which nowadays actors and actresses spend their time during the waits. The greenroom at the Princess's was often visited by distinguished people, among them Planché, the archæologist, who did so much for Charles Kean's productions, and Macready. One night, as with my usual impetuosity I was rushing back to my room to change my dress, I ran right into the white waistcoat of an old gentleman! Looking up with alarm, I found that I had nearly knocked over the great Mr Macready.

"Oh, I *beg* your pardon!" I exclaimed in eager tones. I had always heard from father that Macready was the greatest actor of all, and this was our first meeting. I was utterly abashed, but Mr Macready, looking down with a very kindly smile, only answered: "Never mind! You are a very polite little girl, and you act very earnestly and speak very nicely."

I was too much agitated to do anything but continue my headlong course to my dressing-room, but even in those short moments the strange attractiveness of his face impressed itself on my imagination. I remember distinctly his curling hair, his oddly coloured eyes full of fire, and his beautiful, wavy mouth.

When I first described this meeting with Macready, a disagreeable person wrote to the papers and said that he did not wish to question my veracity, but that it was utterly impossible that Macready could ever have brought himself to go to the Princess's at this time, because of the rivalry between him and Charles Kean. I know that the two actors were not on speaking terms, but very likely Macready had come to see my father or Mr Harley or one of the many members of Kean's company who had once served under him.

The period when I was as vain as a little peacock had come to an end before this. I think my part in "Pizarro" saw the last of it. I was a Worshipper of the Sun, and in a pink feather, pink swathings of muslin, and black arms, I was again struck by my own beauty. I grew quite attached to the looking-glass which reflected that feather! Then suddenly there came a change. *I began to see the whole thing.* My attentive watching of other people began to bear fruit, and the labour and perseverance, care and intelligence which had gone to make these enormous productions dawned on my young mind. *One must see things for oneself.* Up to this time I had loved acting because it was great fun, but I had not loved the grind. After I began to rehearse Prince Arthur in "King John," a part in which my sister Kate had already made a great success six years earlier, I understood that if I did not work, I could not act. And so I wanted to work. I used to get up in the middle of the night and watch my gestures in the glass. I used to try my voice and bring it down and up in the right places. And all vanity fell away from me. At the first rehearsals of "King John" I could not do anything right. Mrs Kean stormed at me, slapped me. I broke down and cried, and then, with all the mortification and grief in my voice, managed to express what Mrs Kean wanted and what she could not teach me by doing it herself.

"That's right, that's right!" she cried excitedly. "You've got it! Now remember what you did with your voice, reproduce it, remember everything, and do it!"

When the rehearsal was over, she gave me a vigorous kiss. "You've done very well," she said. "That's what I want. You're a very tired little girl. Now run home to bed." I shall never forget the relief of those kind words after so much misery, and the little incident often comes back to me now when I hear a young actress say, "I can't do it!" If only she can cry with vexation, I feel sure that she will then be able to make a good attempt at doing it!

There were oppositions and jealousies in the Keans' camp, as in most theatres, but they were never brought to my notice until I played Prince Arthur. Then I saw a great deal of Mr Ryder, who was the Hubert of the production, and discovered that there was some soreness between him and his manager. Ryder was a very pugnacious man—an admirable actor, and in appearance like an old tree that has been struck by lightning, or a greenless, barren rock; he was very strong in his likes and dislikes, and in his manner of expressing them.

"D'ye suppose he engaged me for my powers as an actor?" he used to say of Mr Kean. "Not a bit of it! He engaged me for my damned archæological figure!"

One night during the run of "King John," a notice was put up that no curtain calls would be allowed at the end of a scene. At the end of my scene with Hubert there was tremendous applause, and when we did not appear, the audience began to shout and yell and cheer. I went off to the greenroom, but even from there I could still hear the voices:

"Hubert! Arthur!" Mr Kean began the next scene, but it was of no use. He had to give in and send for us. Meanwhile old Ryder had been striding up and down the greenroom in a perfect fury. "Never mind, ducky!" he kept on saying to me; and it was really quite unnecessary, for "ducky" was just enjoying the noise and thinking it all capital fun. "Never mind! When other people are rotting in their graves, ducky, you'll be up there!" (With a terrific gesture indicative of the dizzy heights of fame.) When the message came to the greenroom that we were to take the call, he strode across the stage to the entrance, I running after him and quite unable to keep up with his long steps.

In "Macbeth" I was again associated with Mr Ryder, who was the Banquo when I was Fleance. I remember that after we had been dismissed by Macbeth: "Good repose the while," we had to go off up a flight of steps. I always stayed at the top till the end of the scene, but Mr Ryder used to go down the other side rather heavily, and Mr Kean, who wanted perfect quiet for the dagger speech, had to keep on saying: "Ssh! ssh!" all through it.

"Those carpenters at the side are enough to ruin any acting," he said one night when he came off.

"I'm a heavy man, and I cant help it," said Ryder.

"Oh, I didn't know it was *you*," said Mr Kean—but I think he did! One night I was the innocent cause of a far worse disturbance. I dozed at the top of the steps and rolled from the top to the bottom with a fearful crash! Another night during a performance of "King John" I got into trouble for not catching Mrs Kean when, as Constance, she sank down on to the ground.

"Here is my throne: bid kings come bow to it!"

I was, for my sins, looking at the audience, and Mrs Kean went down with a *run,* and was naturally very angry with me!

In 1860 the Keans gave up the management of the Princess's Theatre and went to America. They travelled in a sailing vessel, and, being delayed by a calm, had to drink water caught in the sails, the water supply having given out. I believe that although the receipts were wonderful, Charles Kean spent much more than he made during his ten years of management. Indeed, he confessed as much in a public announcement. The Princess's Theatre was not very big, and the seats were low-priced. It is my opinion, however, that no manager with high artistic aims, resolute to carry them out in his own way, can ever make a fortune.

Of the other members of the company during my three years at the Princess's, I remember best Walter Lacy, who was the William Terriss of the time. He knew Madame Vestris, and had many entertaining stories about her. Then there were the Leclercqs, two clever sisters, Carlotta and

24

Rose, who did great things later on. Men, women and children alike worked hard, and if the language of the actors was more Rabelaisian than polite, they were good fellows, and heart and soul devoted to their profession. Their salaries were smaller and their lives were simpler than those of actors now.

Kate and I had been hard at work for some years, but our parents had no notion of our resting. We were now to show what our training had done for us in "A Drawing-room Entertainment."

NOTES TO CHAPTER I

1. *Ellen Terry's ancestry.* Ellen Terry's account of her antecedents is sketchy and not quite accurate. Research into the history of her family has proved that her paternal grandfather was not a builder. He has been identified with a Mr H. B. Terry who lived at Portsmouth, and kept an inn, "The Fortunes of War," in Broad Street. I have not been able to find out when his younger son, Benjamin, born in 1818, went on the stage, but it seems likely that it was before he became engaged to Sarah Ballard, "the daughter of a Scottish minister," who like Mr H. B. Terry resided in Portsmouth. The elopement of the young people to which Ellen Terry refers may have been forced on them by a Scottish minister's objections to an actor as a son-in-law. It is not known whether Miss Sarah Ballard's mother was alive when the attractive Ben Terry (described by the actor John Coleman, who met him on the Worcester Circuit soon after his marriage, as "a handsome fine-looking brown-haired man") carried off her daughter, but if she was, there are grounds for thinking she may have been more sympathetic to the romance than her husband. Mrs Ballard was a Miss Copley, a member of the same family which produced John Singleton Copley, the famous American artist (1735-1815). The strong pictorial element in Ellen Terry's art as an actress, and the affinity she felt throughout her life with painters, have always been attributed to her having been thrown with artists in the impressionable days of her youth, but a factor in it may have been the Copley blood in her veins.

Sarah Ballard probably adopted her handsome young husband's profession from necessity, but she had at least one valuable asset to an actress. She was a good-looker. Coleman was struck, when he met the Terrys on the Worcester Circuit, by her wealth of fair hair, her height, her grace, and her beautiful eyes. She acted under the pseudonym "Miss Yerret," her married name spelled backward, with the addition of an absolutely indispensable second "e."

2. *The Terry family.* Ellen Terry's description of the great theatrical family which her father and mother founded should now be brought up to date. In 1932 only two of their children are still alive. Their younger son Fred, after a long and distinguished career as an actor, and actor-manager, now appears rarely on the stage. An elder son Charles, for many years connected with the theatre as a business-manager, has retired. But the Terry family is in no danger of extinction as a theatrical force. The third generation is represented

on the stage by Kate Terry's daughter, Mabel Terry-Lewis; Charles Terry's children, Beatrice and Minnie; Fred Terry's children, Dennis and Phyllis Neilson-Terry; [1] the fourth by Kate Terry's grandson, John Gielgud, a brilliant young actor who is already in the front rank of his profession. His performances in Shakespeare at the Old Vic Theatre in 1929 and 1930 maintained the reputation of the Terry family for speaking the language of dramatic poetry as if it were their native tongue. This generation is further represented by June Morris and Anthony Hawtrey, grandchildren of Florence Terry, who have adopted the stage as a profession. There is even a member of the fifth generation being trained for it. Robinetta Craig, the grand-daughter of Gordon Craig, and great-grand-daughter of Ellen Terry, may one day keep the torch of the family talent alight, and hand it on to another generation yet unborn.

Ellen Terry's children, who in youth showed a natural aptitude for acting, were on the stage for several years. Gordon Craig promised to become a really great actor, but having discovered at the age of twenty-five that he "was not a second Irving" (his own phrase) he seems to have been discouraged. He left the stage in 1897 and has never acted since. But his determination to "be somebody, and do something" has, owing to the great variety of his talents, borne fruit. He is more famous today than perhaps he would have been if he had devoted himself with the single-heartedness of his master, Irving, to the actor's calling. This is not the place to discuss his position in the world of the theatre. It must suffice to say that he has been a great figure in it for the last thirty years.

Edith Craig may pride herself on having been a *useful* actress in the Lyceum company. Henry Irving early discovered her usefulness, and gave her a series of small but important parts in which he could count on her serving him as an actor with unobtrusive skill and reliability. It is with these qualities that Edith Craig, since she left the stage, has continued to serve the theatre in many different branches. Perhaps no member of the Terry family has worked harder in its service with less reward.

3. *Ellen Terry's First Appearance.* On June 16, 1856, Mr Charles Dodgson (Lewis Carroll) visited the Princess's Theatre. The author of "Alice in Wonderland" had only a month earlier adopted the famous pseudonym chosen, from four names he submitted, by Edmund Yates, the editor of *The Train,* to which Mr Dodgson contributed humorous lyrics. Writing in his diary of the visit to the Princess's, Lewis Carroll says that he "especially admired the acting of the little Mamillius, Ellen Terry, a beautiful little creature, who played with remarkable ease and spirit."

4. *Children on the Stage.* Ellen Terry's statement that children are not allowed by law to appear on the stage until they are ten years old was true in 1906, but now has to be revised. Without a licence, they may not appear until the age of fourteen, nor with one, until the age of twelve.

5. *Rehearsals at the Princess's.* In the year 1928, shortly before Ellen Terry's

---

[1] Since this note was written Dennis Neilson-Terry has died. He succumbed to double pneumonia in July 1932 while on tour in South Africa. At the early age of 37 his distinguished career as an actor and actor-manager came to a tragically sudden end.

eightieth birthday, she received a letter from an old admirer recalling an incident at one of these rehearsals. "A score of years ago a friend told me that when he was quite a little boy he used to go with his mother to rehearsals at the Princess's and was present on one occasion when a little girl was rehearsing Mamillius. During an interval he held out to the little girl a packet of sweets, meaning to offer her some. To his surprise, and boyish indignation, she took the lot!"

The story is very characteristic of Ellen Terry. This was not the only time in her life she "took the lot," not from greed, but from absolute confidence that it was expected of her. It never occurred to her to stint a gift when she was the giver. She gave all recklessly, and took for granted that this was natural in every one.

6. *Dragonetta's Speech*. Edith Craig remembers that when she and her brother were children, their mother used to "give them the shivers" by her delivery of this speech of the bad fairy's. "Her 'broiled for tea' was really terrifying."

7. *Edmund Yates*. Mr Yates also "had no idea" that he was in later years to be the instrument of starting a correspondence between that "precocious child," and another child, in 1859 in the cradle, which was to become famous. It was Yates, who in the year 1892, asked Bernard Shaw, then music critic of *The World*, to answer a letter addressed to him by Ellen Terry.

8. The parts played by Ellen Terry during the period covered by Chapter 1 were: Mamillius ("A Winter's Tale," April 28, 1856); Puck ("A Midsummer Night's Dream," October 15, 1856); William Waddilove ("To Parents and Guardians," September 22, 1857); Jacob Earwig ("Boots at the Swan," September 23, 1857); Fairy Goldenstar ("The White Cat," December 26, 1857); Dragonetta ("The White Cat," January 26, 1858); Karl ("Faust and Marguerite," April 5, 1858); Prince Arthur ("King John," October 18, 1858); Fleance ("Macbeth," November 17, 1858); Genie of the Jewels ("The King of the Castle," (December 28, 1858); Tiger Tim ("If the Cap Fits," June 13, 1859).

CHAPTER II

GROWING UP

(1859–1866)

§ 1

FROM July to September every year the leading theatres in London and the provincial cities were closed for the summer vacation. This plan is still adhered to more or less, but in London, at any rate, some theatres keep their doors open all the year round. During these two months most actors take their holiday, but when we were with the Keans we were not in a position to afford such a luxury. Kate and I were earning good salaries for our age,[1] but the family at home was increasing in size, and my mother was careful not to let us think that there never could be any rainy days. I am bound to say that I left questions of thrift, and what we could afford and what we couldnt entirely to my parents. I received sixpence a week pocket-money, with which I was more than content for many years. Poor we may have been at this time, but, owing to my mother's diligent care and cleverness, we always looked nice and neat. One of the few early dissipations I can remember was a Christmas party in Half Moon Street, where our white muslin dresses were equal to any present. But more love and toil and pride than money had gone to make them. I have a very clear vision of coming home late from the theatre to our home in Stanhope Street, Regent's Park, and seeing my dear mother stitching at those pretty frocks by the light of one candle. It was no uncommon thing to find her sewing at that time, but if she was tired, she never showed it. She was always bright and tender. With the callousness of childhood, I scarcely realised the devotion and ceaseless care that she bestowed on us, and her untiring efforts to bring us up as beautifully as she could. The knowledge came to me later on when, all too early in my life, my own responsibilities came on me and quickened my perceptions. But I was a heartless little thing when I danced off to

---

[1] Of course, all salaries are bigger now than they were in my youth. The "stars" in old days earned large sums—Edmund Kean received two hundred and fifty pounds for four performances—but the ordinary members of a company were paid at a very modest rate.

that party! I remember that when the great evening came, our hair, which we still wore down our backs, was done to perfection, and we really looked fit to dance with a king. As things were, I *did* dance with the late Duke of Cambridge! It was the most exciting Christmas Day in my life.

Our summer holidays, as I have said, were spent at Ryde. We stayed at Rose Cottage (for which I sought in vain when I revisited the place the other day), and the change was pleasant, even though we were working hard. One of the pieces father gave at the theatre to amuse the summer visitors was a farce called "To Parents and Guardians." I played the fat, naughty boy Waddilove, a part which had been associated with the comedian Robson in London, and I remember that I made the unsophisticated audience shout with laughter by entering with my hands covered with jam! Father was capital as the French usher Tourbillon; and the whole thing went splendidly. Looking back, it seems rather audacious for a mere child to have attempted a grown-up comedian's part, but it was excellent practice for that child! It was the success of these little summer ventures at Ryde which made my father think of our touring in "A Drawing-room Entertainment" when the Keans left the Princess's.

The entertainment consisted of two little plays "Home for the Holidays" and "Distant Relations," and they were written, I think, by a Mr Courtney. We were engaged to do it first at the Royal Colosseum, Regent's Park, by Sir Charles Wyndham's father, Mr Culverwell. Kate and I played all the parts in each piece, and we did quick changes at the side worthy of Fregoli! The whole thing was quite a success, and after playing it at the Colosseum we started on a round of visits.

In "Home for the Holidays," which came first in our little programme, Kate played Letitia Melrose, a young girl of about seventeen, who is expecting her young brother home for the holidays. Letitia, if I remember right, is discovered soliloquising somewhat after this fashion: "Dear little Harry! Left all alone in the world, as we are, I feel such responsibility for him. Shall I find him changed, I wonder, after two years' absence? He has not answered my letters lately. I hope he got the cake and toffee I sent him, but I've not heard a word." At this point I entered as Harry, but instead of being the innocent little schoolboy of Letitia's fond imagination, Harry appears in loud peg-top trousers (peg-top trousers were very fashionable in 1860), with a big cigar in his mouth, and his hat worn jauntily on one side. His talk is all of racing, betting, and fighting. Letty is struck dumb with astonishment at first, but the awful change which two years have effected gradually dawns on her. She implores him to turn from his idle, foolish ways. Master Harry sinks on

29

his knees by her side, but just as his sister is about to rejoice and kiss him, he looks up in her face and bursts into loud laughter. She is exasperated, and, threatening to send some one to him who will talk to him in a very different fashion, she leaves the stage. Master Hopeful thereupon dons his dressing-gown and smoking cap, and, lying full length upon the sofa, begins to have a quiet smoke. He is interrupted by the appearance of a most wonderful and grim old woman in blue spectacles —Miss Terrorbody. This is no other than Sister Letty, dressed up in order to frighten the youth out of his wits. She talks and talks, and, after painting vivid pictures of what will become of him unless he alters his "vile ways," leaves him, but not before she has succeeded in making him shed tears, half of fright and half of anger. Later on, Sister Letty, looking from the window, sees a grand fight going on between Master Harry and a butcher-boy, and then Harry enters with his coat off, his sleeves tucked up, explaining in a state of blazing excitement that he "*had* to fight that butcher-boy, because he had struck a little girl in the street." Letty sees that the lad has a fine nature in spite of his folly, and appeals to his better feelings, this time not in vain.

"Distant Relations" was far more inconsequent, but it served to show our versatility, at any rate. I was all things by turns, and nothing long! First I was the page boy who admitted the "relations" (Kate in many guises). Then I was a relation myself—Giles, a rustic. As Giles, I suddenly asked if the audience would like to hear me play the drum, and "obliged" with a drum solo, in which I had spent a great deal of time perfecting myself. Long before this I remember dimly some rehearsal when I was put in the orchestra and taken care of by "the gentleman who played the drum," and how badly I wanted to play it too! I afterwards took lessons from Mr Woodhouse, the drummer at the Princess's.

Both Kate and I, even at this early age, had dreams of playing all Mrs Kean's parts. We knew the words, not only of them, but of every female part in every play in which we had appeared at the Princess's. "Walking on is so dull," the young actress says sometimes to me now, and I ask her if she knows all the parts of the play in which she is "walking on." I hardly ever find that she does. "I have no understudy," is her excuse. Even if a young woman has not been given an understudy, she ought, if she has any intention of taking her profession as an actress seriously, to constitute herself an understudy to every part in the piece! Then she would not find her time as a "super" hang heavy on her hands.

Some of my readers may be able to remember the Stalactite Caverns which used to be one of the attractions at the Colosseum. It was there that I first studied the words of Juliet. To me the gloomy horror of the place was a perfect godsend! Here I could cultivate a creepy, eerie sensation, and get into a fitting frame of mind for the potion scene. Down in this least imposing of subterranean abodes I used to tremble and thrill with passion and terror. Ah, if only in after years, when I played Juliet at the Lyceum, I could have thrilled an audience to the same extent!

After a few weeks at the Colosseum, we began our little tour. It was a very merry, happy time. We travelled a company of five, although only two of us were acting. There were my father and mother, Kate and myself, and Mr Sydney Naylor, who played the very important part of orchestra. We usually journeyed in a carriage. Once we tramped from Bristol to Exeter. Oh, those delightful journeys on the open road! I tasted the joys of the strolling player's existence, without its miseries. I saw the country for the first time.... When they asked me what I was thinking of as we drove along, I remember answering: "Only that I should like to run wild in a wood for ever!" At night we stayed in beautiful little inns which were ever so much more cheap and comfortable than the hotels of today. In some of the places we were asked out to tea and dinner and very much fêted. An odd little troupe we were! Father was what we will call for courtesy's sake "Stage Manager," but in reality he set the stage himself, and did the work which generally falls to the lot of the stage manager and an army of carpenters combined. My mother used to coach us in our parts, dress us, make us go to sleep part of the day so that we might look fresh at night, and look after us generally. Mr Naylor, who was not very much more than a boy, though to my childish eyes he looked quite venerable, besides discoursing eloquent music in the evenings, during the progress of the "Drawing-room Entertainment," would amuse us —me most especially—by being very entertaining himself during our journeys from place to place. How he made us laugh about—well, mostly about nothing at all.

We travelled in this way for nearly two years, visiting a new place every day, and making, I think, about ten to fifteen pounds a performance. Our little pieces were very pretty, but very slight, too; and I can only suppose that the people thought that "never anything can be amiss when simpleness and duty tender it," for they received our entertainment very well. The time had come when my little brothers had to be sent to school, and our earnings came in useful.

§ 2

WHEN the tour came to an end in 1861, I went to London with my father to find an engagement, while Kate joined the stock company at Bristol. We still gave the "Drawing-room Entertainment" at Ryde in the summer, and it still drew large audiences.

In London my name was put on an agent's books in the usual way, and presently he sent me to Madame Albina de Rhona, who had not long taken over the management of the Royal Soho Theatre and changed its name to the Royalty. French workmen had swept and garnished the dusty, dingy place and transformed it into a theatre as dainty and pretty as Madame de Rhona herself. Dancing was Madame's strong point, but she had been very successful as an actress too, first in Paris and Petersburg, and then in London at the St James's and Drury Lane. What made her go into management on her own account I dont know. I suppose she was ambitous, and rich enough for the enterprise.

At this time I was "in standing water," as Malvolio says of Viola when she is dressed as a boy. I was neither child nor woman—a long-legged girl of about thirteen, still in short skirts, and feeling that I ought to have long ones. However, when I set out with father to see Madame de Rhona, I was very smart. I borrowed Kate's new bonnet—pink silk trimmed with black lace—and thought I looked nice in it. So did father, for he said on the way to the theatre that pink was my colour. In fact, I am sure it was the bonnet that made Madame de Rhona engage me on the spot!

She was the first Frenchwoman I had ever met, and I was tremendously interested in her. Her neat and expressive ways made me feel very "small," or rather *big* and clumsy, even at the first interview. A quick-tempered, bright, energetic little woman, she nearly frightened me out of my wits at the first rehearsal by dancing round me on the stage in a perfect frenzy of anger at what she was pleased to call my stupidity. Then something I did suddenly pleased her, and she overwhelmed me with compliments and praise. After a time these became the order of the day, and she soon won my youthful affections. Madame de Rhona was very kind-hearted and generous. To her generosity I owed the first piece of jewellery I ever possessed—a pretty little brooch, which, with characteristic carelessness, I promptly lost! Besides being flattered by her praise and grateful for her kindness, I was filled with great admiration for her. She was a wee thing—like a toy, and her dancing was really exquisite. When I watched the way she moved her hands and feet, despair entered my soul. It was all so precise, so "express and admirable." Her limbs were so dainty and graceful—mine so big and unmanageable! "How long and gaunt I am," I used to say to myself, "and what a pattern of prim prettiness she is!" I was so much ashamed of my large hands, during this time at the Royalty, that I kept them tucked up under my arms! This subjected me to unmerciful criticism from Madame Albina at rehearsals.

"Take down your hands," she would call out. *"Mon Dieu!* It is like an ugly young *poulet* going to roost!"

32

In spite of this, I did not lose my elegant habit for many years! I was only broken of it at last by a friend saying that he supposed I had very ugly hands, as I never showed them! That did it! Out came the hands to prove that they were not so *very* ugly, after all! Vanity often succeeds where remonstrance fails.

The greenroom at the Royalty was a very pretty little place, and Madame Albina sometimes had supper-parties there after the play. One night I could not resist the pangs of curiosity, and I peeped through the keyhole to see what was going on! I chose a lucky moment! One of Madame's admirers was drinking champagne out of her slipper! It was even worth the box on the ear that mother gave me when she caught me. She had been looking all over the theatre for me, to take me home.

My first part at the Royalty was Clementine in "Attar Gull." Of the play, adapted from a story by Eugene Sue, I have a very hazy recollection, but I know that I had one very effective scene in it. Clementine, an ordinary fair-haired ingénue in white muslin, has a great horror of snakes, and, in order to cure her, some one suggests that a dead snake should be put in her room, and she be taught how harmless the thing is for which she has such an aversion. An Indian servant, who, for some reason or other, has a deadly hatred for the whole family, substitutes a live reptile. Clementine appears at the window with the venomous creature coiled round her neck, screaming with terror. The spectators on the stage think that the snake is dead, and that she is only screaming from nerves, but in reality she is being slowly strangled. I began screaming in a frantic, heart-rending manner, and continued screaming, each cry surpassing the last in intensity and agony. At rehearsal I could not get these screams right for a long time. Madame de Rhona grew more and more impatient and at last flew at me like a wild-cat and shook me. I cried, just as I had done when I could not get Prince Arthur's terror right, and then the wild, agonised scream that Madame de Rhona wanted came to me. I *reproduced* it and enlarged it in effect. On the first night the audience applauded the screaming more than anything in the play. Madame de Rhona assured me that I had made a sensation, kissed me and said I was a genius! How sweet and pleasant her flattering words sounded in my young and inexperienced ears I need hardly say.

Looking back at it now, I know perfectly well why I, a mere child of thirteen, was able to give such a realistic display of horror. I had the emotional instinct to start with, no doubt, but if I did it well, it was because I was able to imagine what would be *real* in such a situation. I had never *observed* such horror, but I had previously *realised* it, when, as Arthur, I had imagined the terror of having my eyes put out.

Imagination! imagination! I put it first years ago, when I was asked

33

what qualities I thought necessary for success upon the stage. And I am still of the same opinion. Imagination, industry, and intelligence—"the three I's"—are all indispensable to the actress, but of these three the greatest is, without any doubt, imagination.

After this "screaming" success, which, however, did not keep "Attar Gull" in the bill at the Royalty for more than a few nights, I continued to play under Madame de Rhona's management until February 1862. During these few months new plays were being constantly put on, for Madame was somehow not very fortunate in gauging the taste of the public. It was in the fourth production—"The Governor's Wife"—that, as Letty Briggs, I had my first experience of what is called "stage fright." I had been on the stage more than five years, and had played at least sixteen parts, so there was really no excuse for me. I suspect now that I had not taken enough pains to get word-perfect. I know I had five new parts to study between November 21 and December 26.

Stage fright is like nothing else in the world. You are standing on the stage apparently quite well and in your right mind, when suddenly you feel as if your tongue had been dislocated and was lying powerless in your mouth. Cold shivers begin to creep downwards from the nape of your neck and all up you at the same time, until they seem to meet in the small of your back. About this time you feel as if a centipede, all of whose feet have been carefully iced, has begun to run about in the roots of your hair. The next agreeable sensation is the breaking out of a cold sweat all over. Then you are certain that some one has cut the muscles at the back of your knees. Your mouth begins to open slowly, without giving utterance to a single sound, and your eyes seem inclined to jump out of your head over the footlights. At this point it is as well to get off the stage as quickly as you can, for you are far beyond human help.

Whether everybody suffers in this way or not I cannot say, but it exactly describes the torture I went through in "The Governor's Wife." I had just enough strength and sense to drag myself off the stage and seize a book, with which, after a few minutes, I reappeared and ignominiously read my part. Whether Madame de Rhona boxed my ears or not, I can't remember, but I think it is very likely, for she was very quick-tempered. In later years I have not suffered from the fearsome malady, but even now, after fifty years of stage-life, I never play a new part without being overcome by a terrible nervousness and a torturing dread of forgetting my lines. Every nerve in my body seems to be dancing an independent jig on its own account.

It was at the Royalty that I first acted with Mr Kendal. He and I played together in a comedietta called "A Nice Quiet Day." Soon after,

34

my engagement came to an end, and I went to Bristol, where I gained the experience of my life with a stock company.

§ 3

"I THINK anything, naturally written, ought to be in everybody's way that pretends to be an actor." This remark of Colley Cibber's long ago struck me as an excellent motto for a beginner on the stage. The ambitious boy thinks of Hamlet, the ambitious girl of Juliet, but where shall we find the young actor and actress whose heart is set on being useful?

Usefulness! It is not a fascinating word, and the quality is not one of which the aspiring spirit can dream o' nights, yet on the stage it is the first thing to aim at. Not until we have learned to be useful can we afford to do what we like. The tragedian will always be a limited tragedian if he has not learned how to laugh. The comedian who cannot weep will never touch the highest levels of mirth.

It was in the stock companies that we learned the great lesson of usefulness; we played everything—tragedy, comedy, farce, and burlesque. There was no question of parts "suiting" us; we had to take what we were given.

The first time I was cast for a part in a burlesque I told the stage manager I couldnt sing and I couldnt dance. His reply was short and to the point. "You've got to." And so I sang and danced in a way—a very funny way at first, no doubt. It was admirable training, for it took all the self-consciousness out of me to start with. To end with, I thought it capital fun, and enjoyed burlesque as much as Shakespeare.

What was a stock company? I forget that in these days the question may be asked in all good faith, and that it is necessary to answer it. Well, then, a stock company was a company of actors and actresses brought together by the manager of a provincial theatre to support a leading actor or actress—"a star"—from London. When Edmund Kean, the Kembles, Macready, or Mrs Siddons visited provincial towns, these companies were ready to support them in Shakespeare. They were also ready to play burlesque, farce, and comedy to fill out the bill. Sometimes the "stars" would come for a whole season; if their magnitude were of the first order, for only one night. Sometimes they would rehearse with the stock company, sometimes they wouldnt. There is a story of a manager visiting Edmund Kean at his hotel on his arrival in a small provincial town, and asking the great actor when he would rehearse.

"Rehearse! I'm not going to rehearse. I'm going to sleep!"

"Have you any instructions?"

"Instructions! No! Tell 'em to keep a long arm's length away from me and do their damned worst!"

At Bristol, where I joined Mr J. H. Chute's stock company in 1861, we had no experience of that kind, perhaps because there was no Kean alive to give it to us. And I dont think that our "worst" would have been so very bad. Mr Chute, who had married Macready's half-sister, was a splendid manager, and he contrived to gather round him a company which was something more than "sound."

Several of its members distinguished themselves greatly in after years. Among these I may mention Miss Marie Wilton (now Lady Bancroft) and Miss Madge Robertson (now Mrs Kendal).

Lady Bancroft had left the company before I joined it, but Mrs Kendal was there, and so was Miss Henrietta Hodson (afterwards Mrs Labouchere). I was much struck at that time by Mrs Kendal's singing. Her voice was beautiful. As an example of how anything can be twisted to make mischief, I may quote here an absurd tarradiddle about Mrs Kendal never forgetting in after years that in the Bristol stock company she had to play the singing fairy to my Titania in "A Midsummer Night's Dream." The simple explanation was that she had the best voice in the company, and was of such infinite value in singing parts that no manager in his senses would have taken her out of them. There was no question of my taking precedence of her, or of her playing second fiddle to me.

Miss Hodson was a brilliant burlesque actress, a good singer, and a capital dancer. She had great personal charm, too, and was an enormous favourite with the Bristol public. I cannot exactly call her a "rival" of my sister Kate's, for Kate was the "principal lady" or "star," and Henrietta Hodson the "soubrette," and, in burlesque, the "principal boy." Nevertheless, there were certainly rival factions of admirers, and the friendly antagonism between the Hodsonites and the Terryites used to amuse us all greatly.

We were petted, spoiled, and applauded to our hearts' content, but I dont think it did us any harm. We all had scores of admirers, but their youthful ardour seemed to be satisfied by tracking us when we went to rehearsal in the morning and waiting for us outside the stage-door at night.

When Kate and I had a "benefit" night, they had an opportunity of coming to rather closer quarters, for on these occasions tickets could be bought from members of the company, as well as at the box-office of the theatre.

Our lodgings in Queen Square were besieged by Bristol youths who were anxious to get a glimpse of the Terrys. The Terrys demurely chatted with them and sold them tickets. My mother was most vigilant in her rôle of duenna, and from the time I first went on the stage until I was a grown woman I can never remember going home unaccompanied by either her or my father.

The leading male members of Mr Chute's stock company were Arthur Wood (an admirable comedian), William George Rignold, W. H. Vernon, and Charles Coghlan. At this time Charles Coghlan was acting magnificently, and dressing each of his characters so correctly and so perfectly that most of the audience did not understand it. For instance, as Glavis, in "The Lady of Lyons," he looked a picture of the Directoire fop. He did not compromise in any single detail, but wore the long straggling hair, the high cravat, the eye-glass, bows, jags, and tags, to the infinite amusement of some members of the audience, who could not imagine what his quaint dress meant. Coghlan's clothes were not more perfect than his manner, but both were a little in advance of the appreciation of Bristol playgoers in the 'sixties.

At the Princess's Theatre I had gained my experience of long rehearsals. When I arrived in Bristol I was to learn the value of short ones. Mr Chute took me in hand, and I had to wake up and be alert with brains and body. The first part I played was Cupid in "Endymion." To this day I can remember my lines. I entered as a blind old woman in what is known in theatrical jargon as a "disguise cloak."

> Pity the poor blind—what, no one here?
> Nay then, I'm not so blind as I appear,
> And so to throw off all disguise and sham,
> Let me at once inform you who I am! (throwing off cloak)
> I'm Cupid!

Henrietta Hodson as Endymion and Kate as Diana had a dance with me which used to bring down the house. I wore a short tunic which in those days was considered too scanty to be "quite nice," and carried the conventional bow and quiver.

In another burlesque, "Perseus and Andromeda," I played Dictys; it was in this piece that Arthur Wood used to make people laugh by punning on the line: "Such a mystery (Miss Terry) here!" It was an absurd little joke, but the people used to cheer and applaud.

§ 4

WHILE my stage education was progressing apace, I was, through the influence of a very wonderful family whose acquaintance we made, having my eyes opened to beautiful things in art and literature. Mr Godwin,

37

the architect and archæologist, was living in Bristol when Kate and I were at the Theatre Royal, and we used to go to his house for some of the Shakespeare readings in which our Bristol friends asked us to take part. This house, with its Persian rugs, beautiful furniture, its organ, which for the first time I learned to love, its sense of design in every detail, was a revelation to me, and the talk of its master and mistress made me *think*. At the theatre I was living in an atmosphere which was developing my powers as an actress and teaching me what work meant, but my mind had begun to grasp dimly and almost unconsciously that I must do something for myself—something that all the education and training I was receiving in my profession could not do for me. I was fourteen years old at Bristol, but I now felt that I had never really lived at all before. For the first time I began to appreciate beauty, to observe, to feel the splendour of things, to *aspire!*

I remember that in one of the local papers there had appeared under the headline "Jottings" some very wonderful criticisms of the performances at the theatre. The writer did not indulge in flattery, and in particular he attacked our classical burlesques on the ground that they were ugly. They were discussing "Jottings" one day at the Godwins' house, and Kate said it was absurd to take a burlesque so seriously.

"I dont agree," said our host. "Even a burlesque can be beautiful."

Afterwards he asked me what I thought of "Jottings," and I confessed that there seemed to me a good deal of truth in what had been said. I had cut out all that had been written about us, read it several times, and thought it all very clever, most amusing—and generally right. Later on I found that Mr Godwin and "Jottings" were one and the same!

At the Godwins' I met Mr Barclay, Mr Hine, William Burges the architect, and many other people who made an impression on my young mind. I absorbed their lessons eagerly, and found them of the greatest value later on.

In March 1863 Mr. Chute opened the Theatre Royal, Bath, when, besides a specially written play symbolic of the event, his stock company performed "A Midsummer Night's Dream." Titania was the first Shakespeare part I had played since I left Charles Kean, but I think even in those early days I was more at home in Shakespeare than in anything else. Mr Godwin designed my dress, and we made it at his house in Bristol. He showed me how to damp it and "wring" it while it was wet, tying up the material as the Orientals do in their "tie and dry" process, so that when it was dry and untied, it was all crinkled and clinging. This was the first lovely dress that I ever wore, and I learned a great deal from it.

Almost directly after that appearance at Bath I went to London to fulfill an engagement at the Haymarket Theatre, of which Mr Buckstone was still the manager and Sothern the great attraction. I had played Gertrude Howard in "The Little Treasure" during the stock season at Bristol, and when Mr Buckstone wanted to revive the piece at the Haymarket, he was told about me. I was fifteen at this time, and my sense of humour was as yet ill-developed. I was fond of "larking" and merry enough, but I hated being laughed *at!* At any rate, I could see no humour in Mr Sothern's jokes at my expense. He played my lover in "The Little Treasure," and he was always teasing me—pulling my hair, making me forget my part and look like an idiot. But for dear old Mr Howe, who was my "father" in the same piece, I should not have enjoyed acting in it at all, but he made amends for everything. We had a scene together in which he used to cry, and I used to cry—oh, it was lovely!

Why I should never have liked Sothern, with his wonderful hands and blue eyes, Sothern, whom every one found so fascinating and delightful, I cannot say, and I record it as discreditable to me, not to him. I admired him—I could not help doing that—but I dreaded his jokes, and thought some of them very cruel.

Another thing I thought cruel at this time was the scandal which was talked in the theatre. A change for the better has taken place in this respect—at any rate, in conduct. People behave better now, and in our profession, carried on as it is in the public eye, behaviour is everything. At the Haymarket there were simply no bounds to what was said in the greenroom. One night I remember gathering up my skirts (we were, I think, playing "The Rivals" at the time), making a curtsey, as Mr Chippendale, one of the best actors in old comedy I ever knew, had taught me, and sweeping out of the room with the famous line from another Sheridan play: "Ladies and gentlemen, I leave my character behind me!"

I see now that was very priggish of me, but I am quite as uncompromising in my hatred of scandal now as I was then. Quite recently I had a line to say in "Captain Brassbound's Conversion," which is a very helpful reply to any tale-bearing. "As if any one ever knew the whole truth about anything!" That is just the point. It is only the whole truth which is informing and fair in the long run, and the whole truth is never known.

I regard my engagement at the Haymarket as one of my lost opportunities, which in after years I would have given much to have had over again. I might have learned so much more than I did. I was preoccupied by events outside the theatre. Tom Taylor, who had for some time been a good friend to both Kate and me, had introduced us to Mr Watts, the great painter, and to me the stage seemed a poor place when compared with the wonderful studio where Kate and I were painted as "The Sisters." At the Taylors' house, too, the friends, the arts, the refinements had an enormous influence on me, and for a time the theatre became almost distasteful. Never at any time in my life have I been ambitious, but at the Haymarket I was not even passionately anxious to do my best with every part that came my way—a quality which with me has been a good substitute for ambition. I was just dreaming of and aspiring after another world, a world full of pictures and music and gentle, artistic people with quiet voices and elegant manners. The reality of such a world was Little Holland House, the home of Mr Watts.

So I confess quite frankly that I did not appreciate until it was too late my advantages in serving at the Haymarket with comrades who were the most surpassingly fine actors and actresses in old comedy that I have ever known. There were Mr Buckstone, the Chippendales, Mr Compton, Mr Farren. They one and all thoroughly understood Sheridan. Their bows, their curtseys, their grand manner, the indefinable *style* which they brought to their task, were something to see. We shall never know their like again, and the smoothest old-comedy acting of this age seems rough in comparison. Of course, we suffer more with every fresh decade that separates us from Sheridan. As he gets farther and farther away, the traditions of the performances which he directed become vaguer and vaguer. Mr Chippendale knew these traditions backwards. He might even have known Sheridan himself. Charles Reade's mother did know him, and sat on the stage with him while he rehearsed "The School for Scandal" with Mrs Abingdon, the original Lady Teazle.

Mrs Abingdon, according to Charles Reade, who told the story, had just delivered the line, "How dare you abuse my relations?" when Sheridan stopped the rehearsal.

"No, no, that wont do at all! It mustnt be *pettish*. That's shallow—shallow. You must go up stage with, 'You are just what my cousin Sophy said you would be,' and then turn and sweep down on him like a volcano. 'You are a great bear to abuse my relations! How *dare* you abuse my relations!' "

I hope to refrain, in telling the story of my life, from praising the past at the expense of the present. It is always an easy thing for the old to do, as the young, however sceptical, are unable to test the truth of their elders' eulogies. Yet I must put on record that although I have seen many improvements in actors and acting since I was at the Haymarket, I have never seen old comedy acted as it was acted there.

Not that I was much good at it myself. I played Julia in "The Rivals" very ill; it was too difficult and subtle for me—ungrateful into the bargain—and I even made a blunder in bringing down the curtain on the first night. It fell to my lot to finish the play—in players' language, to speak the "tag." Now, it has been a superstition among actors for centuries that it is unlucky to speak the "tag" in full at rehearsal. So during the rehearsals of "The Rivals," I followed precedent and did not say the last two or three words of my part and of the play, but just "mum, mum, mum!" When the first night came, instead of dropping my voice with the last word in the conventional and proper manner, I ended with an upward inflection, which was right for the sense, but wrong for the curtain.

This unexpected innovation produced utter consternation all round me. The prompter was so much astounded that he thought there was something more coming and did not give the "pull" for the curtain to come down. There was a horrid pause while it remained up, and then Mr Buckstone, the Bob Acres of the cast, who was very deaf and had not heard the upward inflection, exclaimed loudly and irritably: "Eh! eh! What does this mean? Why the devil don't you bring down the curtain?" And he went on cursing until it did come down. This experience made me think more than ever of the advice of an old actor: "Never leave your stage effects to *chance,* my child, but *rehearse,* and find out all about it!"

How I wished I had rehearsed that "tag" and taken the risk of being unlucky!

For the credit of my intelligence I should add that the mistake was a technical one, not a stupid one. The line was a question. It *demanded* an upward inflection; but no play can end like that.

It was not all old comedy at the Haymarket. "Much Ado About Nothing" was put on during my engagement, and I played Hero to Miss Louisa Angell's Beatrice. Miss Angell was a very modern Beatrice, but I, though I say it "as shouldnt," played Hero beautifully! I remember wondering if I should ever play Beatrice. I just *wondered,* that was all. It was the same when Miss Angell played Letitia Hardy in "The Belle's Stratagem," and I was Lady Touchwood. I just wondered! I never felt jealous of other people having bigger parts; I never looked forward consciously to a day when I should have them myself. There was no virtue in it. It was just because I wasnt ambitious.

Louise Keeley, a pretty little woman and clever, took my fancy more than any one else in the company. She was always merry and kind, and I admired her dainty, vivacious acting. In a burlesque called "Buckstone at Home" (in which I played Britannia and came up a trap in a huge pearl, which opened and disclosed me) Miss Keeley was delightful. One evening the Prince and Princess of Wales (now our King and Queen)[1] came to see "Buckstone at Home." I believe it was the very first time they had appeared at a theatre since their marriage. They sat far back

[1] Edward VII and Queen Alexandra.

in the royal box, the ladies and gentlemen of their suite occupying the front seats. Miss Keeley, dressed as a youth, had a song in which she brought forward by the hand some well-known characters in fairy tales and nursery rhymes—Cinderella, Little Boy Blue, Jack and Jill, and so on, and introduced them to the audience in a topical verse. One verse ran·

> Here's the Prince of Happyland,
> Once he dwelt at the Lyceum;
> Here's another Prince at hand,
> But being *invisible,* you cant see him!

Probably the Prince of Wales must have wished the singer at—well, not at the Haymarket Theatre; but the next minute he must have been touched by the loyal greeting that he received. When the audience grasped the situation, every one—stalls, boxes, circle, pit, gallery—stood up and cheered and cheered again. Never was there a more extraordinary scene in a playhouse—such excitement, such enthusiasm! The action of the play came to a full stop, but not the cheers. They grew louder and louder, until the Prince came forward and bowed his acknowledgments. I doubt if any royal personage has ever been so popular in England as he was. Of course he is popular as King too, but as Prince of Wales he came nearer the people. They had more opportunities of seeing him, and they appreciated his untiring efforts to make up by his many public appearances for the seclusion in which the Queen lived.

§ 5

In the middle of the run of "The American Cousin" I left the stage and married. Mary Meredith was the part, and I played it vilely. I was not quite sixteen years old, too young to be married even in those days, when every one married early. But I was delighted, and my parents were delighted, although the disparity of age between my husband and me was very great. It all seems like a dream—not a clear dream, but a fitful one which in the morning one tries in vain to tell. And even if I could tell it, I would not. I was happy, because my face was the type which the great artist who had married me loved to paint. I remember sitting to him in armour for hours, and never realising that it was heavy until I fainted!

The day of my wedding it was very cold. I can always remember what I was wearing on the important occasions of my life.[1] On that day I wore a brown silk gown which had been designed by Holman Hunt,

[1] Notice the definiteness of Ellen Terry's memory of her Mamillius dress described on p. 16.

42

HEAD OF A YOUNG GIRL (ELLEN TERRY)
From the painting by George Frederick Watts, in the collection of Alexander
Henderson, Esq., M.P.

and a quilted white bonnet with a sprig of orange-blossom, and I was wrapped in a beautiful Indian shawl. I "went away" in a sealskin jacket with coral buttons, and a little sealskin cap. I cried a great deal, and Mr Watts said, "Dont cry. It makes your nose swell." The day I left home to be married. I "tubbed" all my little brothers and sisters and washed their fair hair.

Little Holland House, where Mr Watts lived, seemed to me a paradise, where only beautiful things were allowed to come. All the women were graceful, and all the men were gifted. A trio of sisters—Mrs Prinsep—(mother of the painter), Lady Somers, and Mrs Cameron, a pioneer in artistic photography—were known as Beauty, Dash, and Talent. There were two more beautiful sisters, Mrs Jackson and Mrs Dalrymple. Gladstone, Disraeli and Browning were among Mr Watt's visitors. At Freshwater, where I went on a visit soon after my marriage, I first saw Tennyson.

As I write down these great names, I feel apprehensive of rousing expectations in the reader which I shall be unable to satisfy. For my recollections of the men to whom the names belong are very incomplete. I remember thinking that Mr Gladstone was like a volcano at rest; his face was pale and calm, but the calm was the calm of the grey crust of Etna. You looked into the piercing dark eyes and caught a glimpse of the red-hot crater beneath the crust. Years later when I met him at the Lyceum, I had exactly the same impression. Then I became better acquainted with him, and discovered that he was one of the best "audiences" actor or actress could desire. He used often to come to the Lyceum and watch the play from a little seat in the O. P. corner. Henry Irving covered the seat with red baize and hung up curtains so that our great visitor should be protected from draughts. It was not only on account of his deafness that Mr Gladstone preferred this corner close to the actors to a stall or box. He could come and go without attracting attention. But he seldom took advantage of this, nearly always arriving five minutes before the curtain went up, and staying until the end of the play. One bitter winter night I feared he would catch cold, and I lent him a white scarf which he wore with great dignity.

He could always give his whole mind to the thing which claimed his interest at the moment. This made him one of the most comfortable people to talk to that I have ever met. In everything he was thorough. Would that all playgoers were as punctual and as capable of such concentration!

I remember contrasting his punctuality when he came to see "King Lear" with the unpunctuality of another statesman, Lord Randolph Churchill, who came to see the same play the following evening.

He arrived with a party of men friends when the first act was over!

Of Disraeli in those days at Little Holland House I have a vaguer memory than of Gladstone. His name conjures up a garden party; I am struck by the appearance of a man with Jewish features, who wears a garish blue tie. His straggling black curls shake as he walks. The picture melts into one of Henry Irving as Shylock. Both noble Jews. I know I must have admired Disraeli greatly at first sight, for some time afterwards when I saw him walking in Piccadilly on the Green Park side, I crossed the road to have a good look at him. I even went so far as to bump into him to make him raise his head. It was a very little bump! My elbow just touched his, and then I felt embarrassed. He took off his hat, looked at me, and, not recognising me, muttered "I beg your pardon" and passed on. I had had my look, and can see now those quiet, rather indifferent eyes, which didn't open wide.

Tennyson was more to me than a magic-lantern shape, flitting across the blank of my young experience. The first time I saw him he was sitting at the table in his library, and Mrs Tennyson, her very slender hands hidden by thick gloves, was standing on a step-ladder handing him down some heavy books. She was very frail, and reminded me of a slender-stalked tea-rose. After that one time I only remember her lying on a sofa.

In the evenings I went walking with Tennyson over the fields, and he would point out to me the differences in the flight of different birds, and tell me to watch their solid phalanxes turning against the sunset, the compact wedge suddenly narrowing sharply into a thin line. He taught me to recognise the barks of trees and to call wild flowers by their names. He picked me the first bit of pimpernel I ever noticed. Always I was quite at ease with him. He was so wonderfully simple.

A hat that I wore at Freshwater suddenly comes to my remembrance. It was a brown straw mushroom with a dull red feather round it. It was tied under my chin, and I still had my hair down.

It was easy enough for me to believe that Tennyson was a poet. He showed it in everything, although he was entirely free from romantic airs and graces. What a contrast he was to Browning, with his carefully brushed hat, smart coat, and fine society manners!

At the time of my first marriage, when I met these great men, I had never had the advantage—I assume that it *is* an advantage!—of a single day's schooling in a *real school*. What I have learned outside my own profession I have learned from my environment. Perhaps it is this which makes me think environment is more important than education in forming character.

At Freshwater I was still so young that I preferred playing Indians and Knights of the Round Table with Tennyson's sons, Hallam and Lionel, and the young Camerons, to sitting indoors noticing what the poet did and said. I was mighty proud when I learned how to prepare his daily pipe for him. It was a long church-warden, and he liked the stem to be steeped in a solution of sal volatile, or something of that kind, so that it did not stick to his lips. But he and all the others seemed to me very old. There were my young knights waiting for me; and jumping gates, climbing trees, and running paper-chases are pleasant when one is young.

It was not to inattentive ears that Tennyson read his poems. His reading was most impressive, but I think he read Browning's "Ride from Ghent to Aix" better than anything of his own, except, perhaps, "The Northern Farmer." He used to preserve the monotonous rhythm of the galloping horses in Browning's poem, and made the words come out sharply like hoofs upon a road. It was a little comic until one got used to it, but that fault lay in the ear of the hearer. It was the right way and the fine way to read this particular poem, and I have never forgotten it.

In after years I met Tennyson again, when with Henry Irving I acted in two of his plays at the Lyceum. When I come to those plays, I shall have more to say of him. Browning too I met in later years, but only at dinner-parties. I knew him no better than in this early period, when I was Nelly Watts, and heedless of the greatness of great men, "To meet an angel and not be afraid is to be impudent." I dont like to confess to it, but I think I must have been, according to this definition, *very* impudent!

One charming domestic arrangement at Freshwater was the serving of the dessert in a separate room from the rest of the dinner. And such a dessert it always was! Fruit piled high on great dishes in Veronese fashion, not the few nuts and an orange of some English households.

It must have been some years after the Freshwater days, yet before the production of "The Cup," that I saw Tennyson in his carriage outside a jeweller's shop in Bond Street.

"How very nice you look in the daytime," he remarked. "Not like an actress!"

I disclaimed my singularity, and said I thought actresses looked *very* nice in the daytime.

To him and to the others my early romance was always the most interesting thing about me. When I saw them in later times, it seemed as if months, not years, had passed since I was Nelly Watts.

Once, at the dictates of a conscience, perhaps an over-scrupulous conscience, I made a bonfire of my letters. But a few were saved from the burning, more by accident than design. Among them I found yesterday a kind little note from Sir William Vernon Harcourt, which shows me that I must have known him, too, at the time of my first marriage and met him later on when I returned to the stage.

"You cannot tell how much pleased I am to hear that you have been as happy as you deserve to be. The longer one lives, the more one learns not to despair, and to believe that nothing is impossible to those who have courage and hope and youth—I was going to add beauty and genius." (*This is the sort of thing that made me blush—and burn my letters!*)

"My little boy is still the charm and consolation of my life. He is now twelve years old, and though I say it that should not, is a perfect child, and wins the hearts of all who know him."

That little boy, now in His Majesty's Government, is known as the Right Honourable Lewis Harcourt. He married an American lady, Miss Burns of New York.

Many inaccurate stories have been told of my brief married life, and I have never contradicted them—they were so manifestly absurd. Those who can imagine the surroundings into which I, a raw girl, undeveloped in all except my training as an actress, was thrown, can imagine the situation.

Of one thing I am certain. While I was with Signor—the name by which Mr Watts was known among his friends—I never had one single pang of regret for the theatre. This may do me no credit, but it is *true*.

I wondered at the new life, and worshipped it because of its beauty. When it suddenly came to an end, I was thunderstruck; and refused at first to consent to the separation, which was arranged for me in much the same way as my marriage had been.

The whole thing was managed by those kind friends whose chief business in life seems to be the care of others. I dont blame them. There are things for which no one is to blame. "There do exist such things as honest misunderstandings," as Charles Reade was always impressing on me at a later time. There were no vulgar accusations on either side, and the words I read in the deed of separation, "incompatibility of temper"— a mere legal phrase—*more* than covered the ground. Truer still would have been "incompatibility of *occupation*," and the interference of well-meaning friends. We all suffer from that sort of thing. Pray God one be not a well-meaning friend one's self!

"The marriage was not a happy one," they will probably say after my death, but for me it was in many ways very happy indeed. What bitterness there was effaced itself in a very remarkable way.

I saw Mr Watts but once face to face after the separation. We met in the street at Brighton, and he told me that I had grown! That was the last time I spoke to him. But years later, after I had appeared at the

Lyceum and had made some success in the world, I was in the garden of a house which adjoined the new Little Holland House, and Mr Watts, in his garden, saw me through the hedge. It was then that I received from him the first letter that I had had for years. In this letter he told me that he had watched my success with eager interest, and asked me to shake hands with him in spirit. "What success I may have," he wrote, "will be very incomplete and unsatisfactory if you cannot do what I have long been hesitating to ask. If you cannot, keep silence. If you can, one word, 'Yes,' will be enough."

I answered simply, "Yes."

After that he wrote to me again, and for two or three years we corresponded, but I never came into personal contact with him.

As the past is now to me like a story in a book that I once read, I can speak of it easily. But if by doing so I thought that I might give pain or embarrassment to any one else, I should be silent about this long-forgotten time. After careful consideration it does not seem to me that it can be either indiscreet or harmful to let it be known that this great artist honoured and appreciated my efforts to devote myself to my art; that this great man could not rid himself of the pain of feeling that he "had spoiled my life" (a chivalrous assumption of blame for what was, I think, a natural, almost inevitable, catastrophe), and that long after all personal relations had been broken off, he wrote to me gently and kindly, —as sympathetically ignoring the strangeness of the position, as if, to use his own expression, "we stood face to face on the brink of an universal grave."

When this tender kindness was established between us, he sent me a portrait-head that he had done of me when I was his wife. I think it a very beautiful picture. He did not touch it except to mend the edges, thinking it better not to try to improve it by the work of another time.

In one of his letters he writes that "there is nothing in all this that the world might not know." Surely the world is always the better for having a little truth instead of a great deal of falsehood. That is my justification for publishing this, if justification be needed.

If I did not fulfil his prophecy that "in addition to your artistic eminence, I feel that you will achieve a solid social position, make yourself a great woman, and take a noble place in the history of your time," I was the better for his having made it.

If I had been able to look into the future, I should have been less rebellious at the termination of my first marriage. Was I so rebellious, after all? I am afraid I *showed* about as much rebellion as a sheep. But I was miserable, indignant, unable to understand that there could be any justice in what had happened. In 1866 I returned to the stage. I was

47

practically *driven* back by those who meant to be kind—Tom Taylor, my father and mother, and others. *They* looked ahead and saw clearly it was for my good.

It *was* a good thing, but at the time I hated it. And I hated going back to live at home. Mother furnished a room for me, and I thought the furniture hideous. Poor mother!

For years Beethoven always reminded me of mending stockings, because I used to struggle with the large holes in my brothers' stockings upstairs in that ugly room, while downstairs Kate played the "Moonlight Sonata." I caught up the stitches in time to the notes! This was the period when, though every one was kind, I hated my life, hated every one and everything in the world more than at any time before or since.

NOTES TO CHAPTER II

1. *The Summer Vacation.* The practice of closing the London theatres from July to September, which Ellen Terry says was universal in her youth, and still fairly common in 1906, is now obsolete. One explanation may be the disappearance of stable managements, under which a series of plays were acted by more or less permanent companies during the most popular play-going months of the year. Another that suggests itself is that the development of swift transit has brought an increasing number of visitors to London during the summer. The old London theatre public was composed mainly of residents, many of whom migrated to the country during the summer months. The theatres would seem to be as well patronised now in the summer as in the winter, in spite of the institution of "summer time" which prolongs the hours devoted to outdoor amusements.

2. *Rose Cottage.* According to the family records, the Terry company stayed at Bellevue Cottage, Clay Lane, when they visited Ryde. The owner of the cottage was Aunt Lizzie, of the brown pelisse, described by Ellen Terry in Chapter I.

3. *Robson.* Ellen Terry says it was audacious of a mere child to tackle a grown-up comedian's parts, but the full extent of the audacity may not be appreciated by the reader who is ignorant of the fame of Robson in the 'fifties. The dramatic critic of *The Times* hailed him after his appearance in a burlesque of "The Merchant of Venice" as the greatest actor seen on the English stage since Edmund Kean. He was a low comedian, playing the commonest routine of vulgar drollery, yet he made an indelible impression on all who saw him by sudden moments of tragic passion.

4. *Fregoli.* For the benefit of young readers who may not see the point of this allusion, it should be explained that Fregoli was an Italian quick-change artist who met with sensational success when he appeared in the London music-halls at the beginning of this century. He had a rival in Biondi, but maintained his supremacy.

5. *Mrs Terry.* While alluding to the many services rendered by her mother

during the tours of the Drawing-Room Entertainment, Ellen Terry does not mention that she played parts in some of the little pieces in the programme.

6. *Those large hands.* It may well astonish readers who are old enough to remember Ellen Terry that she should ever have been ashamed of her hands. But perhaps they were not so beautiful in youth before she had learned how to us them. Apropos of this speculation, I quote Bernard Shaw's opinion that "Ellen Terry actually invented her own beauty. Her portraits as a girl have hardly anything in them of the wonderful woman who, after leaving the stage for seven years, re-appeared in 1875 and took London by storm."

7. *Mr Godwin.* The first allusion in Ellen Terry's autobiography to "Mr Godwin" (Edward William Godwin, F.S.A.) calls for amplification. It is strange that there is no biography of this brilliant man, who besides being an architect of distinction in the British school which broke away from the pseudo-classic style of the early 19th century period, was a learned archæologist, a pioneer in the reform of domestic furniture and decoration, and the initiator of an æsthetic movement in the theatre which was destined to have a lasting influence. One of the greatest services rendered by Gordon Craig's organ *The Mask*, a journal devoted to the art of the theatre, now deceased, was the reprint in 1908 of Godwin's valuable series of articles on "The Architecture and Costumes of Shakespeare's Plays" which originally appeared in "The Architect" in 1875. The time has come to reprint them once more for the instruction of a generation entirely ignorant of the debt the theatre owes to Godwin.

His career can be only briefly summarised here. Born in Bristol in 1833, he was little more than a boy when he won the three premiums in the competitions for designs for the assize-courts in his native town. At the age of twenty-five he built the Town Hall at Northampton. Another important architectural achievement is the Town Hall at Congleton. Of the many houses Godwin built, the White House in Chelsea, designed for his friend Whistler, is best known. In lending his talents to the service of the theatre Godwin had precursors in the great architects, Serlio, Palladio and Inigo Jones. His wide learning and keen perception of beauty made him dissatisfied both with the archæological and æsthetic standards of production in the theatre of his youth. He expressed some of this dissatisfaction in the criticisms of the productions at Bristol to which Ellen Terry refers.

After Godwin left Bristol for London he continued to practise his profession as architect, but from the year 1875 when he supervised the Bancrofts' production of "The Merchant of Venice" (in which Ellen Terry played Portia) his work for the theatre engrossed him. Its extent is not to be measured by the actual number of productions in which he collaborated. He prepared scene and costume designs for many other plays, and was a prolific writer of articles on his special subject, archæology in relation to the theatre. His most notable achievement was the production of "Helena in Troas" at Hengler's Circus in 1886. He designed and built a theatre on the Greek model within the existing structure, and applied his detailed knowledge of the past to the reconstruction of a Greek performance. A contemporary picture of this production, in which

49

Sir Herbert Tree (who years afterwards acknowledged Godwin as his master) appeared as Paris, suggests that it was quite as remarkable for its beauty as for its accuracy. Godwin died in the autumn of the same year at the age of 53.

Ellen Terry is reticent about the character and personality of the man who, seven years after their first meeting at Bristol, was to bring about the great change in her life, which alienated her from her family, and interrupted her career as an actress for the second time. The reticence is natural. We may respect it, and yet wish ardently that Ellen Terry's genius for flashing down vivid impressions of people had been exercised on Edward Godwin. His contemporaries who wrote about him after his premature death are more eloquent about what he did than about what he was. There are a few faint indications in these obituary notices. "He was learned without having a particle of the Dryasdust about him." "He assumed an air of superiority at times, but he found many who willingly recognised his right to it." "He was a friend of Whistler's, of Sandys's and of Swinburne's, and had a singular fascination for those whom he cared to please." "On a foreign tour he was a delightful companion." "His pale ascetic face, rather resembling that of Cardinal Manning." "A picturesque figure." Those scraps help us to visualise Godwin in 1886. But we should like to see him as he was in 1863, to have a picture of the successful young architect, with his penetrating brown eyes set wide apart, teaching fair-haired little Nelly Terry how to "wring" a dress, discoursing the while, perhaps, on his theories of beauty on the stage. There is an interesting piece of evidence that Godwin had tried to interest little Nelly's first manager Charles Kean in these theories, in a letter to him from Kean, which Ellen Terry preserved. The letter had another interest for her. Godwin had seen her as a child in the part of Puck.

10 March 1858.

MY DEAR MR GODWIN:

Many thanks for your kind offer. I shall stick pretty nearly to Macbeth with some slight alterations of the old scenery ... but I am sure Mr Grieve will be always glad to see you, and I shall always be glad to hear you have been seen. I send you a ticket for "The Corsicans" [1] and another for the last night of "The Midsummer" [2] and the Pantomime. Sincerely yours,

C. KEAN

It is not clear whether by the "mistress" of Godwin's beautiful house in Portland Square, Bristol, Ellen Terry means Godwin's first wife (Sara Young) or the sister who kept house for him after the wife's death. As she died within a few months of the marriage (to the strains of a Prelude by Bach which her husband played on the organ to her at her request) it seems more probable that Ellen Terry is referring to Miss Godwin.

8. *The Marriage to Mr Watts.* "We have to announce the marriage of Miss Ellen Alice Terry, the pleasing young actress who was lately a member of the Haymarket Company. The ceremony was performed on Saturday, the 20th

[1] "The Corsican Brothers."
[2] "A Midsummer Night's Dream."

inst., at the church of St Barnabas, Kensington, by the Rev Dr Hussey, and the name of the gentleman with whom the lady has become united in the bonds of matrimony is Mr G. F. Watts."

This cutting from a newspaper of January, 1864, was preserved by Ellen Terry in some reliquary or other for over forty years. In 1908, when her book was published, she transferred it to her copy, pasting it beneath the reproduction of Watts's picture "The Sisters." There is nothing to be said about the paragraph except that "child" would have been a more accurate description of the bride than "lady," but the place in her book chosen for its last resting place by Ellen Terry invites comment. She may have recalled that the first visit of "The Sisters," Kate and Ellen, to Watts's studio was the first step to the altar of St Barnabas's Church. Mr Watts had seen and admired Kate Terry on the stage, and asked his friend Tom Taylor to bring her to his studio. That her younger and then less famous sister should have accompanied Kate is not surprising. Kate had to be chaperoned, and Mrs Terry, busy at home with her large young family, was no doubt glad to let Nelly take her place. Contemporary descriptions of the sisters at this time confirm the evidence of Watts's picture that there was a very effective contrast in their looks. "The contrast was not one of colouring only, but of type. Clement Scott was conscious of this when he wrote that Kate was a pure English beauty, while Ellen was ideal, mystical and mediæval." If he did not get hold of the right words, he certainly got hold of the right idea.

The moment G. F. Watts clapped eyes on that "ideal" face, he seems to have recognised his ideal of an inspiring model. Like the Emperor Franz Josef of Austria, on a somewhat similar occasion, he turned from the elder sister, who was already in Tom Taylor's imagination the future Mrs Watts, to the younger. The marriage was arranged and all too shortly took place. It is not known whether the elderly artist, elderly that is in comparison with his bride —he was more than twice her age—felt any compunction at the innocent rapture of Ellen Terry at the prospect of living with him at Little Holland House. His first marriage is not even mentioned in his biography, a strange omission, hardly justified by the fact that his biographer was his second wife. But the conjecture that he had an uneasy conscience is reasonable. The late Lady Constance Leslie, who was present at the wedding, once told me that the contrast between the atrabilious bridegroom, walking slowly and heavily up the aisle, and the radiant child bride dancing up it on winged feet, struck her as painful. She recalled the lines:

> Crabbed age and youth
> Cannot live together
> Youth is full of pleasaunce:
> Age is full of care.

Apparently neither Tom Taylor, who had the interests of little Nelly Terry at heart, nor her parents, who adored her, were as sensitive. They were pleased that the child had made such a good marriage. As stage folk they may have regretted the abrupt termination of a career so full of promise, but there is no proof of this.

Ellen Terry, writing of her marriage to Watts in after years, says that in many ways it was a happy one. This was a generous exaggeration, very natural in a woman who on her own confession was always "incapable of sustaining a resentment." Mrs Watts, aged sixteen, may have been too young and flighty to be trusted with the usual prerogatives of a wife, but she was kept in a state of tutelage at Little Holland House, for which neither her youth nor her temperament provide an excuse. "The Signor," as Watts was called by his friends, was surrounded by a little court of married women of his own age, presided over by "Beauty" (Mrs Prinsep), who seem to have made it their business to keep his child-wife in order. She was subjected to a humiliating surveillance and had strict injunctions not to open her mouth in the presence of distinguished guests. No doubt Ellen Terry was a trial to the Signor and his court. The story that she once bounded into the room after a dinner-party at Little Holland House, dressed as Cupid (Cupids in those days were dressed, not undressed) may be apocryphal, but the girl who at Freshwater preferred larking with the young Tennysons to sitting sedately in the drawing-room listening to their father's conversation, is very likely to have incurred the displeasure of crabbed age by some such childish prank.

Nevertheless Mrs Watts appears to have been genuinely surprised and mortified when she found that Mr Watts wanted to get rid of her. She loved and admired him, was happy in his studio where she sat to him almost continuously during her brief married life, and was far too innocent to realise the situation. The exact incident which led to the separation was hushed up by the Little Holland House court. It was discreditable to the husband, not to the wife. That his treatment of her weighed heavily on his conscience is evident in the letters he wrote to her between the years 1882 and 1886. Generous again to a fault, Ellen Terry speaks of his "chivalrous assumption of blame." But there was no assumption about it. He knew he was to blame, and entreated her forgiveness. She exculpated him, but he never exculpated himself, although in one letter he expresses his gratitude that "I shall not carry out of the world the sense that any malediction will follow me now that you do not think unkindly of me."

This strange correspondence, begun after Ellen Terry's divorce and second marriage, proves among other things that Watts was astounded at the development of mental powers in his former wife, the existence of which he had never discerned in her youth. The writer of these wonderful letters to him was the girl he had thought should be seen not heard! She was seen by him to some purpose, let it be admitted. His pictures of her are among his best works, the only ones which have stood the test of time.

9. The parts played by Ellen Terry during the period covered by Chapter II were: Hector Melrose ("Home for the Holidays," 1859); Giles, Harry James, etc. ("Distant Relations," 1859); Mabel Valecrusis ("A Lesson for Life," 1860); Sarah Janes ("Nine Points of the Law," 1861); Puck ("Midsummer's Eve," 1861); Clementine ("Attar Gull," 1861); Sophia Steinbach ("All in the Dark," 1861); Rosetta ("A Thumping Legacy," 1861); Letty Briggs ("The Governor's Wife," 1861); Sophie Western ("Bamboozling,"

1861); Clara ("Matrimony," 1861); Mabel ("A Lesson for Husbands," 1861); Mrs Brinstone ("A Nice Quiet Day," 1861); Florence ("A Chinese Honeymoon," 1862); Louisa Drayton ("Grandfather Whitehead," 1862); Clorinda ("A Family Failing," 1862); Margot ("The Sergeant's Wife," 1862); Sally Potts ("The Eton Boy," 1862); Kate Mapleton ("Nine Points of the Law," 1862); Cupid ("Endymion," 1862); Alice ("Marriage at any Price," 1862); Dictys ("Perseus and Andromeda," 1862); Marie ("The Marble Heart," 1862); Marguerite de Stormberg ("The Angel at Midnight," 1862); Gertrude Howard ("The Little Treasure," 1862); Serena ("Conrad and Medera," 1862); Fanny Fact ("Time Tries All," 1862); Spirit of the Future ("Opening Ceremony at the Theatre Royal, Bath," 1863); Titania ("A Midsummer Night's Dream," 1863); Britannia ("Buckstone at Home," 1863); Hero ("Much Ado About Nothing," 1863); Lady Frances Touchwood ('The Belle's Stratagem," 1863); Desdemona ("Othello," 1863); Mary Ford ("A Lesson for Life," 1863); Isabella ("A Game of Romps," 1863); Flora ("The Duke's Motto," 1863); Nerissa ('The Merchant of Venice," 1863); Constance Belmore ("One Touch of Nature," 1863); Julia Melville ("The Rivals," 1863); Sir Tristram ('King Arthur," 1863); Mary Meredith ("The American Cousin," 1863).

CHAPTER III

AN EARLY RETIREMENT

(1867–1868)

§ 1

Most people know that Tom Taylor was one of the leading play-wrights of the 'sixties as well as the dramatic critic of *The Times,* editor of *Punch,* and a distinguished Civil Servant, but to us he was more than this. He was an institution! I simply cannot remember when I did not know him. It is the Tom Taylors of the world who give children on the stage their splendid education. We never had any education in the strict sense of the word, yet through the Taylors and others, we *were* educated. Their house in Lavender Sweep was lovely. I can hardly bear to go near that part of London now, it is so horribly changed. Where are its green fields and its chestnut-trees? We were always welcome at the Taylors', and every Sunday we heard music and met interesting people—Charles Reade among them. Mrs Taylor had rather a hard outside—she was like Mrs Charles Kean in that respect—and I was often frightened out of my life by her; yet I adored her. She was in reality the most tender-hearted, sympathetic woman, and what an admirable musician! She composed nearly all the music for her husband's plays. Every Sunday there was music at Lavender Sweep, quartet playing, and Clara Schumann at the piano.

Tom Taylor was one of the most benign and gentle of men, a good and loyal friend. At first he was more interested in my sister Kate's career than in mine, as was only natural; for, up to the time of my first marriage, Kate had a present, I, only a future. Before we went to Bristol and played with the stock company, she had made her name. At the St James's Theatre, in 1862, she was playing a small part in a version of Sardou's "Nos Intimes," known then as "Friends and Foes," and in a later day and in another version as "Peril."

Miss Herbert—the beautiful Miss Herbert, as she was appropriately called—had the chief part in the play (Mrs Union), and Kate, although not the understudy, was called upon to play it at a few hours' notice. She had from childhood acquired a habit of studying every part in every play

54

in which she was concerned, so she was as ready as though she had been the understudy. Miss Herbert was not a remarkable actress, but her appearance was wonderful indeed. She was very tall, with pale gold hair and the spiritual, ethereal look which the æsthetic movement loved. When mother wanted to flatter me, she said that I looked like Miss Herbert! Rossetti founded many of his pictures on her, and she and Mrs "Janie" Morris were his favourite types. When any one was the object of Rossetti's devotion, there was no extravagant length to which he would not go in demonstrating it. He bought a white bull because it had "eyes like Janie Morris," and tethered it on the lawn of his home in Chelsea. Soon there was no lawn left—only the bull! He invited people to meet it, and heaped favours on it until it kicked everything to pieces, when he reluctantly had to get rid of it.

His next purchase was a white peacock, which, very soon after its arrival, disappeared under the sofa. In vain did Rossetti "shoo" it out. It refused to budge. This went on for days.

"The lovely creature wont respond to me," said Rossetti pathetically to a friend.

The friend dragged out the bird.

"No wonder! It's *dead!*"

"Bulls dont like me," said Rossetti a few days later, "and peacocks arent homely."

It preyed on his mind so much that he tried to repair the failure by buying some white dormice. He sat them up on tiny bamboo chairs, and they looked sweet. When the winter was over, he invited a party to meet them and congratulate them upon waking up from their long sleep.

"They are awake now," he said, "but how quiet they are! How full of repose!"

One of the guests went to inspect the dormice more closely, and a peculiar expression came over his face. It might almost have been thought that he was holding his nose.

"Wake up, little dormice," said Rossetti, prodding them gently with a quill pen.

"They'll never do *that*," said the guest. "They're *dead*. I believe they have been dead some days!"

Do you think Rossetti gave up live stock after this? Not a bit of it. He tried armadillos and tortoises.

"How are the tortoises?" he asked his man one day, after a long spell of forgetfulness that he had any.

"Pretty well, sir, thank you.... That's to say, sir, there aint no tortoises!"

The tortoises, bought to eat the beetles, had been eaten themselves. At least, the shells were found full of beetles.

And the armadillos? "The air of Chelsea dont suit them," said Rossetti's servant. They had certainly left Rossetti's house, but they had not left Chelsea. All the neighbours had dozens of them! They had burrowed, and came up smiling in houses where they were far from welcome.

This, by the way. Miss Herbert, who looked like the Blessed Damosel leaning out "across the bar of heaven," was not very well suited to the line of parts that she was playing at the St James's, but she was very much admired. During the run of "Friends and Foes" she fell ill. Her illness was Kate's opportunity. From the night that Kate played Mrs Union, her reputation was made.

It was a splendid chance, no doubt, but of what use would it have been to any one who was not ready to use it? Kate, though only about nineteen at this time, was a finished actress. She had been a perfect Ariel, a beautiful Cordelia, and had played at least forty other parts of importance since she had appeared as a tiny Robin in the Keans' production of "The Merry Wives of Windsor." She had not had her head turned by big salaries, and she had never ceased working since she was four years old. No wonder that she was capable of bearing the burden of a piece at a moment's notice. The Americans cleverly say that "the lucky cat *watches*." I should add that the lucky cat *works*. Reputations on the stage—at any rate, enduring reputations—are not made by chance, and to an actress who has not worked hard the finest opportunity in the world will be utterly useless.

Kate's acting, unlike that of Adelaide Neilsen, who was the great popular favourite before Kate came to the front, was scientific. She knew what she was about. There was more ideality than passionate womanliness in her interpretations. For this reason, perhaps, her Cordelia was finer than her Portia or her Beatrice.

She was engaged at one time to a young actor, called Montagu. If the course of that love affair had run smooth, where should I have been? Kate would have been the Terry of the age. But Mr Montagu went to America, and, after five years of life as a matinée idol, died there. Before that, Arthur Lewis had come along. I was glad because he was rich, and during his courtship of my sister I had some riding, of which in my girlhood I was passionately fond.

Tom Taylor had an enormous admiration for Kate, and during her second season as a "star" at Bristol he came down to see her play Juliet and Beatrice and Portia.

From Bristol my sister went to London to become Fechter's "leading lady," and from that time until she made her last appearance in 1867 as Juliet at the Adelphi, her career was a blaze of triumph.

§ 2

It was about this time that I paid my first visit to Paris. I saw the Empress Eugénie driving in the Bois, looking like an exquisite waxwork. Oh, the beautiful *slope* of women at this period! They looked like lovely half-moons, lying back in their carriages. It was an age of elegance —in France particularly—an age of luxury. They had just laid down asphalt for the first time in the streets of Paris, and the quiet of the boulevards was wonderful after the rattling London streets. I often went to three parties a night; but I was in a difficult position, as I could not speak a word of the language. I met Tissot, and Gambard, who had just built Rosa Bonheur a house at Nice.

I liked the Frenchmen because they liked me, but I didn't admire them.

I tried to learn to smoke, but I never took kindly to it and soon gave it up.

What was the thing that made me homesick for London? *Household Words!* The excitement in the 'sixties over each issue of this journal in which Dickens's novels were published serially can be understood only by people who experienced it at the time. Boys used to sell *Household Words* in the streets, and they were often pursued by an eager crowd, for all the world as if they were carrying news of the "latest winner."

Of course I went to the theatre in Paris. I saw Sarah Bernhardt for the first time, and Madame Favart, Croisette, Delaunay, and Got. I never thought Croisette—a superb animal—a "patch" on Sarah, who was at this time as thin as a harrow. Even then I recognised that Sarah was not a bit conventional, and would not stay long at the Comédie. Yet she did not put me out of conceit with the old school. I saw "Les Précieuses Ridicules" finely done, and I said to myself then, as I have often said since: "Old school—new school? What does it matter which, so long as it is *good enough?*"

Madame Favart I knew personally, and she gave me many useful hints. One was never to black my eyes *underneath* when "making up." She pointed out that although this was necessary when the stage was lighted entirely from beneath, it had become ugly and meaningless since the introduction of top lights.

The friend who took me everywhere in Paris landed me one night in the dressing-room of a singer. I remember it because I heard her com-

57

plain to a man of some injustice. She had not got some engagement that she had expected.

"It serves you damn right!" he answered. For the first time I seemed to realise how brutal it was of a man to speak to a woman like that, and I *hated* it.

Long afterwards, in the same city, I saw a man sitting calmly in a *fiacre* and ordering the *cocher* to drive on, although a woman was clinging to the side of the carriage and refusing to let go. She was a strong, splendid creature of the peasant class, bareheaded, with a fine open brow, and she was obviously consumed by resentment of some injustice—mad with it. She was dragged along in one of the busiest streets in Paris, the little Frenchman sitting there smiling. How she escaped death I dont know. Then he became conscious that people were looking, and he stopped the cab and let her get in.

Paris! Paris! Young as I was, I fell under the spell of your elegance, your cleanness, your well-designed streets, your nonchalant gaiety. I drank coffee at Tortoni's. I visited the studio of Meissonier. I stood in the crowd that collected round Rosa Bonheur's "Horse Fair," which was in the Salon that year. I grew dead sick of the endless galleries of the Louvre. I went to the Madeleine at Easter time, and fainted from ecstasy when the Host was raised.... I never fainted again in my life, except once from *anger,* when I heard some friends whom I loved slandering another friend whom I loved more.

Good-bye to Paris and back to London, where I began acting again with only half my heart. I did very well, they said, as Helen in "The Hunchback," the first part I played after my return; but I cared nothing about my success. I was feeling wretchedly ill, and angry too, because they insisted on putting my married name on the bills.

After playing with Kate at Bristol and at the Adelphi in London, I accepted an engagement to appear in a new play by Tom Taylor, called "The Antipodes." It was a bad play, and I had a bad part, but Telbin's scenery was lovely. Telbin was a poet, and he has handed on much of his talent to his son. The younger Telbin painted most of our "Faust" scenery at the Lyceum; the rest was the work of dear Hawes Craven, who so loved his garden and could paint the flicker of golden sunshine for the stage better than any one. I have always been friendly with the scene-painters, perhaps because I have always taken pains about my dresses, and consulted them beforehand about the colour, so that I should not look wrong in their scenes, nor their scenes wrong with my dresses.

The elder Telbin and Albert Moore together did up the New Queen's Theatre, Long Acre, which was opened in October, 1867, under the ostensible management of the Alfred Wigans. I say "ostensible," because

58

Mr Labouchere was behind them, controlling their policy. Miss Henrietta Hodson, whom he afterwards married, played in the burlesques and farces without which no theatre bill in London at that time was complete. The Wigans offered me an engagement, and I stayed with them until 1868, when I again left the stage. During this engagement I acted with Charles Wyndham and Lionel Brough, and, last, but not least, with Henry Irving.

Mrs Wigan, *née* Leonora Pincott, did me the honour to think that I was worth teaching, and took nearly as much pains to improve me as Mrs Kean had done at a different stage in my artistic growth. Her own accomplishments as a comedy actress impressed me more than I can say. I remember seeing her as Mrs Candour, and thinking to myself, "This is absolutely perfect." If I were a teacher I would impress on young actresses never to move a finger or turn the eye without being quite certain that the movement or the glance *tells* something. Mrs Wigan made few gestures, but each one quietly, delicately indicated what the words which followed expressed. And while she was speaking she never frittered away the effect of that silent eloquence.

One of my besetting sins was—nay, still is—the lack of repose. Mrs Wigan at once detected this fault, and at rehearsals would work to make me remedy it. *"Stand still!"* she would shout from the stalls. "Now you're of value!" "Motionless! Just as you are! *That's* right."

Ten years later she came to see me at the Court Theatre, where I was playing in "The House of Darnley," and afterwards wrote me the following very kind and encouraging letter:

December 7, 1877.

DEAR MISS TERRY,—

You have a very difficult part in 'The House of Darnley.' I know no one who could play it as well as you did last night—but *you* could do it much better. You would vex me much if I thought you had no ambition in your art. You are the one young actress of my day who can have her success entirely in her own hands. You have all the gifts for your noble profession, and, as you know, your own devotion to it will give you all that can be learned. I'm very glad my stage direction was useful and pleasant to you, and any benefit you have derived from it is overpaid by your style of acting. You cannot have a 'groove'; you are too much of an artist. Go on and prosper, and if at any time you think I can help you in your art, you may always count on that help from your most sincere well-wisher

LEONORA WIGAN.

Another service that Mrs Wigan did me was to cure me of "fooling" on the stage. *"Did* she?", I think I hear some one interrupt me unkindly at this point! Well, at any rate, she gave me a good fright one night, and

I never forgot it, though I will not say I never fooled again. I think it was in "The Double Marriage," the first play put on at the New Queen's. As Rose de Beaurepaire, I wore a white muslin Directoire dress and looked absurdly young. There was one "curtain" which used to convulse Wyndham. He had a line, "Whose child is this?" and there was I, looking a mere child myself, and with a bad cold in my head too, answering: It's *bine!*" The very thought of it used to send us off into fits of laughter. We hung on to chairs, helpless, limp, and incapable. Mrs. Wigan said if we did it again, she would go in front and hiss us, and she carried out her threat. The very next time we laughed a loud hiss rose from the stagebox. I was simply paralysed with terror.

Dear old Mrs Wigan! The stories that have been told about her would fill a book! She was exceedingly plain, rather like a toad, yet, perversely, she was more vain of her looks than of her acting. In the theatre she gave herself great airs and graces, and outside it hobnobbed with duchesses and princesses.

This fondness for aristocratic society gave additional spice to the story that one day a blear-eyed old cabman in capes and muffler descended from the box of a disreputable-looking growler, and inquired at the stage-door for Leonora Pincott.

"Any lady 'ere of that name?"

"No."

"Well, I think she's married, and changed her name, but she's 'ere right enough. Tell 'er I wont keep 'er a minute. I'm 'er bloody old father!"

§ 3

ONE very foggy night in December 1867—it was Boxing Day, I think— I acted for the first time with Henry Irving. This was a great event in my life, but at the time it passed me by and left "no wrack behind." Ever anxious to improve on the truth, which is often devoid of all sensationalism, people have told a story of Henry Irving promising that if he ever were in a position to offer me an engagement I should be his leading lady. The latest tale of our first meeting was told during my jubilee. Then, to my amazement, I read that on that famous night when I was playing Puck at the Princess's, and caught my toe in the trap, "a young man with dark hair and a white face rushed forward from the crowd of supers and said: 'Never mind, darling. Dont cry! One day you will be queen of the stage.' It was Henry Irving!"

In view of these legends, I ought to assert all the more stoutly that, until I went to the Lyceum Theatre, Henry Irving was nothing to me and I nothing to him. I never consciously thought that he would become a great actor. He had no high opinion of *my* acting! He has said since that he thought me at the Queen's Theatre charming and individual as a woman, but as an actress *hoydenish!* I believe that he hardly spared me even so much definite thought as this. His soul was not more surely in his body than in the theatre, and I, a woman who was at this time caring more about love and life than the theatre, must have been to him more or less unsympathetic. He thought of nothing else, cared for nothing else; worked day and night; went without his dinner to buy a book that might be helpful in studying, or a stage jewel that might be helpful to wear. I remember his telling me that he once bought a sword with a jewelled hilt, and hung it at the foot of his bed. All night he kept getting up and striking matches to see it, shifting its position, rapt in admiration of it.

He had it all in him when we acted together that foggy night, but he could express very little. Many of his defects sprang from his not having been on the stage as a child. He was stiff with self-consciousness; his eyes were dull, his face heavy. The piece we played was Garrick's boiled-down version of "The Taming of the Shrew," and he, as Petruchio, appreciated the humour and everything else far more than I did, as Katharine; yet he played badly, nearly as badly as I did; and how much more to blame I was, for I was at this time much more easy and skilful from a purely technical point of view.

Was Henry Irving impressive in those days? Yes and no. His fierce and indomitable will showed itself in his application to his work. Quite unconsciously I learned from watching him that to do work well, the artist must spend his life in incessant labour, and deny himself every-thing for that purpose. It is a lesson we actors and actresses cannot learn too early, for the bright and glorious heyday of our success must always be brief at best.

Henry Irving, when he played Petruchio, had been toiling in the provinces for eleven years, and not until Rawdon Scudamore in "Hunted Down" had he had any success. Even that was forgotten in his failure as Petruchio. What a trouncing he received from the critics who have since heaped praise on many worse players!

I think this was the peculiar quality in his acting afterwards—a kind of fine temper, like that of the purest steel, produced by the perpetual fight against difficulties. Socrates, it is said, had every capacity for evil in his face, yet he was good, as a naturally good man could never be. Henry Irving at first had everything against him as an actor. He could not speak, he could not walk, he could not *look*. He wanted to do things in a part, and he could not do them. His amazing power was imprisoned, and only after long and weary years did he succeed in setting it free.

A man with a will like that *must* be impressive! To quick-seeing eyes he must, no doubt. But my eyes were not quick, and they were, moreover, fixed on a world outside the theatre. Better than his talent and his will I remember his courtesy. In those days, instead of having our salaries brought to our dressing-rooms, we used to wait in a queue on Treasury Day to receive them. I was always late in coming, and always in a hurry to get away. Very gravely and quietly Henry Irving used to give up his place to me.

I played once more at the Queen's after Katharine and Petruchio. It was in a little piece called "The Household Fairy," and I remember it chiefly through an accident which befell poor Jack Clayton through me. The curtain had fallen on "The Household Fairy," and Clayton was dancing with me on the stage to the music which was being played during the interval, instead of changing his dress for the next piece. This dancing during the entr'acte was very popular among us. Many a burlesque quadrille I had with Terriss and others in later days. On this occasion Clayton suddenly found he was late in changing, and, rushing upstairs to his dressing-room in a hurry, he missed his footing and fell back on his head. This made me very miserable, as I could not help feeling that I was responsible.

Soon afterwards I left the stage for six years. I left it without regret. I was very happy, leading a quiet, domestic life in the heart of the country. When my two children were born, I thought of the stage less than ever. They absorbed all my time, all my interest, all my love.

NOTES TO CHAPTER III

1. *Tom Taylor.* The chief dramatic critic of *The Times* at the date of Kate Terry's triumph at the St James's Theatre was John Oxenford. Taylor was the art critic, but occasionally wrote about plays in Oxenford's place. No doubt when he heard his protégée was going to play Miss Herbert's part, he saw an opportunity for advancing her reputation in London, and laid his plans for noticing her performance. The eulogy which appeared in *The Times* the next morning made the name of Kate Terry famous.

2. *Rossetti.* Ellen Terry's digression to Rossetti, into which she was led by her reference to Miss Herbert, invites a brief allusion to a question many people have asked. Why did Rossetti never paint Ellen Terry? An artist to whom I put the question answered that Ellen Terry was not really the type the Pre-Raphaelites liked. "Too largely built, too vigorous, too Norse. In fact not nearly floppy enough." Yet Graham Robertson in his book of reminiscence, "Time Was," says that she was "the accepted type of the Pre-Raphaelite school," and comments on the strangeness of her never having been painted by any artist belonging to it.

3. *Arthur Lewis.* At the time Arthur Lewis "came along" and fell in love with Kate Terry, he was well known in musical and artistic circles. His house,

Moray Lodge, Campden Hill, was a kind of "salon" in the 'sixties. There the "Moray Minstrels," among whom, George du Maurier, then at the beginning of his brilliant career, shone as a singer and raconteur, used to give entertainments.

4. *Fechter*. Charles Albert Fechter came to London from Paris. He had a great reputation as a perfect stage lover. He played Hamlet as "a pale woebegone Norseman with long flaxen hair, wearing a strange garb, never associated with the part upon the English stage, and making a piratical sweep upon the whole fleet of little theatrical prescriptions" (Charles Dickens). "Fechter's Hamlet was chiefly remarkable for light hair and bad English" (William Winter). His reign at the Lyceum was brief. and was remembered chiefly on account of Kate Terry's Ophelia.

5. *Ellen Terry's Second Retirement*. "She left the stage without hesitation for the best years of her youth to keep house on £3 a week with Edward William Godwin; and was induced to return to it, only by an offer of £40 when she had two children to provide for." (From Bernard Shaw's Preface to "Ellen Terry and Bernard Shaw: A Correspondence") I doubt whether the truth about Ellen Terry's second retirement is quite as simple as Mr Shaw represents. From such facts as are known, and they are few because Ellen Terry spoke about this period of her life with reserve even to those most intimate with her, and then subjectively rather than objectively, very different conclusions can be drawn.

There is no proof that Ellen Terry left the stage in 1868 without hesitation, and voluntarily. It is clear from what she says in her autobiography that from the time she was driven back to her work (after her separation from Watts) she took no pleasure in it, but disillusioned, and suffering from a sense of cruel injustice, she was then unable to take pleasure in anything. "I hated my life, hated every one and everything," she writes. The stage was no more detestable to her than the world. It was while she was in this unhappy frame of mind, kicking against the pricks, that she met Edward Godwin, the friend of those happy days at Bristol, again. It was in his favour that he was a citizen of that artistic paradise from which she had been ignominiously expelled. Who would wish to pry into the secret places of Ellen Terry's heart? But the story that she ran away from her family and the stage at the dictates of love is not the exact truth. The parents of the youthful Mrs Watts were, in spite of their association with the stage, in spite of their having begun their married life unconventionally with an elopement, eminently Victorian in their standards of conduct. An indiscretion of Nelly's—it is said that when Edward Godwin was ill, she stayed to look after him one night instead of returning home—led to a domestic scene, that often acted scene which ends in a door being slammed on an erring daughter. The sequel was that Ellen Terry "set up house" with Edward Godwin somewhere in Hertfordshire. One reason for her abandoning the stage at the same time appears to have been that she had incurred the disapproval of all the friends who had interested themselves in her career as an actress. She may have been influenced too by a genuine wish not to be a source of embarrassment to her family. Her sister Kate, through her marriage, now occupied a social position of some importance. The conclusion that Ellen Terry's retirement was to some extent forced on her is not fantastic, and quite compatible with her statement that she did not regret it, and for a time was blissfully happy.

The effect on her art was probably beneficial. Her friend Graham Robertson argues convincingly in one of the chapters devoted to her in his memoirs that these years of exile from the stage were responsible for the uniqueness of Ellen Terry. "What was it that made her so unlike any other actress? Why had the stage left no mark upon her, for never was woman less stagey and artificial? I think it was because at the most critical and receptive age of nineteen, when most young players are working up towards their first success and living wholly in the world behind the footlights, she left the stage and gave what would be considered her best years to a real life, away in the country, far from theatres and all concerning them." In support of the theory that a peculiar freshness and spontaneity in Ellen Terry's acting might have been lacking without this six years' retirement, an often quoted apothegm of Talma's, may be quoted once more. "Perpetual indulgence in the excitement of impersonation dulls the sympathy and impairs the imaginative faculty of the comedian. His power of observation is weakened, and he is in danger of becoming mechanical and uninspired." Nevertheless a long spell of abstinence from the practice of an art is not to be recommended until there has been enough practice for a solid and enduring technique to be acquired. At the time of her retirement Ellen Terry had had this practice. She had acted continuously during her childhood and adolescence, and could artistically afford a rest.

6. The parts played by Ellen Terry during the period covered by Chapter III were: Helen ("The Hunchback," 1866); Marion Vernon ("A Sister's Penance," 1867); Keziah Mapletop ("A Sheep in Wolf's Clothing," 1867); Margaret Wentworth ("Henry Dunbar," 1867); Madeleine ("The Antipodes," 1867); Kate Dalrymple ("The Little Savage," 1867); Rose de Beaurepaire ("The Double Marriage," 1867); Mrs Mildmay ("Still Waters Run Deep," 1867); Katharine ("Katharine and Petruchio," 1867); Kitty ("The Household Fairy," 1868).

CHAPTER IV

SIX YEARS IN THE COUNTRY

(1868–1874)

§ 1

MY disappearance from the stage must have been a heavy blow to my father and mother, who had urged me to return in 1866 after the failure of my first marriage, and were quite certain that I had a great future. For the first time for years they had no child in the theatre. Marion and Floss, who were afterwards to adopt the stage as a profession, were still at school; Kate had married; and none of their sons had shown any great aptitude for acting. Fred, the youngest, who was afterwards to do so well, was at this time hardly out of petticoats.

My retirement was a very different one from my sister Kate's. I left the stage quietly and secretly, and I was cut off from my family and friends.

Then a dreadful thing happened. A body was found in the river—the dead body of a young woman, very fair and slight and tall. Every one thought it was my body.

I had gone away without a word. No one knew where I was. My own father identified the corpse, and Floss and Marion, at their boarding-school, were put into mourning. Then mother went. She kept her head under the shock of the likeness, and bethought her of "a strawberry mark upon my left arm." (*Really* it was on my left knee.) That settled it, for there was no such mark to be found upon the poor corpse. It was just at this moment that the news came to me in my country retreat that I had been found dead, and I flew up to London to give ocular proof to my poor distracted parents that I was alive. Mother, who had been the only one not to identify the drowned girl, confessed to me that she was so like me that just for a second she, too, was deceived. You see, they knew I had not been very happy since my return to the stage, and when I went away without a word, they were terribly anxious, and prepared to believe the first bad tidings that came to hand. It came in the shape of that most extraordinary likeness between me and that poor soul who threw herself into the river.

65

I was barely twenty when I left the stage for the second time, and I haven't made up my mind yet whether it was good or bad for me, as an actress, to cease from practising my craft for six years. Talma, the great French actor, recommends long spells of rest. This comes in very useful in my defence, yet I am not convinced they are always beneficial. I can't imagine Henry Irving leaving the stage for six months, much less for six years, and I dont think it would have been of the slightest benefit to him. But he had not been on the stage as a child. If I was able to rest so long without rusting, it was, I am sure, because I had been thoroughly trained in the technique of acting long before I reached my twentieth year—an age at which most students are just beginning to wrestle with elementary principles.

Of course, I did not argue in this way at the time! I had no intention of ever acting again when I left the Queen's Theatre. If it is the mark of the artist to love art before everything, to renounce everything for its sake, to think all the sweet human things of life well lost if only he may attain something, do some good, great work—then I was never an artist. I have been happiest in my work when I was working for some one else. I admire those impersonal people who care for nothing outside their own ambition, yet I detest them at the same time, and I have the simplest faith that absolute devotion to another human being means the greatest *happiness*. That happiness for a time was now mine.

I led a most unconventional life, and experienced exquisite delight from the mere fact of being in the country. No one knows what "the country" means until he or she has lived in it. "Then, if ever, come perfect days."

What a sensation it was, too, to be untrammelled by time! Actors must take care of themselves and their voices, husband their strength for the evening work, and when it is over they are too tired to do anything! For the first time I was able to put all my energies into living. Charles Lamb writes that when he left the East India House, he felt embarrassed by the vast estates of time at his disposal, and wished that he had a bailiff to manage them for him, but I knew no such embarrassment when I left the stage. I began gardening, "the purest of human pleasures"; I learned to cook, and in time cooked very well, though my first essay in that difficult art was rewarded with dire and complete failure.

It was a chicken! Now, as all the chickens had names—Sultan, Duke, Lord Tom Noddy, Lady Teazle, and so forth—and as I was very proud of them as living birds, it was a great wrench to kill one at all, to start with. It was the murder of Sultan, not the killing of a chicken. However, at last it was done, and Sultan deprived of his feathers, floured, and

66

MARION AND FLORENCE TERRY

trussed. I had no idea *how* this was all done, but I tried to make him "sit up" nicely like the chickens in the shops.

He came up to the table looking magnificent—almost turkey-like in his proportions.

"Hasnt this chicken rather an odd smell?" some one said.

"How can you!" I answered. "It must be quite fresh—it's Sultan!"

However, when we began to carve, the smell grew more and more potent.

I had cooked Sultan without taking out his in'ards!

There was no dinner that day except bread-sauce, beautifully made, well-cooked vegetables, and pastry like the foam of the sea. I had a wonderful hand for pastry!

My hour of rising at this pleasant place near Mackery End in Hertfordshire was six. Then I washed the babies. I had a perfect mania for *washing* everything and everybody. We had one little servant, and I insisted on washing her head. Her mother came up from the village to protest.

"Never washed her head in my life. Never washed any of my children's heads. And just look at their splendid hair!"

After the washing I fed the animals. There were two hundred ducks and fowls to feed, as well as the children. By the time I had done this, and cooked the dinner, the morning had flown away. After the midday meal I sewed. Sometimes I drove out in the pony-cart. And in the evening I walked across the common to fetch the milk. The babies used to roam where they liked on this common in charge of a bulldog, while I sat and read.

I studied cookery-books instead of parts. Mrs Beeton instead of Shakespeare!

Of course, I thought my children the most brilliant and beautiful children in the world, and, indeed, "this side idolatry," they were exceptional, and they had an exceptional bringing up. They were allowed no rubbishy picture-books, but from the first Japanese prints lined their nursery walls, and Walter Crane was their classic. If injudicious friends gave the wrong sort of present, it was promptly burned. A mechanical mouse in which Edy, my little daughter, showed keen interest and delight, was taken away as being "realistic and common." Only wooden toys were allowed. This severe training proved so effective that when a doll dressed in a violent pink silk dress was given to Edy, she said it was "vulgar"!

By that time she had found a tongue, but until she was two years old she never spoke a word, though she seemed to notice everything with her grave dark eyes. We were out driving when I heard her voice for the first time:

"There's some more."

She spoke quite distinctly. It was almost uncanny.

"More what?" I asked in a trembling voice, afraid that having delivered herself once, she might lapse into dumbness.

"Birds!"

The nursemaid, Essie, described Edy tersely as "a piece," while Teddy, who was adored by every one because he was fat and fair and angelic-looking, she called "the feather of England."

"The feather of England" was considered by his sister a great coward. She used to hit him on the head with a wooden spoon for crying, and exhort him, when he said, "Master Teddy afraid of the dark," to be a *woman!*

I feel that if I go maundering on much longer about my children, some one will exclaim with a witty and delightful author when he saw "Peter Pan" for the seventh time: "Oh, for an hour of Herod!" When I think of little Edy bringing me in minute bunches of flowers all the morning, with the reassuring information that "there are lots more," I could cry. But why should any one be interested in that? Is it interesting that when she dug up a turnip in the garden for the first time, she should have come running to beg me to come quick: "Miss Edy found a radish. It's as big as—as big as *God!*"

When I took her to her first theatre—it was Sanger's Circus—and the clown pretended to fall from the tight-rope, and the drum went bang! she said: "Take me away! take me away! you ought never to have brought me here!" No wonder she was considered a dour child! I immediately and humbly obeyed.

It was truly the simple life we led in Hertfordshire. From scrubbing floors and lighting fires, cooking, gardening, and harnessing the pony, I grew thinner than ever—as thin as a whipping-post, a hurdle, or a haddock! I went to church in blue-and-white cotton, with my servant in silk. "I dont half like it," she said. "Theyll take you for the cook, and me for the lady!"

We kept a goat, a dear fellow whom I liked very much until I caught him one day chasing my daughter. I seized him by his horns to inflict severe punishment; but then I saw that his eyes were exactly like mine, and it made me laugh so much that I let him go and never punished him at all.

"Boo" became an institution in these days. She was the wife of a doctor who kept a private asylum in the neighbouring village, and on his death she tried to look after the lunatics herself. But she wasnt

68

at all successful! They kept escaping, and people didnt like it. This was my gain, for "Boo" came to look after me instead and for the next thirty years I was her only lunatic, and she my most constant companion and dear and loyal friend.

We seldom went to London. When we did, Ted nearly had a fit at seeing so many "we'els go wound." But we went to Normandy, and saw Lisieux, Nantes, Bayeux. Long afterwards, when I was feeling as dry as sand-paper on the stage, I had only to recall some of the divine music I had heard in those great churches abroad to become soft, melted, able to act. I remember in some cathedral we left little Edy sitting down below while we climbed up into the clerestory to look at some beautiful piece of architecture. The choir were practising, and suddenly there rose a boy's voice, pure, effortless, and clear. . . . For years that moment stayed with me. When we came down to fetch Edy, she said:

"Ssh! ssh! Miss Edy has seen the angels!"

Oh, blissful quiet days! How soon they came to an end! Already the shadow of financial trouble fell across my peace. Yet still I never thought of returning to the stage.

One day I was driving in a narrow lane, when the wheel of the pony-cart came off. I was standing there, thinking what I should do next, when a whole crowd of horsemen in "pink" came leaping over the hedge into the lane. One of them stopped and asked if he could do anything. Then he looked hard at me and exclaimed: "Good God! it's Nelly!"

The man was Charles Reade.

"Where have you been all these years?" he said.

"I have been having a very happy time," I answered.

"Well, you've had it long enough. Come back to the stage!"

"No, never!"

"You're a fool! You ought to come back."

Suddenly I remembered the bailiff in the house a few miles away, and I said laughingly: "Well, perhaps, I would think of it if some one would give me forty pounds a week!"

"Done!" said Charles Reade. "I'll give you that, and more, if you'll come and play Philippa Chester in 'The Wandering Heir.' "

He went on to explain that Mrs John Wood, who had been playing Philippa at the New Queen's, of which he was the lessee, would have to relinquish the part soon, because she was under contract to appear else-where. The piece was a great success, and promised to run a long time if he could find a good Philippa to replace Mrs Wood. It was a kind of Rosalind part, and Charles Reade only exaggerated pardonably when he said that I should never have any part better suited to me!

§ 2

In a very short time after that meeting in the lane, it was announced that the new Philippa was to be an actress who was returning to the stage "after a long period of retirement." Only just before the first night did any one guess who it was, and then there was great excitement among those who remembered me. The acclamation with which I was welcomed back on the first night surprised me. The papers were more flattering than they had ever been before. It was a tremendous success for me, and I was all the more pleased because I was following an accomplished actress in the part.

It is curious how often I have "followed" others. I never "created" a part, as theatrical jargon has it, until I played Olivia at the Court, and I had to challenge comparison, in turn, with Miss Marie Wilton, Mrs John Wood and Mrs Kendal. Perhaps it was better for me than if I had had parts specially written for me, and with which no other names were associated.

The hero of "The Wandering Heir," when I first took up the part of Philippa, was played by Edmund Leathes, but afterward by Johnstone Forbes-Robertson. Every one knows how good-looking he is now, but as a boy he was a beautiful creature. Dressed in an indigo blue smock, he looked more like an artist than an actor, and indeed he had great gifts as a painter. In those days began a friendship between us which has lasted unbroken until this moment. His father and mother were delightful people, and very kind to me always.

Every one was kind to me at this time. Friends who I had thought would be estranged by my long absence rallied round me and welcomed me as if it were six minutes instead of six years since I had dropped out of their ken. I was not yet a "made" woman, but I had a profitable engagement, and a delightful one, too, with Charles Reade, and I felt an enthusiasm for my work which had been wholly absent when I had returned to the stage the first time. My children were left in the country at first, but they came up and joined me when, in the year following "The Wandering Heir," I went to the Bancrofts at the Prince of Wales's. I never had the slightest fear of leaving them to their own devices, for they always knew how to amuse themselves, and were very independent and dependable in spite of their extreme youth. I have often thanked heaven since that, with all their faults, my boy and girl have never been lazy, and never felt dull. At this time Teddy always had a pencil in his hand, when he wasnt looking for his biscuit—he was a greedy little thing! —and Edy was hammering clothes on to her dolls with tin-tacks! Teddy said poetry beautifully, and when he and his sister were still tiny mites,

70

they used to go through scene after scene of "As You Like It," for their own amusement, not for an audience, in the Wilderness at Hampton Court. They were by no means prodigies, but it did not surprise me that my son, when he grew up, should be first a good actor, then an artist of originality, and should finally turn all his brains and industry to new developments in the art of the theatre. My daughter has acted also—not enough to please me, for I have a very firm belief in her talents—and has shown again and again that she can design and make clothes for the stage that are both lovely and effective. In all my most successful stage dresses lately she has had a hand, and if I had anything to do with a national theatre, I should, without prejudice, put her in charge of the wardrobe at once!

I may be a proud parent, but I have always refrained from "pushing" my children. They have had to fight for themselves, and to their mother their actual achievements have mattered very little. So long as they were not lazy, I have always felt that I could forgive them anything!

And now Teddy and Edy—Teddy in a minute white piqué suit, and Edy in a tiny kimono, in which she looked as Japanese as everything which surrounded her—disappear from these pages for quite a long time. But all this time, you must understand, they are educating their mother!

§ 3

CHARLES READE, having brought me back to the stage, and being my manager into the bargain, was deeply concerned about my progress as an actress. During the run of "The Wandering Heir" he used to sit in a box every night to watch the play, and would send me round notes between the acts, telling me what I had done ill and what well in the preceding act. Dear, kind, unjust, generous, cautious, impulsive, passionate, gentle Charles Reade. Never have I known any one who combined so many qualities, far asunder as the poles, in one single disposition. He was placid and turbulent, yet always majestic. He was inexplicable and entirely lovable—a stupid old dear, and as wise as Solomon! He seemed guileless, and yet had moments of suspicion and craftiness worthy of the wisdom of the serpent. One moment he would call me "dearest child"; the next, with indignant emphasis, "Madam!"

When "The Wandering Heir" had at last exhausted its great popularity, I went on a tour with Charles Reade in several of his plays. In spite of his many and varied interests, he had entirely succumbed to the magic of the "irresistible theatre," and it used to strike me as rather pathetic to see a man of his intellectual power and originality working the stage sea at nights, in company with a rough lad, in his dramatic

71

version of "Hard Cash." In this play, which was known as "Our Seaman," I had a part which I could not bear to be paid twenty-five pounds a week for acting. I knew that the tour was not a financial success, and I ventured to suggest that it would be good economy to get some one else for Susan Merton. For answer I got a fiery "Madam, you are a rat! You desert a sinking ship!" My dear old companion, Boo, who was with me, resented this very much: "How can you say such things to my Nelly?"

"Your Nelly!" said Charles Reade. "I love her a thousand times better than you do, or any puling woman." Another time he grew white with rage, and his dark eyes blazed, because the same "puling woman" said very lightly and playfully: "Why did poor Nell come home from rehearsal looking so tired yesterday? You work her too hard." He thought this unfair, as the work had to be done, and flamed out at us with such violence that it was almost impossible to identify him with the kind old gentleman of the Colonel Newcome type whom I had seen stand up at the Tom Taylors', on Sunday evenings, and sing "The Girl I Left Behind Me" with such pathos that he himself was moved to tears. But, though it was a painful time for both of us, it was almost worth while to quarrel with him, because when we made it up he was sure to give me some "treat"—a luncheon, a present, or a drive. We both felt we needed some jollification because we had suffered so much from being estranged. He used to say that there should be no such word as "quarrel," and one morning he wrote me a letter with the following postscript written in big letters:

THERE DO EXIST SUCH THINGS AS HONEST MISUNDERSTANDINGS.

There, my Eleanora Delicia (this was his name for me, my real, full name being Ellen Alicia), stick that up in some place where you will often see it. Better put it on *your looking-glass*. And if you can once get those words into your noddle, it will save you a world of unhappiness.

I think he was quite right about this. Would that he had been as right in his theories about stage management! He was a rare one for realism. He had *preached* it in all his plays, and when he produced a one-act play, "Rachael the Reaper," in front of "The Wandering Heir," he began to practise what he preached—jumped into reality up to the neck!

He began by buying *real* pigs, *real* sheep, a *real* goat, and a *real* dog. *Real* litter was strewn all over the stage, much to the inconvenience of the unreal farm-labourer, Charles Kelly, who could not compete with it, although he looked as like a farmer as any actor could. They all looked their parts better than the real wall which ran across the stage,

72

piteously naked of *real* shadows, owing to the absence of the *real* sun, and, of course, deficient in the painted shadows which make a painted wall look so like the real thing.

Never, never can I forget Charles Reade's arrival at the theatre in a four-wheeler with a goat and a lot of little pigs. When the cab drew up at the stage-door, the goat seemed to say, as plainly as any goat could: "I'm dashed if I stay in this cab any longer with these pigs!" and while Charles Reade was trying to pacify it, the piggies escaped! Unfortunately, they didnt all go in the same direction, and poor dear Charles Reade had a "divided duty." There was the goat, too, in a nasty mood. Oh, his serious face, as he decided to leave the goat and run for the pigs, with his loose trousers, each one a yard wide at least, flapping in the wind!

"That's a relief, at any rate," said Charles Kelly, who was watching the flight of the pigs. "I shant have those damned pigs to spoil my acting as well as the damned dog and the damned goat!"

How we all laughed when Charles Reade returned from the pig-hunt to rehearsal with the brief direction to the stage manager that the pigs would be "cut out."

The reason for the real wall was made more evident when the real goat was tied up to it. A painted wall would never have stood such a strain.

On the first night, the real dog bit Kelly's real ankles, and in real anger he kicked the real animal by a real mistake into the orchestra's real drum!

So much for realism as practised by Charles Reade! There was still something to remind him of the experiment in Rachael, the circus goat. Rachael—he was no she, but what of that?—was given the free run of the garden of Reade's house at Knightsbridge. He had everything that any normal goat could desire—a rustic stable, a green lawn, the best of food. Yet Rachael pined and grew thinner and thinner. One night when we were all sitting at dinner, with the French windows open on to the lawn because it was a hot night, Rachael came prancing into the room, looking happy, lively, and quite at home. All the time, while Charles Reade had been fashing himself to provide every sort of rural joy for his goat, the ungrateful beast had been longing for the naphtha lights of the circus, for lively conversation and the applause of the crowd.

You cant force a goat any more than you can force a child to live the simple life. "N'Yawk's the place," said the child of a Bowery tenement in New York, on the night of her return from an enforced sojourn in Arcady. She hated picking daisies, and drinking rich new milk made her sick. When the kind teacher who had brought her to the country strove to impress her by taking her to see a cow milked, she remarked wither-ingly to the man who was milking: "Gee! You put it in!"

Rachael's sentiments were of the same type, I think. "Back to the circus!" was his cry, not "Back to the land!"

I hope, when he felt the sawdust under his feet again (I think Charles Reade sent him back to the ring), he remembered his late master with gratitude. To how many animals, and not only four-footed ones, was not Charles Reade generously kind, and to none of them more kind than to Ellen Terry.

NOTES TO CHAPTER IV

1. *Ellen Terry in Hertfordshire.* Ellen Terry's first Hertfordshire home was a cottage on Gusterwood Common. Later Edward Godwin built a house for his family at Harpenden, where they were living at the time of the eventful meeting with Charles Reade. This was not the cause of Ellen Terry's separa-tion from Godwin, as might be thought from some accounts of the incident. Gordon Craig, for example, implies in his biography of his mother that if Charles Reade had not come leaping over the hedge in a scarlet coat "like some ludicrous Mephistopheles" tempting her back to the stage, she might have gone on living a quiet, domestic life at Harpenden indefinitely. There is no reason to think that Godwin had any objection to her returning to the stage. Later in the year 1874 when she received an offer from Charles Calvert, manager of the Princes Theatre, Manchester, to appear there as Juliet and Rosalind (an offer which came to nothing), Godwin made designs for her dresses, and as has already been said (Note 7 to Chapter II) worked in the same theatre with her when the Bancrofts produced "The Merchant of Venice" in 1875. Graham Robertson's statement that at Harpenden Ellen Terry was far from the theatres, and all concerning them, is a romantic exaggeration, since Godwin was there, with the theatre in his head and heart. However, it appears that as time went on Ellen Terry herself romanticised these days, at least when she was speaking of them to a romantic listener. Some puzzling discrepancies in the impressions she gave different people, equally intimate with her, of her experiences, thoughts and feelings, in her retirement, may be explained by the ease with which she could always identify herself with different people's conceptions of her character and temperament. To put it more clearly, it came naturally to Ellen Terry to dramatise herself. So there are hundreds of Ellen Terries, all genuine in their way, for there was in this extraordinary rich and varied nature an abundance of material for their creation.

The Arcadian bliss of Harpenden was in jeopardy long before Charles Reade leapt over the hedge into Ellen Terry's life. The young mother had other troubles than those financial ones which had culminated in bailiffs. Her future was uncertain, and she was worried about it on account of her children. In the conversation with Charles Reade she records they are not mentioned, yet it is clear that it was the thought of them which made her see reason in Reade's remark: "You ought to come back"—not his reason, but another. It is very doubtful whether she felt the magnetic pull of the theatre at that moment as her son surmises. Indeed her distaste for the stage, the result not of her life at Harpenden, but of the miserable years preceding it, is still so strong that at first she impulsively rejects Charles Reade's proposal with "No, never," and after she has considered it, names terms she is half hopeful will be an obstacle. Charles Reade's *"Done"* ended the struggle between her inclinations and her sense of duty.

2. *Edy and the doll.* Edy's reception of the doll in the bright pink silk dress recalls a story of her father told me by his niece Mrs Godwin-Davies who is still living in Bristol. "One little episode stands out in my memory. I was about eight and my sister about four. We were sent for from the nursery to see Uncle Ted, and when we appeared, well washed and decked out in organdy muslin and big blue sashes, he was shocked, and said to Mother: 'My God, Annie, how dare you dress your children in such appalling clothes!' We both went away in tears."

3. *Charles Reade.* Gordon Craig in "Ellen Terry and Her Secret Self" says he cannot explain why after all these years he should dislike the thought of Charles Reade so much. The explanation may be that Reade disliked Edward Godwin, and thought he had a bad influence on Ellen Terry. She tells the reader in this chapter how Reade impressed her at this time. The publication of Malcolm Elwin's biography of Reade, with extracts from his note-books, has made it possible to add how Ellen Terry impressed Reade: "Ellen Terry, a character such as neither Molière nor Balzac, I believe, had the luck to fall in with. Soft and yielding on the surface, egotistical below. *Varia et mutabilis,* always wanting something 'dreadful bad' today, which she does not want tomorrow, especially if you are weak enough to give it her, or get it her. Hysterical, sentimental, hard as a nail in money matters, but velvet on the surface. A creature born to please and to deceive. *Enfant gatée, et enfant terrible."*

At a later date, Reade made the following comment on this note:

"This was written while she was under the influence of ———. Since then, greatly improved: the hardness below is melting away. In good hands a very amiable creature but dangerous to the young. Downright fascinating. Even I, who look coldly on from senile heights, am delighted by her."

Reade's description of Ellen Terry's physical features is better known. It was served up so often in her life-time that it lost its savour, but as the new generation of readers has not been surfeited with it, it is brought out again, without apology:

"Ellen Terry is an enigma. Her eyes are pale, her nose rather long, her mouth nothing particular. Complexion a delicate brickdust, her hair rather like tow. Yet somehow she is *beautiful.* Her expression *kills* any pretty face you see beside her. Her figure is lean and bony; her hand masculine in size and form. Yet she is a pattern of fawn-like grace. Whether in movement or repose, grace pervades the hussy."

75

"The hussy" had an enthusiastic reception from the audience at the New Queen's Theatre the night she made her re-appearance in "The Wandering Heir" (February 28, 1874, the day after her twenty-sixth birthday). The play, inspired by the famous Tichborne case, had been running successfully for some time with Mrs John Wood as Philippa Chester, and now curiosity to see Ellen Terry in the part gave it a new lease of life. It was transferred to Astley's Theatre in the following April.

"A few days after Ellen Terry's death her daughter found a piece of paper labelled 'My Friends.' In this roll of honour which there was evidence was of very recent date, the name of Charles Reade was written first. Directly underneath it was the name of Bernard Shaw" (From "Ellen Terry and Bernard Shaw: A Correspondence").

4. The parts played by Ellen Terry during the period covered by Chapter IV were: Philippa Chester ("The Wandering Heir," 1874); Susan Merton ("Never Too Late to Mend," 1874); Helen Rolleston ("Our Seaman," 1874); Volante ("The Honeymoon," 1874); Kate Hardcastle ("She Stoops to Conquer," 1874).

Chapter V

BACK TO THE THEATRE

(1874–1875)

§ 1

THE relation between author and actor is a very important element in the life of the stage. It is the way with some dramatists to despise those who interpret their plays, to accuse us of ruining their creations, to suffer disappointment and rage because we do not, or cannot, carry out their ideas.

Other dramatists admit that we players can teach them something; but I have noticed that it is generally in "the other fellow's" play that we can teach them, not in their own!

As they are necessary to us, and we to them, the great thing is to reduce friction by sympathy. The actor should understand that the author can be of use to him; the author, on his side, should believe that the actor can be of service to the author, and sometimes in ways which only a long and severe training in the actor's trade can discover.

The first author with whom I had to deal, at a critical point in my progress as an actress, was Charles Reade, and he helped me enormously. He might, and often did, make twelve suggestions that were wrong; but against them he would make one that was so right that its value was immeasurable and unforgettable.

It is through the dissatisfaction of a man like Charles Reade that an actress *learns*—that is, if she is not conceited. Conceit is an insuperable obstacle to all progress. On the other hand, it is of little use to take criticism in a slavish spirit and to act on it without understanding it. Charles Reade constantly wrote and said things to me which were not absolutely just criticism; but they directed my attention to the true cause of the faults which he found in my performance, and put me on the way to mending them.

A letter which he wrote me during the run of "The Wandering Heir" was such a wonderful lesson to me that I am going to quote it almost in full, in the hope that it may be a lesson to other actresses— "happy in this, they are not yet so old but they can learn"; unhappy in

77

this, that they have never had a Charles Reade to give them a trouncing!

Well, the letter begins with sheer eulogy. Eulogy is nice, but one does not learn anything from it. Had dear Charles Reade stopped after writing "womanly grace, subtlety, delicacy, the variety yet invariable truthfulness of the facial expression, compared with which the faces beside yours are wooden, uniform dolls," he would have done nothing to advance me in my art; but this was only the jam in which I was to take the powder!

Here followed more jam—with the first taste of the powder:

I prefer you for my Philippa to any other actress, and shall do so still, even if you will not, or cannot, throw more vigour into the lines that need it. I do not pretend to be as good a writer of plays as you are an actress, but I do pretend to be a great judge of acting in general. And I know how my own lines and business ought to be rendered infinitely better than any one else, except the Omniscient. It is only on this narrow ground I presume to teach a woman of your gifts. If I teach you Philippa, you will teach me Juliet; for I am very sure that when I have seen you act her, I shall know a vast deal more about her than I do at present.

No great quality of an actress is absent from your performance. Very often you have *vigour*. But in other places where it is as much required, or even more, you turn *limp*. You have limp lines, limp business, and in Act III limp exits instead of ardent exits.

Except in the actual word used, he was perfectly right. I was not *limp*, but I was exhausted. By a natural instinct, I had produced my voice scientifically almost from the first, and I had found out for myself many things, which in these days of Delsarte systems and the science of voice-production, are taught. But when, after my six years' absence from the stage, I came back, and played a long and arduous part, I found that my breathing was still not right. This accounted for my exhaustion, or limpness and lack of vigour, as Charles Reade preferred to call it.

As for the "ardent" exits, how right he was! That word set me on the track of learning the value of moving off the stage with a swift rush. I had always had the gift of being rapid in movement, but to *have* a gift, and to *use* it, are two very different things.

I never realised that I was rather quick in movement until one day when I was sitting on a sofa talking to the famous throat specialist, Dr Morell Mackenzie. In the middle of one of his sentences I said: "Wait a minute while I get a glass of water." I was out of the room and back so soon that he said, "Well, go and get it then!" and was amazed when he saw that the glass was in my hand and that I was sitting down again!

Consider! That was one of Charles Reade's favourite expressions, and just hearing him say the word used to make me consider, and think, and come to conclusions—perhaps not always the conclusions that he wished, but suggested by him.

In this matter of "ardent" exit, he wrote:

The swift rush of the words, the personal rush, should carry you off the stage. It is in reality as easy as shelling peas, if you will only go by the right method instead of by the wrong. You have overcome far greater difficulties than this, yet night after night you go on suffering ignoble defeat at this point. Come, courage! You took a leaf out of Reade's dictionary at Manchester, and trampled on two difficulties—impossibilities, you called them. That was on Saturday. Monday you knocked the poor impossibilities down. Tuesday you kicked them where they lay. Wednesday you walked placidly over their prostrate bodies!

The difficulty that he was now urging me to knock down was one of *pace,* and I am afraid that in all my stage life subsequently I never quite succeeded in kicking it or walking over its prostrate body!

Looking backward, I remember many times when I failed in rapidity of utterance, and was "pumped" at moments when swiftness was essential. Pace is the soul of comedy, and to elaborate lines at the expense of pace is disastrous. Curiously enough, I have met and envied this gift of pace in actors who were not conspicuously talented in other respects, and no Rosalind that I have ever seen has had enough of it. Of course, it is not a question of swift utterance only, but of swift thinking. I am able to think more swiftly on the stage now than at the time Charles Reade wrote to me, and I only wish I were young enough to take advantage of it. But youth thinks *slowly,* as a rule.

Vary the pace. Charles Reade was never tired of saying this, and, indeed, it is one of the foundations of all good acting.

You don't seem quite to realize, he writes in the letter before me, that uniformity of pace leads inevitably to languor. You should deliver a pistol-shot or two. Remember Philippa is a fiery girl; she can snap. If only for variety, she should snap James' head off when she says, "Do I *speak* as if I loved them!"

My memories of the part of Philippa are rather vague, but I know that Reade was right in insisting that I needed more "bite" in the passages when I was dressed as a boy. Though he complimented me on my self-denial in making what he called "some sacrifice of beauty" to pass for a boy, "so that the audience cant say, 'Why, James must be a fool not to see she is a girl,'" he scolded me for my want of bluntness.

Fix your mind on the adjective "blunt" and the substantive "pistol-shot"; they will do you good service.

They did! And I recommend them to any one who finds it hard to overcome monotony of pace and languor of diction.

When you come to tell old Surefoot about his daughter's love, the letter goes on, you should fall into a positive imitation of his manner: crest motionless, and hands in front, and deliver your preambles with a nasal twang. But at the second invitation to speak out, you should cast this to the winds, and go into the other extreme of bluntness and rapidity. When you meet him after the exposure, you should speak as you are coming to him and stop him in mid-career, and *then* attack him. You should also (in Act II) get the pearls back into the tree before you say: "Oh, I hope he did not see me!"

Yes, I remember that in both these situations I used to muddle and blur the effect by doing the business and speaking at the same time. By acting on Reade's suggestion I gained confidence in making a pause.

After the beating, wait at least ten seconds longer than you do—to rouse expectation—and when you do come on, make a little more of it. You ought to be very pale indeed—even to enter with a slight totter, done moderately, of course; and before you say a single word, you ought to stand shaking and with your brows knitting, looking almost terrible. Of course, I do not expect or desire to make a melo-dramatic actress of you, but still I think you capable of any effect, provided *it is not sustained too long.*

A truer word was never spoken. It has never been in my power to *sustain.* In private life, I cannot sustain a hatred or a resentment. On the stage, I can pass swiftly from one effect to another, but I cannot fix *one,* and dwell on it, with that superb concentration which seems to me the special attribute of the tragic actress. To sustain, with me, is to lose the impression that I have created, not to increase its intensity.

The last passage of the third act is just a little too hurried. Break the line. "Now, James—for England and liberty!"

I remember that I never could see that he was right about that, and if I cant see a thing I cant do it. The author's idea must become mine before I can carry it out—at least, with any sincerity, and obedience without sincerity would be of small service to an author. It must be despairing to him, if he wants me to say a line in a certain way, to find that I always say it in another; but I cant help it. I have tried to act passages as I have been told, just *because* I was told and without conviction, and I have failed miserably and have had to go back to my own way.

Climax is reached not only by rush but by increasing pace. Your exit speech is a failure at present, because you do not vary the pace of its delivery. Get by yourself for one half-hour—if you can! Get by the seaside, if you can, since there it was Demosthenes studied eloquence and overcame mountains—not mole-hills like this. Being by the seaside, study those lines by themselves: "And then let them find their young gentleman, and find him quickly, for London shall not hold me long—no, nor England either."

Study to speak these lines with great volubility and fire, and settle the exact syllable to run at.

I remember that Reade, with characteristic generosity, gave me ten pounds and sent me to the seaside in earnest, as he suggests my doing, half in fun, in the letter. "I know you won't go otherwise," he said, "because you want to insure your life or do something of that sort. Here! go to Brighton—go anywhere by the sea for Sunday! Dont thank me! It's all for Philippa."

As I read these notes of his on anti-climax, monotony of pace, and all the other offences against scientific principles of acting which I committed in this one part, I feel more strongly than ever how important it is to master these principles. Until you have learned them and practised them you cannot afford to discard them. There is all the difference in the world between departure from recognised rules by one who has learned to obey them, and neglect of them through want of training or want of skill or want of understanding. Before you can be eccentric you must know where the circle is.

Nowadays acting is less scientific (except in the matter of voice-production) than it was when I was receiving hints, cautions, and advice from my two dramatist friends, Charles Reade and Tom Taylor; and the leading principles to which they attached importance have come to be regarded as old-fashioned and superfluous. This attitude is comparatively harmless in the interpretation of those modern plays in which parts are made to fit the actors and personality is everything. But those who have been led to believe that they can make their own rules find their mistake when they come to tackle Shakespeare or any of the standard dramatists in which the actors have to fit themselves to the parts. Then, if ever, technique is avenged!

All my life the thing which has struck me as wanting on the stage is *variety*. Some people are "tone-deaf," and they find it physically impossible to observe the law of contrasts. But even a physical deficiency can be overcome by that faculty for taking infinite pains which may not be genius but is certainly a good substitute for it.

When it comes to pointing out an example, Henry Irving is the monument, the great mark set up to show the genius of *will*. For years he worked to overcome the dragging leg, which seemed to attract more attention from some small-minded critics (sharp of eye, yet how dull of vision!) than all the mental splendour of his impersonations. He toiled, and he overcame this defect, just as he overcame his difficulty with vowels, and the self-consciousness which in the early stages of his career used to hamper and incommode him. His *self* was to him on a first night what the shell is to a lobster on dry land. In "Hamlet," when we first acted together after that long-ago Katharine and Petruchio period at the Queen's, he used to discuss with me the secret of my freedom from self-consciousness; and I suggested a more swift entrance on the stage from the dressing-room. I told him that, in spite of the advantage in ease which I had gained through having been on the stage when still a mere child, I should be paralysed with fright from over-acute realisation of the audience if I stood at the wing for ten minutes, as he was in the habit of doing. He did not heed me then, nor during the run of our next play, "The Lady of Lyons"; but when it came to Shylock, a quite new part to him, he tried the experiment, and, as he told me, with great comfort to himself and success with the audience.

Only a great actor finds the difficulties of the actor's art infinite. Even up to the last five years of his life, Henry Irving was striving, striving. He never rested on old triumphs, never found a part in which there was no more to do. Once when I was touring with him in America, at the time when he was at the highest point of his fame, I watched him one day in the train—always a delightful occupation, for his face provided many pictures a minute—and being struck by a curious look, half puzzled, half despairing, asked him what he was thinking about.

"I was thinking," he answered slowly, "how strange it is that I should have made the reputation I have as an actor, with nothing to help me—with no equipment. My legs, my voice—everything has been against me. For an actor who cant walk, cant talk, and has no face to speak of, I've done pretty well."

And I, looking at that splendid head, those wonderful hands, the whole strange beauty of him, thought, "Ah, you little know!"

§ 2

THE brilliant story of the Bancroft management of the old Prince of Wales's Theatre was more familiar twenty years ago than it is now. I think that few of the youngest playgoers who point out, on the first nights of important productions, a remarkably striking figure of a man with erect carriage, white hair, and flashing dark eyes—a man whose eye-glass, manners, and clothes all suggest Thackeray and Major Pendennis, in spite of his success in keeping abreast of everything modern—few playgoers, I say, who point this man out as Sir Squire Bancroft could give any adequate account of what he did for the English theatre in the 'seventies. Nor do the public who see an elegant little lady starting for a drive from a certain house in Berkeley Square realize that this is Marie Wilton, afterwards Mrs Bancroft, now Lady Bancroft, the comedienne who created the heroines of Tom Robertson, and, with her husband, brought what is called the cup-and-saucer drama to absolute perfection.

We players know quite well and accept with philosophy the fact that when we have done we are forgotten. We are sometimes told that we live too much in the public eye and enjoy too much public favour and attention; but at least we make up for it by leaving no trace of our short and merry reign behind us when it is over!

I have never, even in Paris, seen anything more admirable than the ensemble of the Bancroft productions. Every part in the domestic comedies, the presentation of which, up to 1875, they had made their policy, was played with such point and finish that the more rough, uneven, and emotional acting of the present day has not produced anything so good in the same line. The Prince of Wales's Theatre was the most fashionable in London, and there seemed no reason why the Robertson vogue should not last for ever.

But that's the strange thing about theatrical success. However great, it is limited in its duration, as we found out at the Lyceum twenty years later. It was not only because the Bancrofts were ambitious that they determined on a Shakespearean revival in 1875: they felt that you can give the public too much even of a good thing, and thought that a complete change might bring their theatre new populaity as well as new prestige.

I, however, thought little of this at the time. After my return to the stage in "The Wandering Heir," and my tour with Charles Reade, my interest in the theatre again declined. It has always been my fate or my nature—perhaps they are really the same thing—to be very happy or very miserable. At this time I was very miserable. I was worried to death by domestic troubles and financial difficulties. The house in which I first lived in London, after I left Hertfordshire, had been stripped of some of its most beautiful treasures by the brokers. Pressure was being put on me by well-meaning friends to leave this house and make a great change in my life. Everything was at its darkest when Mrs Bancroft came to call on me and offered me the part of Portia in "The Merchant of Venice."

I had, of course, known her before, in the way that all people in the theatre seem to know each other, and I had seen her act; but on this day, when she came to me as a kind of messenger of Fate, the harbinger of the true dawn of my success, she should have had for me some special and extraordinary significance. I could invest that interview now with many dramatic features, but my memory, either because it is bad or because it is good, corrects my imagination.

"May I come in?"

An ordinary remark, truly, to stick in one's head for thirty-odd years! But it was made in such a *very* pretty voice—one of the most silvery voices I have ever heard from any woman except the late Queen Victoria, whose voice was like a silver stream flowing over golden stones.

The smart little figure—Mrs Bancroft was, above all things, *petite*—dressed in black—elegant Parisian black—came into a room which had been almost completely stripped of furniture. The floor was covered with Japanse matting, and at one end was a cast of the Venus of Milo, almost the same colossal size as the original.

Mrs Bancroft's wonderful grey eyes examined it curiously. The room, the statue, and I myself must all have seemed very strange to her. I wore a dress of some deep yellow woollen material which my little daughter used to call the "frog dress," because it was speckled with brown like a frog's skin. It was cut like a Viollet-le-Duc tabard, and had not a trace of the fashion of the time. Mrs Bancroft, however, did not look at me less kindly because I wore æsthetic clothes and was painfully thin. She explained that they were going to put on "The Merchant of Venice" at the Prince of Wales's, that she was to rest for a while for reasons connected with her health; that she and Mr Bancroft had thought of me for Portia.

Portia! It seemed too good to be true! I was a student when I was young. I knew not only every word of the part, but every detail of that period of Venetian splendour in which the action of the play takes place. I had studied Vecellio.

Mrs Bancroft told me that the production would be as beautiful as money and thought could make it. The artistic side of the venture was to be in the hands of Mr Godwin.

"Well, what do you say?" said Mrs Bancroft. "Will you put your shoulder to the wheel with us?"

I answered incoherently and joyfully, that of all things, I had been wanting most to play in Shakespeare; that in Shakespeare I had always felt I would play for half the salary; that—oh, I dont know what I said! Probably it was all very foolish and unbusinesslike, but the engagement was practically settled before Mrs Bancroft left the house, although I was charged not to say anything about it yet.

But theatre secrets are generally *secrets de polichinelle*. When I went to Charles Reade's house at Albert Gate on the following Sunday for one of his regular Sunday parties, he came up to me at once with a knowing look and said:

"So you've got an engagement."

84

"I'm not to say anything about it."

"It's in Shakespeare!"

"I'm not to tell."

"But I know. I've been thinking it out. It's 'The Merchant of Venice.'"

"Nothing is settled yet. It's on the cards."

"I know! I know!" said wise old Charles. "Well, you'll never have such a good part as Philippa Chester!"

"No, Nelly, never!" said Mrs Seymour, who happened to overhear this. "They call Philippa a Rosalind part. Rosalind! Rosalind is not to be compared with it!"

Between Mrs Seymour and Charles Reade there existed a friendship of that rare sort about which it is easy for people who are not at all rare, unfortunately, to say ill-natured things. Charles Reade worshipped Laura Seymour, and she understood him and sympathised with his work and his whims. She died before he did, and he never got over it. The great success of one of his last plays, "Drink," an adaptation from the French, in which Charles Warner is still thrilling audiences to this day, meant nothing to him because she was not alive to share it. The epitaph which he had inscribed over her grave is characteristic of the man, the woman, and their friendship:

HERE LIES THE GREAT HEART OF
LAURA SEYMOUR

I liked Mrs Seymour so much that I was hurt when I found that she had instructed Charles Reade to tell Nelly Terry "not to paint her face" in the daytime, and I was young enough to enjoy revenging myself in my own way. We used to play childish games at Charles Reade's house sometimes, and with "Follow my leader" came my opportunity. I asked for a basin of water and a towel and scrubbed my face with a significant thoroughness. The rules of the game meant that every one had to follow my example! When I had dried my face I powdered it, and then darkened my eyebrows. I wished to be quite frank about the harmless little bit of artifice which Mrs Seymour had exaggerated. She was now hoist with her own petard, for, being heavily made up, she could not and would not follow the leader. After this, Charles Reade acquitted me of the use of "pigments red," but he still kept up a campaign against "Chalky," as he humorously christened my powder-puff. "Dont be pig-headed, love," he wrote to me once; "it is because Chalky does not improve you that I forbid it. Trust unprejudiced and friendly eyes and drop it altogether."

Although Mrs Seymour was naturally prejudiced where Charles Reade's work was concerned, she only spoke the truth, pardonably exaggerated, about the part of Philippa Chester. I know no part which is a patch on it for effectiveness; yet there is little in it of the stuff which endures. The play itself was too unbusiness-like ever to become a classic.

Not for years afterwards did I find out that I was not the "first choice" for Portia. The Bancrofts had tried the Kendals first, with the idea of making a double engagement; but the negotiations failed. Perhaps the rivalry between Mrs Kendal and me might have become of more significance had she appeared as Portia at the Prince of Wales's and preferred Shakespeare to domestic comedy. In after years she played Rosalind—I never did, alas!—and quite recently acted with me in "The Merry Wives of Windsor"; but the best of her fame will always be associated with such plays as "The Squire," "The Ironmaster," "Lady Clancarty," and many more plays of that type. When she played with me in Shakespeare she laughingly challenged me to come and play with her in a modern piece, a domestic play, and I said, "Done!" but it has not been done yet, although in Mrs Clifford's "The Likeness of the Night" there was a good medium for the experiment. I found Mrs Kendal wonderful to act with. No other English actress has such extraordinary skill. Of course, people have said we are jealous of each other. "Ellen Terry Acts with Lifelong Enemy," proclaimed an American newspaper in five-inch type, when we played together as Mistress Page and Mistress Ford in Mr Tree's Coronation production of "The Merry Wives of Windsor." But the enmity did not seem to worry us as much as the newspaper men over the Atlantic had represented.

It was during this engagement in 1902 that a young actor who was watching us coming in at the stage-door at His Majesty's one day is reported to have said: "Look at Mr Tree between his two 'stars'!"

"You mean Ancient Lights!" answered the witty actress to whom the remark was made.

It was long before these days that Mrs Kendal decided not to bring her consummately dexterous and humorous workmanship to the task of playing Portia, and left the field open for me. I had had some success in other parts, and had tasted the delight of knowing that audiences liked me, and had liked them back again. But never until I appeared as Portia at the Prince of Wales's had I experienced that awe-struck feeling which comes, I suppose, to no actress more than once in a life-time—the feeling of the conqueror. In homely parlance, I knew that I had "got them" at the moment when I spoke the speech beginning, "You see me, Lord Bassanio, where I stand."

"What can this be?" I thought. "*Quite* this thing has never come to me before! *This is different!* It has never been quite the same before."

It was never to be quite the same again.

Elation, triumph, being lifted on high by a single stroke of the mighty wing of glory—call it by any name, think of it as you like—it was as Portia that I had my first and last sense of it. And, while it made me happy, it made me miserable because I foresaw, as plainly as my own success, another's failure.

Charles Coghlan, an actor whose previous record was fine enough to justify his engagement as Shylock, showed that night the fatal quality of *indecision.*

A worse performance than his, carried through with decision and attack, might have succeeded, but Coghlan's Shylock was not even bad. It was *nothing.*

You could hardly hear a word he said. He spoke as though he had a sponge in his mouth, and moved as if paralysed. The perspiration poured down his face; yet what he was doing no one could guess. It was a case of moral cowardice rather than incompetency. At rehearsals no one had entirely believed in him, and this, instead of stinging him into a resolution to triumph, had made him take fright and run away.

People felt that they were witnessing a great play with a great part cut out, and "The Merchant of Venice" ran for three weeks!

It was a pity, if only because a more gorgeous and complete little spectacle had never been seen on the English stage. Veronese's "Marriage in Cana" had inspired many of the stage pictures, and the expenditure in carrying them out had been lavish.

In the casket scene I wore a dress like almond-blossom. I was very thin, but Portia and all the ideal *young* heroines of Shakespeare ought to be thin. Fat is fatal to romance!

I played the part more stiffly and more slowly at the Prince of Wales's than I did in later years. I moved and spoke slowly. The clothes seemed to demand it, and the setting of the play developed the Italian feeling in it, and let the English Elizabethan element take care of itself. The silver casket scene with the Prince of Aragon was retained, and so was the last act, which had hitherto been cut out in nearly all stage versions.

I have tried five or six different ways of treating Portia, but the way I think best is not the one which finds the heartiest response from my audiences. (Has there ever been a dramatist, I wonder, whose parts admit of so many different interpretations as do Shakespeare's?) There lies his immortality as an acting force. For times change, and parts have to be acted differently for different generations. Some parts are not sufficiently universal for this to be possible, but every ten years an actor can reconsider a Shakespeare part and find new life in it for his new purpose and new audiences.

The æsthetic movement, with all its faults, was responsible for a great deal of true enthusiasm for anything beautiful. It made people welcome the Bancrofts' production of "The Merchant of Venice" with an appreciation which took the practical form of an offer to keep the performances going by subscription, as the general public was not supporting them. Sir Frederick and Lady Pollock, James Spedding, Edwin Arnold, Sir Frederick Leighton and others made the proposal to the Bancrofts, but nothing came of it.

Short as the run of the play was, it was a wonderful time for me. Every one seemed to be in love with me! I had sweethearts by the dozen, known and unknown. Most of the letters written to me I destroyed long ago, but the feeling of sweetness and light with which some of them filled me can never be destroyed. The task of reading and answering letters has been a heavy one all my life, but it would be ungrateful to complain of it. To some people expression is life itself. Half my letters begin: "I cannot help writing to tell you," and I believe that this is the simple truth. I, for one, should have been poorer, though my eyes might have been stronger, if they *had* been able to help it.

There turns up today, out of a long-neglected box, a charming note about "The Merchant of Venice" from some unknown friend.

"Playing to such houses," he wrote, "is not an encouraging pursuit; but to give to human beings the greatest pleasure that they are capable of receiving must always be worth doing. You have given me that pleasure, and I write to offer you my poor thanks. Portia has always been my favourite heroine, and I saw her last night as sweet and lovely as I had always hoped she might be. I hope that I shall see you again in other Shakespearean characters, and that nothing will tempt you to withhold your talents from their proper sphere."

The audiences may have been scanty, but they were wonderful. O'Shaughnessy, Watts-Dunton, Oscar Wilde, Alfred Gilbert, and, I think, Swinburne were there. A poetic and artistic atmosphere pervaded the front of the house as well as the stage itself.

§ 3

I HAVE read in some of the biographies of me that have been published from time to time, that I was chagrined at Coghlan's fiasco because it brought my success as Portia so soon to an end. As a matter of fact, I never thought about it. I was just sorry for clever Coghlan, who was deeply hurt and took his defeat hardly and moodily. He wiped out the public recollection of it to a great extent by his Evelyn in "Money," his Sir Charles Pomander in "Masks and Faces," and his Claude Melnotte in "The Lady of Lyons," which he played with me at the Princess's Theatre for one night only in the August following the withdrawal of "The Merchant of Venice."

I have been credited with great generosity for appearing in that single performance of "The Lady of Lyons." It was said that I wanted to help Coghlan to reinstate himself, and so on. Very likely there was some such feeling in the matter, but there was also a good part and good remuneration! I remember that I played Lytton's proud heroine better then than I did at the Lyceum five years later, and Coghlan was more successful as Melnotte than Henry Irving. But I was never really good in the part. I tried in vain to have sympathy with a lady who was addressed as "haughty cousin," yet whose very pride had so much inconsistency. How could any woman fall in love with a cad like Melnotte, I used to ask myself despairingly. The very fact that I tried to understand Pauline was against me. There is only one way to play her, and to be distracted by questions of sincerity and consistency means that you will miss that way for a certainty!

I missed it, and fell between two stools. Finding that it was useless to depend upon feeling, I groped after the definite rules which had always governed the delivery of Pauline's fustian, and the fate that commonly overtakes those who try to put old wine into new bottles overtook me.

I knew, for instance, exactly how the following speech ought to be done, but I never could do it. It occurs in the fourth act, where Beauséant, after Pauline has been disillusioned, thinks it will be an easy matter to induce the proud beauty to fly with him:

"Go! (*White to the lips.*) Sir, leave this house! It is humble; but a husband's roof, however lowly, is, in the eyes of God and man, the temple of a wife's honour. (*Tumultuous applause.*) Know that I would rather starve— aye, *starve*—with him who has betrayed me than accept *your* lawful hand, even were you the prince whose name he bore. (*Hurrying on quickly to prevent applause before the finish.*) Go!"

It is easy to laugh at Lytton's rhetoric, but very few dramatists have had a more complete mastery of theatrical situations, and that is a good thing to be master of. Why the word "theatrical" should have come to be used in a contemptuous sense I cannot understand. "Musical" is a word of praise in music; why not "theatrical" in a theatre? A play in any age which holds the boards so continuously as "The Lady of Lyons" deserves more recognition than the ridicule of those who think that the world has moved on because our playwrights write more naturally than Lytton wrote. The merit of the play lay, not in its bombast, but in its situations.

Before Pauline I had played Clara Douglas in a revival of "Money," and I found her far more interesting and possible. To act the *balance* of the girl was keen enjoyment; it foreshadowed some of that greater enjoyment I was to have in after years when playing Hermione—another well-judged, well-balanced mind, a woman who is not passion's slave, who never answers on the spur of the moment, but from the depths of reason and of comprehension. I didn't agree with Clara Douglas's sentiments but I saw her point of view, and that was everything.

Tom Taylor, like Charles Reade, never hesitated to speak plainly to me about my acting, and, after the first night of "Money," wrote me a letter full of hints and caution and advice:

As I expected, you put feeling into every situation which gave you the opportunity, and the truth of your intention and expression seemed to bring a note of nature into the horribly sophisticated atmosphere of that hollow and most claptrappy of all Bulwerian stage offences. Nothing could be better than the appeal to Evelyn in the last act. It was sweet, womanly and earnest, and rang true in every note.

But you were nervous and uncomfortable in many parts for want of sufficient rehearsal. These passages you will, no doubt, improve in nightly. I would only urge on you the great importance of studying to be quiet and composed, and not fidgeting. There was especially a trick of constantly twiddling with and looking at your fingers which you should, above all, be on your guard against...I think, too, you showed too evident feeling in the earlier scene with Evelyn. A blind man must have read what you felt—your sentiment should be more masked.

Laura (Mrs. Taylor) absolutely hates the play. We both thought——detestable in his part, false in emphasis, violent and coarse. Generally the fault of the performance was, strange to say for that theatre, overacting, want of repose, point, and finish. With you in essentials I was quite satisfied, but *quiet*—not so much movement of arms and hands. Bear this in mind for improvement; and go over your part to yourself with a view to it.

The Allinghams have been here today. They saw you twice as Portia, and were charmed. Mrs Allingham wants to paint you. Allingham tells me that Spedding is going to write an article on your Portia, and will include Clara Douglas. I am going to see Salvini in "Hamlet" tomorrow morning, but I would call in Charlotte Street between one and two, on the chance of seeing you and talking it over, and amplifying what I have said.

Ever your true old friend,
TOM TAYLOR.

A true old friend indeed he was! I have already tried to convey how much I owed to him—how he stood by me and helped me in difficulties, and said generously and unequivocably, at the time of my separation from my first husband, that "the poor child was not to blame."

90

I was very fond of my own father, but in many ways Tom Taylor was more of a father to me than my father in blood. Father was charming, but Irish and irresponsible. I think he loved my sister Floss and me most because we were the lawless ones of the family! It was not in his temperament to give wise advice and counsel. Having bequeathed to me light-heartedness and a sanguine disposition, and trained me splendidly for my profession in childhood, he became in after years a very cormorant for adulation of me!

"Duchess, you might have been anything!" was his favourite comment, when I was not living up to his ideas of my position and attainments. And I used to answer: "I've played my cards for what I want."

Years afterwards, when he and mother used to come to first nights at the Lyceum, the grossest flattery of me after the performance was not good enough for them.

"How proud you must be of her!" some one would say. "How well this part suits her!"

"Yes," father would answer, in a sort of "is-that-all-you-have-to-say" tone. "But she ought to play Rosalind!"

To him I owe the gaiety of temperament which has enabled me to dance through the most harsh and barren passages of my life, just as he used to make Kate and me dance along the sordid London streets as we walked home from the Princess's Theatre. He would make us come under his cloak, partly for warmth, partly to hide from us the stages of the journey home. From the comfortable darkness one of us would cry out:

"Oh, I'm so tired! Arent we nearly home? Where are we, father?"

"You know Schwab, the baker?"

"Yes, yes!"

"Well, we're *not* there yet!"

As I grew up, this teasing, jolly, insouciant Irish father of mine was relieved of some of his paternal duties by Tom Taylor. It was not Nelly alone whom Tom Taylor fathered. He adopted the whole family.

At Lavender Sweep, with the horse-chestnut blossoms strewing the drive and making it look like a tessellated pavement, all of us were always welcome, and Tom Taylor would often come to our house and ask mother to grill him a bone! Such intimate friendships are seldom possible in our busy profession, and there was never another Tom Taylor in my life.

When we were not in London and could not go to Lavender Sweep to see him, he wrote almost daily to us. He was angry when other people criticised me, but he did not spare criticism himself.

"Dont be Nelly Know-all," I remember his saying once. "*I saw you* floundering out of your depths tonight on the subject of butterflies! The man to whom you were talking is one of the greatest entomologists in Europe, and must have seen through you at once."

When William Black's "Madcap Violet" was published, common report said that the heroine had been drawn from Ellen Terry, and some of the reviews made Taylor furious.

"It's disgraceful! I shall deny it. Never will I let it be said of you that you could conceive any vulgarity. I shall write and contradict it. Indiscreet, high-spirited, full of surprises, you may be, but vulgar—never! I shall write at once."

"Dont do that," I said. "Cant you see that the author hasnt described me, but only men in 'New Men and Old Acres'?" As this was Tom Taylor's own play, his rage against "Madcap Violet" was very funny! "There am I, just as you wrote it. My actions, manners, and clothes in the play are all reproduced. You ought to feel pleased, not angry."

When his play "Victims" was being rehearsed at the Court Theatre, an old woman and old actress who had, I think, been in the preceding play was not wanted. The day the management gave her her dismissal, she met Taylor outside the theatre, and poured out a long story of distress. She had not a stocking to her foot, she owed her rent, she was starving. Wouldnt Mr Taylor tell the management what dismissal meant to her? Wouldnt he get her taken back? Mr Taylor would try, and Mr Taylor gave her fifteen pounds in the street then and there! Mrs Taylor wasnt surprised. She only wondered it wasnt thirty!

"Tom the Adapter" was the Terry dramatist for many years. Kate played in many of the pieces which, some openly, some deviously, he brought into the English theatre from the French. When Kate married, my turn came, and the interest that he had taken in my sister's talent he transferred in part to me, although I dont think he ever thought me her equal. Floss made her first appearance in the child's part in Taylor's play "A Sheep in Wolf's Clothing," and Marion her first appearance as Ophelia in his version of "Hamlet"—perhaps "perversion" would be an honester description! Taylor introduced a "fool" who went about whacking people, including the Prince, by way of brightening up the tragedy.

I never saw my sister's Ophelia, but I know it was a fine send-off for her and that she must have looked lovely. Oh, what a pretty young girl she was! Her golden-brown eyes exactly matched her hair, and she was the winsomest thing imaginable! From the first she showed talent.

From Taylor's letters I find—and, indeed, without them I could not have forgotten—that the good, kind friend never ceased to work in our interests. "I have recommended Flossy to play Lady Betty in the country." "I have written to the Bancrofts in favour of Forbes-Robertson for

Bassanio." (Evidently this was in answer to a request from me. Naturally, the Bancrofts wanted some one of higher standing, but was I wrong about J. Forbes-Robertson? I think not!) "The mother came to see me the other day. I was extremely sorry to hear the bad news of Tom." (Tom was the black sheep of our family, but a fascinating wretch, all the same.) "I rejoice to think of your coming back," he writes another time, "to show the stage what an actress should be." "A thousand thanks for the photographs. I like the profile best. It is most Paolo Veronesish and gives the right notion of your Portia, although the colour hardly suggests the golden gorgeousness of your dress and the blonde glory of the hair and complexion.... I hope you have seen the quiet little boxes at ———'s foolish article." (This refers to an article which attacked my Portia in *Blackwood's Magazine*.) "Of course, if ——— found his ideal in ——— he must dislike you in Portia, or in anything where it is a case of grace and spontaneity and Nature against affectation, over-emphasis, stilt, and false idealism—in short, utter lack of Nature. How *can* the same critic admire both? However, the public is with you, happily, as it is not always when the struggle is between good art and bad."

I quote these dear letters from my friend, not in my praise, but in his. Until his death in 1880, he never ceased to write to me sympathetically and encouragingly; he rejoiced in my success the more because he had felt himself in part responsible for my marriage and its unhappy ending, and had perhaps feared that my life would suffer. Every little detail about me and my children, or about any of my family, was of interest to him. He was never too busy to give an attentive ear to my difficulties. " 'Think of you lovingly if I can'!" he writes to me at a time when I had taken a course for which all blamed me, perhaps·because they did not know enough to pardon enough—*savoir tout c'est tout pardonner.* "Can I think of you otherwise than lovingly? *Never,* if I know you and myself!"

Tom Taylor got through an enormous amount of work. Dramatic critic and art critic for the *Times,* he was also editor of *Punch* and a busy playwright. Every one who wanted an address written or a play altered came to him, and his house was a kind of Mecca for pilgrims from America and from all parts of the world. Yet he all the time occupied a position in a Government office, and often walked from Whitehall to Lavender Sweep when his day's work was done. He was an enthusiastic amateur actor, his favourite part being Adam in "As You Like It," perhaps because tradition says this was a part that Shakespeare played; at any rate, he was very good in it. Gilbert and Sullivan, in very far-off days, used to be concerned in these amateur theatricals. Their names were not associated then, but Kate and I established a prophetic link by carrying on a mild flirtation, I with Arthur Sullivan, Kate with W. S. Gilbert!

Taylor never wasted a moment. He pottered, but thought deeply all the time; and when I used to watch him plucking at his grey beard, I realised that he was just as busy as if his pen had been plucking at his paper. Many would-be writers complain that the necessity of earning a living in some other and more secure profession hinders them from achieving anything. What about Taylor at the Home Office, Charles Lamb at East India House, and Rousseau copying music for bread? It all depends on the point of view. A young lady in Chicago, who has written some charming short stories, told me how eagerly she was looking forward to the time when she would be able to give up teaching and devote herself entirely to a literary career. I wondered, and said I was never sure whether absolute freedom in such a matter *was* desirable. Perhaps Charles Lamb was all the better for being a slave at the desk for so many years.

"Ah, but then, Charles Lamb wrote so little!" was the remarkable answer.

Taylor did not write "so little." He wrote perhaps too much, and I think his heart was too strong for his brain. He was far too simple and lovable a being to be great. The atmosphere of gaiety which pervaded Lavender Sweep arose from his generous, kindly nature, which insisted that it was possible for every one to have a good time.

Once, when we were rushing to catch a train with him, Kate hanging on to one arm and I on to the other, we all three fell down the station steps. "Now, then, none of your jokes!" said a cross man behind us, who seemed to attribute our descent to rowdyism. Taylor stood up with his soft felt hat bashed over one eye, his spectacles broken, and laughed, and laughed, and laughed!

Lavender Sweep was a sort of house of call for every one of note. Mazzini stayed there for some time, and Steele Mackaye, the American actor who played that odd version of "Hamlet" at the Crystal Palace with Polly as Ophelia. Perhaps a man with more acute literary conscience than Taylor would not have condescended to "write up" Shakespeare; perhaps a man of more independence and ambition would not have wasted his really fine accomplishment as a playwright for ever on adaptations. That was his weakness—if it was a weakness. He lived entirely for his age, and so was more prominent in it than Charles Reade, for instance, whose name, no doubt, will live longer.

He put himself at the mercy of Whistler, once, in some Velasquez controversy of which I forget the details, but they are all set out, for those who like mordant ridicule, in "The Gentle Art of Making Enemies."

When Tom Taylor criticised acting he wrote as an expert, and he

94

often said illuminating things to me about actors and actresses which I could apply over again to some of the players with whom I have been associated since. "She is a curious example," he said once of an actress of great conscientiousness, "of how far seriousness, sincerity, and weight will supply the place of almost all the other qualities of an actress." When a famous classic actress reappeared as Rosalind, he described her performance as "all minute-guns and *minauderies, . . .* a foot between every word, and the intensity of the emphasis entirely destroying all the spontaneity and flow of spirits which alone excuse and explain; . . . as unlike Shakespeare's Rosalind, I will stake my head, as human personation could be!"

There was some talk at that time (the early 'seventies) of my playing Rosalind at Manchester for Mr Charles Calvert, and Tom Taylor urged me to do it. "Then," he said charmingly, "I can sing my stage Nunc Dimittis." The whole plan fell through, including a project for me to star as Juliet to the Romeo of a lady!

I have already said that the Taylors' home was one of the most softening and culturing influences of my early life. Would that I could give an impression of the dear host at the head of his dinner-table, dressed in black silk knee-breeches and velvet cutaway coat—a survival of a politer time, not an affectation of it—beaming on his guests with his *very* brown eyes!

Lavender is still associated in my mind with everything that is lovely and refined. My mother nearly always wore the colour, and the Taylors lived at Lavender Sweep! This may not be an excellent reason for my feelings on the subject, but it is reason good enough.

"Nature repairs her ravages," it is said, but not all. New things come into one's life—new loves, new joys, new interests, new friends—but they cannot replace the old. When Tom Taylor died, I lost a friend the like of whom I never had again.

NOTES TO CHAPTER V

1. *Ellen Terry's entrances.* Ellen Terry's reference to her suggestion to Henry Irving that he should make "a more swift entrance on the stage from the dressing-room" is interesting. Her custom of leaving her entrance to the very last moment, which often filled lookers-on in her dressing-room with nervous terror that she would be late, and drove the call-boy at the Lyceum to fib about the nearness of her cue—"They're at the quarrel scene, now, Miss Terry" and so on—was wrongly attributed to mere recklessness. She had a very good reason for it as this passage proves.

2. *Portia in 1875.* After the publication of "Childe Harold" Byron woke one morning to find himself famous. Ellen Terry had a similar experience

after her first appearance as Portia. There was never any question after this appearance that she was an actress of the first rank, yet many stage historians give the impression that her career before Henry Irving engaged her as his leading lady in 1878 was insignificant, and that it is improbable she would have achieved a great position apart from Irving. Ellen Terry, who never over-rated her successes, says that as Portia at the Prince of Wales's she had her first and last sense of "being lifted on high by a single stroke of the mighty wing of glory," and contemporary accounts of her triumph make the statement perfectly credible. Yet today Portia is reckoned a second-rate part, and if actresses fail to make much of it, Shakespeare is blamed. A Portia about whom poets, painters and scholars raved is inconceivable in 1932. A painter (Graham Robertson) writes that Ellen Terry was *par excellence* "the Painter's Actress," and appealed to the eye before the ear; her gesture and pose were eloquence itself. "Her charm held every one but I think pre-eminently those who loved pictures." This throws some light on the subjugation of the painters in the audience at the Prince of Wales's. The poets were probably entranced by hearing the true Shakespearean music. The scholars? Well, they may have been struck by the young actress's penetration into the meaning of the words behind the music. And all, ordinary playgoing men and women as well as the artists, fell in love with the enchanting personality of the new Portia.

3. *The Private Life of Portia.* The house at which Mrs Bancroft called to offer Ellen Terry the part of Portia was in Taviton Street. It had been decorated and furnished with great care by Edward Godwin, while Ellen Terry was on tour with Charles Reade, but by the date of Mrs Bancroft's visit, the brokers had made it a desert. In describing the interview with Mrs Bancroft, in her book, Ellen Terry forgot a little detail she always remembered when telling the story to her children. "When Mrs Bancroft saw the Venus, she ejaculated 'Dear me!' in her best comedy manner, and, really rather startled by the enormous size of the cast, made the farcially shocked gesture of putting her hand to her eyes."

It was at Taviton Street that Ellen Terry's final breach with Edward Godwin occurred. Hence her allusion to domestic troubles. I have the authority of an old friend of Godwin's for the story that in "a fit of pique" he left the house, and soon afterwards married Miss Beatrix Phillips, one of his pupils, a young girl still at school. She was the daughter of John Bernie Phillips, the sculptor who executed the frieze on the podium of the Albert Memorial. There is further evidence of that self-confessed inability of Ellen Terry's to sustain a resentment, by which her first husband benefited, in her subsequent attitude towards Edward Godwin. Admiration for it remains unaffected by the consideration that there may have been faults on both sides. If Godwin was not "an easy person to live with," neither was Ellen Terry, as the history of her marriages proves. Writing to a friend of the Harpenden days she had met unexpectedly again after a twenty years' separation, she says: "The times, of which you were part, were my best times, my happiest times. I can never think of him but at his best, and when he died, he thought only

96

so of me. I could never suffer again I think as I have suffered, but I joy in the remembrance of him. He loved me, and I loved him, and that, I suppose, is the reason we so cruelly hurt each other. He went away and shut the door after him. It seems like that to me, but *he knows."*

Well might the friend who was honoured with this confidence reply: "If I wish to express the friendship I feel for you it is not because you are a great actress, perhaps the greatest, but because you are a woman who has preserved uninjured by time whatever was good in the past with a deep tenderness and undying remembrance, letting what was evil vanish." The date of these letters is 1890, four years after Edward Godwin's death.

After the separation he continued to design Ellen Terry's dresses. In her archives there is a delightful little note from him, written during a performance of "The Cup" at the Lyceum. It is illustrated by drawings of the attitudes that are, and are not, archæologically justified in an actress representing a Greek priestess of the period of the play. "This, and this, but never *that."*

Godwin's grave is at Norleigh, near Witney in Oxfordshire. No stone marks it as he was known by his friends to have a strong objection to gravestones. For many years the late Lady Archibald Campbell, a devout admirer of Godwin's (he directed the once famous performances by the "Pastoral Players" in her park at Coombe in which she took part) made the grave her care. An anonymous sonnet, the manuscript of which was preserved by Ellen Terry with other relics may have been published at the time of his death, but I have been unable to find it in print. It is printed now as an appropriate epitaph for "an inheritor of unfulfilled renown."

> A man of men, born to be genial King,
> By frank election of the artist kind,
> Attempting all things, and on anything
> Setting the signet of a master mind.
> What others dreamed amiss, he did aright:
> His dreams were visions of art's golden age:
> Yet self-betrayed, he fell in Fortune's spite,
> His royal birthright sold for scanty wage.
> The best of comrades, winning old and young.
> With keen audacious charm, dandling the fool
> That pleased his humour, but with scathing tongue
> For blatant pedants of the bungler school.
> They tell me he had faults—I know of one:
> Dying too soon, he left his best undone.

There is something ironical in the fact that in a very few years Edward William Godwin's memory survived only because his widow married James McNeill Whistler. Ellen Terry was prohibited by the strange code of manners and morals which regulated the society in which she grew up from paying any public tribute to that memory. What she could not do for herself in life her daughter and I have tried after her death to do for her, feeling certain our effort will command sympathy in an age with a less hypocritical standard of discretion than the one its immediate predecessor set up. The reader who still adheres to this standard, would do well to ponder Ellen Terry's words: "Surely the world is always the better for having a little truth instead of a great deal of falsehood."

4. The parts played by Ellen Terry during the period covered by Chapter V were: Portia ("The Merchant of Venice," 1875); Clara Douglas ("Money," 1875); Mrs Honeyton ("A Happy Pair," 1875); Pauline ("The Lady of Lyons," 1875); Mabel Vane ("Masks and Faces," 1875).

CHAPTER VI

EVENTFUL YEARS

(1876-1878)

§ 1

MY engagement with the Bancrofts lasted a little over a year. After Portia there was nothing momentous about it. I found Clara Douglas difficult, but I enjoyed playing her. I found Mabel Vane easy, and I enjoyed playing her, too, although there was less to be proud of in my success here. Almost any actress of average ability could have walked away with a part demanding such very simple womanly emotion. At this time friends who had fallen in love with Portia used to gather at the Prince of Wales's and applaud me in a manner more vigorous than judicious. It was their fault that it got about that I had hired a claque to clap me! Now, it seems funny, but at the time I was deeply hurt at the insinuation, and it cast a shadow over what would otherwise have been a very happy time.

It is the way of the public sometimes to keep all their enthusiasm for an actress who is doing well in a minor part, and to withhold it from the actress who is playing the leading part. I dont say for a minute that Mrs Bancroft's Peg Woffington in "Masks and Faces" was not appreciated and applauded, but I know that my Mabel Vane was received with a warmth out of all proportion to the merits of my performance, and that this angered some of Mrs Bancroft's admirers, and made them the bearers of ill-natured stories. Any unpleasantness that it caused between us personally was of the briefest duration. It would have been odd indeed if I had been jealous of her, or she of me. Apart from all else, I had met with my little bit of success in such a different field, and she was almost another Madame Vestris in popular esteem.

When I was playing Blanche Hayes in "Ours," I nearly killed Mrs Bancroft with the bayonet which it was part of the business of the play for me to "fool" with. I charged as usual; either she made a mistake and moved to the right instead of to the left, or I made a mistake. Anyhow, I wounded her in the arm. She had to wear it in a sling, and I felt very badly about it, all the more because of the ill-natured stories of its being no accident.

Miss Marie Tempest is perhaps the actress of the present day who reminds me a little of what Mrs Bancroft was at the Prince of Wales's, but neither nature nor art succeed in producing two actresses exactly alike. At her best Mrs Bancroft was unapproachable. I think that the best thing I ever saw her do was the farewell to the boy in "Sweethearts." It was exquisite!

In "Masks and Faces" Taylor and Reade had collaborated, and the exact share of each in the result was left to one's own discernment. I remember saying to Taylor one night at dinner when Reade was sitting opposite me, that I wished he (Taylor) would write me a part like that. "If only I could have an original part like Peg!"

Charles Reade, after fixing me with his amused and *very* glittering eye, said across the table: "I have something for your private ear, Madam, after this repast!" And he came up *with* the ladies, sat by me, and, calling me "an artful toad"—a favourite expression of his for me!—told me that *he,* Charles Reade and no other, had written every line of Peg, and that I ought to have known it. I *didn't* know, as a matter of fact, but perhaps it was stupid of me. There was more of Tom Taylor in Mabel Vane.

I played five parts in all at the Prince of Wales's, and I think I may claim that the Bancrofts found me a *useful* actress—ever the height of my ambition! They wanted Byron—the author of "Our Boys"—to write me a part in the new play, which they had ordered from him, but when "Wrinkles" turned up there was no part which they felt they could offer me, and I think Coghlan was also not included in the cast. At any rate, he was free to take me to see Henry Irving act. Coghlan was always raving about Irving at this time. He said that one evening spent in watching him act was the best education an actor could have. Seeing other people act, even if they are not Irvings, is always an education to us. I have never been to a theatre yet without learning something. It must have been in the spring of 1876 that I received this note:

Will you come in our box on Tuesday for Queen Mary? Ever yours,
CHARLES T. COGHLAN.

I accepted the invitation. I saw Irving's King Philip.

Well, I can only say that he never did anything better to the day of his death. Never shall I forget his expression and manner when Miss Bateman, as Queen Mary (she was *very* good, by the way), was pouring out her heart to him. The horrid, dead look, the cruel unresponsiveness, the indifference of the creature! While the poor woman protested and wept, he went on polishing his ring! Then the tone in which he asked: "Is dinner ready?"

It was the perfection of quiet malignity and cruelty. I was just spell-bound by a study in cruelty, which seemed to me a triumphant assertion of the power of the actor to create as well as to interpret, for Tennyson does not suggest half what Henry Irving did.

We talk of progress, improvement, and advance; but when I think of Henry Irving's Philip, I begin to wonder if Oscar Wilde was not profound as well as witty when he said that a great artist moves in a cycle of masterpieces, of which the last is no more perfect than the first. Only the memory of Irving's Petruchio stops me. But, then, he had not found himself. He was not an artist.

"Why did Whistler paint him as Philip?" some one once asked me. How dangerous to "ask why" about any one so freakish as Jimmy Whistler. But I answered then, and would answer now, that it was because, as Philip, Henry, in his dress without much colour (from the common point of view), his long, gray legs, and Velasquez-like attitude, looked like the kind of thing which Whistler loved to paint. Velasquez had painted a real Philip of the same race. Whistler would paint the actor who had created the Philip of the stage.

I have a note from Whistler written to Henry at a later date which refers to the picture, and suggests portraying him in all his characters. It is common knowledge that the sitter never cared much about the por-trait. Henry had a strange affection for the wrong picture of himself. He disliked the Bastien Lepage, the Whistler, and the Sargent, which never even saw the light. He adored the weak, handsome picture by Millais, which I must admit, all the same, held the mirror up to one of the characteristics of Henry's face—its extreme refinement. Whistler's Philip probably seemed to him not nearly showy enough.

I knew Whistler, by the way, long before he painted the Philip. He gave me the most lovely dinner-set of blue and white china that any woman ever possessed, and a set of Venetian glass, too good for a world where glass is broken. He sent my little girl a tiny Japanese kimono when Liberty was hardly a name. Many of his friends were my friends. He was with the dearest of those friends, Edward Godwin, when he died.

The most remarkable men I have known were Whistler and Oscar Wilde. This does not imply that I liked them better or admired them more than others, but there was something about both of them more instantaneously individual and audacious than it is possible to describe.

§ 2

W_HEN_ I went with Coghlan to see Henry Irving's Philip I was no stranger to his acting. I had been present with Tom Taylor at the famous first night at the Lyceum in 1874, when Henry Irving put his fortune, counted not in gold, but in years of scorned delights and laborious days —years of constant study and reflection, of Spartan self-denial, and deep melancholy—I was present when he put it all to the touch "to win or lose it all." This is no exaggeration. Hamlet was by far the greatest part that he had ever played, or was ever to play. If he had failed—but why pursue it? He could not fail.

Yet the success on the first night at the Lyceum in 1874 was not of that electrical kind which has greeted the momentous achievements of some actors. The first two acts were received with indifference. The people could not see how packed they were with superb acting—perhaps because the new Hamlet was so simple, so quiet, so free from the exhibition of actors' artifices which used to bring down the house in "Louis XI" and in "Richelieu," but which were really the *easy* things in acting, and in "Richelieu" (in my opinion) not especially well done. In "Hamlet" Henry Irving did not go to the audience. He made them come to him. Slowly but surely attention gave place to admiration, admiration to enthusiasm, enthusiasm to triumphant acclaim.

I have seen many Hamlets—Fechter, Charles Kean, Rossi, Frederick Haas, Forbes-Robertson, and my own son, Gordon Craig, among them— but they were not in the same hemisphere! I refuse to go and see Hamlets now. I want to keep Henry Irving's fresh and clear in my memory until I die.

When he engaged me to play Ophelia in 1878 he asked me to go down to Birmingham to see the play, and that night I saw what I shall always consider the *perfection* of acting. This Hamlet had been wonderful in 1874. In 1878 it was far more wonderful. It has been said that when Henry Irving had the "advantage" of my Ophelia, his Hamlet "improved." I dont think so. He was always quite independent of the people with whom he acted.

The Birmingham night he knew I was there. He played—I say it without vanity—for me. We players are not above that weakness, if it be a weakness. If ever anything inspires us to do our best it is the presence in the audience of some fellow-artist who must in the nature of things know more completely than any one what we intend, what we do, what we feel. The response from such a member of the audience flies across the footlights to us like a flame. I felt it once when I played Olivia

102

before Eleonora Duse. I felt that she felt it once when she played Marguerite Gauthier for me.

When I read "Hamlet" now, everything that Henry did in it seems to me more absolutely right, even than I thought at the time. I would give much to be able to record it all in detail, but writing is not the medium in which this can be done. Sometimes I have thought of giving readings of "Hamlet," for I can remember every tone of Henry's voice, every emphasis, every shade of meaning that he saw in the lines and made manifest to the discerning. Yes, I think I could give some pale idea of what his Hamlet was if I read the play.

"Words! words! words!" What is it to say, for instance, that the cardinal qualities of his Prince of Denmark were strength, delicacy, distinction? There was never a touch of commonness. Whatever he did or said, blood and breeding pervaded him.

His "make-up" was very pale, and this made his face beautiful when one was close to him, but at a distance it gave him a haggard look. Some said he looked twice his age.

He kept three things going at the same time—the antic madness, the sanity, the sense of the theatre. The last was to all that he imagined and thought, what charity is said by St Paul to be to all other virtues.

He was never cross or moody—only melancholy. His melancholy was as simple as it was profound. It was touching, too, rather than defiant. You never thought that he was wantonly sad and enjoying his own misery.

He neglected no *coup de théâtre* to assist him, but who notices the servants when the host is present?

For instance, his first entrance as Hamlet was, as we say in the theatre, very much "worked up." He was always a tremendous believer in processions, and rightly. It is through such means that Royalty keeps its hold on the feeling of the public, and makes its mark as a Figure and a Symbol. Henry Irving understood this. Therefore, to music so apt that it was not remarkable in itself, but merely a contribution to the general excited anticipation, the Prince of Denmark came on to the stage. I understood later on at the Lyceum what days of patient work had gone to the making of that procession.

At its tail, when the excitement was at fever heat, came the solitary figure of Hamlet, looking extraordinarily tall and thin. The lights were turned down—another stage trick—to help the effect that the figure was spirit rather than man.

He was weary. His cloak trailed on the ground. He did *not* wear the miniature of his father obtrusively round his neck! His attitude was one which I have seen in a common little illumination to the "Reciter," compiled by Dr Pinches (Henry Irving's old schoolmaster). Yet how right to have taken it, to have been indifferent to its humble origin! Nothing could have been better when translated into life by Irving's genius.

The hair looked blue-black, like the plumage of a crow; the eyes burning—two fires veiled as yet by melancholy. But the appearance of the man was not single, straight or obvious, as it is when I describe it—any more than his passions throughout the play were. I only remember one moment when his intensity concentrated itself in a straightforward unmistakable emotion, without side-current or back-water. It was when he said:

> The play's the thing
> With which to catch the conscience of the King,

and, as the curtain came down, was seen to be writing madly on his tablets against one of the pillars.

"We must start this play a living thing," he used to say at rehearsals, and he worked until the skin grew tight over his face, until he became livid with fatigue, yet still beautiful, to get the opening lines said with individuality, suggestiveness, speed, and power.

> *Bernardo:* Who's there?
> *Francisco:* Nay, answer me; stand, and unfold yourself.
> *Bernardo:* Long live the King!
> *Francisco:* Bernardo?
> *Bernardo:* He.
> *Francisco:* You come most carefully upon your hour.
> *Bernardo:* 'Tis now struck twelve; get thee to bed, Francisco.
> *Francisco:* For this relief much thanks; 'tis bitter cold . . .

And all that he tried to make others do with these lines, he himself did with every line of his own part. Every word lived.

Some said: "Oh, Irving only makes Hamlet a love poem!" They said that, I suppose, because in the Nunnery scene with Ophelia he was the lover above the prince and the poet. With what passionate longing his hands hovered over Ophelia at her words:

> Rich gifts wax poor when givers prove unkind.

His advice to the players was not advice. He did not speak it as an actor. Nearly all Hamlets in that scene give away the fact that they are actors, and not dilettanti of royal blood. Irving defined the way he would have the players speak as an *order,* an instruction of the merit of which he was regally sure. There was no patronising flavour in his acting here, not a touch of "I'll teach you how to do it." He was swift—swift and simple—pausing for the right word now and again, as in the phrase "to hold as 'twere the mirror up to nature." His slight pause and eloquent gesture when the all-embracing word "Nature" came in answer to his call, were exactly repeated unconsciously years later by the Queen of Roumania (Carmen Sylva). She was telling us the story of a play that she had written. The words rushed out swiftly, but occasionally she would wait for the one that expressed her meaning most comprehensively and exactly, and as she got it, up went her hand in triumph over her head. 'Like yours in 'Hamlet,' " I told Henry at the time.

I knew this Hamlet both ways—as an actress from the stage, and as an actress putting away her profession for the time as one of the audience—and both ways it was superb to me. Tennyson, I know, said it was not a perfect Hamlet. I wonder, then, where he hoped to find perfection!

James Spedding, considered a fine critic in his day, said Irving was "simply hideous...a monster!" Another of these fine critics declared that he never could believe in Irving's Hamlet after having seen "part (sic) of his performance as a murderer in a commonplace melodrama." Would one believe that any one could seriously write so stupidly as that about the earnest effort of an earnest actor, if it were not quoted by some of Irving's biographers?

Some criticism, however severe, however misguided, remains within the bounds of justice, but what is one to think of the *Quarterly* Reviewer who declared that "the enormous pains taken with the scenery had ensured Mr Irving's success"? The scenery was of the simplest. No money was spent on it even when the play was revived at the Lyceum after Colonel Bateman's death. Henry's dress probably cost him about £2!

My Ophelia dress was made of material which could not have cost more than 2s. a yard, and not many yards were wanted, as I was at the time thin to vanishing point! I have the dress still, and, looking at it the other day, I wondered what leading lady now would condescend to wear it.

At all its best points, Henry's Hamlet was susceptible of absurd imitation. Think of this well, young actors, who are content to play for safety, to avoid ridicule at all costs, to be "natural"—oh, word most vilely abused! What sort of *naturalness* is this of Hamlet's?

O villain, villain, smiling damned villain!

Henry Irving's imitators could make people burst with laughter when they took off his delivery of that line. And, indeed, the original, too, was almost provocative of laughter—rightly so, for such emotional indignation has its funny as well as its terrible aspect. The mad, and all are mad who have, as Socrates put it, "a divine release from the common ways of men," may speak ludicrously, even when they speak the truth.

All great acting has a certain strain of extravagance which the imitators catch hold of. They give us the eccentric body without the sublime soul.

From the first I saw this extravagance, this bizarrerie in Henry Irving's acting. I noticed, too, its infinite variety. In "Hamlet," during the first scene with Horatio, Marcellus and Bernardo, he began by being very absent and distant. He exchanged greetings sweetly and gently, but he was the visionary. His feet might be on the ground, but his head was towards the stars "where the eternal are." Years later he said to me of another actor in "Hamlet": "*He* would never have seen the ghost." Well, there was never any doubt that Henry Irving saw it, and it was through his acting in the Horatio scene that he made us sure.

As a bad actor befogs Shakespeare's meaning, so a good actor illuminates it. Bit by bit as Horatio talks, Hamlet comes back into the world. He is still out of it when he says:

> My father! Methinks I see my father.

But the dreamer becomes attentive, sharp as a needle, with the words:

> For God's love, let me hear.

Irving's face, as he listened to Horatio's tale, blazed with intelligence. He cross-examined the men with keenness and authority. His mental deductions as they answered were clearly shown. With "I would I had been there" the cloud of unseen witnesses with whom he had before been communing again descended. For a second or two Horatio and the rest did not exist for him.... So onward to the crowning couplet:

> ... foul deeds will rise,
> Though all the earth o'erwhelm them to men's eyes.

After having been very quiet and rapid, very discreet, he pronounced these lines in a loud, clear voice, dragged out every syllable as if there never could be an end to his horror and his rage.

I had been familiar with the scene from my childhood—I had studied it; I had heard from my father how Macready acted in it, and now I found that I had a *fool* of an idea of it! That's the advantage of study, good people, who go to see Shakespeare acted. It makes you know sometimes what is being done, and what you never dreamed would be done when you read the scene at home.

As one of the audience I was much struck by Irving's treatment of interjections and exclamations in "Hamlet." He breathed the line: "O, that this too, too solid flesh would melt," as one long yearning, and,

"O horrible, O horrible! most horrible!" as a groan. When we first went to America his address at Harvard touched on this very subject, and it may be interesting to know that what he preached in 1885 he had practised as far back as 1874.

On the question of pronunciation, there is something to be said which I think in ordinary teaching is not sufficiently considered. Pronunciation should be simple and unaffected, but not always fashioned rigidly according to a dictionary standard. No less an authority than Cicero points out that pronunciation must vary widely according to the emotions to be expressed; that it may be broken or cut with a varying or direct sound, and that it serves for the actor the purpose of colour to the painter, from which to draw variations. Take the simplest illustration. The formal pronunciation of A-h is "Ah," of O-h, "Oh," but you cannot stereotype the expression of emotion like this. These exclamations are words of one syllable, but the speaker who is sounding the gamut of human feeling will not be restricted in his pronunciation by dictionary rule. It is said of Edmund Kean that he never spoke such ejaculations, but always sighed or groaned them. Fancy an actor saying:

"My Desdemona! Oh! oh! oh!"

Words are intended to express feelings and ideas, not to bind them in rigid fetters; the accents of pleasure are different from the accents of pain, and if a feeling is more accurately expressed as in nature by a variation of sound not provided by the laws of pronunciation, then such imperfect laws must be disregarded and nature vindicated!

It was of the address in which these words occur that a Boston hearer said that it was felt by every one present that "the truth had been spoken by a man who had learned it through living and not through theory."

I leave his Hamlet for the present with one further reflection. It was in *courtesy* and *humour* that it differed most widely from other Hamlets that I have seen and heard of. This Hamlet was never rude to Polonius. His attitude towards the old Bromide was that of one who should say: "You dear, funny old simpleton, whom I have had to bear with all my life—how terribly in the way you seem now." With what slightly amused and cynical playfulness this Hamlet said: "I had thought some of Nature's journeymen had made men and not made them well; they imitated humanity so abominably."

Hamlet was by far his greatest triumph, although he would not admit it himself—preferring in some moods to declare that his finest work was done in Macbeth, which was almost universally disliked.

§ 3

ALTHOUGH I was now earning a good salary, I still lived in lodgings at Camden Town, took an omnibus to and from the theatre, and denied myself all luxuries. I did not take a house until I went to the Court Theatre. It was then, too, that I had my first cottage—a wee place at Hampton Court where my children were very happy. They used to give performances of "As You Like It" for the benefit of the Palace custodians—old Crimean veterans, most of them—and when the children had grown up these old men would still ask affectionately after "little Miss Edy" and "Master Teddy," forgetting the passing of time.

My little daughter was a very severe critic! I think if I had listened to her, I should have left the stage in despair. She saw me act for the first time as Mabel Vane, but no compliments were to be extracted from her.

"You *did* look long and thin in your grey dress."

"When you fainted I thought you was going to fall into the orchestra —you was so *long*."

In "New Men and Old Acres" I had to play the piano while I conducted a conversation consisting on my side chiefly of haughty remarks to the effect that "blood would tell," to talk naturally and play at the same time. I "shied" at the lines, became self-conscious, and either sang the words or altered the rhythm of the tune to suit the pace of the speech. I grew anxious about it, and was always practising it at home. After much hard work Edy used to wither me with:

"*That's* not right!"

Teddy was of a more flattering disposition, but very obstinate when he chose. I remember "wrastling" with him for hours over a little Blake poem which he had learned by heart, to say to his mother:

When the voices of children are heard on the green,
   And laughing is heard on the hill,
My heart is at rest within my breast,
   And everything else is still.
Then come home, my children, the sun is gone down,
   And the dews of the night arise,
Come, come, leave off play, and let us away,
   Till morning appears in the skies.

No, no, let us play, for yet it is day,
   And we cannot go to sleep.
Besides, in the sky the little birds fly,
   And the hills are all covered with sheep . . .

All went well until the last line. Then he came to a stop. *Nothing* would make him say sheep!

With a face beaming with anxiety to please, looking adorable, he would offer any word but the right one.

"And the hills are all covered with—"

"With what, Teddy?"

"Master Teddy dont know."

"Something white, Teddy."

"Snow?"

"No, no. Does snow rhyme with 'sleep'?"

"Paper?"

"No, no. Now, I am not going to the theatre until you say the right word. What are the hills covered with?"

"People."

"Teddy, you're a very naughty boy."

At this point he was put in the corner. His first suggestion when he came out was:

"Grass? Trees?"

"Are grass or trees white?" said the despairing mother with her eye on the clock, which warned her that, after all, she would have to go to the theatre without winning.

Meanwhile, Edy was murmuring: *"Sheep,* Teddy," in a loud aside, but Teddy would *not* say it, not even when both he and I burst into tears!

At Hampton Court the two children, dressed in blue and white check pinafores, their hair closely cropped—the little boy fat and fair (at this time he bore a remarkable resemblance to Lawrence's portrait of the youthful King of Rome), the little girl thin and dark—ran as wild as though the desert had been their playground instead of the gardens of this old palace of kings! They were always ready to show visitors (not so numerous then as now) the sights; prattled freely to them of "mummie," who was acting in London, and showed them the new trees which they had assisted the gardeners to plant in the wild garden, and christened after my parts. A silver birch was Iolanthe, a maple Portia, an oak Mabel Vane. Through their kind offices many a stranger found it easy to follow the intricacies of the famous Maze. It was a fine life for them, surely, this unrestricted running to and fro in the gardens, with the great Palace as a civilising influence!

It was for their sake that I was most glad of my increasing prosperity in my profession. My engagement with the Bancrofts was exchanged at the close of the summer season of 1876 for an even more profitable one with Mr John Hare at the Court Theatre.

I had learned a great deal at the Prince of Wales's, notably that the art of playing in modern plays in a tiny theatre was quite different from the art of playing in the classics in a big theatre. The methods for big and little theatres are alike, yet quite unlike. I had learned breadth in

Shakespeare at the Princess's, and had had to employ it again in romantic plays for Charles Reade. The pit and gallery were the audience which we had to reach. At the Prince of Wales's I had to adopt a more delicate, more subtle, more intimate style. But the breadth had to be there just the same—as seen through the wrong end of the microscope. In acting one must possess great strength before one can be delicate in the right way. Too often weakness is mistaken for delicacy.

§ 4

Mr Hare was one of the best stage managers that I have met during the whole of my long experience in the theatre. He was snappy in manner, extremely irritable if anything went wrong, but he knew what he wanted, and he got it. No one has ever surpassed him in the securing of a perfect *ensemble*. He was the Meissonier among the theatre artists. Very likely he would have failed if he had been called upon to produce "King John," but what better evidence of his talent than that he knew his line and stuck to it?

The members of his company were his, body and soul, while they were rehearsing. He gave them fifteen minutes for lunch, and any actor or actress who was foolish or unlucky enough to be a minute late, was sorry afterwards. Mr Hare was peppery and irascible, and lost his temper easily.

Personally, I always got on well with my new manager, and I ought to be grateful to him, if only because he gave me the second great opportunity of my career—the part of Olivia in Wills's play from "The Vicar of Wakefield."

I had known Wills before this through the Forbes-Robertsons. He was at one time engaged to one of the girls, but it was a good thing it ended in smoke. With all his charm Wills was not cut out for a husband. He was Irish all over—the strangest mixture of the aristocrat and the sloven. He could eat a large raw onion every night like any peasant, yet his ideas were magnificent and instinct with refinement.

A true Bohemian in money matters, he made a great deal out of his plays, and yet never had a farthing to bless himself with!

In the theatre he was charming—from an actor's point of view. He interfered very little with the stage-management, and did not care to sit in the stalls and criticise. But he would come quietly to me and tell me things which were most illuminating, and he paid me the compliment of weeping at the wing while I rehearsed "Olivia."

I was generally weeping, too, for Olivia, more than any part, touched me to the heart. I cried too much in it, just as I cried too much later on in the Nunnery scene in "Hamlet," and in the last act of "Charles I." My real tears on the stage have astonished some people, and have been the envy of others, but they have often been a hindrance to me. I have had to *work* to restrain them.

Oddly enough, although "Olivia" was such a great success at the Court, it has never made much money since. The play could pack a tiny theatre; it could never appeal in a big way to the masses. In itself, it has a sure message—the love story of an injured woman is one of the cards in the stage pack which it is always safe to play—but against this there is a bad last act, one of the worst I have ever acted in. It was always being tinkered with, but patching and alteration only seemed to make things worse.

Mr Hare produced "Olivia" perfectly. Marcus Stone designed the clothes, and I found my dresses—both faithful and charming as reproductions of the eighteenth century spirit—stood the advance of time and the progress of ideas when I played the part later at the Lyceum. I had not to alter anything. Henry Irving discovered the same thing about the scenery and stage-management. They could not be improved upon. There was very little scenery at the Court, but a great deal of taste and care in selection.

Every one was "Olivia" mad. The Olivia cap shared public favour with the Langtry bonnet. That most lovely and exquisite creature, Mrs Langtry, could not go out anywhere, at the dawn of the 'eighties, without being the nucleus of a crowd. It was no rare thing to see the crowd, to ask its cause, to receive the answer, "Mrs Langtry!" and to look in vain for the nucleus.

This was all the more remarkable, and honourable to public taste, too, because Mrs Langtry's was not a showy beauty. Her hair was the colour that it had pleased God to make it; her complexion was her own; in evening-dress she did not display nearly as much of her neck and arms as was the vogue, yet they outshone all other necks and arms through their own perfection.

I am aware that the professional critics and the public did not transfer to Mrs Langtry, the actress, the homage that they had paid to Mrs Langtry, the beauty, but I can only speak of the simplicity with which she approached her work, of her industry, and utter lack of vanity about her powers. When she played Rosalind (which my daughter, the best critic of acting *I* know, tells me was in many respects admirable), she wrote to me:

DEAR NELLY,—I bundled through my part somehow last night, a disgraceful performance, and *no* waist-padding! Oh, what an impudent wretch you must think me to attempt such a part! I pinched my arm once or twice

III

last night to see if it was really me. It was so sweet of you to write me such a nice letter, and then a telegram, too! Yours ever, dear Nell,

LILLIE.

Just at this time there was a great dearth on the stage of people with lovely speech, and Lillie Langtry had it. I can imagine that she spoke Rosalind's lines beautifully, and that her clear, grey eyes and frank manner, too well-bred to be hoydenish, must have been of great value.

To go back to "Olivia." Like all Hare's productions, it was perfectly cast. Where all were good, it will be admitted, I think, by every one who saw the production, that Terriss was the best. "As you stand there, whipping your boot, you look the very picture of vain indifference," Olivia says to Squire Thornhill in the first act, and never did I say it without thinking how absolutely *to the life* Terriss had got it.

As I look back, I remember no figure in the theatre more remarkable than Terriss. He was one of those heaven-born actors who, like Kings by divine right, can, up to a certain point, do no wrong. Very often, like the "inspired idiot," Mrs Pritchard, he did not know what he was talking about. Yet he "got there," while many cleverer men stayed behind. He had unbounded impudence, yet so much charm that no one could ever be angry with him. Sometimes he reminded me of a butcher-boy flashing past, whistling, on the high seat of his cart, or of Phaëthon driving the chariot of the sun—pretty much the same thing, I imagine! When he was "dressed up" Terriss was spoiled by fine feathers; when he was in rough clothes, he looked a prince.

He always commanded the love of his intimates as well as that of the outside public. To the end he was "Sailor Bill"—a sort of grown-up midshipmite, whose weaknesses provoked no more condemnation than the weaknesses of a child. In the theatre he had the tidy habits of a sailor. He folded up his clothes and kept them in beautiful condition; and of a young man who had proposed for his daughter's hand he said: "The man's a blackguard! Why, he throws his things all over the room! The most untidy chap I ever saw!"

Terriss had had every sort of adventure by land and sea before I acted with him at the Court. He had been midshipman, tea-planter, engineer, sheep-farmer, and horse-breeder. He had, to use his own words, "hobnobbed with every kind of queer folk, and found myself in extremely queer predicaments." The adventurous, dare-devil spirit of the roamer, the veritable gipsy, always looked out of his insolent eyes. Yet, audacious as he seemed, no man was ever more nervous on the stage. On a first night he was shaking all over with fright, in spite of his confident and dashing appearance.

His bluff was colossal. Once when he was a little boy and wanted money, he said to his mother: "Give me £5 or I'll jump out of the window." And she at once believed that he meant it, and cried out: "Come back, come back! and I'll give you anything."

He showed the same sort of "attack" with audiences. He made them believe in him the moment he stepped on to the stage.

His conversation was extremely entertaining—and, let me add, ingenuous. One of his favourite reflections was: "Tempus fugit! So make the most of it. While you're alive, gather roses; for when you're dead, you're dead a damned long time."

He was a perfect rider, and loved to do cowboy "stunts" in Richmond Park while riding to the "Star and Garter."

When he had presents from the front, which happened every night, he gave them at once to the call-boy or the gas-man. To the women-folk, especially the plainer ones, he was always delightful. Never was any man more adored by the theatre staff. And children, my own Edy included, were simply *daft* about him. A little American girl, daughter of William Winter, the famous critic, when staying with me in England, announced gravely when we were out driving:

"I've gone a mash on Terriss."

There was much laughter. When it had subsided, the child said gravely:

"Oh, you can laugh, but it's true. I wish I was hammered to him!"

Perhaps if he had lived longer, Terriss would have lost his throne. He died as a beautiful youth, a kind of Adonis, although he was fifty years old when he was stabbed at the stage-door of the Adelphi Theatre.

Terriss had a beautiful mouth. That predisposed me in his favour at once! I have always been "cracked" on pretty mouths! I remember that I used to say "Naughty Teddy!" to my own little boy just for the pleasure of seeing him put out his under-lip, when his mouth looked lovely!

At the Court Terriss was still under thirty, but doing the best work of his life. He *never* did anything finer than Squire Thornhill, although he was clever in later years as Henry VIII. His gravity as Flutter in "The Belle's Stratagem" was very fetching; as Bucklaw in "Ravenswood" he looked magnificent, and, of course, as the sailor hero in Adelphi melodrama he was as good as could be. But it is as Thornhill that I like best to remember him. He was precisely the handsome, reckless, unworthy creature that good women are fools enough to love.

In the Court production of "Olivia," both my children walked on to the stage for the first time. Teddy had such red cheeks that they made all the *rouged* cheeks look quite pale! Little Edy gave me a bunch of real flowers that she had picked in the country the day before.

Young Norman Forbes-Robertson was the Moses of the original cast.

He played the part again at the Lyceum. How charming he was! And how very, very young! He at once gave promise of being a good actor, and of having done the right thing in following his brother on to the stage. At the present day I consider him the only actor on the stage who can play Shakespeare's fools as they should be played.

§5

I HAVE not the faintest recollection of "Brothers," the play by Coghlan, in which I see by the evidence of an old play-bill that I made my first appearance under Mr Hare's management.

Charles Coghlan seems to have been consistently unlucky. Yet he was a good actor and a brilliant man. I always enjoyed his companionship; found him a pleasant, natural fellow, absorbed in his work, and not at all the "dangerous" man that some people represented him.

Within less than a month from the date of the production of "Brothers," "New Men and Old Acres" was put into the Court bill. It was not a new play, but the public at once began to crowd to see it, and I have heard that it brought Mr Hare £30,000. My part, Lilian Vavasour, had been played in the original production by Mrs Kendal, but it had been written for me by Tom Taylor when I was at the Haymarket, and it suited me very well. The revival was well acted all round. Charles Kelly was splendid as Mr Brown, and H. B. Conway, a young actor whose good looks were talked of everywhere, was also in the cast. He was a descendant of Lord Byron's, and had a look of the *handsomest* portraits of the poet. With his bright hair curling tightly all over his well-shaped head, his beautiful figure, and charming presence, Conway created a sensation in the 'eighties almost equal to that made by the more famous beauty, Lillie Langtry.

As an actor he belonged to the Terriss type, but he was not nearly as good as Terriss. Of his extraordinary failure in "Faust" I shall say something when I come to the Lyceum productions.

After "New Men and Old Acres," Mr Hare tried a posthumous play by Lord Lytton—"The House of Darnley." It was *not* a good play, and I was *not* good in it, although the pleasant adulation of some of my friends has made me out so. The play met with some success. It was during its run that Mr Hare commissioned Wills to write "Olivia."

§6

I HAD met Charles Kelly before this engagement at the Court Theatre. He had acted with me after my return to the stage in 1874, both in

London and in the provinces, in Charles Reade's plays. His real name was Charles Wardell, and he had not been bred an actor but a soldier. He was in the 66th Regiment and fought in the Crimean War. His father was a clergyman, vicar of Winlaton, Northumberland—a charming parson of an old-fashioned type, a friendship with Sir Walter Scott in his past, and in his present, when I became acquainted with him, many relics of Scott to remind one of that past. Charlie, physically a manly bulldog sort of man, possessed as an actor great tenderness and humour. Owing to his lack of training he had to be very carefully suited with a part, but given one that was in his line, he could do as well as many actors twenty years ahead of him in experience. In such parts as Mr Brown in "New Men and Old Acres," and the farmer father in Reade's adaptation of Tennyson's "Dora," he was at his best. He would certainly have made as great a success as Burchell in "Olivia" as Terriss made as Thornhill, but he was piqued at not being offered the leading part of the Vicar, which was given to Herman Vezin, and stubbornly refused to play Burchell. Alas! many actors are just as blind to their true interests.

Charles Kelly and I were married during the run of "Olivia." After I left the Court Theatre for the Lyceum we continued to tour together in the provinces when the Lyceum was closed. These tours were very successful, but I never had to work harder in my life! On one of these tours I played Beatrice in "Much Ado About Nothing" for the first time. Kelly's Benedick was in many ways a splendid performance, perhaps better for the play than the more subtle and deliberate performance Henry Irving gave at the Lyceum.

After a performance of "Dora" at Liverpool, Charles Reade wrote:

Nincompoop!
What have you to fear from me for such a masterly performance! Be assured nobody can appreciate your value and Mr Kelly's as I do. It is well played all round.

NOTES ON CHAPTER VI

1. *Blanche Hayes in "Ours."* This was the first part in which Bernard Shaw saw Ellen Terry. The event is recorded in his preface to "Ellen Terry and Bernard Shaw: A Correspondence": "When I came to London ... (1876) I hastened to the famous little theatre off Tottenham Court Road, where the Scala Theatre now stands, to see the Cup and Saucer drama of Robertson handled by the Bancrofts. The play was 'Ours,' and in it I saw Ellen Terry for the first time. She left on me an impression of waywardness; of not quite fitting into her part, and not wanting to; and she gave no indication of her full power for which the part afforded no scope. As her portraits had pre-

pared me to find her interesting and singular (I have never been susceptible to mere prettiness) I was less struck than I should have been if she had been quite new to me."

2. *Carmen Sylva.* In a copy of Carmen Sylva's "Thoughts of a Queen" belonging to Ellen Terry there is a note in her handwriting giving a more detailed impression of the royal author: "Beautiful creature, Elizabeth Queen of Roumania. She read a play to H. I. and E. T., and was exquisitely impressive and expressive. She translated as she read, standing up, and her movements were grandly simple. Her face glowed with intelligence. The voice a little hard, but not sharp. Her very beautiful eyes glittered. The mouth well cut—a little too firm. The hands beautiful, and she used them delicately, and slowly. She had arranged her effects to perfection, and most folk would not have perceived the arrangement. A gracious, simple woman, every inch a Queen. She was tall and finely proportioned."

3. *"I had studied it."* This reference of Ellen Terry's to study invites a comment on a distinction, not realized now-a-days, between memorizing and studying. It can be seen from this passage that Ellen Terry had studied the part of Hamlet. This does not imply she had learned it by heart. She had been trained in a school in which the study of great parts, not with the object of playing them but with that of developing dramatic perception, was considered essential in the player's education.

4. *John Hare as "stage-manager."* Ellen Terry is writing of days when the terminology of the theatre was somewhat different. The stage-manager of yesterday is the "producer" of today. The stage-manager of today is the "prompter" of yesterday. The office of assistant-stage-manager did not exist in 1876. His duties were performed by the call-boy.

5. *Lilian Vavasour.* It was as Lilian Vavasour in "New Men and Old Acres" that Ellen Terry "completely conquered" Bernard Shaw, convincing him that here was the woman for the new drama which was still "in the womb of time waiting for Ibsen to impregnate it."

6. *Ellen Terry's Second Marriage.* The belated divorce proceedings taken by G. F. Watts had left Ellen Terry free to marry again. Watts has been severely censured for not taking these proceedings earlier at the time of Ellen Terry's elopement with Godwin. Perhaps it was for this he feared a "malediction" as well as for treating his young wife harshly. But I have no data for an explanation of the delay. It may be known to some of Ellen Terry's friends whether Watts would have applied for a divorce earlier had she wished it, and he been convinced it would be to her benefit, but I am in the dark about it, and am willing to make the charitable assumption that the question of divorce did not arise until after Ellen Terry's separation from Godwin. No doubt one of her motives then for deciding to marry was a desire, in her children's interests, to regularize her position. Yet it is conceivable that she was strongly attracted by Charles Wardell. All through her life the man of brains competed for her affections with the man of brawn. But this man of brawn, although a good fellow in some ways—he had a genuine affection for his wife's children, who for a time bore his name—had a violent and

jealous temper which Ellen Terry eventually found intolerable. She implies in this chapter that her second husband had no notion of playing second fiddle as an actor. He fancied himself as a leading man. This justifies the presumption that he was mortified by her engagement at the Lyceum, which threatened his position as her leading man. It is known that he resented the friendship with Henry Irving which was the sequel to the engagement. Ellen Terry continued to tour with her husband until 1880. In 1881 there was a judicial separation. In 1885 Charles Wardell died. Ellen Terry paid his debts, and for years supported the sisters of his first wife! One happy result of her second unhappy marriage was that it healed the breach between her and her family which had caused both great pain. In a letter at this time to an old friend Ellen Terry writes of her joy at the reconciliation: "Thank God, mother is alive, and I can atone to her for the pain I unintentionally caused her."

7. The parts played by Ellen Terry during the period covered by Chapter VI were: Blanche Hayes ("Ours," 1876); Kate Hungerford ("Brothers," 1876); Lilian Vavasour ("New Men and Old Acres," 1876); Georgina Vesey ("Money," 1877); Lady Teazle ("School for Scandal," 1877); Lady Juliet ("The House of Darnley," 1877); Mrs Merryweather ("Victims," 1878); Olivia ("Olivia," 1878); Iris ("The Cynic's Defeat," 1878); Dora ("Dora," 1878).

CHAPTER VII

WORK AT THE LYCEUM

(1878–1880)

§ 1

IT was during the run of "Olivia" that Henry Irving became sole lessee of the Lyceum Theatre. For a long time he had been contemplating the step, but it was one of such magnitude that it could not be taken in a hurry. I daresay he found it difficult to separate from Mrs Bateman and from her daughter, who had for such a long time been his "leading lady." He had to be a little cruel, not for the last time in a career devoted unremittingly and unrelentingly to his art and his ambition.

It was said in later years that rich ladies financed Henry Irving's ventures. The only shadow of foundation for this statement is that at the beginning of his tenancy of the Lyceum, the Baroness Burdett-Coutts lent him a certain sum of money, every farthing of which was repaid during the first few months of his management.

The first letter that I ever received from Henry Irving was written on July 20th, 1878, from 15a, Grafton Street, the house in which he lived during the entire period of his Lyceum management.

DEAR MISS TERRY,—I look forward to the pleasure of calling upon you on Tuesday next at two o'clock.

With every good wish, believe me, Yours sincerely,

HENRY IRVING.

The call was in reference to my engagement as Ophelia. Very characteristic I see it now to have been of Henry to have been content to take my powers as an actress more or less on trust. A mutual friend, Lady Pollock, had told him that I was the very person for him, that "all London" was talking of my Olivia, that I had acted well in Shakespeare with the Bancrofts, that I should bring to the Lyceum Theatre what players call "a personal following." Henry chose his friends as carefully as he chose his company and his staff. He believed in Lady Pollock implicitly, and he did not—it is possible that he could not—come and see my Olivia for himself.

I was living in Longridge Road, Earls Court, at the time of this memorable visit from Henry Irving. I cant recall our conversation about the engagement, but I know I noticed the great change that had taken place in the man since I had last met him in 1867. Then he was really almost ordinary looking—with a moustache, an unwrinkled face, and a sloping forehead. The only wonderful thing about him was his melancholy. Once, when I was playing the piano in the greenroom at the Queen's Theatre, he came in and listened. I remember being made aware of his presence by his sigh—the deepest, profoundest, sincerest sigh I have ever heard from any human being. He asked me if I would not play the piece again.

The incident impressed itself on my mind, inseparably associated with a picture of him as he looked at thirty—a picture by no means pleasing. He looked conceited, and almost savagely proud of the isolation in which he lived. There was a touch of exaggeration in his appearance—a dash of Werther, with a few flourishes of Jingle! Nervously sensitive to ridicule, self-conscious, suffering deeply from his inability to express himself through his art, Henry Irving, in 1867, was a very different person from the Henry Irving who called on me at Longridge Road in 1878.

In ten years he had found himself, and so lost himself—lost, I mean, much of that stiff, ugly, self-consciousness which had encased him as the shell encases the lobster. His forehead had become more massive, and the very outline of his features had altered. He was a man of the world, whose strenuous fighting now was to be done as a general—not, as hitherto, in the ranks. His manner was very quiet and gentle. "In quietness and confidence shall be your strength," says the Psalmist. That was always like Henry Irving.

And here, perhaps, is the place to say that I, of all people, can perhaps appreciate him least justly, although I was his associate on the stage for a quarter of a century, and was on the terms of the closest friendship with him for almost as long a time. He had precisely the qualities that I never find likable.

He was an egotist—an egotist of the great type, *never* "a mean egotist," as he was once slanderously described—and all his faults sprang from egotism, which is in one sense, after all, only another name for greatness. So much absorbed was he in his own achievements that he was unable or unwilling to appreciate the achievements of others. I never heard him speak in high terms of the great foreign actors and actresses who from time to time visited England. It would be easy to attribute this to jealousy, but the easy explanation is not the true one. He simply would not give himself up to appreciation. Perhaps appreciation is a *wasting* though a generous quality of the mind and heart, and best left to lookers-on, who have plenty of time to develop it.

I was with him when he saw Sarah Bernhardt act for the first time. The play was "Ruy Blas," and it was one of Sarah's bad days. She was walking through the part listlessly, and I was angry that there should be any ground for Henry's indifference. The same thing happened years later, when I took him to see Eleonora Duse. The play was "La Locandiera," in which to my mind she is not at her very best. He was surprised at my enthusiasm. There was an element of justice in his attitude towards the performance which infuriated me, but I doubt if he would have shown more enthusiasm if he had seen her at her very best.

As the years went on he grew very much attached to Sarah Bernhardt, and admired her as a colleague whose managerial work in the theatre was as dignified as his own, but of her superb powers as an actress, I dont believe he ever had a glimmering notion!

Perhaps it is not true, but, as I believe it to be true, I may as well state it: *It was never any pleasure to him to see the acting of other actors and actresses.* All the same, Salvini's Othello I know he thought magnificent, but he would not speak of it.

What I have written so far I have written merely to indicate the qualities in Henry Irving's nature, which were unintelligible to me, perhaps because I have always been more woman than artist. He always put the theatre first. He lived in it, he died in it. He possessed none of what I may call my homely qualities—the love of children, the love of a home, the dislike of solitude. I have always thought it hard to find my inferiors. He was sure of his high place. He was far simpler than I in some ways. He would talk, for instance, in such an ingenuous way to painters and musicians that I blushed for him.

He never pretended. One of his biographers has said that he posed as being a French scholar. Such a thing, and all things like it, were impossible to his nature. If it were necessary in one of his plays to say a few French words, he took infinite pains to learn them and said them beautifully.

He once told me that in the early part of his career, before I knew him, he had been jeered at, and hooted, because of his thin legs. The first service I did him was to tell him they were beautiful.

"What do you want with fat, podgy, prize-fighter legs!" I expostulated.

Praise to some people at certain stages of their career is more helpful than blame. I admired the very things in Henry for which other people criticised him. I believe this helped him.

I brought help, too, in pictorial matters. Henry Irving had had little training in such matters. I had had a great deal. Judgment about colours, clothes and lighting must be *trained*. I had learned from Mr Watts, from Mr Godwin, and from other artists, until a sense of decorative effect had become second nature to me.

§ 2

Now for the Lyceum rehearsals of November, 1878. Although Henry Irving had played Hamlet for over two hundred nights in London, and for I dont know how many nights in the provinces, he always rehearsed in cloak and rapier. This careful attention to detail came back to my mind years afterwards, when he gave readings of Macbeth. He never gave a public reading without first going through the entire play at his hotel.

At the first rehearsal of Hamlet he read every one's part except mine, which he skipped, and the power that he put into each part was extraordinary. He threw himself so thoroughly into it that his skin contracted and his eyes shone. His lips grew whiter and whiter, and his skin more and more drawn as time went on, until he looked livid but still beautiful.

He never got at anything *easily,* and often I felt angry that he should waste so much of his strength in trying to teach people to do things in the right way. Very often it only ended in his producing actors who gave colourless, feeble and unintelligent imitations of him. There were exceptions, of course.

When it came to the last ten days before the date named for the production of "Hamlet," and my scenes with him were still unrehearsed, I grew very anxious and miserable. I was still a stranger in the theatre, and in awe of Henry Irving personally; but I plucked up courage, and said:

"I am very nervous about my first appearance with you. Couldnt we rehearse *our* scenes?"

"*We* shall be all right," he answered, "but we are not going to run the risk of being bottled up by a gas-man or a fiddler."

When I spoke, I think he was taking a band rehearsal. Although he did not understand a note of music, he felt, through intuition, what the music ought to be, and would pull it about and have alterations made. No one was cleverer than Hamilton Clarke, Henry's first musical director, and a most gifted composer, at carrying out his instructions. Hamilton Clarke often grew angry and flung out of the theatre, saying that it was quite impossible to do what Mr Irving required.

"Patch it together, indeed!" he used to say to me indignantly, when

121

I was told off to smooth him down. "Mr Irving knows nothing about music, or he couldnt ask me to do such a thing."

But the next day he would return with the score altered on the lines suggested by Henry, and would confess that the music was improved. "Upon my soul, it's better! The 'Guv'nor' was perfectly right."

His Danish march in "Hamlet," his Brocken music in "Faust," and his music for "The Merchant of Venice" were all, to my mind, exactly *right*. The brilliant gifts of Clarke, before many years had passed, "o'erleaped" themselves, and he ended his days in a lunatic asylum.

The only person who did not profit by Henry's ceaseless labours was poor Ophelia. When the first night came, I did not play the part well, although the critics and the public were pleased. To myself I *failed*. I had not rehearsed enough. I can remember one occasion when I played Ophelia really well. It was in Chicago some ten years later. At Drury Lane, in 1896, when I played the mad scene for Nelly Farren's benefit, and took farewell of the part for ever, I was just *damnable!*

Ophelia only *pervades* the scenes in which she is concerned until the mad scene. This was a tremendous thing for me, who am not capable of *sustained* effort, but can perhaps manage a *cumulative* effort better than most actresses. I have been told that Ophelia has "nothing to do" at first. I found so much to do! Little bits of business which, slight in themselves, contributed to a definite result, and kept me always in the picture.

Like all Ophelias before (and after) me, I went to the madhouse to study wits astray. I was disheartened at first. There was no beauty, no nature, no pity in most of the lunatics. Strange as it may sound, they were too *theatrical* to teach me anything. Then, just as I was going away, I noticed a young girl gazing at the wall. I went between her and the wall to see her face. It was quite vacant, but the body expressed that she was waiting, waiting. Suddenly she threw up her hands and sped across the room like a swallow. I never forgot it. She was very thin, very pathetic, very young, and the movement was as poignant as it was beautiful.

I saw another woman laugh with a face that had no gleam of mirth anywhere—a face of pathetic and resigned grief.

My experiences convinced me that the actor must imagine first and observe afterwards. It is no good observing life and bringing the result to the stage without selection, without a definite idea. The idea must come first, the realism afterwards.

Perhaps because I was nervous and irritable about my own part from insufficient rehearsal, perhaps because his responsibility as lessee weighed upon him, Henry Irving's Hamlet on the first night at the Lyceum seemed to me less wonderful than it had at Birmingham. At rehearsals he had been the perfection of grace. On the night itself, he dragged his leg and seemed stiff from self-consciousness. He asked me later on if I thought the ill-natured criticism of his walk was in any way justified, and if he really said "Gud" for "God," and the rest of it. I said straight out that he *did* say his vowels in a peculiar way, and that he *did* drag his leg.

I begged him to give up that dreadful, paralysing waiting at the side for his cue, and after a time he took my advice. He was never obstinate in such matters. His one object was to *find out,* to *test* suggestion, and follow it if it stood his test.

He was very diplomatic when he meant to have his own way. He never blustered or enforced or threatened. My first acquaintance with this side of him was made over my dress for Ophelia. He had heard that I intended to wear black in the mad scene, and he intended me to wear white. When he first mentioned the subject, I had no idea that there would be any opposition. He spoke of my dresses, and I told him that as I was very anxious not to be worried about them at the last minute, they had been got on with early and were now finished.

"Finished! That's very interesting! Very interesting. And what—er— what colours are they?"

"In the first scene I wear a pinkish dress. It's all rose-coloured with her. Her father and brother love her. The Prince loves her—and so she wears pink."

"Pink," repeated Henry thoughtfully.

"In the nunnery scene I have a pale, gold, amber dress—the most beautiful colour. The material is a church brocade. It will 'tone down' the color of my hair. In the last scene I wear a transparent, black dress."

Henry did not wag an eyelid.

"I see. In mourning for her father."

"No, not exactly that. I think *red* was the mourning colour of the period. But black seems to me *right*—like the character, like the situation."

"Would you put the dresses on?" said Henry gravely.

At that minute Walter Lacy came up, that very Walter Lacy who had been with Charles Kean when I was a child, and who now acted as adviser to Henry Irving in his Shakespearean productions.

"Ah, here's Lacy. Would you mind, Miss Terry, telling Mr Lacy what you are going to wear?"

Rather surprised, but still unsuspecting, I told Lacy all over again. Pink in the first scene, yellow in the second, black—

You should have seen Lacy's face at the word "black." He was going to burst out, but Henry stopped him. He was more diplomatic than that!

"Ophelias generally wear *white,* dont they?"

"I believe so," I answered, "but black is more interesting."

"I should have thought you would look much better in white."

"Oh, no!" I said.

And then they dropped the subject for that day. It *was* clever of him! The next day Lacy came up to me:

"You didnt really mean that you are going to wear black in the mad scene?"

"Yes, I did. Why not?"

"*Why not!* My God! Madam, there must be only one black figure in this play, and that's Hamlet!"

I did feel a fool. What a blundering donkey I had been not to see it before! I was very thrifty in those days, and the thought of having been the cause of needless expense worried me. So instead of the crêpe de Chine and miniver, which had been used for the black dress, I had for the white dress Bolton sheeting and rabbit, and I believe it looked better.

The incident, whether Henry was right or not, led me to see that, although I knew more of art and archæology in dress than he did, he had a finer sense of what was right for the *scene*. After this he always consulted me about the costumes, but if he said: "I want such and such a scene to be kept dark and mysterious," I knew better than to try and introduce pale-coloured dresses into it.

Henry always had a fondness for "the old actor," and would engage him in preference to the tvro any day. "I can trust them," he explained briefly.

In the cast of "Hamlet" Mr Forrester, Mr Chippendale, and Tom Mead worthily repaid the trust. Meade, in spite of a terrible excellence in "Meadisms"—he substituted the most excruciatingly funny words for Shakespeare's when his memory of the text failed—was a remarkable actor. His voice as the Ghost was beautiful, and his appearance splendid. With his deep-set eyes, hawk-like nose, and clear brow, he reminded me of the Rameses head in the British Museum.

We had young men in the cast, too. There was one very studious youth who could never be caught loafing. He was always reading, or busy in the greenroom studying by turns the pictures of past actor-humanity with which the walls were peopled, or the present realities of actors who came in and out of the room. Although he was so much younger then, Mr Pinero looked much as he does now. He played Rosencrantz very neatly. Consummate care, precision, and brains characterised his work as an actor always, but his chief ambition lay another way. Rosencrantz and the rest were his school of stage-craft.

Kyrle Bellew, the Osric of the production, was another man of the future, though we did not know it. He was very handsome, a tremendous lady-killer! He wore his hair rather long, had a graceful figure, and a good voice, as became the son of a preacher who had the reputation of saying the Lord's Prayer so dramatically that his congregation sobbed.

Frank Cooper, a descendant of the Kembles, another actor who has risen to eminence since, played Laertes. It was he who first led me onto the Lyceum stage. Twenty years later he became my leading man on the first tour I had taken independently of Henry Irving since my tours with Charles Kelly.

§ 3

WHEN I am asked what I remember about the first ten years at the Lyceum, I can answer in one word: *Work*. I was hardly ever out of the theatre. What with acting, rehearsing, and studying—twenty-five reference books were a "simple coming-in" for one part—I sometimes thought I should go blind and mad. It was not only for my parts at the Lyceum that I had to rehearse. From August to October I was still touring in the provinces on my own account. My brother George acted as my business manager. His enthusiasm was not greater than his loyalty and industry. When we were playing in small towns he used to rush into mv dressing-room after the curtain was up and say excitedly:

"We've got twenty-five more people in our gallery than the ——— Theatre opposite!"

Although he was very delicate, he worked for me like a slave. When my tours with Mr Kelly ended in 1880 and I promised Henry Irving that in future I would go to the provincial towns with him, my brother was given a position at the Lyceum, where, I fear, his scrupulous and uncompromising honesty often got him into trouble. Perquisites, or "perks," as they are called in domestic service, are one of the heaviest additions to a manager's working expenses, and George tried to fight the system. He hurt no one so much as himself.

One of my productions in the provinces was an English version of "Frou-Frou," made for me by my dear friend Mrs Comyns Carr, who for many years designed the dresses that I wore in different Lyceum plays. "Butterfly," as "Frou-Frou" was called when the play was produced in English, went well; indeed, the Scots of Edinburgh received it with overwhelming enthusiasm. It served my purpose at the time, but when I saw Sarah Bernhardt play the part I wondered that I had had the presumption to meddle with it. It was not a case of my having a different view of the character and playing it according to my imagination, as it was, for instance, when Duse played "La Dame aux Camélias," and gave a performance that one could not say was *inferior* to Bernhardt's, although it was so utterly *different*. No people in their right senses could have accepted my "Frou-Frou" instead of Sarah's. What I lacked technically in it was *pace*.

Of course, it is partly the language. English cannot be phrased as rapidly as French. But I have heard foreign actors, playing in the English tongue, show us this rapidity, this warmth, this fury—call it what you will—and have just wondered why we are, most of us, so deficient in it.

Fechter had it, so had Edwin Forrest. When strongly moved, their passions and their fervour made them swift. The more Henry Irving felt, the more deliberate he became. I said to him once: "You seem to be hampered in the vehemence of passion." "I *am*," he answered. This is what crippled his Othello, and made his scene with Tubal in "The Merchant of Venice" the least successful *to him*. What it was to the audience is another matter. But he had to take refuge in speechless rage when he would have liked to pour out his words like a torrent.

In the company which Charles Kelly and I took round the provinces in 1880 were Henry Kemble and Charles Brookfield. Young Brookfield was just beginning life as an actor, and he was so brilliantly funny off the stage that he was always a little disappointing *on* it. My old manageress, Mrs Wigan, first brought him to my notice, writing in a charming little note that she knew him "to have a power of *personation* very rare in an unpractised actor," and that if we could give him varied practice, she would feel it a courtesy to her.

I had reason to admire Mr Brookfield's "powers of personation" when I was acting at Buxton. He and Kemble had no parts in one of our plays, so they amused themselves during their "off" night by hiring bath-chairs and pretending to be paralytics! We were acting in a hall, and the most infirm of the invalids visiting the place to take the waters were wheeled in at the back, and up the centre aisle. In the middle of a very pathetic scene I caught sight of Kemble and Brookfield in their bath-chairs, and could not *speak* for several minutes.

Mr Brookfield does not tell this little story in his "Random Reminiscences." It is about the only one that he has left out! To my mind he is the prince of story-tellers. All the cleverness that he should have put into his acting and his play-writing (of which since those early days he has done a great deal) he seems to have put into his life. I remember him more clearly as a delightful companion than an actor, and he won my heart at once by his kindness to my little daughter Edy, who accompanied me on this tour. He has too great a sense of humour to resent my inadequate recollection of him. Did he not in his own book quote gleefully from an obituary notice published on a false report of his death, the summary: "Never a great actor, he was invaluable in small parts. But after all it is at his club that he will be most missed!"

In the last act of "Butterfly," when the poor woman is dying, her husband shows her a locket with a picture of her child in it. Night after night we used a "property" locket, but on my birthday, when we happened to be playing the piece, Charles Kelly bought a silver locket and put inside it two little coloured photographs of my children, Edy and Teddy, and gave it to me on the stage instead of the "property" one. When I opened it, I burst into very real tears! I have often wondered since if the audience that night knew that they were seeing *real* instead of assumed emotion! Probably the difference did not tell at all.

At Leeds we produced "Much Ado About Nothing." I never played Beatrice as well again. When I began to "take soundings" from life for my conception of her, I found in my friend Anne Codrington (now Lady Winchilsea) what I wanted. There was before me a Beatrice—as fine a lady as ever lived, a great-hearted woman—beautiful, accomplished, merry, tender. When Nan Codrington came into a room it was as if the sun came out. She was the daughter of an admiral, and always tried to make her room look as like a cabin as she could. "An excellent musician," as Benedick hints Beatrice was, Nan composed the little song that I sang at the Lyceum in "The Cup," and very good it was, too.

§ 4

WHEN Henry Irving put on "Much Ado About Nothing"—a play which he may be said to have revived for me, as he never really liked the part of Benedick—I was not the same Beatrice at all. A great actor can do nothing badly, and there was very much to admire in Henry Irving's Benedick. But he gave me little help. Beatrice must be swift, swift, swift! Owing to Henry's rather finicking, deliberate method as Benedick, I could never put the right pace into my part. I was also feeling unhappy about it, because I had been compelled to give way about a traditional "gag" in the church scene, with which we ended the fourth act. In my own production we had scorned this gag, and let the curtain come down on Benedick's line: "Go, comfort your cousin; I must say she is dead, and so farewell." When I was told that we were to descend to the buffoonery of:

> *Beatrice:* Benedick, kill him—kill him if you can.
> *Benedick:* As sure as I'm alive, I will!

I protested, and implored Henry not to do it. He said that it was necessary: otherwise the "curtain" would be received in dead silence. I assured him that we had often had seven and eight calls without it. I used every argument, artistic and otherwise. Henry, according to his custom, was gentle, would not discuss it much, but remained obdurate. After holding out for a week, I gave in. "It's my duty to obey your orders, and do it," I said, "but I do it under protest." Then I burst into tears. It was really for his sake just as much as for mine. I thought it must bring such disgrace on him! Looking back on the incident, I find that the most humorous thing in connection with it was that the critics, never reluctant to accuse Henry of "monkeying" with Shakespeare if they could find cause, never noticed the gag at all!

Such disagreements occurred very seldom. In "The Merchant of Venice" I found that Henry Irving's Shylock necessitated an entire revision of my conception of Portia, especially in the trial scene, but here there was no point of honour involved. I had considered, and still am of the same mind, that Portia in the trial scene ought to be very *quiet*. I saw an extraordinary effect in this quietness. But as Henry's Shylock was quiet, I had to give it up. His heroic saint was splendid, but it wasn't good for Portia.

Of course, there were always injudicious friends to say that I had not "chances" enough at the Lyceum. Even my father said to me after "Othello":

"We must have no more of these Ophelias and Desdemonas!"

"Father!" I cried out, really shocked.

"They're second fiddle parts—not the parts for you, Duchess."

"Father!" I gasped out again, for really I thought Ophelia a pretty good part, and was delighted at my success in it.

But granting these *were* "second fiddle" parts, I want to make quite clear that I had my turn of "first fiddle" ones. "Romeo and Juliet," "Much Ado About Nothing," "Olivia," and "The Cup" all gave me finer opportunities than they gave Henry. In "The Merchant of Venice" and in "Charles I" they were at least equal to his.

I have sometimes wondered what I should have accomplished without Henry Irving. I might have had "bigger" parts, but it doesn't follow that they would have been better ones, and if they had been written by contemporary dramatists my success would have been less durable. "No actor or actress who doesn't play in the 'classics'—in Shakespeare or old comedy—will be heard of long," was one of Henry Irving's sayings, by the way, and he was right.

It was a long time before we had much talk with each other. In the "Hamlet" days, Henry Irving's melancholy was appalling. I remember feeling as if I had laughed in church when he came to the foot of the stairs leading to my dressing-room, and caught me sliding down

From a photograph by Lewis Carroll

MR AND MRS BENJAMIN TERRY
The Father and Mother of Ellen Terry

the banisters! He smiled at me, but didnt seem able to get over it.

"Lacy," he said some days later, "what do you think! I found her the other day sliding down the banisters."

Keats writes in one of his marvellous letters that the poet lives not in one, but in a thousand worlds, and this is true of the actor of great imagination. He forms in these worlds many different natures. What was the real Henry Irving, I used to speculate!

His religious upbringing always left its mark on him, though no one could be more "raffish" and mischievous than he when entertaining friends at supper in the Beefsteak-room, or chaffing his valued adjutants, Bram Stoker and Loveday. H. J. Loveday, our stage manager, was, I think, as absolutely devoted to Henry as any one except his fox-terrier, Fussy. Loveday's loyalty made him agree with everything that Henry said, however preposterous, and didnt Henry trade on it sometimes!

Once while he was talking to me, when he was making up, he absently took a white lily out of a bowl on the table and began to stripe and dot the petals with the stick of grease-paint in his hand. He pulled off one or two of the petals, and held it out to me.

"Pretty flower, isnt it?"

"Oh, dont be ridiculous, Henry!" I said.

"You wait!" he said mischievously. "We'll show it to Loveday."

Loveday was sent for on some business connected with the evening's performance. Henry held out the flower obtrusively, but Loveday wouldnt notice it.

"Pretty, isnt it?" said Henry carelessly.

"Very," said Loveday. "I always like those lilies. A friend of mine has his garden full of them, and he says they're not so difficult to grow if only you give 'em enough water."

Henry's delight at having "taken in" Loveday was childish. But sometimes I think Loveday must have seen through these innocent jokes, only he wouldnt have spoiled "the Guv'nor's" bit of fun for the world.

When Henry first met him he was conducting an orchestra. I forget the precise details, but I know that he gave up this position to follow Henry, that he was with him during the Bateman régime at the Lyceum, and that when the Lyceum became a thing of the past, he still kept the post of stage manager. He was literally "faithful unto death," for it was only at Henry's death that his service ended.

Bram Stoker, whose recently published "Reminiscences of Irving" have told, as well as it ever *can* be told, the history of the Lyceum Theatre under Irving's direction, was as good a servant in the front of the theatre as Loveday was behind scenes. Like a true Irishman, he has given me some lovely blarney in his book. He has also told *all* the stories that I might have told, and described every one connected with the Lyceum except himself. I can fill *that* deficiency to a certain extent by saying that he is one of the most kind and tender-hearted of men. He filled a difficult position with great tact, and was not so universally abused as most business managers, because he was always straight with the company, and never took a mean advantage of them.

Stoker and Loveday were daily, nay, hourly, associated for many years with Henry Irving; but, after all, did they or any one else *really* know him? And what was Henry Irving's attitude? I believe myself that he never wholly trusted his friends, and never admitted them to his intimacy, although they thought he did, which was the same thing to *them*.

From his childhood up, Henry was lonely. His chief companions in youth were the Bible and Shakespeare. He used to study "Hamlet" in the Cornish fields, when he was sent out by his aunt, Mrs Penberthy, to call in the cows. One day, when he was in one of the deep, narrow lanes common in that part of England, he looked up and saw the face of a sweet little lamb gazing at him from the top of the bank. The symbol of the lamb in the Bible had always attracted him, and his heart went out to the dear little creature. With some difficulty he scrambled up the bank, slipping often in the damp, red earth, threw his arms round the lamb's neck and kissed it.

The lamb bit him!

Did this set-back in early childhood influence him? I wonder! He had another such set-back when he first went on the stage, and for some six weeks in Dublin was subjected every night to groans, hoots, hisses, and cat-calls from audiences who resented him because he had taken the place of a dismissed favourite. In such a situation an actor is not likely to take stock of *reasons*. Henry Irving only knew that the Dublin people made him the object of violent personal antipathy. "I played my parts not badly for me," he said simply, "in spite of the howls of execration with which I was received."

The bitterness of this Dublin episode was never quite forgotten. It coloured Henry Irving's attitude towards the public. When he made his humble little speeches of thanks to them before the curtain, there was always a touch of pride in the humility. Perhaps he would not have received adulation in quite the same dignified way if he had never known what it was to wear the martyr's "shirt of flame."

§ 5

My chief difficulty in giving a consecutive narrative of my first years at the Lyceum is that Henry Irving looms across them, reducing all events, all feelings, all that happened, and all that was suggested, to insignificance.

Let me speak *generally* of his method of procedure in producing a play.

First he studied it for three months himself, and nothing in that play would escape him. Some one asked him a question about "Titus Andronicus." "God bless my soul!" he said. "I never read it, so how should I know!" The Shakespearean scholar who had questioned him was a little shocked—a fact which Henry Irving, the closest observer of men, did not fail to notice.

"When I am going to do 'Titus Andronicus,' or any other play," he said to me afterwards, "I shall know more about it than A—— or any other student."

There was no conceit in this. It was just a statement of fact. And it may not have been an admirable quality in Henry Irving but all his life he only took an interest in the things which concerned the work that he had in hand. When there was a question of his playing Napoleon, his room at Grafton Street was filled with Napoleonic literature. Busts of Napoleon, pictures of Napoleon, relics of Napoleon were everywhere. Then, when another play was being prepared, the busts, however fine, would probably go down to the cellar. It was not *Napoleon* who interested Henry Irving, but *Napoleon for his purpose*—two very different things.

His concentration during his three months' study of the play which he had in view was marvellous. When, at the end of the three months, he called the first rehearsal, he read the play exactly as it was going to be done on the first night. He knew exactly by that time what he personally was going to do on the first night, and the company did well to notice how he read his own part, for never again until the first night, though he rehearsed with them, would he show his conception so fully and completely.

These readings, which took place sometimes in the greenroom or Beefsteak-room at the Lyceum, sometimes at his house in Grafton Street, were wonderful. Never were the names of the characters said by the reader, but never was there the slightest doubt as to which was speaking. Henry Irving swiftly, surely, acted every part in the piece as he read. While he read, he made notes as to the position of the characters and the order of the crowds and processions. At the end of the first reading he gave out the parts.

The next day there was the "comparing" of the parts. It generally took place on the stage, and we sat down for it. Each person took his own character, and took up the cues to make sure that no blunder had been made in writing them out. Parts at the Lyceum were written, or printed, never typed.

These first two rehearsals—the one devoted to the reading of the play, and the other to the comparing of the parts—were generally arranged for Thursday and Friday. Then there was two days' grace. On Monday came the first stand-up rehearsal on the stage.

We then did one act straight through, and, after that, straight through again, even if it took all day. There was no luncheon interval. People took a bite when they could, or went without. Henry himself generally went without. The second day exactly the same method was pursued with the second act. All the time Henry gave the stage his personal direction, gave it keenly, and gave it whole. He was the sole superintendent of his rehearsals, with Mr Loveday as his working assistant, and Mr Allen as his prompter. This despotism meant much less wasted time than when actor-manager, "producer," literary adviser, stage manager, and any one who likes to offer a suggestion, are all competing in giving orders and advice to a company.

Henry Irving never spent much time on the women in the company, except in regard to position. Sometimes he would ask me to suggest things to them, to do for them what he did for the men. The men were as much like him when they tried to carry out his instructions as brass is like gold; but he never grew weary of "coaching" them, down to the most minute detail. Once during the rehearsals of "Hamlet" I saw him growing more and more fatigued with his efforts to get the actors who opened the play to perceive his meaning. He wanted the first voice to ring out like a pistol shot.

"*Who's there?*"

"Do give it up," I said. "It's no better!"

"Yes, it's a little better," he answered quietly, "and so it's worth doing."

From the first the scenery, or substitute scenery, was put upon the stage for rehearsal, and the properties, or substitute properties, were to hand.

After each act had been gone through twice each day, it came to half an act once in a whole day, because of the development of detail. There was no detail too small for Henry Irving's notice. He never missed anything that was cumulative—that would contribute something to the whole effect.

The messenger who came in to announce something always needed a great deal of rehearsal. There were processions, and half processions, quiet bits when no word was spoken. There was *timing*. Nothing was left to chance.

In the master carpenter, Arnott, a Yorkshireman, we had a splendid

132

man. He inspired confidence at once through his strong, able personality, and, as time went on, deserved it through all the knowledge he acquired and through his excellence in never making a difficulty.

"You shall have it," was no bluff from Arnott. You *did* "have it."

We could not find precisely the right material for one of my dresses in "The Cup." At last, poking about myself in quest of it, I came across the very thing at Liberty's—a saffron silk with a design woven into it by hand with many-coloured threads and little jewels. I brought a yard to rehearsal. It was declared perfect, but I declared the price prohibitive.

"It's twelve guineas a yard, and I shall want yards and yards!"

In these days I am afraid they would not only put such material on to the leading lady, but on to the supers too! At the Lyceum *wanton* extravagance was unknown.

"Where can I get anything at all like it?"

"You leave it to me," said Arnott. "I'll get it for you. That'll be all right."

"But, Arnott, it's a hand-woven Indian material. How *can* you get it?"

"You leave it to me," Arnott repeated in his slow, quiet, confident way. "Do you mind letting me have this yard as a pattern?"

He went off with it, and before the dress rehearsal had produced about twenty yards of silk, which on the stage looked better than the twelve-guinea original.

"There's plenty more if you want it," he said dryly.

He had had some raw silk dyed the exact saffron. He had had two blocks made, one red and the other black, and the design had been printed, and a few cheap spangles had been added to replace the real jewels. My toga looked beautiful.

This was but one of the many emergencies to which Arnott rose with talent and promptitude.

With the staff of the theatre he was a bit of a bully—one of those men not easily roused, but being vexed, "nasty in the extreme!" As a craftsman he had wonderful taste, and could copy antique furniture so that one could not tell the copy from the original.

The great aim at the Lyceum was to get everything "rotten perfect," as theatrical slang has it, before the dress rehearsal. Father's test of being rotten perfect was not a bad one. "If you can get out of bed in the middle of the night and do your part, you're perfect. If you cant, you dont really know it!"

Henry Irving applied some such test to every one concerned in the production. I cannot remember any play at the Lyceum which did not begin punctually and end at the advertised time, except "Olivia," when some unwise changes in the last act led to delay

He never hesitated to discard scenery if it did not suit his purpose and could not be changed in the allotted time. There was enough scenery rejected in "Faust" to have furnished three productions, and what was finally used for the famous Brocken scene cost next to nothing.

Even the best scene-painters sometimes think more of their pictures than of scenic effects. Henry would never accept anything that was not right *theatrically* as well as pictorially. His instinct in this was unerring and incomparable.

I remember that at one scene-rehearsal every one was fatuously pleased with the scenery. Henry sat in the stalls talking about everything *but* the scenery. It was hard to tell what he thought.

"Well, are you ready?" he asked at last.

"Yes, sir."

"My God! Is that what you think I am going to give the public?"

Never shall I forget the astonishment of stage manager, scene-painter, and staff! It was never safe to indulge in too much self-satisfaction beforehand with Henry. He was always liable to drop such bombs!

He believed very much in "front" scenes, seeing how necessary they were to the swift progress of Shakespeare's diverging plots. These cloths were sometimes so wonderfully painted and lighted that they constituted scenes of remarkable beauty. The best of all were the Apothecary scene in "Romeo and Juliet" and the exterior of Aufidius's house in "Coriolanus."

We never had electricity installed at the Lyceum until Daly took the theatre. When I saw the effect on the faces of the electric footlights, I entreated Henry to have the gas restored, and he did. We used gas footlights and gas limes there until we left the theatre for good in 1902.

To this I attribute much of the beauty of our lighting. I say "our" because this was a branch of Henry's work in which I was always his chief helper. Until electricity has been greatly improved and developed, it can never be to the stage what gas was. The thick softness of gaslight, with the lovely specks and motes in it, so like *natural* light, gave illusion to many a scene which is now revealed in all its naked trashiness by electricity.

§ 6

The superficial in the art of acting often attracts the superficial critic. I think this is what made some people think Irving was at his best in such parts as Louis XI, Dubosc, and Richard III. He could have played Louis XI three times a day "on his head," as the saying is. In "The Lyons Mail," Dubosc the wicked man was easy enough—but Lesurques, the *good* man in the same play, was difficult. Any actor, skilful in the

134

tricks of the business, can play the drunkard; but to play a good man sincerely, as he did here, to show that double thing, the look of guilt which an innocent man wears when accused of crime, requires great acting, for *"the look"* is the outward and visible sign of the inward and spiritual emotion—and this delicate emotion can only be perfectly expressed when the actor's heart and mind and soul and skill are in absolute accord.

In dual parts Irving depended little on make-up. Make-up was, indeed, always his servant, not his master. He knew its uselessness when not informed by the *spirit*. "The letter" (and in characterisation "make-up" is the letter) "killeth—the spirit giveth life." Irving's Lesurques was different from his Dubosc because of the way he held his shoulders, because of his expression. He always took a deep interest in crime (an interest which his sons have inherited), and often went to the police-court to study the faces of the accused. He told me that the innocent man generally looked guilty and hesitated when asked a question, but that the round, wide-open eyes corrected the bad impression. The result of this careful watching was seen in his expression as Lesurques. He opened his eyes wide. As Dubosc he kept them half closed.

Our productions from 1878 to 1887 were "Hamlet," "The Lady of Lyons," "Eugene Aram," "Charles I," "The Merchant of Venice," "Iolanthe," "The Cup," "The Belle's Stratagem," "Othello," "Romeo and Juliet," "Much Ado About Nothing," "Twelfth Night," "Olivia," "Faust," "Raising the Wind," and "The Amber Heart." I give this list to keep myself straight. My mental division of the years at the Lyceum is *before* "Macbeth," and *after*. I divide them thus because I consider "Macbeth" the most important of all our productions. I judge it by the amount of preparation and thought that it cost us and by the discussion which it provoked.

Of the characters played by Henry Irving in the plays of the first division—in the pre-Macbeth period—I reckon Hamlet his greatest triumph. That may be because it was the only part that was big enough for him. It was more difficult, and he had more scope in it than in any other. If there had been a finer part than Hamlet, that particular part would have been his finest.

When one praises an actor in this way, one is always open to accusations of prejudice, hyperbole, uncritical gush, unreasoned eulogy, and the rest. Must a careful and deliberate opinion *always* deny a great man genius? If so, no careful and deliberate opinions from me!

I have no doubt in the world of Irving's genius—no doubt that he is with David Garrick and Edmund Kean, rather than with other actors of great talents and great achievements—actors who rightly won high opinions from the multitude of their day, but who have not left behind them an impression of that inexplicable thing we call genius.

Since my great comrade died I have read many estimates of him, and nearly all of them denied what I assert. "Now, who shall arbitrate?" I find no contradiction of my testimony in the fact that he was not appreciated for a long time, that some found him an acquired taste, that others mocked and derided him.

My father, who worshipped Macready, put Irving above him because of Irving's *originality*. The old school were not usually so generous. Fanny Kemble thought it necessary to write as follows of one who had had his share of misfortune and failure before he came into his kingdom and made her jealous, I suppose, for the dead kings among her kindred:

I have seen some of the accounts and criticisms of Mr. Irving's acting, and rather elaborate ones of his Hamlet, which, however, give me no very distinct idea of his performance, and a very hazy one indeed of the part itself as seen from the point of view of his critics. Edward Fitzgerald wrote me word that he looked like my people, and sent me a photograph to prove it, which I thought much more like Young than my father or uncle. *I have not seen a play of Shakespeare's acted I do not know when. I think I should find such an exhibition extremely curious as well as entertaining.*

Now, shall I put on record what Henry Irving thought of Fanny Kemble! If there is a touch of malice in my doing so, surely the passage that I have quoted justifies it.

Having lived with Hamlet nearly all his life, studied the part when he was a clerk, dreamed of a day when he might play it, the young Henry Irving saw that Mrs Butler, the famous Fanny Kemble, was going to give a reading of the play. His heart throbbed high with anticipation, for in those days TRADITION was everything—the name of Kemble a beacon and a star.

The studious young clerk went to the reading.

An attendant came on the platform and made trivial and apparently unnecessary alterations in the position of the reading desk. A glass of water and a book were placed on it.

After a portentous wait, on swept a lady with an extraordinarily flashing eye, a masculine and muscular outside. Pounding the book with terrific energy, as if she wished to knock the stuffing out of it, she announced in thrilling tones:

" 'HAM—A—LETTE.'
By
will—y—am Shak—es—peare."

136

"I suppose this is all right," thought the young clerk, a little dismayed at the fierce and sectional enunciation.

Then the reader came to Act 1, Sc. 2, which a certain old actor (to leave the Kemble reading for a minute), with but a hazy notion of the text, used to begin:

Although of Hamlet, our dear brother's death,
The memory be—memory be—(What *is* the damned colour?) *green* . . .

Well, when Fanny Kemble came to this scene the future Hamlet began to listen more intently.

Gertrude: Let not thy mother lose *her* prayers, *Ham—a—lette*.
Hamlet: I shall in all respects obey *you,* madam (obviously with a fiery flashing eye of hate upon the King).

When he heard this and more like it, Henry Irving exercised his independence of judgment and refused to accept Fanny Kemble's view of the gentle, melancholy, and well-bred Prince of Denmark.

He was a stickler for tradition, and always studied it, followed it, sometimes to his own detriment, but he was not influenced by the Kemble Hamlet, except that for some time he wore the absurd John Philip feather, which he would have been much better without!

Let me pray that I, representing the old school, may never look on the new school with the patronising airs of "Old Fitz"[1] and Fanny Kemble. I wish that I could *see* the new school of acting in Shakespeare, however. Shakespeare must be kept up, or we shall become a third-rate nation!

Henry told me this story of Fanny Kemble's reading without a spark of ill-nature, but with many a gleam of humour. He told me at the same time of the wonderful effect that Adelaide Kemble (Mrs Sartoris) used to make when she recited Shelley's lines, beginning:

Good-night—Ah, no, the hour is ill
Which severs those it should unite.
Let us remain together still—
Then it will be *good-night!*

§ 7

I HAVE already said that I never could cope with Pauline Deschappelles in "The Lady of Lyons," and why Henry wanted to play Melnotte was a mystery. Claude Melnotte after Hamlet! Oddly enough, Henry was always attracted by fustian. He simply revelled in the big speeches. The play was beautifully staged; the garden scene alone probably cost as much as the whole of "Hamlet." The march past the window of the appar-

[1] Edward FitzGerald.

ently unending army—that good old trick which sends the supers flying round the back-cloth to cross the stage again and again—created a superb effect. The curtain used to go up and down as often as we liked and chose to keep the army marching! The play ran some time, I suppose because even at our worst the public found *something* in our acting to like.

As Ruth Meadowes in "Eugene Aram" I had very little to do, but what there was, was worth doing. The last act, like the last act of "Ravenswood," gave me opportunity. It was staged with a great appreciation of grim and poetic effect. Henry always thought that the dark, overhanging branch of the cedar was like the cruel outstretched hand of Fate. He called it the Fate Tree, and used it in "Hamlet," in "Eugene Aram," and in "Romeo and Juliet."

In "Eugene Aram," the Fate Tree drooped low over the graves in the churchyard. On one of them Henry used to be lying in a black cloak as the curtain went up on the last act. Not until a moonbeam struck the dark mass did you see that it was a man.

He played all such parts well. Melancholy and the horrors had a peculiar fascination for him, especially in these early days. But his recitation of the poem "Eugene Aram" was finer than anything he did in the play, especially when he did it in a frock-coat. No one ever looked so well in a frock-coat! He was always ready to recite it, would do it after supper, anywhere. We had a talk about it once, and I told him that it was *too much* for a room. No man was ever more willing to listen to suggestion or less obstinate about taking advice. He immediately moderated his methods when reciting in *a room,* making it all less theatrical. The play was a good repertory play, and we did it later on in America with success. There the part of Houseman was played by Terriss, who was quite splendid in it, and at Chicago my little boy Teddy made his second appearance on any stage as Joey, a gardener's boy. He had, when still a mere baby, come on to the stage at the Court in "Olivia," and this must be counted his *first* appearance, although the chroniclers, ignoring both that and Joey in "Eugene Aram," *say* he never appeared at all until he played an important part in "The Dead Heart."

It is because of Teddy that "Eugene Aram" is associated in my mind with one of the most beautiful sights upon the stage that I ever saw in my life. He was about ten or eleven at the time, and as he tied up the stage roses, his cheeks, untouched by rouge, put the reddest of them to shame! He was graceful and natural; he spoke his lines with ease, and smiled all over his face! "A born actor!" I said, although Joey was my son. Whenever I think of him in that stage garden, I weep for pride, and for sorrow, too, because before he was thirty my son had left the stage—he who had it all in him. I have good reason to be proud of what he has done since, but I regret the lost actor *always*.

Henry Irving could not at first keep away from melancholy pieces. Henrietta Maria was another sad part for me, but I used to play it well, except when I cried too much in the last act. The play had been one of the Bateman productions, and I had seen Miss Isabel Bateman as Henrietta Maria and liked her, although I could not find it possible to follow her example and play the part with a French accent! I constantly catch myself saying of Henry Irving, "That is by far the best thing that he ever did." I could say it of some things in "Charles I"—of the way he gave up his sword to Cromwell, of the way he came into the room in the last act and shut the door behind him. It was not a man coming on to a stage to meet some one. It was a king going to the scaffold, quietly, unobtrusively, and courageously. However often I played that scene with him, I knew that when he first came on he was not aware of my presence nor of any *earthly* presence: he seemed to be already in heaven.

Much has been said of his "make-up" as Charles I. Edwin Long painted him a triptych of Vandyck heads, which he always had in his dressing-room, and which is now in my possession. He used to come on to the stage looking precisely like the Vandyck portraits, but not because he had been busy building up his face with wig-paste and similar atrocities. His make-up in this, as in other parts, was the process of *assisting subtly and surely the expression from within.* It was elastic, and never hampered him. It changed with the expression. As Charles, he was assisted by Nature, who had given him the most beautiful Stuart hands, but his clothes most actors would have consigned to the dust-bin! Before we had done with Charles I—we played it together for the last time in 1902— these clothes were really threadbare. Yet he looked in them every inch a king.

His care of detail may be judged from the fact that in the last act his wig was not only greyer, but had far less hair in it. I should hardly think it necessary to mention this if I had not noticed how many actors seem to think that an effect of age may be procured by the simple expedient of dipping their heads, covered with mats of flourishing hair, into a flour-barrel!

Unlike most stage kings, he never seemed to be *assuming* dignity. He was very, very simple.

Wills has been much blamed for making Cromwell out to be such a wretch—a mean blackguard, not even a great bad man. But in plays the villain must not compete for sympathy with the hero, or both fall to the ground! I think that Wills showed himself in this play, at any rate in the last act, a great playwright. It gave us both wonderful opportunities, yet very few words were spoken.

Some people thought me at my best in the camp scene in the third act, where I had even fewer lines to speak. I was proud of it myself when I found that it had inspired Oscar Wilde to write me this lovely sonnet:

> In the lone tent, waiting for victory,
> She stands with eyes marred by the mists of pain,
> Like some wan lily overdrenched with rain;
> The clamorous clang of arms, the ensanguined sky,
> War's ruin, and the wreck of chivalry
> To her proud soul no common fear can bring;
> Bravely she tarrieth for her Lord, the King,
> Her soul aflame with passionate ecstasy.
> O, hair of gold! O, crimson lips! O, face
> Made for the luring and the love of man!
> With thee I do forget the toil and stress,
> The loveless road that knows no resting place,
> Time's straitened pulse, the soul's dread weariness,
> My freedom, and my life republican!

That phrase "wan lily" represented perfectly what I had tried to convey, not only in this part but in Ophelia. I hope I thanked Oscar enough at the time. Now he is dead, and I cannot thank him any more....I had so much *bad* poetry written to me that these lovely sonnets from a real poet should have given me the greater pleasure. "He often has the poet's heart, who never felt the poet's fire." There is more good *heart* and kind feeling in most of the verses written to me than real poetry.

"One must discriminate," even if it sounds unkind. At the time that Whistler was having one of his most undignified "rows" with a sitter over a portrait and wrangling over the price, another artist was painting frescoes in a cathedral for nothing. "It may be sad that it should be so," a friend said to me, "but *one must discriminate*. The man haggling over the sixpence is the greater artist!"

§ 8

ANOTHER sonnet from Oscar Wilde—to Portia this time—is the first document that I find in connection with "The Merchant," as the play was always called by the theatre staff.

> I marvel not Bassanio was so bold
> To peril all he had upon the lead,
> Or that proud Aragon bent low his head,
> Or that Morocco's fiery heart grew cold;

140

For in that gorgeous dress of beaten gold,
Which is more golden than the golden sun,
No woman Veronese looked upon
Was half so fair as thou whom I behold.
Yet fairer when with wisdom as your shield
The sober-suited lawyer's gown you donned,
And would not let the laws of Venice yield
Antonio's heart to that accursed Jew—
O, Portia! take my heart; it is thy due:
I think I will not quarrel with the Bond.

Henry Irving's Shylock dress was designed by Sir John Gilbert. It was never replaced, and only once cleaned by Henry's dresser and valet, Walter Collinson. Walter, I think, replaced "Doody," Henry's first dresser at the Lyceum during the run of "The Merchant of Venice." Walter like Doody was a wig-maker by trade. It was Doody who, on being asked his opinion of a production, said that it was fine—"not a *join* [1] to be seen anywhere!" It was Walter who was asked by Henry to say which he thought his best part. Walter could not be "drawn" for a long time. At last he said Macbeth.

This pleased Henry immensely, for he fancied himself in Macbeth more than in any other part.

"It is generally conceded to be Hamlet," said Henry.

"Oh, no, sir," said Walter, "Macbeth. You sweat twice as much in that."

In appearance Walter was very like Shakespeare's bust in Stratford Church. He was a most faithful and devoted servant, and was the only person with Henry Irving when he died. Quiet in his ways, discreet, gentle, and very quick, he was the ideal dresser.

The Lyceum production of "The Merchant of Venice" was not so strictly archæological as the Bancrofts' had been, but it was very gravely beautiful and effective. If less attention was paid to details of costume and scenery, the play itself was arranged and acted very attractively, and always went with a swing. To the end of my partnership with Henry Irving it was a safe "draw" both in England and America. By this time I must have played Portia over a thousand times. In a severe criticism of my performance in *Blackwood's Magazine* it was suggested that I showed too much of a "coming-on" disposition in the Casket Scene. This affected me for years, and made me self-conscious and uncomfortable. At last I lived it down. Any suggestion of *indelicacy* in my treatment of a part always blighted me. Mr Dodgson (Lewis Carroll, of the immortal "Alice

[1] A "join" in theatrical wig-makers' parlance is the point where the frontpiece of the wig ends and the actor's forehead begins.

in Wonderland") once brought a little girl to see me in "Faust." He wrote and told me that she had said (where Margaret begins to undress): "Where is it going to stop?" and that perhaps, in consideration of the fact that it could affect a mere child disagreeably, I ought to alter my business!

I had known dear Mr Dodgson for years and years. He was as fond of me as he could be of any one over the age of ten, but I was *furious*. "I thought you only knew *nice* children," was all the answer I gave him. "It would have seemed awful for a *child* to see harm where harm is; how much more so when she sees it where harm is not."

But I felt ashamed and shy whenever I played that scene. It was the Casket Scene over again.

Mr Dodgson was one of my earliest friends among literary folk. I cant remember a time when I didnt know him. He saw Kate and me act as children, and gave us a copy of "Alice in Wonderland." He always gave any new young friend "Alice" at once. It was his way of following up the introduction and establishing pleasant relations. The "Alice" ceremony was gone through with every member of the Terry family, and in later years with their children.

Mr Dodgson was an ardent playgoer. He took the keenest interest in all the Lyceum productions, frequently writing to me to point out slips in the dramatist's logic which only he would ever have noticed! He did not even spare Shakespeare. I think he wrote these letters for fun, as some people make puzzles, anagrams, or Limericks!

Now I'm going to put before you a "Hero-ic" puzzle of mine, but please remember I do not ask for your solution of it, as you will persist in believing, if I ask your help in a Shakespeare difficulty, that I am only jesting! However, if you won't attack it yourself, perhaps you would ask Mr Irving some day how *he* explains it?

My difficulty is this:—Why in the world did not Hero (or at any rate Beatrice on her behalf) prove an "alibi" in answer to the charge? It seems certain that she did *not* sleep in her room that night; for how could Margaret venture to open the window and talk from it, with her mistress asleep in the room? It would be sure to wake her. Besides Borachio says, after promising that Margaret shall speak with him out of Hero's chamber window, "I will so fashion the matter that Hero shall be absent." (*How* he could possibly manage any such thing is another difficulty, but I pass over that.) Well then, granting that Hero slept in some other room that night, why didn't she say so? When Claudio asked her: "What man was he you talked with yesternight out at your window betwixt twelve and one?" Why doesn't she reply: "I talked with no man at that hour, my lord. Nor was I in my chamber yesternight, but in another, far from it, remote." And this she could, of course, prove by the evidence of the housemaids, who must have known that she had occupied another room that night.

But even if Hero might be supposed to be so distracted as not to remember where she had slept the night before, or even whether she had slept *anywhere*, surely *Beatrice* has her wits about her; And when an arrangement was made, by which she was to lose, for one night, her twelve-months' bedfellow, is it conceivable that she didn't know *where* Hero passed the night? Why didn't *she* reply:

> But good my lord sweet Hero slept not there:
> She had another chamber for the nonce.
> 'Twas sure some counterfeit that did present
> Her person at the window, aped her voice,
> Her mien, her manners, and hath thus deceived
> My good Lord Pedro and this company?

With all these excellent materials for proving an "alibi" it is incomprehensible that no one should think of it. If only there had been a barrister present, to cross-examine Beatrice!

"Now, ma'am, attend to me, please, and speak up so that the jury can hear you. Where did you sleep last night? Where did Hero sleep? Will you swear that she slept in her own room? Will you swear that you do not know where she slept?" I feel inclined to quote old Mr. Weller and to say to Beatrice at the end of the play (only I'm afraid it isnt etiquette to speak across the footlight):

"Oh, Samivel, Samivel, vy vornt there a halibi?"

Mr Dodgson's kindness to children was wonderful. He *really* loved them and put himself out for them. The children he knew who wanted to go on the stage were those who came under my observation, and nothing could have been more touching than his ceaseless industry on their behalf.

I want to thank you, he wrote to me in 1894 from Oxford, as heartily as words can do it for your true kindness in letting me bring D. behind the scenes to you. You will know without my telling you what an intense pleasure you thereby gave to a warm-hearted girl, and what love (which I fancy you value more than mere admiration) you have won from her. Her wild longing to try the stage will not, I think, bear the cold light of day when once she has tried it, and has realised what a lot of hard work and weary waiting and "hope deferred" it involves. She doesn't, so far as I know, absolutely need, as N. does, to earn money for her own support. But I fancy she will find life rather a *pinch,* unless she can manage to do something in the way of earning money. So I dont like to advise her strongly *against* it, as I would any one who had no such need.

Also thank you, thank you with all my heart for all your great kindness to N. She does write so brightly and gratefully about all you do for her and say to her.

"N." has since achieved great success on the music-halls and in pantomime. "D." is a leading lady!

This letter to my sister Floss is characteristic of his "Wonderland" style when writing to children:

CH. CH., January, 1874.

MY DEAR FLORENCE,—

Ever since that heartless piece of conduct of yours (I allude to the affair of the Moon and the blue silk gown) I have regarded you with a gloomy interest, rather than with any of the affection of former years—so that the above epithet "dear" must be taken as conventional only, or perhaps may be more fitly taken in the sense in which we talk of a "dear" bargain, meaning to imply how much it has cost us; and who shall say how many sleepless nights it has cost me to endeavour to unravel (a most appropriate verb) that "blue silk gown"?

Will you please explain to Tom about that photograph of the family group which I promised him? Its history is an instructive one, as illustrating my habits of care and deliberation. In 1867 the picture was promised him, and an entry made in my book. In 1869, or thereabouts, I mounted the picture on a large card, and packed it in brown paper. In 1870, or 1871, or thereabouts, I took it with me to Guilford, that it might be handy to take with me when I went up to town. Since then I have taken it two or three times to London, and on each occasion (having forgotten to deliver it to him) I brought it back again. This was because I had no convenient place in London to leave it in. But *now* I have found such a place. Mr Dubourg has kindly taken charge of it—so that it is now much nearer to its future owner than it has been for seven years. I quite hope, in the course of another year or two, to be able to remember to bring it to your house: or perhaps Mr Dubourg may be calling even sooner than that and take it with him. You will wonder why I ask you to tell him instead of writing myself. The obvious reason is that you will be able, from sympathy, to put my delay in the most favourable light—to make him see that, as hasty puddings are not the best of puddings, so hasty judgments are not the best of judgments, and that he ought to be content to wait even another seven years for his picture, and to sit "like patience on a monument, smiling at grief." This quotation, by the way, is altogether a misprint. Let me explain it to you. The passage originally stood, "*They* sit like patients on the Monument, smiling at Greenwich." In the next edition "Greenwich" was printed short, "Green[h]," and so got gradually altered into "grief." The allusion of course is to the celebrated Dr Jenner, who used to send all his patients to sit on top of the Monument (near London Bridge) to inhale fresh air, promising them that, when they were well enough, they should go to "Greenwich Fair." So of course they always looked out towards Greenwich, and sat smiling to think of the treat in store for them. A play was written on the subject of their inhaling the fresh air, and was for some time attributed to Shakespeare, but it is certainly not in his style. It was called "The Wandering Air," and was lately revived at the Queen's

Theatre. The custom of sitting on the Monument was given up when Dr Jenner went mad, and insisted on it that the air was worse up there and that the *lower* you went the *more airy* it became. Hence he always called those little yards, below the pavement, outside the kitchen windows, "*the kitchen airier*," a name that is still in use.

All this information you are most welcome to use, the next time you are in want of something to talk about. You may say you learned it from "a distinguished etymologist," which is perfectly true, since any one who knows me by sight can easily distinguish me from all other etymologists.

What parts are you and Polly now playing?

Believe me to be (conventionally)
Yours affectionately,
L. DODGSON.

This Dodgson digression has led me far from Portia and the Casket Scene, and I want to return to them for a moment. In that "Blackwood's" article, which I still think was unfair as well as unkind, I was blamed for showing too plainly that Portia loves Bassanio before he has actually won her, yet I had Shakespeare's warrant for this "business." He makes Portia say *before* Bassanio chooses the right casket:

One half of me is yours—the other half yours—*All yours!*

Surely this suggests that she is not concealing her passion like a Victorian prude and that Bassanio had most surely won her love, though not yet the right to be her husband.

Dr Furnivall, a great Shakespearean scholar, was so kind as to write me the following letter about Portia:

Being founder and director of the New Shakespeare Society, I venture to thank you most heartily for your most charming and admirable impersonation of our poet's Portia, which I witnessed tonight with a real delight. You have given me a new light on the character, and by your so pretty by-play in the Casket Scene have made bright in my memory for ever the spot which almost all critics have felt dull, and I hope to say this in a new edition of "Shakespeare."

(He did say it, in "The Leopold" edition.)

Again those touches of the wife's love in the advocate when Bassanio says he'd give up his wife for Antonio, and when you kissed your hand to him behind his back in the Ring bit—how pretty and natural they were! Your whole conception and acting of the character are so true to Shakespeare's lines that one longs he could be here to see you. A lady gracious and graceful, handsome, witty, loving and wise, you are his Portia to the life.

That's the best of Shakespeare, I say. His characters can be interpreted in at least eight different ways, and of each way some one will say: "That is Shakespeare!" The German actress plays Portia as a low comedy part. She wears an eighteenth-century law wig, horn spectacles, a cravat (this last anachronism is not confined to Germans), and often a moustache! There is something to be said for it all, though I should not like to play the part that way myself.

Lady Pollock, who first brought me to Henry Irving's notice as a possible leading lady, thought my Portia better at the Lyceum than it had been at the Prince of Wales's.

Thanks, my dear Valentine and enchanting Portia, she writes to me in response to a photograph that I had sent her, but the photographers don't see you as you are, and have not the poetry in them to do you justice ... You were especially admirable in the Casket Scene. You kept your by-play quieter, and it gained in effect from the addition of repose—and I rejoiced that you did not kneel to Bassanio at "My Lord, my governor, my King." I used to feel that too much like worship from any girl to her affianced, and Portia's position being one of command, I should doubt the possibility of such an action ...

I think I received more letters about my Portia than about all my other parts put together. Many of them came from university men. One old playgoer wrote to tell me that he liked me better than my former instructress, Mrs Charles Kean. "She mouthed it as she did most things. ... She was a staid, sentimental 'Anglaise,' and more than a little stiffly pokerish."

Henry Irving's Shylock was generally conceded to be full of talent and reality, but some of his critics could not resist saying that this was *not* the Jew that Shakespeare drew! Now, who is in a position to say what *is* the Jew that Shakespeare drew? I think Henry Irving knew as well as most! Nay, I am sure that in his age he was the only person able to decide.

Some said his Shylock was intellectual, and appealed more to the intellect of his audiences than to their emotions. Surely this is talking for the sake of talking. I recall so many things that touched people to the heart! For absolute pathos, achieved by absolute simplicity of means, I never saw anything in the theatre to compare with Shylock's return home over the bridge to his deserted house after Jessica's flight.

A younger actor, producing "The Merchant of Venice" in recent years, asked Irving if he might borrow this bit of business. "By all means," said Henry. "With great pleasure."

"Then, why didnt you do it?" inquired my daughter bluntly when the actor was telling us how kind and courteous Henry had been in allowing him to use his stroke of invention.

146

"What do you mean?" asked the astonished actor.

My daughter told him that Henry had dropped the curtain on a stage full of noise, and light, and revelry. When it went up again the stage was empty, desolate, with no light but a pale moon, and all sounds of life at a great distance—and then over the bridge came the weary figure of the Jew. This marked the passing of the time between Jessica's elopement and Shylock's return home. It created an atmosphere of silence, and the middle of the night.

"*You* came back without dropping the curtain," said my daughter, "and so it wasnt a bit the same."

"I couldnt risk dropping the curtain for the business," answered the actor, "*because it needed applause to take it up again!*"

Henry Irving never grew tired of a part, never ceased to work at it, just as he never gave up the fight against his limitations. His diction, as the years went on, grew far clearer when he was depicting rage and passion. His dragging leg dragged no more. To this heroic perseverance he added an almost childlike eagerness in heeding any suggestion for the improvement of his interpretations which commended itself to his imagination and his judgment. From a blind man came the most illuminating criticism of his Shylock. The sensitive ear of the sightless hearer detected a fault in Henry Irving's method of delivering the opening line of his part:

"Three thousand ducats—well!"

"I hear no sound of the usurer in that," the blind man said at the end of the performance. "It is said with the reflective air of a man to whom money means very little."

The justice of the criticism appealed strongly to Henry. He revised his reading not only of the first line, but of many other lines in which he saw now that he had not been enough of the money-lender.

In more recent years he made one change in his dress. He asked my daughter—whose cleverness in such things he fully recognised—to put some stage jewels on to the scarf that he wore round his head when he supped with the Christians.

"I have an idea that, when he went to that supper, he'd like to flaunt his wealth in the Christian dogs' faces. It will look well, too—'like the toad, ugly and venomous,' wearing precious jewels on his head!"

The scarf, witnessing to that untiring love of throwing new light on his impersonations which distinguished Henry to the last, is now in my daughter's possession. She values no relic of him more unless it be the wreath of oak-leaves that she made him for "Coriolanus."

9

"The Merchant of Venice" was acted two hundred and fifty consecutive nights on the occasion of the first production. On the hundredth night every member of the audience was presented with Henry Irving's acting edition of the play bound in white vellum—a solid and permanent souvenir, paper, print and binding all being of the best. The famous Chiswick Press did all his work of this kind. On the title page was printed:

> I count myself in nothing else so happy
> As in a soul remembering my good friends.

At the close of the performance which took place on Saturday, February 14, 1880, Henry entertained a party of 350 to supper on the stage. This was the first of those enormous gatherings which afterwards became an institution at the Lyceum.

It was at this supper that Lord Houghton surprised us all by making a very sarcastic speech about the stage and actors generally. It was no doubt more interesting than the "butter" which is usually applied to the profession at such functions, but every one felt that it was rather rude to abuse long runs when the company were met to celebrate a hundredth performance!

Henry Irving's answer was delightful. He spoke with good sense, good humour and good breeding, and it was all spontaneous. I wish that a phonograph had been in existence that night, and that a record had been taken of the speech. It would be so good for the people who have asserted that Henry Irving always employed journalists (when he could not get Poets Laureate!) to write his speeches for him! The voice was always the voice of Irving, if the hands were sometimes the hands of the professional writer. When Henry was thrown on his debating resources he really spoke better than when he prepared a speech, and his letters prove, if proof were needed, how finely he could write! Those who represent him as dependent in such matters on the help of literary hacks are just ignorant of the facts.

NOTES TO CHAPTER VII

1. *Longridge Road*. Although Ellen Terry received a good salary at the Prince of Wales's Theatre, and a better one at the Court, she appears to have been hard up for some time after leaving her home in Taviton Street. She writes in Chapter VI of living in lodgings at Camden Town and going to the Prince of Wales's by 'bus. There is evidence she had borrowed money in the rainy days, and when the fine ones came she lived carefully, cheaply, and humbly, still feeling the pinch of poverty, until she had paid her debts. From

lodgings at Camden Town she moved to lodgings in Finborough Road, Earl's Court. Later she took a house in Longridge Road, also in Earl's Court, which was not all bricks and mortar in those days. Market gardens still survived.

The number of Ellen Terry's house was 33. At 36, opposite, there lived with his family a young man who had just entered University College. He was not one of those who have eyes, and see not. He was indeed abnormally observant. The morning after the new tenants of 33 had moved in, he caught "the flicker of an elbow in the bay-window of the dining-room," and writing of the vision nearly fifty years afterwards says that "even so little of the owner was fascinating." She went this way and that, handling a broom. One way brought her nearer the window. More than the elbow now to see! "A dazzling shape." The young man, enraptured, called his sisters, and they too gazed.

"All ignorant as we were of the theatre and its stars, we had no guess at her identity, and she was dubbed 'The Greek Lady' till we learned that she was Ellen Terry, then appearing at The Court Theatre." D. S. MacColl, from whose "Batch of Memories" I have been allowed to quote this, gives a charming impression, the kind of impression we get only from painters, of a daily event in Longridge Road at this time:

" . . . Each morning when the Greek Lady went off to rehearsal, there was a scene as pretty as anything she played upon the stage. She appeared upon the steps like April morning, lifting wide eloquent lips, hooded eyes and breathless face to the light. She raised and kissed two little tots who were to be known as Edith and Gordon Craig. She greeted the next-door neighbours, family of a Rabbinical scholar, who had promptly become slaves of her apparition, and stood ready on the pavement. Her cushions were brought out, placed and patted in the open carriage; herself installed; the air became tender and gay with wavings and blown kisses; the wheels revolved, and greyness descended once more on Longridge Road."

The MacColl family felt that with this "Phantom of Delight," the figure of that "manly bulldog sort of man," Charles Kelly, did not fit in. "We resented the conjunction for her as a false concord." When a year had passed, that too substantial figure disappeared, and a new figure was seen in Longridge Road, "spare, and grim-jaunty in close-fitting short jacket, and tilted wide-a-wake; Henry Irving."

Other memorable figures could be seen in Longridge Road at this time. After Ellen Terry, shedding brightness on the air, had driven off to rehearsal, one could see an invalid emerge from another of those sad-coloured brick houses, to make one of his last excursions in a bath-chair. This was Charles Mackay, author of "Cheer Boys, Cheer." In his wake would sometimes trip a couple, bright as enamel in face and dress against the drab portico. They were Marie Corelli and her half-brother, Eric Mackay. From another doorway would sweep out a stalwart figure, all ulster, "deer-stalker," and beard: George MacDonald. Longridge Road was dull only in colour in the early 'eighties.

2. *Henry Irving.* The many references to Irving as man, actor, and man-

ager, in the pages of Ellen Terry's book are amplified in the appendix to Chapter XIII. This gives a more complete study of him, compiled by Ellen Terry at various dates, but as it deals mainly with Irving in the last days of the Lyceum, and describes the situation in 1903 when the long and famous Irving-Terry partnership was finally broken, it has been appended to the chapter covering that period.

3. *More Woman than Artist.* Ellen Terry honestly thought this was true, and the passage in which it occurs confirms the impression given by many who knew her well (her son Gordon Craig and one of her most famous correspondents, Bernard Shaw, have both helped to fix it in people's minds) that she was not devoted heart and soul to her vocation as an actress, and would have been quite ready at any time to sacrifice it to her life as a human being. It is impossible to identify this theoretical Ellen Terry, in whom Ellen Terry herself believed, with the Ellen Terry of fact. Except for a brief period in her youth, her work (like Eleanora Duse, she never spoke of her "art," but of her "work") was always the most important thing in her life. For its sake she "scorned delights and lived laborious days." She imagined she was a home-loving person, yet she spent the greater part of her time at home nursing her energy for rehearsals and performances in the theatre. She imagined she was a good housewife, yet her home was best ordered when she left its management to others. It is significant that while her domestic partnerships were of short duration, her artistic partnership with Irving lasted for over twenty years.

More light is thrown on her attitude to her work by this confession found recently in one of her notebooks:

"I love to work, and I love to dream. *I had my dream right off.* Foolish to suppose I could dream again, but I could never give up hoping—in little matters, in big matters. I must hope to the end. That will be my end— when hopes goes. I have always felt people were worth it. Perhaps 'my mistake'! But there is *always work.*"

4. *Ellen Terry's last appearance as Ophelia.* Ellen Terry's opinion that when she played Ophelia at Drury Lane for the last time in 1896 she was "just damnable" conflicts with her son's impression that she was marvellous. One of the best of Gordon Craig's early woodcuts represents Ellen Terry as Ophelia. It bears the inscription: "To the Divine Ophelia of Drury Lane."

5. *The Brocken Music in "Faust."* Ellen Terry made a slip here. The incidental music for "Faust," including that for the "Brocken" scene, was composed by Meredith Ball, Hamilton Clarke's successor at the Lyceum. When this chapter appeared in "M. A. P.," Mr Ball wrote to the Editor (the late T.P. O'Connor) to point out the slip, and Ellen Terry sent a letter of apology: "As he (Mr Ball) is one of the most amiable of created men, I know he will forgive me for having forgotten for the moment that it was he who wrote our music for Faust." There was possibly an intentional touch of irony in this courteous reference to Mr Ball, as he was a peppery little man, and his correction of Ellen Terry's mistake had been made in a far from amiable manner.

6. *Irving's Shylock*. Graham Robertson, like many frequenters of the Lyceum, was not convinced that Irving's reading of Shylock was right. In "Time Was," he writes that this "heroic aristocratic martyr upset the balance of the play and ruined Portia's Trial Scene. How small and mean sounded her quibbling tricky speeches when addressed to a being who united the soul of Savonarola and the bearing of Charles I with just a touch of Lord Beaconsfield that made for mystery. After her best effect, we momentarily expected the doge to rise, exclaiming: 'My dear sir, pray accept the apology of the Court for any annoyance that this young person has caused you. By all means take as much of Antonio as you think proper, and if we may throw in a prime cut off Bassanio, and the whole of Gratiano, we shall regard your acceptance of the same as a favour!"

The scarf made by Edith Craig which Irving wore in the part in later years is now in the Ellen Terry Memorial Museum at Smallhythe (Kent).

7. *The Beefsteak Room*. This room at the Lyceum Theatre where Irving entertained so many distinguished guests had been the last meeting place of "The Sublime Society of Beefsteaks" a club which was in existence in the reign of Queen Anne, and is believed to have been founded at an earlier date. Its history is uncertain before the year 1735 when John Rich, the manager of Covent Garden Theatre, gave its members accommodation there. Hogarth, George Colman, Colley Cibber and George, Prince of Wales, were among the famous "Beefsteaks" of the Covent Garden days. When the theatre was burned down early in the 19th century the Beefsteaks moved to the Bedford Coffee House, and thence to the newly built Lyceum. When that theatre too was burned down, a spacious room was provided for the Beefsteaks in another Lyceum on the same site. "The whole of the room was panelled in old English oak, portraits of past and present members graced the walls, and the original gridiron, rescued from the ruins caused by two fires, occupied the centre of the ceiling." In spite of this splendour, the prestige of the club began to decline, and by 1867 it was bankrupt. The furniture and portraits were sold at Christie's, and the room was used for the storage of theatre properties until Irving became manager of the Lyceum. He restored it, and it became the scene of gatherings as distinguished as those of its palmiest days. Ellen Terry refers to some of Irving's Beefsteak guests in Chapter XII.

8. *The phonograph*. Eight years after the night when Ellen Terry wished a "phonograph had been in existence," Irving heard one for the first time. Writing to Ellen Terry (who was on holiday in Berlin) in August 1888, he describes it as "a most extraordinary instrument phenomenon. You speak into it, and everything is recorded, voice, tone, intonation, everything. You turn a little wheel, and forth it comes, and can be repeated ten thousands of times. Only fancy what this suggests. Wouldn't you like to have heard the voice of Shakespeare, or Jesus Christ? I only wished that I could hear *your* voice."

When a record was made of Irving's voice he was shocked and horrified at the result. "Is *that* my voice? My God!" Ellen Terry kept the wax matrix for some years. Then it came to pieces in a housemaid's hand. She herself made records later when the device of reproducing them from the matrix had been invented, but they are all unsatisfactory, even when judged by the standard of the time, and give no idea of the quality of her voice.

9. *Ellen Terry's Portia.* There is a vast amount of evidence of the long and profound study Ellen Terry gave to her parts. She continued to give it, long after they had become old parts. I have found a cutting from an Italian essay on "The Merchant of Venice," dated 1903, with comments in her writing which shows she was still interested in anything which threw new light on the play. The writer of the article made the ingenious suggestion that the song in the Casket Scene: "Tell me where is fancy bred" had been deliberately selected by Portia in order to guide Bassanio to the choice of the right casket. "I like this idea," writes Ellen Terry. "And why shouldn't Portia sing the song herself? She could make the four rhymes, 'bred, head, nourished, fed,' set the word 'lead' ringing in Bassanio's ears. A woman of Portia's sort couldnt possibly remain passive in such a crisis in her life."

10. The parts played by Ellen Terry during the period covered by Chapter VII were: Ophelia ("Hamlet," 1878); Lady Anne ("Richard III," Act I, 1879); Ruth Meadowes ("Eugene Aram," 1879); Henrietta Maria ("Charles I," 1879); Frou-Frou ("Butterfly," 1879); Iolanthe ("Iolanthe," 1880); Beatrice ("Much Ado About Nothing," at Leeds, 1880).

CHAPTER VIII

THE LYCEUM IN THE 'EIGHTIES

(1880–1883)

§ I

THE play with which the Lyceum reopened in the autumn of 1880 was "The Corsican Brothers." Henry Irving had not played the dual rôle of Louis and Fabien del Franchi before, and he had to compete with old playgoers' memories of Charles Kean and Fechter. Wisely enough he made of it a "period" play, emphasising its old-fashioned atmosphere. In 1891, when the play was revived, the D'Orsay costumes were noticed, and considered piquant and charming. In 1880 I am afraid they were regarded with indifference as merely antiquated.

The grace and elegance of Henry as the sophisticated brother I shall never forget. There was something in *him* to which the manners and custom, the whole florid style of the D'Orsay period appealed, and he spoke the stilted language with as much ease as he wore the cravat and the tight-waisted full-breasted coat. Such a line as,

'Tis she! Her footstep beats upon my heart!

were not absurd from his lips.

The sincerity of the period, he felt, lay in its elegance. A rough movement, a too undeliberate speech, and the absurdity of the thing might be given away. It was in fact given away by Terriss as Château-Renaud, who was not the smooth, graceful, courteous villain that Alfred Wigan had been and that Henry wanted. He told me that he paid Miss Fowler, an actress who in other respects was not very remarkable, an enormous salary because she could look the high-bred lady of elegant manners.

It was in "The Corsican Brothers" that tableau curtains were first used at the Lyceum. They were made of red plush, which suited the old decoration of the theatre. Those who only saw the Lyceum after its renovation in 1881 do not realize perhaps that before that date it was decorated in dull gold and dark crimson, and had funny boxes with high fronts like old-fashioned church pews. One of these boxes was rented annually by the Baroness Burdett-Coutts. It was rather like the toy cardboard theatre which children used to be able to buy for sixpence. The effect was sombre, but I think I liked it better than the cold, light, shallow, bastard Pompeian decoration of later days.

§ 2

In Hallam Tennyson's life of his father, I find that I described "The Cup" as a "great little play." After thirty years (nearly) I stick to that. Its chief fault was that it was not long enough, for it involved a tremendous production, tremendous acting, had all the heroic size of tragedy, and yet was all over so quickly that we could play a long play like "The Corsican Brothers" with it in a single evening.

Tennyson read the play to us at Eaton Place. There were present Henry Irving, Ellen Terry, William Terriss, Mr Knowles, who had arranged the reading, my daughter Edy, who was then about nine, Hallam Tennyson, *and* a dog, I think Charlie, for the days of Fussie were not yet.

Tennyson, like many poets, read in a monotone, rumbling on a low note in much the same way that Shelley is said to have screamed on a high one. For the women's parts he changed his voice suddenly, climbing up into a key which he could not sustain. In spite of this I was beginning to think how impressive it all was, when I looked up and saw Edy, who was sitting on Henry's knee, looking over his shoulder at young Hallam and laughing, and Henry, instead of reproaching her, on the broad grin. There was much discussion as to what the play should be called, and as to whether the names "Synorix" and "Sinnatus" would be confused.

"I dont think they will," I said, for I thought this was a very small matter for the poet to worry about.

"I do!" said Edy in a loud clear voice, "I havent known one from the other all the time!"

"Edy, be good!" I whispered.

Henry, mischievous as usual, was delighted at Edy's independence, but her mother was unutterably ashamed.

"Leave her alone," said Henry, "she's quite right."

Tennyson at first wanted to call the play "The Senator's Wife," then thought of "Sinnatus and Synorix," and finally agreed with us that "The Cup" was the best, as it was the simplest, title.

The production was one of the most beautiful things that Henry Irving ever accomplished. It has been described again and again, but none of the descriptions are very successful. There was a vastness, a spaciousness of proportion about the scene in the Temple of Artemis which I never saw again upon the stage until my son attempted something like

154

it in the Church Scene that he designed for my production of "Much Ado About Nothing" in 1903.

A great deal of the effect was due to the lighting. The gigantic figure of the many-breasted Artemis, placed far back in the scene-dock, loomed through a blue mist, while the foreground of the picture was in yellow light. The thrilling effect always to be gained on the stage by the simple expedient of a great number of people doing the same thing in the same way at the same moment, was seen in "The Cup," when the stage was filled with a crowd of women who raised their arms about their heads with a large, rhythmic, sweeping movement and then bowed to the goddess with the regularity of a regiment saluting.

At rehearsals there was one girl who did this movement with peculiar grace. She always wore a black velveteen dress and I called her "Hamlet." I used to chaff her about wearing such a grand dress at rehearsals, but she was never to be seen in any other. The girls at the theatre told me that she was very poor, and that underneath her black velveteen dress, which she wore summer and winter, she had nothing but a pair of stockings and a chemise. Not long after the first night of "The Cup" she disappeared. I made inquiries about her, and found that she was dying in hospital. I went several times to see her. She looked so beautiful in the little white bed. Her great eyes, black, with weary white lids, used to follow me as I left the hospital ward, and I could not always tear myself away from their dumb beseechingness, but would turn back and sit down again by the bed. Once she asked me if I would leave something belonging to me that she might look at until I came again. I took off the amber and coral beads that I was wearing at the time and gave them to her. Two days later I had a letter from the nurse telling me that poor "Hamlet" was dead—that just before she died, with closed eyes, and gasping for breath, she sent her love to her "dear Miss Terry," and wanted me to know that the tall lilies I had brought her on my last visit were to be buried with her, but that she had wiped the coral and amber beads and put them in cotton-wool, to be returned to me when she was dead. Poor "Hamlet"!

Quite as wonderful as the Temple Scene was the setting of the first act, which represented the rocky side of a mountain with a glimpse of a fertile table-land and a pergola with vines growing over it at the top. The acting in this scene all took place on different levels. The hunt swept past on one level; the entrance to the temple was on another. A goatherd played upon a pipe. Scenically speaking, it was not Greece, but Greece in Sicily, Capri, or some such hilly region.

Henry Irving was not able to look like the full-lipped, full-blooded

Romans such as we see in long lines in marble at the British Museum, so he conceived his own type of the blend of Roman intellect and sensuality with barbarian cruelty and lust. Tennyson was not pleased with him as Synorix! *How* he failed to delight in it as a picture I can't conceive. With a pale, pale face, bright red hair, gold armour and a tiger-skin, a diabolical expression and very thin crimson lips, Henry looked handsome and sickening at the same time. *Lechery* was written across his forehead.

The first act was well within my means; the second was beyond them, but it was very good for me to try and do it. I had a long apostrophe to the goddess with my back turned to the audience, and I never tackled anything more difficult. My dresses, designed by Mr Godwin, one of them with the toga made of that wonderful material which Arnott had printed, were simple, fine and free.

I wrote to Tennyson's son Hallam, after the first night, that I knew his father would be delighted with Henry's splendid performance, but was afraid he would be disappointed in me.

DEAR CAMMA, he answered, I have given your messages to my father, but believe me, who am not 'common report,' that he will thoroughly appreciate your noble, *most* beautiful and imaginative rendering of 'Camma.' My father and myself hope to see you soon, but not while this detestable cold weather lasts. We trust that you are not now really the worse for that night of nights.

With all our best wishes.

Yours ever sincerely,
HALLAM TENNYSON.

I quite agree with you as to H. I.'s Synorix.

The music of "The Cup" was not up to the level of the rest. Lady Winchilsea's setting of "Moon on the field and the foam," written within the compass of eight notes, for my poor singing voice, which will not go up high nor down low, was effective enough, but the music as a whole was too "chatty" for a severe tragedy. One night when I was singing my very best:

Moon, bring him home, bring him home,
Safe from the dark and the cold,

some one in the audience *sneezed*. Every one burst out laughing, and I had to laugh too. I did not even attempt the next line.

"The Cup" was called a failure, yet it ran 125 nights, and every night the house was crowded! On the hundredth night I sent Tennyson the Cup itself. I had it made in silver from Mr Godwin's design—a three-handled cup, pipkin-shaped, standing on three legs.

156

"The Cup" and "The Corsican Brothers" together made the bill too heavy and too long, even at a time when we still "rang up" at 7:30; and in the April following the production of Tennyson's beautiful tragedy— which I think in sheer poetic intensity surpasses "Becket," although it is not nearly so good a play—"The Belle's Stratagem" was substituted for "The Corsican Brothers." This was the first real rollicking comedy that a Lyceum audience had ever seen, and the way they laughed did my heart good. I had had enough of tragedy and the horrors by this time, and I could have cried with joy at that rare and welcome sight—an audience rocking with laughter. On the first night the play opened propitiously enough with a loud laugh due to the only accident of the kind that ever happened at the Lyceum. The curtain went up before the staff had "cleared," and Arnott, Jimmy and the rest were seen running for their lives out of the centre entrance!

People said that it was so clever of me to play Camma and Letitia Hardy (the comedy part in "The Belle's Stratagem") on the same evening. They used to say the same kind thing, "only more so," when Henry played Jingle in "Raising the Wind," and Matthias in "The Bells." But I never liked doing it. A *tour de force* is always more interesting to the looker-on than to the person who is accomplishing it. One feels no pride in such an achievement, which ought to be possible to any one calling himself an actor. Personally, I never play comedy and tragedy on the same night without a sense that one is spoiling the other.

Henry Irving was immensely funny as Doricourt. We had sort of Beatrice and Benedick scenes together, and I began to notice what a lot his *face* did for him. There have only been two faces on the stage in my time—his and Duse's.

My face has never been of much use to me, but my *pace* has filled the deficiency sometimes, in comedy at any rate. In "The Belle's Stratagem" the public had face and pace together, and they seemed to like it.

There was one scene in which I sang "Where are you going to, my pretty maid?" I used to act it all the way through and give imitations of Doricourt—ending up by chucking him under the chin. The house rose at it!

I was often asked at this time when I went out to a party if I would not sing that dear little song from "The Cup." When I said I didnt think it would sound very nice without the harp, as it was only a chant on two or three notes, some one would say:

"Well, then, the song in 'The Belle's Stratagem'! *That* has no accompaniment!"

"No," I used to answer, "but it isn't a song. It's a look here, a gesture there, a laugh anywhere, *and* Henry Irving's face everywhere!"

Miss Winifred Emery came to us for "The Belle's Stratagem" and played the part that I had played years before at the Haymarket. She was bewitching, and in her white wig in the ball-room, beautiful as well. She knew how to bear herself on the stage instinctively, and could dance a minuet to perfection. The daughter of Sam Emery, a great comedian in a day of great comedians, and the granddaughter of *the* Emery, it was not surprising that she should show aptitude for the stage.

Mr Howe was another new arrival in the Lyceum company. He was at his funniest as Mr Hardy in "The Belle's Stratagem." It was not the first time that he had played my father in a piece (we had acted father and daughter in "The Little Treasure"), and I always called him "Daddy." The dear old man was much liked by every one. He had a tremendous pair of legs, was bluff and bustling in manner, though courtly too, and cared more about gardening than acting. He had a little farm at Isleworth and because of this and of his stout gaitered legs, Henry called him "the agricultural actor." He was a good old port and whisky drinker, but he could carry his liquor like a Regency man.

He was a walking history of the stage. "Yes, my dear," he used to say to me, "I was in the original cast of the first performance of 'The Lady of Lyons,' which Lord Lytton gave Macready as a present, and I was the original François when 'Richelieu' was produced. Lord Lytton wrote this part for a lady, but at rehearsal it was found that there was a good deal of movement awkward for a lady to do, so I was put into it."

"What year was it, Daddy?"

"God bless me, I must think.... It must have been about a year after Her Majesty took the throne."

For forty years and nine months Daddy Howe had acted at the Haymarket Theatre! When he was first there, the theatre was lighted with oil lamps, and when a lamp smoked or went out, one of the servants of the theatre came on and lighted it up again during the action of the play.

Of Henry Irving as an actor Howe once said to me that at first he was prejudiced against him because he was so different from the other great actors that he had known.

"'This isn't a bit like Iago,' I said to myself when I first saw him in 'Othello.' That was at the end of the first act. But he had commanded my attention to his innovations. In the second act I found myself deeply interested in watching and studying the development of his conception. In the third act I was fascinated by his originality. By the end of the

158

play I wondered that I could ever have thought that the part ought to be played differently."

Daddy Howe was the first member of the Lyceum company who got a reception from the audience on his entrance as a public favourite. He remained with us until his death, which took place on our fourth American tour in 1893.

§ 3

EVERY one has commended Henry Irving's kindly courtesy in inviting Edwin Booth to come and play with him at the Lyceum Theatre. Booth was having a wretched season at the Princess's, which was, when he went there, a theatre on the down-grade, and under a thoroughly commercial management. The great American actor, through much domestic trouble and bereavement, had more or less "given up" things. At any rate he had not the spirit which can combat such treatment as he received at the Princess's, where the pieces in which he appeared were "thrown" on to the stage with every mark of assumption that he was not going to be a success.

Yet, although he accepted with gratitude Henry Irving's suggestion that he should migrate from the Princess's to the Lyceum and appear there three times a week as Othello with the Lyceum company and its manager to support him, I cannot be sure that Booth's pride was not more hurt by this magnificent hospitality than it ever could have been by disaster. It is always more difficult to *receive* than to *give*.

Few people thought of this, I suppose. I did, because I could imagine Henry Irving in America in the same situation—accepting the hospitality of Booth. Would not he too have been melancholy, quiet, unassertive, *almost* as uninteresting and uninterested as Booth was?

I saw him first at a benefit performance at Drury Lane. I came to the door of the room where Henry was dressing, and Booth was sitting there with his back to me.

"Here's Miss Terry," said Henry as I came round the door. Booth looked up at me swiftly. I have never in any face, in any country, seen such wonderful eyes. There was a mystery about his appearance and his manner—a sort of pride which seemed to say: "Don't try to know me, for I am not what I have been." He seemed broken, and devoid of ambition.

At rehearsal he was very gentle and apathetic. Accustomed to playing Othello with stock companies, he had few suggestions to make about the stage-management. The part was to him more or less of a monologue.

"I shall never make you black," he said one morning. "When I take

159

your hand I shall have a corner of my drapery in my hand. That will protect you."

I am bound to say that I thought of Mr Booth's "protection" with some yearning the next week when I played Desdemona to *Henry's* Othello. Before he had done with me I was nearly as black as he.

Booth was a melancholy, dignified Othello, but not great as Salvini was great. Salvini's Hamlet made me scream with mirth, but his Othello was the grandest, biggest, most glorious thing. We often prate of "reserved force." Salvini had it, for the simple reason that his was the gigantic force which may be restrained because of its immensity. Men have no need to dam up a little purling brook. If they do it in acting, it is tame, absurd and pretentious. But Salvini held himself in, and still his groan was like a tempest, his passion huge.

The fact is that, apart from Salvini's personal genius, the foreign temperament is better fitted to deal with Othello than the English. Shakespeare's French and Italians, Greeks and Latins, medievals and barbarians, fancifuls and reals, all have a dash of Elizabethan Englishmen in them, but not Othello.

Booth's Othello was very helpful to my Desdemona. It is difficult to preserve the simple, heroic blindness of Desdemona to the fact that her lord mistrusts her, if her lord is raving and stamping under her nose! Booth was gentle in the scenes with Desdemona until *the* scene where Othello overwhelms her with the foul word and destroys her faith.

My greatest triumph as Desdemona was not gained with the audience but with Henry Irving! He found my endeavours to accept comfort from Iago so pathetic that they brought the tears to his eyes. It was the oddest sensation when I said "Oh, good Iago, what shall I do to win my lord again?" to look up—my own eyes dry, for Desdemona is past crying then —and see Henry's eyes at their biggest, and most luminous, soft and full of tears! He was, in spite of Iago and in spite of his power of identifying himself with the part, very deeply moved by my acting. But he knew how to turn it to his purpose: he obtrusively took the tears with his fingers and blew his nose with much feeling, softly and long (so much expression there is, by the way, in blowing the nose on the stage), so that the audience might think his emotion a fresh stroke of hypocrisy.

Every one liked Henry's Iago. For the first time in his life he knew what it was to win unanimous praise. Nothing could be better, I think, that Mr Walkley's [1] description: "Daringly Italian, a true compatriot of the Borgias, or rather, better than Italians, that devil incarnate, an Englishman Italianate."

One adored him, devil though he was. He was so full of charm, so

[1] Mr A. B. Walkley, then dramatic critic of *The Times*.

sincerely the "honest" Iago, peculiarly sympathetic with Othello, Desdemona, Roderigo, *all* of them—except his wife. It was only in the soliloquies and in the scenes with his wife that he revealed his devil's nature. Could one ever forget those grapes which he plucked in the first act, and slowly ate, spitting out the seeds, as if each one represented a worthy virtue to be put out of his mouth? His Iago and his Romeo in different ways proved his power to portray *Italian* passions—the passions of lovely, treacherous people, who will either sing you a love sonnet or stab you in the back—you are not sure which!

We played "Othello" for six weeks, three performances a week, to guinea stalls, and could have played it longer. Each week Henry and Booth changed parts. For both of them it was a change *for the worse.*

Booth's Iago seemed deadly commonplace after Henry's. He was always the snake in the grass; he showed the villain in all the scenes. He could not resist the temptation of making ornate effects.

Henry Irving's Othello was condemned almost as universally as his Iago was praised. For once I find myself with the majority. He screamed and ranted and raved—lost his voice, was slow where he should have been swift, incoherent where he should have been strong. I could not bear to see him in the part. It was painful to me. Yet night after night he achieved in the speech to the Senate one of the most superb and beautiful bits of acting of his life. It was *wonderful*. He spoke the speech, beaming on Desdemona all the time. The gallantry of the thing is indescribable.

I think his failure as Othello was one of the unspoken bitternesses of Henry's life. When I say "failure" I am of course judging him by his own standard, and using the word to describe what he was to himself, not what he was to the public. On the last night, he rolled up the clothes that he had worn as the Moor one by one, carefully laying one garment on top of the other, and then, half-humorously and very deliberately said, *"Never again!"* Then he stretched himself with his arms above his head and gave a great sigh of relief.

Mr. Pinero was excellent as Roderigo in this production. He was always good in the "silly ass" type of part and no one could say of him that he was playing himself!

Desdemona is not counted a big part by actresses, but I loved playing it. Some nights I played it beautifully. My appearance was right—I was such a poor wraith of a thing. But let there be no mistake—it took strength to act this weakness and passiveness of Desdemona's. I soon found that, like Cordelia, she has plenty of character.

Reading the play the other day, I studied the opening scene. It is the finest opening to a play I know.

161

How many times Shakespeare draws fathers and daughters, and how little stock he seems to take of *mothers!* Portia and Desdemona, Cordelia, Rosalind and Miranda, Lady Macbeth, Queen Katherine and Hermione, Ophelia, Jessica, Hero, and many more are daughters of *fathers,* but of their mothers we hear nothing. My own daughter called my attention to this fact quite recently, and it is really a singular one. Of mothers of sons there are plenty of examples. Constance, Volumnia, the Countess Rousillon, Gertrude; but if there are mothers of daughters at all, they are poor examples, like Juliet's mother and Mrs Page. I wonder if in all the many hundreds of books written on Shakespeare and his plays this point has been taken up? I once wrote a paper on the "Letters in Shakespeare's Plays," and congratulated myself that they had never been made a separate study. The very day after I first read my paper in Glasgow, a lady wrote to me from Oxford and said I was mistaken in thinking that there was no other contribution to the subject. She enclosed an essay of her own which had either been published, or read before some society. Probably some one else has dealt with Shakespeare's patronage of fathers and neglect of mothers! I often wonder what the mothers of Goneril, Regan and Cordelia were like! I think Lear must have married twice.

§ 4

"ROMEO AND JULIET" was the first of Henry Irving's great Shakespearean productions. "Hamlet" and "Othello" had been mounted with care, but, in spite of statements that I have seen to the contrary, they were not true reflections of Irving as a producer. In beauty I do not think that "Romeo and Juliet" surpassed "The Cup," but it was very sumptuous, impressive and Italian. It was the most *elaborate* of all the Lyceum productions. In it Henry first displayed his mastery of crowds. The brawling of the rival houses in the streets, the procession of girls to wake Juliet on her wedding morning, the musicians, the magnificent reconciliation of the two houses which closed the play, every one on the stage holding a torch, were all treated with a marvellous sense of pictorial effect.

Henry once said to me: " 'Hamlet' could be played anywhere on its acting merits. It marches from situation to situation. But 'Romeo and Juliet' proceeds from picture to picture. Every line suggests a picture. It is a dramatic poem rather than a drama, and I mean to treat it from that point of view."

While he was preparing the production, he revived "The Two Roses," a comedy in which as Digby Grant he had made a great success years before. I rehearsed the part of Lottie two or three times, but Henry released me because I was studying Juliet; and, as he said, "You've got to do all you know with it."

Perhaps the sense of this responsibility weighed on me. Perhaps I was neither young enough nor old enough to play Juliet. I read everything that had ever been written about her before I had myself decided what she was. It was a dreadful mistake. That was the first thing wrong with my Juliet—lack of original impulse.

As for the second and the third and the fourth—well, I am not more than common vain, I trust, but I see no occasion to write them *all* down.

It was perhaps the greatest opportunity that I had yet had at the Lyceum. I studied the part at my cottage at Hampton Court in a bedroom looking out over the park. There was nothing wrong with *that*. By the way, how important it is to be careful about environment and everything else when one is studying. One ought to be in the country, but not all the time.... It is good to go about and see pictures, hear music, and watch everything. One should be very much alone, and should study early and late—all night, if need be, even at the cost of sleep. Everything that one does or thinks or sees will have an effect upon the part, precisely as on an unborn child.

I wish now that instead of reading how this and that actress had played Juliet, and cracking my brain over the different readings of her lines and making myself familiar with the different opinions of philosophers and critics, I had gone to Verona, and just *imagined*. Perhaps the most wonderful description of Juliet, as she should be acted, occurs in Gabriele d' Annunzio's "Il Fuoco." In the book an Italian actress tells her friend how she played the part when she was a girl of fourteen in an open-air theatre near Verona. Could a girl of fourteen play such a part? Yes, if she were not youthful, only young with the youth of the poet, tragically old as some youth is.

Now I understand Juliet better. Now I know how she should be played. But time is inexorable. At sixty, know what one may, one cannot play Juliet.

I know that Henry Irving's production of "Romeo and Juliet" has been attributed to my ambition. What nonsense! Henry Irving now had in view the production of all Shakespeare's actable plays, and naturally "Romeo and Juliet" would come as early as possible in the programme.

The music was composed by Sir Julius Benedict, and was exactly right. There was no *leit-motiv,* no attempt to reflect the passionate emotion of the drama, but a great deal of Southern gaiety. At a rehearsal which had lasted far into the night I asked Sir Julius, who was very old, if he wasnt sleepy.

"Sleepy! Good heavens, no! I never sleep more than two hours. It's the end of my life, and I don't want to waste it in sleep!"

There is generally some "old 'un" in a company now who complains of insufficient rehearsals, and says, perhaps, "Think of Irving's rehearsals! They were the real thing." While we were rehearsing "Romeo and Juliet" I remember that Mrs Stirling, a charming and ripe old actress whom Henry had engaged to play the nurse, was always groaning out that she had not rehearsed enough.

"Oh, these modern ways!" she used to say. "We never have any rehearsals at all. How am I going to play the Nurse?"

She played it splendidly none the less. Indeed, she as the Nurse and old Tom Mead as the Apothecary—the two "old 'uns" romped away with the chief honours.

I had one battle with Mrs Stirling over "tradition." It was in the scene beginning—

> The clock struck twelve when I did send the nurse,
> And yet she is not here . . .

Tradition said that Juliet must go on coquetting and clicking over the Nurse to get the news of Romeo out of her. Tradition said that Juliet must give imitations of the Nurse on the line "Where's your mother?" in order to get that cheap reward, "a safe laugh." I felt that it was wrong. I felt that Juliet was angry with the Nurse. Each time she delayed in answering I lost my temper, with genuine passion. At "Where's your mother?" I spoke with indignation, tears and rage. We were a long time coaxing Mrs Stirling to let the scene be played on these lines, but this was how it *was* played eventually.

She was the only Nurse that I have ever seen who did not play the part like a female pantaloon. She did not assume any great decrepitude. In the "Cords" scene, where the Nurse tells Juliet of the death of Paris, she did not play for comedy at all, but was very emotional. Her parrot scream when she found me dead was horribly real and effective.

Years before, I had seen Mrs Stirling act at the Adelphi with Benjamin Webster, and had cried out: *"That's* my idea of an actress!" In those days she was playing Olivia (in a version of the "Vicar of Wakefield" by Tom Taylor), Peg Woffington, and other parts of the kind. She swept on to the stage and in that magical way, never, never to be learned, *filled* it. She had such breadth of style, such a lovely voice, such a beautiful expressive eye! When she played the Nurse at the Lyceum her voice had become a little jangled and harsh, but her eye was still bright and her art had not abated—not one little bit! Nor had her charm. Her smile was the most fascinating, irresistible thing imaginable.

164

ELLEN TERRY AS JULIET

The production was received with abuse by the critics. It was one of our failures, yet it ran a hundred and fifty nights!

Henry Irving's Romeo had more bricks thrown at it even than my Juliet! I remember that not long after we opened, a well-known politician who had enough wit, and knowledge of the theatre to have taken a more original view, came up to me and said:

"I say, E. T., why is Irving playing Romeo?"

I looked at him amazed. "You should ask me why I am playing Juliet! Why are we any of us doing what we have to do?"

"Oh, *you're* all right. But Irving!"

"I don't agree with you," I said. I was growing a little angry by this time. "Besides, who would you have play Romeo?"

"Well, it's so obvious. You've got Terriss in the cast."

"Terriss!"

"Yes, I dont doubt Irving's intellectuality, you know. But as Romeo he reminds me of a pig who has been taught to play the fiddle. He does it cleverly, but he would be better employed in squealing. He cannot shine in the part like the fiddler. Terriss in this case is the fiddler."

I was furious. "I am sorry you dont realise," I said, "that the worst thing Henry Irving could do would be better than the best of any one else."

When dear Terriss did play Romeo at the Lyceum two or three years later to the Juliet of Mary Anderson, he attacked the part with a good deal of fire. He was young, truly, and stamped his foot a great deal, was vehement and passionate. But it was so obvious that there was no intelligence behind his reading. He did not know what the part was about, and all the finer shades of meaning in it he missed. Yet the majority, with my political friend, would always prefer a Terriss as Romeo to a Henry Irving.

I am not going to say that Henry's Romeo was good. What I do say is that some bits of it were as good as anything he ever did. In the big emotional scene (in the Friar's cell), he came to grief precisely as he had done in Othello. He screamed, grew slower and slower, and looked older and older. When I begin to think it over I see that he often failed in such scenes through his very genius for impersonation. An actor of commoner mould takes such scenes rhetorically—recites them, and gets through them with some success. But the actor who impersonates, feels, and lives such anguish or passion or tempestuous grief, does for the moment in imagination nearly die. Imagination impeded Henry Irving in what are known as "strong" scenes.

He was a perfect Hamlet, a perfect Richard III, a perfect Shylock, except in the scene with Tubal, where I think his voice failed him. He was an imperfect Romeo; yet, as I have said, he did things in the part which were equal to the best of his perfect Hamlet.

His whole attitude before he met Juliet was beautiful. He came on from the very back of the stage and walked over a little bridge with a book in his hand, sighing and dying for Rosaline. In Iago he had been Italian. Then he was the Italy of Venice. As Romeo he was the Italy of Tuscany. His clothes were as Florentine as his bearing. He ignored the silly tradition that Romeo must wear a feather in his cap. In the course of his study of the part he had found that the youthful fops and gallants of the period put in their hats anything that they had been given—some souvenir of love. And he wore in his hat a sprig of crimson oleander.

It is not usual, I think, to make much of the Rosaline episode. Henry Irving chose with great care a tall dark girl to represent Rosaline at the ball. Can I ever forget his face when suddenly in pursuit of *her* he saw *Juliet*. . . . Once more I reflect that a *face* is the chiefest equipment of the actor.

I know they said he looked too old—was too old for Romeo. In some scenes he looked aged as only a very young man can look. He was not boyish; but ought Romeo to be boyish?

I am not supporting the idea of an elderly Romeo. When it came to the scenes where Romeo "poses" and is poetical but insincere, Henry *did* seem elderly. He couldn't catch the youthful pose of melancholy with its extravagant expression. It was in the repressed scenes, where the melancholy was sincere, the feeling deeper, and the expression slighter, that he was at his best.

"He may be good, but he isn't Romeo," is a favorite type of criticism. But I have seen Duse and Bernhardt in "La Dame aux Camélias," and cannot say which is Marguerite Gauthier. Each has her own view of the character, and each *is* it *according to her imagination*.

According to his imagination, Henry Irving was Romeo.

Again in this production he used his favourite "fate" tree. It gloomed over the street along which Romeo went to the ball. It was in the scene with the Apothecary. Henry thought that it symbolised the destiny hanging over the lovers.

It is usual for Romeo to go in to the dead body of Juliet lying in Capulet's monument through a gate on the *level*, as if the Capulets were buried but a few feet from the road. At rehearsals Henry kept on saying: "I must go *down* to the vault." After a great deal of consideration he had an inspiration. He had the exterior of the vault in one scene, the entrance to it down a flight of steps. Then the scene changed to the interior of the vault, and the steps now led from a height above the stage. At the close of the scene, when the Friar and the crowd came rushing down into the tomb, these steps were thronged with people, each one holding a torch, and the effect was magnificent.

At the opening of the Apothecary Scene, when Balthazar comes to tell Romeo of Juliet's supposed death, Henry was marvellous. His face grew whiter and whiter.

Then she is well and nothing can be ill;
Her body sleeps in Capulet's monument.

It was during the silence after those two lines that Henry Irving as Romeo had one of those sublime moments which an actor only achieves once or twice in his life. The only thing that I ever saw to compare with it was Duse's moment when she took Kellner's card in "Magda." There was absolutely no movement, but her face grew white, and the audience knew what was going on in her soul, as she read the name of the man who years before had seduced and deserted her.

As Juliet I did not *look* right. My little daughter Edy, a born arch-æologist, said: "Mother, you oughtnt to have a fringe." Yet, strangely enough, Henry himself liked me as Juliet. After the dress rehearsal he wrote to me that "beautiful as Portia was, Juliet leaves her far, far behind. Never anybody acted more exquisitely the part of the performance which I saw from the front. 'Hie to high fortune,' and 'Where spirits resort' were simply incomparable. . . . Your mother looked very radiant last night. I told her how proud she should be, and she was. . . . The play will be, I believe, a mighty 'go,' for the beauty of it is bewildering. I am sure of this, for it dumbfounded them all last night. Now you—we—must make our task a delightful one by doing everything possible to make our acting easy and comfortable. We are in for a long run."

To this letter he added a very human postscript: "I have determined not to see a paper for a week—I know they'll cut me up, and I don't like it!"

Yes, he *was* cut up, and he didn't like it, but a few people knew. One of them was Mr Frankfort Moore, the novelist, who wrote to me of this "revealing Romeo, full of originality and power."

"Are you affected by adverse criticism?" I was asked once. I answered then and I answer now, that legitimate adverse criticism has always been of use to me if only because it "gave me to think" furiously. Seldom does the outsider, however talented as a writer and observer, recognise the actor's art, and often we are told that we are acting best when we are showing the works most plainly, and denied any special virtue when we are concealing our method. Professional criticism is most helpful, chiefly because it induces one to criticise oneself. "Did I give that impression to any one? Then there must have been something wrong somewhere."

The "something" is often a perfectly different blemish from that to which the critic drew attention.

Unprofessional criticism is often more helpful still, but alas! one's friends are to one's faults more than a little blind, and to one's virtues very kind! It is through letters from people quite unknown to me that I have sometimes learned valuable lessons. During the run of "Romeo and Juliet" some one wrote and told me that if the dialogue at the ball could be taken in a lighter and *quicker* way, it would better express the manner of a girl of Juliet's age. The same unknown critic pointed out that I was too slow and studied in the Balcony Scene. She—I think it was a woman —was perfectly right.

On the hundredth night, although no one liked my Juliet very much, I received many flowers, little tokens, and poems. To one bouquet was pinned a note which ran:

To Juliet,

As a mark of respect and esteem
From the Gasmen of the Lyceum Theatre.

That alone would have made my recollections of "Romeo and Juliet" pleasant. But there was more. At the supper on the stage after the hundredth performance, Sarah Bernhardt was present. She said nice things to me, and I was enraptured that my "vraies larmes" should have pleased and astonished her! I noticed that she hardly ever moved, yet all the time she gave the impression of swift, butterfly movement. While talking to Henry she took some red stuff out of her bag and rubbed it on her lips! This frank "making-up" in public was a far more astonishing thing in the 'eighties than it would be now. But I liked Miss Sarah for it, as I liked her for everything.

How wonderful she looked in those days! She was as transparent as an azalea, only more so; like a cloud, only not so thick. Smoke from a burning paper describes her more nearly! She was hollow-eyed, thin, almost consumptive-looking. Her body was not the prison of her soul, but its shadow.

On the stage she has always seemed to me more a symbol, an ideal, an epitome, than a *woman*. It is this quality which makes her so easy in such lofty parts as Phèdre. She is always a miracle. Let her play "L'Aiglon," and while matter-of-fact members of the audience are wondering if she looks *really* like the unfortunate King of Rome, and deciding against her and in favour of Maude Adams who did look the boy to perfection, more imaginative spectators see in Sarah's performance a truth far bigger than a mere physical resemblance.

It is this extraordinary decorative and symbolic quality of Sarah's which makes her transcend all personal and individual feeling on the stage. No one plays a love scene better, but it is a *picture* of love that she gives, a strange exotic picture rather than a suggestion of the ordinary human passion as felt by ordinary human people. She is exotic—well, what else should she be? One does not, at any rate one should not, quarrel with an orchid and call it unnatural because it is not a buttercup or a cowslip.

I have spoken of the face as the chief equipment of the actor. Sarah Bernhardt contradicts this at once. Her face does little for her. Her walk is not much. Nothing about her is more remarkable than the way she gets about the stage without one ever seeing her move. By what magic does she triumph without two of the richest possessions that an actress can have? Eleanora Duse has them. Her walk is the walk of the peasant, fine and free. She has the superb carriage of the head which goes with that fearless movement from the hips. And her face! There is nothing like it, nothing! But it is as the real woman, a particular woman, that Duse triumphs most. Her Cleopatra was insignificant compared with Sarah's. She is not so pictorial.

How futile it is to make comparisons! Better far to thank heaven for both these great actresses.

I have found in one of my old diaries some impressions of Sarah recorded when they were fresh and I transcribe them to supplement what I have written today about her.

Saturday, June 11.—To see "Miss Sarah" as "Cléopâtre." She was inspired! The essence of Shakespeare's "Cleopatra." I went round and implored her to do Juliet. She said she was too old. She can *never* be old. "Age cannot wither her."

June 18.—Again to see Sarah—this time "La Dame aux Camélias." Fine, marvellous. Her writing the letter, and the last act the best.

July 11.—*Telegraph* says "Frou-frou" was "never at any time a character in which she (Sarah) excelled." Dear me! When I saw it I thought it wonderful. It made me ashamed of ever having played it.

Sarah Bernhardt has shown herself the equal of any man as a manager. Her productions are always beautiful; she chooses her company with discretion, and sees to every detail of the stage-management. In this respect she differs from all other foreign artists that I have seen. I have always regretted that Duse should play as a rule with such a mediocre company and should be apparently so indifferent to her surroundings. In "Adrienne Lecouvreur" it struck me that the careless stage-management utterly ruined the play, and I could not bear to see Duse as Adrienne beautifully dressed while the Princess and the other Court ladies wore cheap red velveteen and white satin and brought the pictorial level of the performance down to that of a "fit-up."

"Miss Sarah" (my own particular name for her), and I have always been able to understand one another, although I hardly know a word of French and her English is scanty. She too, liked my Juliet—she and Henry Irving! Well, that was charming, although I could not like it myself, except for my "Cords" scene, of which I shall always be proud.

§ 5

My dresser, Sarah Holland, came to me, I think, during the run of "Romeo and Juliet." I never had any other dresser at the Lyceum except Sally's sister Lizzie, who dressed me during the first few years. Sally stuck to me loyally until the Lyceum days ended. Then she perceived "a divided duty." On one side was "the Guv'nor" with "the Guv'nor's" valet Walter, to whom she was devoted; on the other was a precarious in and out job with me, for after the Lyceum I never knew what I was going to do next. She chose to go with Henry, and it was she and Walter who dressed him for the last time when he lay dead in the hotel bedroom at Bradford.

Sally Holland's two little daughters "walked on" in "Romeo and Juliet." Henry always took an interest in the children in the theatre, and was very kind to them. One night as we came down the stairs from our dressing-rooms to go home—the theatre was quiet and deserted—we found a small child sitting forlornly and patiently on the lowest step.

"Well, my dear, what are you doing here?" said Henry.

"Waiting for mother, sir."

"Are you acting in the theatre?"

"Yes, sir."

"And what part do you take?"

"Please, sir, first I'm a water-carrier, then I'm a little page, and then I'm a virgin."

Henry and I sat down on the stairs and laughed until we cried! Little Flo Holland was one of the troops of "virgins" who came to wake Juliet on her bridal morn. As time went on she was promoted to more important parts, but she never made us laugh so much again.

Her mother was a "character," a dear character. She had an extraordinarily open mind, and was ready to grasp each new play as it came along as a separate and entirely different field of operations! She was also extremely methodical, and only got flurried once in a blue moon. When we went to America and made the acquaintance of that dreadful thing, a "one-night stand," she was as precise and particular about having every-

The faithful
"Sally" =
(Sarah Holland =)
"Sans Gêne" =
"Nance Oldfield ="

[*Ellen Terry's Lettering*]

thing nice and in order for me as if we were going to stay in the town a month. Down went my neat square of white drugget; all the lights in my dressing-room were arranged as I wished. Everything was unpacked and ironed. One day when I came into some American theatre to dress I found Sally nearly in tears.

"What's the matter with you, Sally?" I asked.

"I 'avent 'ad a morsel to heat all day, dear, and I cant 'eat my iron."

"Eat your iron, Sally! What *do* you mean?"

" 'Ow am I to iron all this, dear?" wailed Sally, picking up my Nance Oldfield apron and a few other trifles. "It wont get 'ot."

Until then I really thought that Sally was being sardonic about an iron as a substitute for victuals!

When she first began to dress me, I was very thin, so thin that it was really a grief to me. Sally would comfort me in my thin days by the terse compliment:

"Beautiful and fat tonight, dear."

As the years went on and I grew fat, she made a change in the compliment:

"Beautiful and thin tonight, dear."

Mr Fernandez played Friar Laurence in "Romeo and Juliet." He was a very nervous actor, and it used to paralyse him with fright when I knelt down in the friar's cell with my back to the audience and put safety pins in the drapery I wore over my head to keep it in position while I said the lines,

> Are you at leisure, holy father, now
> Or shall I come to you at evening mass?

Not long after the production of "Romeo and Juliet" I saw the performance of a Greek play—the "Electra," I think—by some Oxford students. A young woman veiled in black with bowed head was brought in on a chariot. Suddenly she lifted her head and looked round, revealing a face of such pure classic beauty and a glance of such pathos that I called out:

"What a supremely beautiful girl!"

Then I remembered that there were no women in the cast! The face belonged to a young Oxford undergraduate, Frank Benson.

We engaged him to play Paris in "Romeo and Juliet," when George Alexander, the original Paris, left the Lyceum for a time. Already Benson gave promise of turning out quite a different person from the others. He had not nearly so much of the actor's instinct as Terriss, but one felt that he had far more earnestness. He was easily distinguished as a man with a purpose, one of those workers who "scorn delights and live laborious days." Those laborious days led him at last to the control of two or three companies, all travelling through Great Britain playing a Shakespearean repertory. A wonderful organiser, a good actor (oddly enough, the more difficult the part the better he is—I like his *Lear*), and a man who has always been associated with high endeavour, Frank Benson's name is honoured all over England. He was only at the Lyceum for this one production, but he always regarded Henry Irving as the source of the good work that he did afterwards.

"Thank you very much," he wrote to me after his first night as Paris, "for writing me a word of encouragement. . . . I was very much ashamed and disgusted with myself all Sunday for my poverty-stricken and thin performance. . . . I think I was a little better last night. Indeed I was much touched at the kindness and sympathy of all the company and their efforts to make the awkward new boy feel at home. . . . I feel doubly grateful to you and Mr. Irving for the light you shed from the lamp of art on life now that I begin to understand the labour and weariness the process of trimming the lamp entails."

§ 6

OUR success with "The Belle's Stratagem" had pointed to comedy, to Beatrice and Benedick in particular, because in Mrs Cowley's old comedy we had had some scenes of the same type. I have already told of my first appearance as Beatrice at Leeds, and said that I never played the part so well again; but the Lyceum production was a great success, and Beatrice a great personal success for me. It is only in comedy that people seem to know what I am driving at!

The stage-management of the play was very good; the scenery nothing out of the ordinary except for the Church Scene. There was no question that it *was* a church, hardly a question that old Mead was a Friar. Henry had the art of making ceremonies seem very real.

Johnston Forbes-Robertson made his first appearance at the Lyceum as Claudio. I had not acted with him since "The Wandering Heir," and his improvement as an actor in the ten years that had gone by since then was marvellous. I had once said to him that he had far better stick to his painting and become an artist instead of an actor. His Claudio made me "take it back." It was beautiful. I have seen many young actors play the part since then, but not one of them made it anywhere near as convincing. Forbes-Robertson put a touch of Leontes into it, a part which some years later he was to play magnificently, and through the subtle indication of consuming and insanely suspicious jealousy made Claudio's offensive conduct explicable at least. On the occasion of the performance at Drury Lane which the theatrical profession organised in 1906 in honour of my Stage Jubilee, one of the items in the programme was a scene from "Much Ado About Nothing." I then played Beatrice for the last time, and Forbes-Robertson played his old part of Claudio.

The Lyceum company was not a permanent one. People used to come, learn something, go away, and come back at a larger salary! Miss Emery left for a time, and then returned to play Hero and other parts. I liked her Hero better than Miss Millward's. Miss Millward had a sure touch; strength, vitality, interest; but somehow she was commonplace in this part.

Henry used to spend hours and hours teaching people. I used to think impatiently: "Acting cant be taught." Gradually I learned to modify this conviction and to recognise that there are two classes of actors:

1. Those who can only do what they are taught.
2. Those who cannot be taught, but can be helped by suggestion to work out things for themselves.

Henry said to me once: "What makes a popular actor? Physique! What makes a great actor? Imagination and sensibility." I tried to believe it. Then I thought to myself: "Henry himself is not quite what is understood by 'an actor of physique,' and certainly he is popular. And that he is a great actor I know. He certainly has both imagination and 'sense and sensibility.'" After the lapse of years I begin to wonder if Henry was ever really *popular*. It came naturally to most people to dislike his acting. They found it queer, as some found the art of Whistler queer. But he forced them, almost against their will and nature, out of dislike into admiration. They had to come up to him, for never would he go down to them. This is not popularity.

Brain allied with the instinct of the actor tells, but stupidity allied with the instinct of the actor tells more than brain alone. I have sometimes seen a clever man who was not a born actor play a small part with his brains, and have felt that the cleverness was telling more with the actors on the stage than with the audience.

Terriss, like Mrs Pritchard, if we are to believe what Dr Johnson said of her, often did not know what on earth he was talking about! One morning we went over and over one scene in "Much Ado"—at least a dozen times I should think—and each time when Terriss came to the speech beginning:

What needs the bridge much broader than the flood,

he managed to give a different emphasis. First it would be:
"What! *Needs* the bridge much broader than the flood!" Then:
"What needs the bridge *much* broader than the flood."
After he had been floundering about for some time, Henry said:

"Terriss, what's the meaning of that?"

"Oh, get along, Guv'nor, *you* know!"

Henry laughed. He never could be angry with Terriss, not even when he came to rehearsal full of absurd excuses. One day, however, he was so late that it was past a joke, and Henry spoke to him sharply.

"I think you'll be sorry you've spoken to me like this, Guv'nor," said Terriss, casting down his eyes.

"Now no hanky-panky tricks, Terriss."

"Tricks, Guv'nor! I think you'll regret having said that when you hear that my poor mother passed away early this morning."

And Terriss wept.

Henry promptly gave him the day off. A few weeks later, when Terriss and I were looking through the curtain at the audience just before the play began, he said to me gaily:

"See that dear old woman sitting in the fourth row of the stalls. That's my mother."

The wretch had quite forgotten that he had killed her!

He was the only person who ever ventured to "cheek" Henry, yet he never gave offence, not even when he wrote a letter of this kind:

My dear Guv.,—

I hope you are enjoying yourself, and in the best of health. I very much want to play 'Othello' with you next year (don't laugh). Shall I study it up, and will you do it with me on tour if possible? Say *yes,* and lighten the drooping heart of yours sincerely,

WILL TERRISS.

I have never seen any one at all like Terriss, and my father said the same. The only actor of my father's day, he used to tell me, who had a touch of the same insouciance and lawlessness was Leigh Murray, a famous *jeune premier.*

One night he came into the theatre soaked from head to foot.

"Is it raining, Terriss?" said some one who noticed that he was wet.

"Looks like it, doesnt it?" said Terriss carelessly.

Later it came out that he had jumped off a steamboat into the Thames and saved a little girl's life.

Mr Pinero, who was no longer a member of the Lyceum company when "Much Ado" was produced, wrote to Henry after the first night that it was "as perfect a representation of a Shakespearean play as I conceive to be possible. I think," he added, "that the work at your theatre does so much to create new playgoers—which is what we want, far more I fancy than we want new theatres and perhaps new plays."

A playgoer whose knowledge of the English stage extended over a period of fifty-five years, wrote another nice letter about "Much Ado"

which was passed on to me because it had some nice things about me
in it.

SAVILE CLUB,
January 13, 1883.
MY DEAR HENRY,—

I were an imbecile ingrate if I did not hasten to give you my warmest
thanks for the splendid entertainment of last night. Such a performance is not
a grand entertainment merely, or a glorious pastime, although it was all that.
It was, too, an artistic display of the highest character, elevating in the vast
audience their art instinct—as well as purifying any developed art in the possession of individuals.

I saw the Kean revivals of 1855-57, and I suppose "The Winter's Tale" was
the best of the lot. But it did not approach last night. . . .

I was impressed more strongly than ever with the fact that the plays
of Shakespeare were meant to be *acted*. The man who thinks that he can
know Shakespeare by reading him is a shallow ass. The best critic and scholar
would have been carried out of himself last night into the poet's heart, his
mind-spirit . . . The Terry was glorious. . . . The scenes in which she appeared
—and she was in eight of the sixteen—reminded me of nothing but the blessed
sun that not only beautifies but creates. But she never acts so well as when
I am there to see! That is a real lover's sentiment, and all lovers are vain
men.

Terriss has "come on" wonderfully, and his Don Pedro is princely and
manly.

I have thus set down, my dear Irving, one or two things merely to show
that my gratitude to you is not that of a blind gratified idiot, but of one
whose intimate personal knowledge of the English stage entitles him to say
what he owes to you.

I am   Affectionately yours,
                                        A. J. DUFFIELD.

In 1891, when we revived "Much Ado," Henry's Benedick was far
more brilliant than it was at first. In my diary, January 5, 1891, I wrote:

Revival of "Much Ado about Nothing." Went most brilliantly. Henry
has vastly improved upon his *old* rendering of Benedick. Acts larger now
—not so "finicking." His model (of manner) is the Duke of Sutherland.
VERY good. I did some parts better, I think—made Beatrice a nobler woman.
Yet I failed to please myself in the Church Scene.

Two days later.—Played the Church Scene all right at last. More of a
blaze. The little scene in the garden, too, I did better (in the last act). Beatrice
has *confessed* her love, and is now *softer*. Her voice should be beautiful now,
breaking out into playful defiance now and again, as of old. The last scene,
too, I made much more merry, happy, *soft*.

January 8.—I must make Beatrice more *flashing* at first, and *softer*
afterwards. This will be an improvement upon my old reading of the part.

She must be always *merry* and by turns scornful, tormenting, vexed, self-communing, absent, melting, teasing, brilliant, indignant, *sad-merry*, thoughtful, withering, gentle, humorous, and gay, Gay, *Gay!* Protecting (to Hero), motherly, very intellectual—a gallant creature and complete in mind and feature.

After a run of two hundred and fifty nights, "Much Ado," although it was still drawing fine houses, was withdrawn as we were going to America, for the first time, in the autumn (of 1883) and Henry wanted to rehearse the plays that we were to do in the States by reviving them in London at the close of the summer season. It was during these revivals that I played Jeannette in "The Lyons Mail"—not a big part, and not well suited to me, but I played it well enough to support my theory that whatever I have *not* been, I *have* been a useful actress.

I always associate "The Lyons Mail" with old Mead, whose performance of the father, Jerome Lesurques, was one of the most impressive things that this fine actor did with us. (Before Henry was ever heard of, Mead had played Hamlet at Drury Lane!) Indeed when Mead "broke up," Henry put aside "The Lyons Mail" for many years because he dreaded playing Lesurques' scene with his father without Mead.

In the days just before the break-up, which came about because Mead was old, and—I hope there is no harm in saying of him what can be said of many men who have done finely in the world—too fond of "the wine when it is red," Henry used to suffer great anxiety in the scene, because he never knew what Mead was going to do or say next. When Jerome Lesurques is forced to suspect his son of the murder, he has a line:

Am I mad, or dreaming? Would I were.

Mead one night gave this less romantic reading:

Am I mad or *drunk?* Would I were!

The last episode in the eventful history of "Meadisms" occurred in "The Lyons Mail" when Mead came on to the stage in his own top-hat, went over to the sofa, and lay down, apparently for a nap! Not a word could Henry get from him, and Henry had to play the scene by himself. He did it in this way:

"You say, father, that I," etc. "I answer you that it is false!"

Mead had a remarkable *foot*. Norman Forbes called it an *architectural* foot. Bunions and gout combined to give it a gargoyled effect! One night, I forget whether it was in this play or another, Henry, pawing the ground with his foot before an "exit"—one of the mannerisms which his imitators delighted to burlesque—came down on poor old Mead's foot, bunion, gargoyles and all! Hardly had Mead stopped cursing under his breath than on came Tyars, and brought down *his* weight heavily on the same foot. Directly Tyars came off the stage he looked for Mead in the wings and offered an apology.

"I beg your pardon. I'm really awfully sorry, Mead."

"Sorry! Sorry indeed!" the old man snorted. "It's a damned conspiracy!"

It was the dignity and gravity of Mead which made everything he said so funny. I am afraid that those who never knew him will wonder where the joke comes in.

I forget what year he left us for good, but in a letter of Henry's dated September, 1888, written during a provincial tour of "Faust," when I was ill and my sister Marion played Margaret instead of me, I find this allusion to him:

"Wenman does the Kitchen Witch now (I altered it this morning) and Mead the old one—the 'Climber.' Poor old chap, he'll not climb much longer!"

NOTES TO CHAPTER VIII

1. *Irving's* Othello. The bundle of clothes Irving rolled up on the last night of his appearance as Othello appears to have been rescued by Ellen Terry. Years afterwards she wore Othello's green and gold robe in the ballroom scene in "Romeo and Juliet" when she played the Nurse in Doris Keane's production at the Lyric Theatre. This part of Irving's Othello dress is preserved in the Ellen Terry Memorial Museum.

2. *Pinero's Roderigo.* Edith Craig, who can remember Pinero as an actor, says that his performances were distinguished by the same cleverness as those given in more recent times by another actor-dramatist, Miles Malleson. "Both mixed their fooling with brains." Malleson, in Edith Craig's opinion, is the best Shakespeare clown on the modern stage.

3. *Shakespeare's Fathers.* Sir Arthur Quiller-Couch drew attention this year (1932), in a lecture delivered in April, to the fact that daughters in Shakespeare are allowed fathers, but seldom mothers. He had forgotten, or perhaps may not have known, that Ellen Terry had anticipated him.

4. *The Letters in Shakespeare's Plays.* This was the first of Ellen Terry's now famous lectures on Shakespeare. Their history is given in Part II, Chapter II.

5. *Irving's Romeo.* The well-known politician who angered Ellen Terry by his criticism of this performance was the late Henry Labouchere.

6. *Sarah Holland.* In Ellen Terry's copy of her autobiography the story of Sally (her dresser) and the iron is annotated. "I am sure old Sally will be hurt to the heart by my making her leave out her 'h's'. Some damned kind friend will explain it to her, or she probably would not understand. So I shall put back most of the 'h's' in the next edition, only keeping 'ot and 'eat." Sally

has been dead many years, and the old version of the story has been retained, in order that the reader may have in this note, a charming little piece of evidence of Ellen Terry's kind-heartedness and consideration.

7. The parts played by Ellen Terry during the period covered by Chapter VIII were: Camma ("The Cup," 1881); Letitia Hardy (The Belle's Stratagem, 1881); Desdemona ("Othello," 1881); Juliet ("Romeo and Juliet," 1882); Jeannette ("The Lyons Mail," 1883); Clementine ("Robert Macaire," 1883).

CHAPTER IX

THE LYCEUM IN THE 'EIGHTIES (*Continued*)

(1884–1887)

§ 1

IN order of time my first tour in America with Henry Irving and the Lyceum company ought to come next, but it has seemed to me a better arrangement to continue the chronicle of the productions at the Lyceum to "Macbeth," and leave my American experiences to a later chapter. I think I have said before that "Macbeth" marks a turning-point in the history of the Lyceum, and now I want to emphasise it. The theatre and Henry Irving, and I too, I think, were then at the zenith. We had climbed to the maturity of our success, "wherewith being crowned, crooked eclipses 'gainst our glory" fought, and

Time that gave, did now the gift confound.

We had a little set-back in our climb in July 1884 when Henry produced "Twelfth Night." It was one of the least successful of Henry's Shakespearean productions. Terriss looked all wrong as Orsino; many other people were miscast. Henry said to me a few years later when he thought of doing "The Tempest," "I cant do it without three great comedians. I ought never to have attempted 'Twelfth Night' without them."

We had the curious experience of being "booed" on the first night. The chief reason was that people resented Henry's attempt to reserve the pit. He thought that the public wanted it. When he found that it was against their wish he had to give in.

His speech after the hostile reception of "Twelfth Night" was the only mistake that I ever knew him make. He was furious, and showed it. Instead of accepting the verdict, he denounced the first-night audience for giving it. He simply could not understand it!

My old friend Rose Leclercq, who was in Charles Kean's company at the Princess's when I made my first appearance on the stage, joined the Lyceum company to play Olivia. Strangely enough she had lost the touch for this kind of part. She, who had made one of her early successes as the spirit of Astarte in "Manfred," was known to a later generation of play-goers as the aristocratic dowager of stately presence and incisive repartee. Her son, Fuller Mellish, was also in the cast as Curio, and when we played "Twelfth Night" in America was promoted to the part of Sebastian. In London my brother Fred played it. Directly Fred walked on to the stage, looking as like me as possible, yet a *man* all over, he was a success. I dont think that I have ever seen any success so unmistakable and instantaneous.

In America "Twelfth Night" was liked far better than in London, but I never liked it. I thought our production dull, lumpy and heavy. Henry's Malvolio was fine and dignified, but not good for the play. I was handicapped as Viola by physical pain. On the first night I had a bad thumb—I thought it was a whitlow—and had to carry my arm in a sling. It grew worse every night, and I felt so sick and faint from pain that I played most of my scenes sitting in a chair. One night Dr Stoker, Bram Stoker's brother, came round between the scenes, and, after looking at my thumb, said:

"We'll soon put that right. I'll cut it for you."

He lanced it then and there, and I went on with my performance. George Stoker, who was just going off to Ireland, could not see the job through, but the next day I was in for the worst illness I ever had in my life. It was blood-poisoning, and the doctors were in doubt for a time as to whether they would not have to amputate my arm. They said that if George Stoker had not lanced the thumb so promptly, I *should* have lost my arm.

A disagreeable incident in connection with my illness was that a member of my profession made it the occasion of an unkind allusion (in a speech at the Social Science Congress) to "actresses who feign illness and have straw laid down before their houses, while behind the drawn blinds they are having riotous supper-parties, dancing the can-can and drinking champagne." Upon being asked for "name," the speaker would neither assert nor deny that she was referring to Ellen Terry (whose poor arm at the time was as big as her waist, and *that* has never been very small!).

I think we first heard of the affair on our second voyage to America, during which I was still so ill that they thought I might never see Quebec, and Henry wrote a letter to the press—a "scorcher." He showed it to me on the boat. When I had read it, I tore it up and threw the bits into the sea.

"It hasnt injured me in any way," I said. "Any answer would be undignified."

Henry did what I wished in the matter, but, unlike me, he never forgot it, and never forgave. If the speech-maker chanced to come into a room where he was, he walked out. He showed the same spirit in the last days of his life, long after our partnership had come to an end. A literary club, not a hundred yards from Hyde Park Corner, "blackballed" me (although I was qualified for election under the rules) for reasons with which I was never favoured. The committee, a few months later, wished Henry Irving to be the guest of honour at one of the club dinners. The invitation was declined and the reason given.

§ 2

THE first night of "Olivia" at the Lyceum in 1885 was about the only *comfortable* first night that I have ever had! I was familiar with the part, and two of the cast, Terriss and Norman Forbes, were the same as at the Court, which made me feel all the more at home. Henry left a great deal of the stage-management to us, for he knew that he could not improve on Mr Hare's production. Only he insisted on altering the last act, and made a bad matter worse. The division into two scenes wasted time, and nothing was gained by it. *Never* obstinate, Henry saw his mistake and restored the original end after a time. It was weak and unsatisfactory but not pretentious and bad like the last act he presented at the first performance.

We took the play too slowly at the Lyceum. That was often a fault there. Because Henry was slow, the others took their time from him, and the result was bad.

The lovely scene of the vicarage parlour, in which we used a harpsichord and were accused of pedantry for our pains, did not look so well at the Lyceum as at the Court. The stage was too big for it.

The critics said that I played Olivia better at the Lyceum, but I did not feel this myself.

At first Henry did not rehearse the Vicar at all well. One day when he was stamping his foot in the manner of Mathias in "The Bells," my little Edy, who was a terrible child *and* a wonderful critic, said:

"Dont go on like that, Henry. Why dont you talk as you do to me and Teddy? At home you *are* the Vicar."

The child's frankness did not offend Henry, because it was illuminating. A blind man had changed his Shylock; a child changed his Vicar. When the first night came he gave a simple, lovable performance. Many people now understood and liked him as they had never done before.

In this, as in other plays, he used to make his entrance in the *skin* of the part. No need for him to shake a ladder at the side to work himself up as Macready is said to have done. He walked on, and was the simple-minded old clergyman, just as he walked on a prince in "Hamlet," a king in "Charles I," and a saint in "Becket."

"Olivia" has always been a family play. Edy and Ted walked on the stage for the first time in the Court production. In later years Ted played Moses, and Edy made her first appearance in a speaking part as Polly Flamborough. She has since played both Sophia and the Gipsy. My brother Charlie's little girl Beatrice made her first appearance as Bill; my sister Floss played Olivia on a provincial tour and mv sister Marion played it at the Lyceum when I was ill.

I saw Floss play it, and took from her a lovely and sincere bit of "business." In the third act, where the Vicar has found his erring daughter and has come to take her away from the inn, I had always hesitated at my entrance as if I were not quite sure what reception my father would give me after what had happened. Floss in the same situation came running in and went straight to her father, quite sure of his love if not of his forgiveness.

I did *not* take some business which Marion did on Terriss's suggestion. When Thornhill tells Olivia that she is not his wife, I used to thrust him away with both hands as I said—"Devil!"

"It's very good, Nell, very fine," said Terriss to me, "but believe me, you miss a great effect there. You play it grandly, of course, but at that moment you miss it. As you say 'Devil!' you ought to strike me full in the face."

"Oh, don't be silly, Terriss," I said, "she's not a pugilist."

Of course I saw, apart from what was dramatically fit, what would happen.

However Marion, very young, very earnest, very dutiful, anxious to please Terriss, listened eagerly to the suggestion during an understudy rehearsal.

"No one could play this part better than your sister Nell," said Terriss to the attentive Marion, "but as I always tell her, she does miss one great effect. When Olivia says 'Devil!' she ought to hit me bang in the face."

"Thank you for telling me," said Marion gratefully.

"It will be much more effective," said Terriss.

It *was*. When the night came for Marion to play the part she struck out, and Terriss had to play the rest of the scene with a handkerchief held to his bleeding nose!

I think it was as Olivia that Eleonora Duse first saw me act. She had thought of playing the part herself some time, but she said: *"Never now!"* No letter about my acting ever gave me the same pleasure as this from her:

MADAME,—Avec Olivia vous m'avez donné bonheur et peine. *Bonheur* par votre art qui est noble et sincère ... *peine* car je sens la tristesse au cœur quand je vois une belle généreuse nature de femme, donner son âme à l'art—comme vous le faites—quand c'est la vie même, *votre* cœur même qui parle tendrement, douleureusement, noblement *sous* votre jeu. Je ne puis me débarrasser d'une certaine tristesse quand je vois des artistes si nobles et hauts tels que vous et Irving. ... Si vous êtes si forts de soumettre (avec un travail continu) la vie à l'art, il faut donc vous admirer comme des forces de la nature même qui auraient pourtant le droit de vivre pour elles-mêmes et non pour la foule. Je n'ose pas vous déranger, Madame, et d'ailleurs j'ai tant à faire aussi qu'il m'est impossible de vous dire de vive voix tout le grand plaisir que vous m'avez donné, mais puisque j'ai senti votre cœur, veuillez, chère Madame, croire au mien qui ne demande pas mieux dans cet instant que de vous admirer et de vous le dire tant bien que mal d'une manière quelconque. Bien à vous.

E. DUSE.

When I wrote to Duse the other day to ask her permission to publish this much-prized letter, she answered:

BUENOS AYRES,
September 11, 1907.

CHÈRE ELLEN TERRY,—

Au milieu du travail en Amérique, je reçois votre lettre envoyée à Florence.

Vous me demandez de publier mon ancienne lettre amicale. Oui, chère Ellen Terry; ce que j'ai donné vous appartient; ce que j'ai dit, je le peux encore, et je vous aime et admire comme toujours. ...

J'espère que vous accepterez cette ancienne lettre que j'ai rendue plus claire et un peu mieux écrite. Vous en serez contente avec moi car, ainsi faisant, j'ai eu le moyen de vous dire que je vous aime et de vous le dire deux fois.

A vous de cœur,
E. DUSE.

Dear, noble Eleanora Duse, great woman, great artist—I can never appreciate you in words, but I store the delight that you have given me by your work, and the personal kindness that you have shown me, in the treasure-house of my heart!

When I celebrated my stage jubilee you travelled all the way from Italy to support me on the stage at Drury Lane. When you stood near me, looking so beautiful with wings in your hair, the wings of glory they seemed to me, I could not thank you, but we kissed each other and you understood!

§ 3

"CLAP-TRAP" was the verdict passed by many on the Lyceum "Faust," yet Margaret was the part I liked better than any other—outside Shakespeare.

I played it beautifully sometimes. The language was often very common-place—not nearly as poetic or dramatic as that of "Charles I"—but the character was all right—simple, touching, real.

The Garden Scene I know was unsatisfactory. It was a bad, weak love-scene, but George Alexander as Faust played it admirably. Indeed he always acted like an angel with me; he was so malleable, ready to do anything. He was launched into the part at very short notice, after H. B. Conway's failure on the first night. Poor Conway! It was Coghlan as Shylock all over again.

Henry called a rehearsal the next day, a Sunday, I think. The company stood about in groups on the stage while Henry walked up and down, speechless, but humming a tune occasionally, always a portentous sign with him. The scene set was the Brocken Scene, and Conway stood at the top of the slope as far away from Henry as he could get! He looked abject. His handsome face was very red, his eyes full of tears. He was terrified at the thought of what was going to happen. The actor was summoned to the office, and presently Loveday came out and said that Mr George Alexander would play Faust the following night. Alec had been wonderful as Valentine the night before, and as Faust he more than justified Henry's belief in him. After that he never looked back. He had come to the Lyceum for the first time in 1882, an unknown actor from a stock company in Glasgow, to play Caleb Decie in "The Two Roses." He then left us for a time, returned for "Faust," and remained in the Lyceum company for some years playing all Terriss's parts.

Alexander had the romantic quality which was lacking in Terriss, but there was a kind of shy modesty about him which handicapped him when he played Squire Thornhill in "Olivia." "Be more dashing, Alec!" I used to say to him. "Well, I do my best," he said. "At the hotels I chuck all the barmaids under the chin, and pretend I'm a dog of a fellow for the sake of this part!" Conscientious, dear, delightful Alec! No one ever deserved success more than he did or used it better when it came, as the history of the St James's Theatre under his management proves. He had the good luck to marry a wife who was clever as well as charming, and could help him.

The original cast of "Faust" was never improved upon. What Martha was ever so good as Mrs Stirling? The dear old lady's sight had failed since "Romeo and Juliet," but she was very clever at concealing it. When she let Mephistopheles in at the door, she used to drop her work on the floor so that she could find her way back to her chair. I never knew why she dropped it—she used to do it so naturally with a start when Mephistopheles knocked at the door—until one night when it was in

184

my way and I picked it up, to the confusion of poor Mrs Stirling, who nearly walked into the orchestra.

"Faust" was abused a good deal as a pantomime, a distorted caricature of Goethe, and a thoroughly inartistic production. But it proved the greatest of all Henry's financial successes. The Germans who came to see it, oddly enough, did not scorn it nearly as much as the English who were so sensitive on behalf of the Germans, and the Goethe Society wrote a tribute to Henry Irving after his death, acknowledging his services to Goethe!

It is a curious paradox in the theatre that the play for which every one has a good word is often the play which no one is going to see, while the play which is apparently disliked and run down is crowded every night.

Our preparations for the production of "Faust" included a delightful "grand tour" of Germany. Henry, with his accustomed royal way of doing things, took a party which included my daughter Edy, Mr and Mrs Comyns Carr, and Mr Hawes Craven, who was to paint the scenery. We bought nearly all the properties used in "Faust" in Nuremberg, and many other things which we did not use, that took Henry's fancy. One beautifully carved escutcheon, the finest armorial device I ever saw, he bought at this time and presented it in after years to the famous American connoisseur, Mrs Jack Gardiner. It hangs now in one of the rooms of her house at Boston.

It was when we were going in the train along one of the most beautiful stretches of the Rhine that Sally Holland, who accompanied us as my maid, said:—

"Uncommon pretty scenery, dear, I must say!"

When we laughed, she added:

"Well, dear, _I_ think so!"

During the run of "Faust," Henry visited Oxford and gave his address on "Four Actors" (Burbage, Betterton, Garrick, Kean). He met there one of the many people who had recently been attacking him on the ground of too long runs and too much spectacle. He wrote me an amusing account of the duel between them:

I had supper last night at New College after the affair. A— was there, and I had it out with him—to the delight of all.

"_Too much decoration,_" etc., etc.

I asked him what there was in "Faust" in the matter of appointments, etc., that he would like left out?

Answer: Nothing.

"Too long runs."

"You, sir, are a poet," I said. "Perhaps it may be my privilege some day to produce a play of yours. Would you like it to have a long run or a short one?" (Roars of laughter.)

Answer: "Well—er—well, of course, Mr Irving, you—well—well, a short run, of course for *art*, but—"

"Now, sir, you're on oath," said I. "Suppose that the fees were rolling in £10 and more a night—would vou rather the play were a failure or a success?"

"Well, well, as *you* put it—I must say—er—I would rather my play had a *long* run!"

A— floored!

He has all his life been writing articles running down good work and crying up the impossible, and I was glad to show him up a bit!

The Vice-Chancellor made a most lovely speech after the address—an eloquent and splendid tribute to the stage.

Bourchier presented the address of the "Undergrads." I never saw a young man in a greater funk—because, I suppose, he had imitated me so often!

From the address:

"We have watched with keen and enthusiastic interest the fine intellectual quality of all these representations from Hamlet to Mephistopheles with which you have enriched the contemporary stage. To your influence we owe deeper knowledge and more reverent study of the master mind of Shakespeare."

All very nice indeed!

I never cared much for Henry's Mephistopheles—a twopence coloured part, anyway. Of course he had his moments—he had them in every part—but they were few. One of them was in the Prologue, when he wrote in the student's book, "Ye shall be as gods knowing good and evil." He never looked at the book, and the nature of the *spirit* appeared suddenly in a most uncanny fashion. Another was in the Spinning-wheel Scene when Faust defies Mephistopheles, and he silences him with, "*I am a spirit.*" Henry looked to grow a gigantic height—to hover over the ground instead of walking on it. It was terrifying.

I made valiant efforts to learn to spin before I played Margaret. My instructor was Mr Albert Fleming, who, at the suggestion of Ruskin, had recently revived hand-spinning and hand-weaving in the North of England. I had always hated that obviously "property" spinning-wheel in the opera, and Margaret's unmarketable thread. My thread always broke, and at last I had to "fake" my spinning to a certain extent; but at least I worked my wheel right, and gave an impression that I could spin my pound of thread a day with the best.

Two operatic stars did me the honour to copy my Margaret dress—Madame Albani and Madame Melba. It was rather odd, by the way, that many mothers who took their daughters to see the opera of "Faust" would not bring them to see the Lyceum play. One of these mothers was Princess Mary of Teck, a constant patron of most of our plays.

Other people "missed the music." The popularity of an opera will often kill a play, although the play may have existed before the music was ever thought of. The Lyceum "Faust" held its own against Gounod. I liked our incidental music to the action much better. It was taken from many different sources and welded into an effective and beautiful whole by our clever musical director, Mr Meredith Ball.

In many ways "Faust" was our heaviest production. About four hundred ropes were used, each rope with a name. The list of properties and instructions to the carpenters became a joke among the theatre staff. When Henry first took "Faust" into the provinces, the head carpenter at Liverpool, Myers by name, being something of a humorist, copied out the list on a long thin sheet of paper, which rolled up like a royal proclamation. Instead of "God save the Queen!" he wrote at the foot, with many flourishes: "God help Bill Myers!"

The crowded houses at "Faust" were largely composed of "repeaters," as Americans call those charming playgoers who come to see a play again and again. We found favour with the artists and musicians too, even in "Faust"! Here is a nice letter I got during the run from that gifted singer and good woman, Madame Antoinette Sterling:—

My dear Miss Terry,—

I was quite as disappointed as yourself that you were not at St James's Hall last Monday for my concert.... Jean Ingelow said she enjoyed the afternoon very much....

I wonder if you would like to come to luncheon some day and have a little chat with her? But perhaps you already know her. I love her dearly. She has one fault—she never goes to the theatre. Oh my! What she misses, poor thing, poor thing! We have already seen "Faust" twice, and are going again soon, and shall take the George Macdonalds this time. The Holman Hunts were delighted. He is one of the most interesting and clever men I have ever met, and she is very charming and clever too. How beautifully plain you write! Give me the recipe.

With many kind greetings,
Believe me sincerely yours,
Antoinette Sterling MacKinlay.

My girl Edy was one of the angels in the vision in the last act of "Faust," an event which Henry commemorated in a little rhyme that he sent me on Valentine's Day with some beautiful flowers:

> White and red roses,
> Sweet and fresh posies,
> One bunch for Edy, *Angel* of mine—
> One bunch for Nell, my dear Valentine.

Mr Toole produced a burlesque on the Lyceum "Faust," called "Faust-and-Loose." Henry did not care for burlesques as a rule and in this one he particularly disliked Fred Leslie's exact imitation of him. Face, spectacles, voice—everything was like Henry except the ballet-skirt Leslie wore. Marie Linden gave a really clever imitation of me as Margaret. She and her sister Laura both had the trick of taking me off. I recognised the truth of Laura's caricature in the burlesque of "The Vicar of Wakefield" when as Olivia she made her entrance, leaping impulsively over a stile!

There was an absurd chorus of girl "mashers" in "Faust-and-Loose," dressed in tight black satin coats, who besides dancing and singing had lines in unison, such as "No, no!" "We will!" As one of these girls Violet Vanbrugh made her first appearance on the stage. In her case "we will!" proved prophetic. It was her plucky "I will get on" which finally landed her in her present eminent position.

Violet Barnes was the daughter of Prebendary Barnes of Exeter, who, when he found his daughter stage-struck, behaved far more wisely than most parents. He gave her £100 and sent her to London with her old nurse to look after her, saying that if she really "meant business" she would find an engagement before the £100 was gone. Violet had inherited some talent from her mother, who was a very clever amateur actress, and the whole family were fond of getting up entertainments. But Violet didn't know quite how far £100 would go, or wouldnt go. I happened to call on her at her lodgings near Baker Street one afternoon, and found her having her head washed, and crying bitterly all the time! She had come to the end of the £100, she had not got an engagement, and thought she would have to go home defeated. There was something funny in the tragic situation. Vi was sitting on the floor, drying her hair, crying, and drinking port wine to cure a cold in her head!

I told her not to be a goose, but to cheer up and come and stay with me until something turned up. We packed the old nurse back to Devonshire. Violet came and stayed with me, and in due course something did turn up. Mr Toole came to dinner, and Violet, acting on my instructions to ask every one she saw for an engagement, asked Mr Toole! He said, "That's all right, my dear. Of course. Come down and see me tomorrow." Dear old Toole! The kindliest of men! Violet was with him for some time, and played at his theatre in Mr Barrie's first piece "Walker London." Seymour Hicks, and Mary Ansell (afterwards Mrs Barrie) were also in the cast.

This was all I did to "help" Violet Vanbrugh, now Mrs Arthur Bourchier and one of our best actresses, in her stage career. She helped herself, as most people do who get on. I am afraid that I have discouraged more stage aspirants than I have encouraged. Perhaps I have snubbed really talented people, so great is my horror of girls taking to the stage as a profession when they dont realise what they are about. I once told an elderly aspirant that it was quite useless for any one to go on the stage who had not either great beauty or great talent. She wrote saying that my letter had been a great relief to her, as now she was not discouraged. "I have *both.*"

§ 4

HENRY IRVING has often been attacked for not preferring Robert Louis Stevenson's "Macaire" to the version which he actually produced in 1883. It would have been hardly more unreasonable to complain of his producing "Hamlet" in preference to Mr Gilbert's "Rosencrantz and Guildenstern." Stevenson's "Macaire" may have all the literary quality that is claimed for it, but it is frankly a burlesque, a skit, a *satire* on the real Macaire. The Lyceum was *not* a burlesque house! Why should Henry have done it?

It was funny to see Toole and Henry rehearsing together for "Macaire." Henry was always *plotting* to be funny. When Toole as Jacques Strop hid the dinner in his pocket, Henry, after much labour, thought of his hiding the plate inside his waistcoat. There was much laughter later on when Macaire, playfully tapping Strop with his stick, cracked the plate, and the pieces fell out! Toole hadnt to bother about such subtleties, and Henry's deep-laid plans for getting a laugh must have seemed funny to dear Toole, who had only to come on and say "Whoop!" and the audience roared!

Henry's death as Macaire was one of a long list of splendid deaths. Macaire knows the game is up, and makes a rush for the French windows at the back of the stage. The soldiers on the stage shoot him before he gets away. Henry did not drop, but turned round, swaggered impudently down to the table, leaned on it, then suddenly rolled over, dead.

The production of Byron's "Werner" for one matinée was to do some one a good turn, and when Henry did a "good turn," he did it magnificently.[1] We rehearsed the play as carefully as if we were in for a long run. Beautiful dresses were made for me by my friend Alice Carr. But when we had given that one matinée, they were put away for ever. The play may be described as gloom, gloom, gloom. It was worse than "The Iron Chest."

[1] *From my Diary, June* 1, 1887.—"Westland-Marston Benefit at the Lyceum. A triumphant success entirely due to the genius and admirable industry and devotion of H. I., for it is just the dullest play to read as ever was! He made it *intensely* interesting."

189

While Henry was occupying himself with "Werner," I was pleasing myself with "The Amber Heart," a play by Alfred Calmour, a young man who was at this time Wills's secretary. I wanted to do it, not only to help Calmour, but because I believed in the play and liked the part of Ellaline. I had thought of giving a matinée of it at some other theatre, but Henry, who at first didnt like my doing it at all, said: "You must do it at the Lyceum. I cant let you, or it, go out of the theatre."

So we had the matinée at the Lyceum. Mr Willard and Mr Beerbohm Tree were in the cast, and it was a great success. For the first time Henry saw me act—a whole part from the "front" at least, for he had seen and liked scraps of my Juliet from the "side." Although he had known me such a long time, my Ellaline seemed to come quite as a surprise. "I wish I could tell you of the dream of beauty that you realised," he wrote after the performance. He bought the play for me, and I continued to do it "on and off" here and in America until 1902.

Many people said that I was good but the play was rubbish. This was hard on Alfred Calmour. He had created the opportunity for me, and few plays with the beauty of "The Amber Heart" have come my way since. "He thinks it's all his doing!" said Henry. "If he only knew!" "Well, that's the way of authors," I answered. "They imagine so much more about their work than we put into it, that although we may seem to the outsider to be creating, to the author we are, at our best, only doing our duty by him."

Our next production was "Macbeth." Meanwhile we had visited America three times. I must now give some account of my tours in America, of my friends there, and of some of the impressions that the vast, wonderful country made on me.

NOTES TO CHAPTER IX

1. *Ellen Terry and Stage Aspirants.* "To him that newly cometh to change his life, let not an easy entrance be granted, but as the Apostle saith: 'Try the spirits if they be of God'." This method, prescribed by St Benedict in his Rule, of testing the genuineness of a monastic vocation, was the method adopted by Ellen Terry of testing the genuineness of a stage vocation.

For example, when a young schoolgirl, resolved to become an actress, was brought to see Ellen Terry by her grandmother for advice, she was told to go away and study three important Shakespeare parts for at least a year. "Come back to me then, and we can begin to talk about your going on the stage." The girl had the grit not to be discouraged. She returned to Ellen Terry at the end of the year, not only word-perfect in the parts, but able to show that she had studied them with industry and intelligence. Then Ellen

Terry believed in her vocation for the stage, and helped her to adopt it as a profession.

She makes light of the help she gave Violet Vanbrugh, and does not mention any of the other actresses, now famous, to whom she was a generous friend in the hard days of their obscure novitiate. The American reader will be particularly interested to know that Lynn Fontanne, one of the most brilliant actresses on the American stage today, was taken into Ellen Terry's home in much the same way as Violet Vanbrugh at an earlier time, and "kept going" with little jobs, one of which was to read to Ellen Terry in the afternoons, until she had got a footing in the theatre. I have found an entry in one of Ellen Terry's diaries referring to the difficulty the youthful Lynn had in earning a living on the stage: "Must get Lynn more money. It's wicked . . . She is so intelligent."

Ellen Terry was not given to boasting, when some young actress, whose talent she had been swift to recognise and appreciate in her novice days, "made good," that she had discovered her. It is indeed a rather foolish habit, as the most any of us can do is to proclaim the talent that has discovered itself, and we have had the perspicacity to recognise. The homage due to Ellen Terry is for fearlessness in speaking her mind about talent in the early stages of its development. She spoke it with enthusiasm, but the enthusiasm was always tempered with good sense. For example, she wept for joy over the great talent displayed by a raw student in the Elocution class at the Royal Academy in the recitation of a speech from "Richard II"; then went home and wrote in her diary: "She has to work. Her life must be given to it, and then she will—well, she will achieve just as high as she works." The subsequent career of the student, Lena Ashwell, proved this a true prophecy.

2. *Werner.* The reference to Irving's production of Byron's "Werner" is interesting in view of Bernard Shaw's refusal to attend Irving's funeral in Westminster Abbey "on the public ground that Literature had no place at Irving's graveside." Literature was not so poorly represented in Irving's productions at the Lyceum as this implies. It is not even true that Irving entirely neglected contemporary dramatic literature. He produced three plays by Tennyson, a contemporary poet, a record, which, as the present Poet Laureate, John Masefield, like Tennyson, a dramatist, could testify, no actor today seems anxious to beat.

3. *The Amber Heart.* "Oh, the Amber Heart, the Amber Heart, the Amber Heart!" Shaw writes in a letter to Ellen Terry, his gorge rising more at each repetition. Yet out of this puerile piece, written in the tawdriest verse, loading with ornament sentiments of ludicrous banality, Ellen Terry contrived to create something beautiful and sincere. Michael Angelo is said by Vasari to have made a statue out of snow "which was superb," but that was nothing to Ellen Terry's feat in making a woman out of Calmour's sweetstuff.

4. *The Private Life of Ellen Terry in the 'Eighties.* Writing of the period when she was in the heyday of her popularity as an actress, Ellen Terry says little about her life outside the theatre. This seems the right place for a note on one of its occupations, the bringing up of her children. Arduous as her

work at the Lyceum was, she did not neglect her duty to them. She was all the same by no means a foolish fond mother. Her letters to her daughter (at the schoolgirl age), full of candid, yet helpful criticism, are sufficient proof that she was guiltless of "spoiling" her children, although in after years her son, conscious of having been consistently "spoiled" all his life by adoring women included his mother among them. After giving consideration to his conviction that "the blessed lady, my mother, no more knew how to bring up a boy than she knew how to swim," I find myself wondering whether the problem of bringing up this particular boy, whose character was indeterminate in his abnormally prolonged chrysalis days, would have been tackled more successfully by a father. The speculation reminds me that as a general rule men of genius in their childhood and adolescence have owed more to their mothers than to their fathers.

Ellen Terry, perhaps mindful of the holes left in her culture by her lack of ordinary education, sent the "little tots" of Longridge Road to school early. The school she chose was in Foxton Road, Earls Court; it was kept by a Mrs Cole, a lady with ideas which in the 'eighties were considered advanced. She was a supporter of the new women's movement, and thought that girls ought to have as good an education as boys. She also seems to have been a pioneer of co-education. She took pupils of both sexes. Among the schoolmates of Ellen Terry's tots at Foxton Road, were Walter Raleigh, three of the Sickerts, and the children of Sir Edwin Arnold. Edith Craig tells me that her brother and she, when they first entered the school, were the most backward of the pupils in all but drawing, music and Shakespeare. In 1883 when Ellen Terry went on her first American tour, Edy became a boarder at the school, which had grown in size and reputation and been moved into larger premises; her brother was sent to a school for boys only in Kent. Later the girl's education was continued in Gloucestershire at the home of Mrs Cole's sister, Mrs Malleson, and the boy's at Bradfield. The boy's was interrupted, or enriched, according to the point of view, by a tour in America. In Chicago in 1885 he played the small part of a gardener's boy in "Eugene Aram." "Why the dickens I was not kept to the stage from that time onwards if it was an actor they wanted, it is difficult to discover" he writes in 1932, and speculates it was because his mother was badly advised by friends who did not know that actors need not be sent to schools or colleges. Be that as it may—it is conceivable that Ellen Terry took advice, but not that she acted on it against her own convictions—Edward Wardell, as he was known in those chrysalis days was sent to school and college. From college (Heidelberg) he was also sent away, a punishment for an escapade, which owing to its innocent character, his mother thought far too severe. In 1889, at the age of seventeen, the boy who had been a failure at school and college, became a success on the stage. His first appearance in "The Dead Heart" is chronicled with pride by Ellen Terry in Chapter XII. His success suggests that even if an actor "need not be sent to school," it does him no harm.

Edith Craig, after her school-days in London and Gloucestershire, was sent to Germany to study music. Under Hollander in Berlin she made good progress as a pianist, but rheumatism, from which she had suffered from early childhood, settled the doubtful question of her vocation.

During this period of the children's education, to which, as I hope this note will show, Ellen Terry devoted more care than many a mother with no profession to distract her, there is evidence in her diaries and letters that they were never out of her thoughts. She could always find time to write to Edy, and those wise, tender, yet at times unsparingly critical letters, which have been carefully preserved, ought to be published one day for other reasons than that mothers and daughters alike could learn much from them. They show Ellen Terry as she was when the chameleon element in her nature, which made her swift to take the colour and form of some subjective image of her in another's mind, was passive. Edy from childhood seems to have been able to view her mother's personality objectively. This, I take it, is the explanation of the great simplicity and unpretentiousness of the relations between them.

I quote a few brief extracts from letters to Edy, written to her in Germany in the year 1887 when Ellen Terry was at the height of her fame and popularity. She could not at this time walk in the streets of London, or in those of other towns in England and Scotland, without being mobbed. This manifestation of public interest was not of the spurious kind, worked up by highly paid press-agents, with which we have become familiar since the day of the cinema dawned. Ellen Terry in the 'eighties did not know what an actress's press-agent was, and did not need one. She had not to court publicity. It wooed her spontaneously, and she did not snub its suit. She liked being "made a fuss of," as she put it, but was far too sensible to exaggerate its importance. There are few references to it in the letters to Edy.

In 1887 there is a question of Edy's accompanying her mother on her next American tour:

"And so America—the going to America is what you most desire? Well then, work away now. You must give up some of your present pleasures, and work at your German, and *speak* it. I shall not be able to gratify this wish of your heart, which is for your own pleasure, if you dont gratify the wish of *my* heart (which is for your own benefit) and make good use of the present time, and work."

Nevertheless, the mother is quite aware that all work and no play might make Edy a dull girl: what she fears is that the balance is uneven:

"My dearest, in the hope that you will work all the harder for this extra 'lark,' I send you the Sophia dress so that you may go to the Bal Masqué. It will arrive in a few days—a wig also."

Edy is only just eighteen at this time, and mindful of the free and easy life she had led as a child and her limited experience of the world outside her school, and the theatre, Ellen Terry adds:

"Remember you must be more reserved with a pack of folk you don't know *well* (and one changes one's first opinion of some people) than with old friends and people who know *you*. You know I used (long ago) to have to tell you to keep a little steadier in shops and places where strangers were about."

Another "remember" concerns Edy and her "bear-leader" in Germany, Mabel Malleson:

"Remember, my dear darling, not to (just from thoughtlessness) give too much trouble and anxiety to Mabel, for she is so very conscientious that you will have to guard against being selfish in regard to her, and if you only know this, and think of it, I'm in the best hopes you will remember not to forget! ... By the way I've asked the doctors, and you must on no account drink beer, even of the *smallest* kind! Claret, or any wine of the country, but not beer. (A glass once a moon would not hurt, just to *feel German!*)"

"Oh you bad girl about writing that letter to the German actor! Be careful, my pet. It's all well enough with N. I know him pretty well (know too that he's a young monkey) but be careful, for I would be vexed if some fool or other thought you vulgar.

Tell me something of how you like your life, and of the music and drawing—whether you think you'll get on well in these two things with your two new masters, and which you like best—*not* the personality of either of 'em, but let's hear of their attainments, and their teaching powers."

Ellen Terry in the rôle of Lord Chesterfield, which like other rôles she transfigured into something much better than itself, is seen in one of her most lovable aspects. Re-reading these letters after the lapse of years, Edith Craig said: "If I could have done all Mother advised me to do, been all she wanted me to be, I should now be a very splendid and wise woman."

Many of Ellen Terry's most enduring friendships were formed at this period. I have quoted in the preface a remark of Bernard Shaw's that one day it will be discovered that every famous man of the last quarter of the 19th century, provided he were a theatre-goer, was in love with Ellen Terry. Yet she was not exclusively attractive to the male. The young women of the 'eighties and 'nineties adored her. She is described in a notice of "The Amber Heart" as the "especial friend of her own sex," and an allusion is made to the girls in the audience "dressed up to the portrait of the graceful lady which is a treasured thing in most artistic homes." A great deal of this adoration may have been mere *Schwärmerei*, but some of it had deep roots. There were young women who persisted in "saying it with flowers," with presents, letters and poems too, until they had succeeded in making the personal acquaintance of their goddess. Some were rewarded at last by being admitted to the inner circle of intimate friends. By my Terry time, the beginning of the 20th century, they were firmly established there. Each one was convinced that she was *the* one, a conviction which became a nuisance to Ellen Terry, when some who held it exacted more of her than she could give. Yet even these misguided women who exaggerated their importance in her life, and often behaved selfishly and inconsiderately, were genuinely devoted to her, and their devotion, unlike that of the majority of her men friends, stood the test of time.

In the 'eighties, the man who was on terms of the closest intimacy with her was Henry Irving. She was, in the first phase of their friendship, his "leading lady" in life as well as in the theatre, and in both the position brought her mingled happiness and unhappiness. Even when the happiness predominated, she appears to have resented as a woman the egotism which as Irving's colleague in the theatre she could not help admiring. The original of the letter from him she quotes on page 232 expressing his sense of her value to him, and his contrition for appearing ungrateful for her advice and help, bears the pathetic comment in her writing: "How seldom!" But it was by no means seldom that he wrote to her lovingly and tenderly. If these letters were sincere, there can be no doubt that he loved her, although he loved himself and his calling as an actor, which were really inseparable, more. The nature of her affection for him is more obscure. Her analysis of his character, given at the end of Chapter XIII, suggests that she was repelled by some of his qualities. She admired him more as an actor and a worker than as a man. The frequent recurrence of an entry in her diary for 1887: "Quarrelled with Henry" makes one think that there was already a rift within the lute which was eventually to silence the incidental lovers' music in the drama of their friendship. Another recurring entry: "To the Grange with Henry to dinner" reminds me to add that in the late 'eighties Irving took a house with a large garden at Brook Green, rebuilt it and furnished it. He sometimes entertained his friends there, but never lived in it. The garden was laid out on the lines of Ellen Terry's garden at Harpenden, one sign of many that she cherished the memory of her Hertfordshire idyll.

Her children were christened and confirmed at this period. Lady Gordon, an old friend of Ellen Terry's, and Henry Irving, acted as godmother and godfather at the christening of the boy, the explanation of Henry and Gordon being added to the name Edward by which he had been called from infancy after his father. Edith received the additional names of Geraldine and Ailsa; Geraldine she derived from her godmother, Mrs Stephen Coleridge, Ailsa from Ailsa Craig. During a tour in Scotland in the early 'eighties, Ellen Terry, in the company of Henry Irving and her boy, had visited Ailsa Craig. "What a good stage name!" Ellen Terry said: "A pity *you* can't have it, Ted. I shall give it to Edy." It was given to Edy at her christening, by her godfather, Henry Irving, and the "Craig" was appended to her brother's Christian names also. Edy was known as "Ailsa Craig" when she first went on the stage. Subsequently, to avoid confusion with another actress who had taken the name, she dropped the "Ailsa," in favour of Edith.

A trait of Ellen Terry's, which cannot be ignored in any faithful and comprehensive study of her complex character, is illustrated by this entry in her diary after Edy's confirmation in Exeter Cathedral: "Edith confirmed today (January 11, 1887) by the Bishop of Exeter (Dr Bickersteth). A private single ceremony by the Bishop for Edith. Strange! Over thirty years ago Father and Mother (with Kate and me) *walked* (necessity!) from Bristol to Exeter, and now today my child is given half-an-hour's private talk with the Bishop before her confirmation, Praise God from whom *all* blessings flow."

5. The parts played by Ellen Terry during the period covered by Chapter IX were: Viola ("Twelfth Night," 1884); Margaret ("Faust," 1885); Peggy ("Raising the Wind," 1886); Ellaline ("The Amber Heart," 1887); Josephine ("Werner," 1887); Mary Jane ("Wool-Gathering," 1887).

CHAPTER X

AMERICA

§ 1

THE first time that there was any talk of my going to America was, I think, in 1874, when I was playing in "The Wandering Heir." Dion Boucicault wanted me to go, and dazzled me with figures, but I expect the cautious Charles Reade influenced me against accepting the engagement.

When I did go in 1883, I was thirty-five and had an assured position in my profession. It was the first of eight tours, seven of which I went with Henry Irving. The last was in 1907 after his death. I also went to America one summer on a pleasure trip. The tours lasted three months at least, seven months at most. After a rough calculation, I find that I have spent not quite five years of my life in America. Five out of sixty is not a large proportion, yet I often feel that I am half American. This says a good deal for the hospitality of a people who can make a stranger feel so completely at home in their midst. Perhaps it also says something for my adaptableness!

"When we do not speak of things with a partiality full of love, what we say is not worth being repeated." That was the answer of a courteous Frenchman who was asked for his impressions of a country. In any case it is imprudent to give one's impressions of America. The country is so vast and complex that even those who have amassed mountains of impressions soon find that there still are mountains more! I have lived in New York, Boston and Chicago for a month at a time, and have felt that to know any of these great cities even superficially would take a year. I have become acquainted with this and that class of American, but I realise that there are thousands of other classes that remain unknown to me.

I set out in 1883 from Liverpool on board the *Britannic* with the fixed conviction that I should never, never return. For six weeks before we started, the word America had only to be breathed to me, and I burst into floods of tears! I was leaving my children, my bullfinch, my parrot, my "aunt" Boo, whom I never expected to see alive again, just because she said I never would; and I was going to face the unknown dangers

of the Atlantic and of a strange, barbarous land. Our farewell performances in London had cheered me up a little—though I wept copiously
at every one—by showing us that we should be missed. Henry Irving's
position seemed to be confirmed and ratified by all that took place before
his departure. The dinners he had to eat, the speeches that he had to
make and to listen to, were really terrific!

One speech at the Rabelais Club had, it was said, the longest perora-
tion on record. It was this kind of thing: Where is our friend Irving
going? He is not going like Nares to face the perils of the far North.
He is not going like A—— to face something else. He is not going to
China, etc.,—and so on. After about the hundredth "he is not going,"
Lord Houghton, who was one of the guests, grew very impatient and
interrupted the orator with: "Of course he isnt! He's going to New York
by the Cunard Line. It'll take him about a week!"

Many people came to see us off at Liverpool, but I only remember
seeing Mrs Langtry and Oscar Wilde. It was at this time that Oscar
Wilde had begun to curl his hair in the manner of the Prince Regent.
"Curly hair to match the curly teeth," said some one who disliked him.
Oscar Wilde *had* ugly teeth, and he was not proud of his mouth. He used
to put his hand to his mouth when he talked so that it should not be
noticed. His brow and eyes were very beautiful.

Well, I was not "disappointed in the Atlantic," as Oscar Wilde was
the first to say, though many people have said it since.

My first voyage was a voyage of enchantment to me. The ship was
laden with pig-iron, and she rolled and rolled and rolled. She could
never roll too much for me! I have always been a splendid sailor, and I
feel jolly at sea. The sudden leap from home into the wilderness of
waves does not give me any sensation of melancholy.

What I thought I was going to see when I arrived in America I
hardly remember. I had a vague idea that American women wore red
flannel shirts and carried bowie knives, and that I might be sandbagged
in the street! From somewhere or other I had derived an impression
that New York was an ugly, noisy place.

Ugly! When I first saw that marvellous harbour I nearly cried—it
was so beautiful. Whenever I come now to the unequalled approach to
New York I wonder what Americans must think of the approach from
the sea to London! How different are the mean, flat, marshy banks of
the Thames and the wooden toy lighthouse at Dungeness to the vast,
spreading Hudson with its busy multitude of steamboats, and ferryboats,
its wharf upon wharf, and its tall statue of Liberty dominating all the
racket and bustle of the sea traffic of the world!

That was one of the few times in America when I did not miss the poetry of the past. The poetry of the present, gigantic, colossal and enormous, made me forget it. The "sky-scrapers"—what a brutal name it is when one comes to think of it!—so splendid in the landscape now, did not exist in 1883, but I find it difficult to divide my early impressions from my later ones. There was Brooklyn Bridge though, hung up high in the air like a vast spider's web.

Between 1883 and 1893 I noticed a great change in New York and other cities. In ten years they seemed to have grown with the energy of tropical plants. But between 1893 and 1907 I saw no evidence of such feverish increase. It is possible that the Americans are arriving at a stage when they can no longer beat the records! There is a vast difference between one of the old New York brownstone houses and one of the fourteen-storied buildings near the river, but between this and the Times Square Building or the still more amazing Flatiron Building, which is said to oscillate at the top—it is so far from the ground—there is very little difference. I hear that they are now beginning to build downwards into the earth, but this will not change the appearance of New York for a long time.

I had not to endure the wooden shed in which most people landing in America have to struggle with the Custom-house officials—a struggle as brutal as a "round in the ring," as Paul Bourget describes it. We were taken off the *Britannic* in a tug, and Mr Abbey, Laurence Barrett, and many other friends met us—including the much-dreaded reporters.

They were not a bit dreadful, but very quick to see what kind of a man Henry was. In a minute he was on the best of terms with them. He assumed what I used to call his best "Jingle" manner—a manner full of refinement, bonhomie, elegance and geniality.

"Have a cigar—have a cigar." That was the first remark of Henry's, which put every one at ease. He also wanted to be at ease and have a good smoke. It was just the right merry greeting to the press representatives of a nation whose sense of humour is far more to be relied on than its sense of reverence.

"Now come on, all of you!" he said to the interviewers. He talked to them all in a mass and showed no favouritism. It says much for his tact and diplomacy that he did not "put his foot in it." The Americans are suspicious of servile adulation from a stranger, yet are very sensitive to criticism.

"These gentlemen want to have a few words with you," said Henry to me when the reporters had done with him. Then with a mischievous expression he whispered: "Say something pleasant! Merry and bright!"

Merry and bright! I felt it! The sense of being a stranger entering a strange land, the rushing sense of loneliness and foreignness was overpowering my imagination. I blew my nose hard and tried to keep back my tears, but the first reporter said: "Can I send any message to your friends in England?"

I answered: "Tell them I never loved 'em so much as now," and burst into tears! No wonder that he wrote in his paper that I was a "woman of extreme nervous sensibility." Another of them said that "my figure was spare almost to attenuation." America soon remedied that. I began to put on flesh before I had been in the country a week, and it was during my fifth American tour that I became really fat for the first time in my life.

When we landed I drove to the Hotel Dam, Henry to the Brevoort House. There was no Diana on the top of the Madison Square Building then. The building did not exist, to cheer the heart of a new arrival as the first evidence of beauty in the city. There were horse trams instead of cable cars, but a quarter of a century has not altered the peculiarly dilapidated carriages in which one drives from the dock, the muddy sidewalks, and the cavernous holes in the cobble-paved streets. Had the elevated railway, the first sign of *power* that one notices after leaving the boat, begun to thunder over the streets? I cannot remember New York without it.

I missed then, as I miss now, the numberless *hansoms* of London plying in the streets for hire. People in New York get about in the tram cars, unless they have their own carriages. The hired carriage is rare and takes advantage of the lack of competition to charge two dollars (8s.) for a journey which in London would not cost fifty cents (2s.)!

I cried for two hours at the Hotel Dam! Then my companion, Miss Harries, came bustling in with: "Never mind! here's a piano!" and sat down and played "Annie Laurie" very badly until I screamed with laughter. Before the evening came my room was a bower of roses, and my dear friends in America have been throwing bouquets at me in the same lavish way ever since. I had quite cheered up when Henry came to take me to see some minstrels who were performing at the Star Theatre, the very theatre where in a few days we were to open. I didnt understand many of the jokes which the American comedians made that night, but I liked their dry, cool way of making them.

§ 2

THERE were very few theatres in New York when we first went there. All that part of the city which is now "up town" did not exist, and what was then "up" is now more than "down" town. The American stage has changed almost as much. In those days their most distinguished

200

actors were playing Shakespeare or old comedy, and their new plays were chiefly "imported" goods. Even then there was a liking for local plays which showed the peculiarities of the different States, but they were more violent and crude than now. The original American genius and the true dramatic pleasure of the people is, I believe, in such plays, where very complete observation of certain phases of American life and very real pictures of manners are combined with comedy almost childlike in its naïveté. The sovereignty of the young girl which is such a marked feature in social life is reflected in American plays.

This is by the way.

What I want to make clear is that in 1883 there was no living American drama as there is now, that such productions of romantic plays and Shakespeare as Henry Irving brought over from England were unknown, and that the extraordinary success of our first tours would be impossible now. We were the first and we were pioneers, and we were *new*. To be new is everything in America.

Such palaces as the Hudson Theatre, New York, were not dreamed of when we were at the Star, which was, however quite equal to any theatre in London in front of the footlights. The stage itself, the lighting appliances, and the dressing-rooms were inferior.

Henry made his first appearance in America in "The Bells." He was not at his best on the first night, but he could be pretty good even when he was not at his best. I watched him from a box. Nervousness made the company very slow. The audience was a splendid one—discriminating and appreciative. We felt that the Americans *wanted* to like us. We felt in a few days so extraordinarily at home. The first sensation of entering a foreign city was quickly wiped out.

The difference in atmosphere disappears directly one understands it. I kept on coming across duplicates of "my friends in England." "How this girl reminds me of Alice." "How like that one is to Gill!" We had transported the Lyceum three thousand miles—that was all.

On the second night in New York it was my turn. "Command yourself. This is the time to show you can act!" I said to myself as I went on to the stage of the Star Theatre, dressed as Henrietta Maria. But I could not command myself. I played badly and cried too much in the last act. But the people liked me, and they liked the play, perhaps because it is historical; and the Americans are passionately fond of history. The audience took up many points which had been ignored in London. I had always thought Henry as Charles I most moving when he made that involuntary effort to kneel to his subject, Moray, but the Lyceum audiences had never seemed to notice it. In New York the audience burst out into the most sympathetic spontaneous applause that I have ever heard in a theatre.

I know that there are some advanced stage reformers who think applause "vulgar," and would suppress it in the theatre if they could. If they ever succeed they will suppress a great deal of good acting. It is said that the American actor, Edwin Forrest, once walked down to the footlights and said to the audience very gravely and sincerely: "If you dont applaud, I cant act," and I do sympathise with him. Applause is an instinctive, unconscious act expressing the sympathy between actors and audience. Just as our art demands more instinct than intellect in its exercise, so we demand of those who watch us an appreciation of the simple unconscious kind which finds an outlet in clapping rather than the cold, intellectual approval which would self-consciously think applause derogatory. I have yet to meet the actor who was *sincere* in saying that he disliked applause.

§ 3

My impression of the way American women dressed in 1883 was not favourable. Some of them wore Indian shawls and diamond earrings. They dressed too grandly in the street and too dowdily in the theatre. All this has changed. The stores in New York are now the most beautiful in the world, and the women are dressed to perfection. They are as clever at the *demi-toilette* as the Parisian, and the extreme neatness and smartness of their street clothes are very refreshing after the floppy, blowsy, trailing dresses, accompanied by the inevitable feather boa of which English girls now seem so fond. The universal white "waist" is very pretty and trim on the American girl. It is one of the distinguishing marks of a land of the free, a land where "class" hardly exists. The girl in the store wears the white waist; so does the rich girl on Fifth Avenue. It may cost anything from seventy-five cents to fifty dollars!

London when I come back from America always seems at first like an ill-lighted village, strangely tame, peaceful and backward. Above all, I miss the sunlight of America, and the clear blue skies of an evening.

"Are you glad to get back?" said an English friend.

"Very."

"It's a land of vulgarity, isnt it?"

"Oh yes, if you mean by that a wonderful land—a land of sunshine and light, of happiness, of faith in the future!" I answered. I saw no misery or poverty there. Every one looked happy. What hurts me on coming back to England is the *hopeless* look on so many faces; the dejection and apathy of the people standing about in the streets. Of course there is poverty in New York, but not among the Americans. The Italians, the Russians, the Poles—all the host of immigrants washed in daily on the bosom of the Hudson—these are poor, but you dont see them unless you go Bowery-ways, and even then you cant help feeling that in their sufferings there is always hope. The barrow man of today is the millionaire of tomorrow! Vulgarity? I saw little of it. I thought that the people who had amassed large fortunes used their wealth beautifully.

When a man is rich enough to build himself a big new house, he remembers some old house which he once admired, and he has it imitated with all the technical skill and care that can be had in America. This accounts for the odd jumble of styles in Fifth Avenue, along the lakeside in Chicago, in the new avenues in St Louis and elsewhere. One millionaire's house is modeled on a French château, another on an old Colonial house in Virginia, another on a monastery in Mexico, another is like an Italian palazzo. And these imitations are never weak or pretentious. The architects in America seem to me to be far more able than ours, or else they have a freer hand and more money. It is sad to remember that Mr Stanford White was one of the best of these splendid architects.

It was Stanford White with Saint-Gaudens—that great sculptor, whose work dignifies nearly all the great cities in America—who had most to do with the Exhibition buildings of the World's Fair in Chicago in 1893. It was odd to see that fair dream city rising out of the lake, so far more beautiful in its fleeting beauty than the Chicago of the stockyards and the Pit which had provided the money for its beauty. The millionaires did not interfere with the artists at all. They gave their thousands—and stood aside. The result was one of the loveliest things conceivable. Saint-Gaudens and the rest did their work as well as though the buildings were to endure for centuries instead of being burned in a year to save the trouble of pulling them down!

Saint-Gaudens gave me a cast of his medallion of Bastien-Lepage, and wrote to a friend of mine that "Bastien had 'le cœur au métier.' So has Miss Terry, and I will place that saying in the frame that is to replace the present unsatisfactory one." He was very fastidious about this frame, and took a lot of trouble to get it right. It must have been very irritating to Saint-Gaudens when he fell a victim to that extraordinary official puritanism which sometimes exercises a petty censorship over works of art in America. The medal that he made for the World's Fair was rejected at Washington because it had on it a beautiful little nude figure of a boy holding an olive branch, emblematical of young America.

I think a commonplace wreath and some lettering were substituted.

Saint-Gaudens did the fine bas-relief of Robert Louis Stevenson which was chosen for the monument in St Giles' Cathedral, Edinburgh. He gave my daughter a medallion cast from this, because he knew that she was a great lover of Stevenson. The bas-relief was dedicated to his friend Joe Evans. I knew Saint-Gaudens first through Joe Evans, an artist who, while he lived, was to me and to my daughter the dearest of all in America. His character was so fine and noble—his nature so perfect. Many were the birthday cards he did for me, original in design, beautiful in execution. Whatever he did he put the best of himself into it. I wrote to my daughter soon after his death:—

I heard on Saturday that our dear Joe Evans is dangerously ill. Yesterday came the worst news. Joe was not happy, but he was just heroic, and this world wasn't half good enough for him. I keep on getting letters about him. He seems to have been so glad to die. It was like a child's funeral, I am told, and all his American friends seem to have been there—Saint-Gaudens, Taber, etc. A poem about the dear fellow by Mr. Gilder has one very good line in which he says the grave "might snatch a brightness from his presence there." I thought that was very happy, the love of light and gladness being the most remarkable thing about him, the dear sad Joe.

Robert Taber, the actor, dear, and rather sad too, was a great friend of Joe's. They both came to me first in the shape of a little book in which was inscribed, "Never anything can be amiss when simpleness and duty tender it." "Upon this hint I spake," the book began. It was all the work of a few boys and girls who from the gallery of the Star Theatre, New York, had watched Irving's productions and learned to love him and me. Joe Evans had done a lovely picture by way of frontispiece of a group of eager heads hanging over the gallery's edge, his own and Taber's among them. Eventually Taber came to England and acted with Henry Irving in "Peter the Great."

Like his friend Joe, he too was heroic. His health was bad and his life none too happy—but he struggled on. His career was cut short by consumption, and he died in the Adirondacks in 1904.

I cannot speak of all my friends in America, or anywhere, for the matter of that, *individually*. My personal friends are so many, and they are *all* wonderful—wonderfully staunch to me! I have "tried" them so, and they have never given me up as a bad job.

My first friends of all in America were Mr Bayard, afterwards the American Ambassador in London, and his sister, Mrs Benoni Lockwood, her husband and their children. Now after all these years they are still my friends, and I can hope for none better to the end.

William Winter, poet and critic, was one of the first to write of

Henry with whole-hearted appreciation. But all the criticism in America, favourable and unfavourable, surprised us by the scholarly knowledge it displayed. In Chicago the notices were worthy of the *Temps* or the *Journal des Débats*. There was no attempt to force the personality of the writer into the foreground nor to write a style that should attract attention to the critic and leave the thing criticised to take care of itself. William Winter, and, of late years, Alan Dale, have had their personalities associated with their criticisms, but they are exceptions. Curiously enough the art of acting appears to bore most dramatic critics, the very people who might be expected to be interested in it. The American critics, however, at the time of our early visits, were keenly interested, and showed it by their observation of many points which our English critics had passed over. For instance, writing of "Much Ado about Nothing," one of the American critics said of Henry in the Church Scene that "something of him as a subtle interpreter of doubtful situations was exquisitely shown in the early part of this fine scene by his suspicion of Don John—felt by him alone, and expressed only by a quick covert look, but a look so full of intelligence as to proclaim him a sharer in the secret with his audience."

"Wherein does the superiority lie?" wrote another critic, in comparing our productions with those which had been seen in America up to 1884. "Not in the amount of money expended, but in the amount of brains;—in the artistic intelligence and careful and earnest pains with which every detail is studied and worked out. Nor is there any reason why Mr Irving or any other foreigner should have a monopoly of either intelligence or pains. They are common property, and one man's money can buy them as well as another's. The defect in the American manager's policy heretofore has been that he has squandered his money upon high salaries for a few of his actors, and costly, because unintelligent, expenditure for mere dazzle and show."

William Winter soon became a great personal friend of ours, and visited us in England. He was another of the *sad* people I met in America. He could have sat upon the ground and told "sad stories of the deaths of kings" with the best. He was very familiar with the poetry of the *immediate* past—Cowper, Coleridge, Gray, Wordsworth, Shelley, Keats, and the rest. He *liked* us, so everything we did was right to him. He could not help being guided entirely by his feelings. If he disliked a thing, he had no use for it. Some men can say, "I hate this play, but of its kind it is admirable." Willie Winter could never take that point of view. In England he loved going to see graveyards, and knew where every poet was buried.

His children came to stay with me in London. When we were all coming home from the theatre one night after "Faust" (the year must have been 1886) I said to little Willie:

"Well, what do you think of the play?"

"Oh my!" said he, "it takes the cake."

"Takes the *cake!*" said his little sister scornfully. "It takes the ice-cream!"

"Wont you give me a kiss?" said Henry to the same young miss one night. "No, I *wont* with all that blue stuff on your face." (He was made up for Mephistopheles.) Then, after a pause: "But why—why don't you *take* it!" She was only five years old at the time!

§ 4

For "quite a while" during the first tour I stayed in Washington with my friend Miss Olive Seward, and all the servants of that delightful household were coloured. This was my first introduction to the negroes, whose presence, perhaps more than anything else in the country, makes America seem foreign to European eyes. They are more sharply divided into high and low types than white people, and are not in the least alike in their types. It is safe to call any coloured man "George." They all love it, perhaps because of George Washington, and most of them are really named George. I never met such perfect service as they can give. *Some* of them are delightful. The beautiful voice of the "darkey" is so attractive, so soothing, and they are so deft and gentle. Some of the women are beautiful, and all the young appeared to me to be well-formed. As for the babies! I washed two or three little piccaninnies when I was in the South, and the way they rolled their gorgeous eyes at me was "too cute," or, as we should say in British-English, "fascinating."

At this Washington house, the servants danced a cake-walk for me—the coloured cook, a magnificent type, who "took the cake," saying: "That was because I chose a good handsome boy to dance with, Missie."

They sang too. Their voices were beautiful—with such illimitable power, yet as sweet as treacle.

The little page-boy had a pet of a woolly head. Henry once gave him a tip—"fee," as they call it in America—and said: "There, that's for a new wig when this one is worn out," gently pulling the astrakhan-like hair. The tip would have bought him many wigs, I think!

"Why, Uncle Tom, how your face shines tonight!" said my hostess to one of the very old servants.

"Yes, Missie, glycerine and rose-water, Missie!"

He had taken some from her dressing-table to shine up his face in honour of me! A shiny complexion is considered a great beauty among the negroes! The dear old man! He was very bent and very old; and looked like one of the logs that he used to bring in for the fire—a log from some hoary, lichened tree whose life was long since past. He would produce a pin from his head when you wanted one; he had them stuck in his pad of white woolly hair: "Always handy then, Missie," he would say.

"Ask them to sing 'Sweet Violets,' Uncle Tom."

He was acting as a sort of master of the ceremonies at the entertainment the servants were giving me.

"Dont think they know dat, Miss Olly."

"Why, I heard them singing it the other night!" And she hummed the tune.

"Oh, dat was 'Sweet Vio-*letts,*' Miss Olly!"

Washington was the first city I had seen in America where the people did not hurry, and where the social life did not seem entirely the work of women. The men asserted themselves here as something more than machines in the background untiringly turning out the dollars, while their wives and daughters give luncheons and teas at which only women are present.

Beautifully as the women dress, they talk very little about clothes. I was much struck by their culture—by the evidence that they had read far more and developed a more fastidious taste than most young English-women. Yet it is all mixed up with extraordinary naïvety.

The vivacity, the appearance, at least, of reality, the animation, the energy of American women delighted me. They are very sympathetic, too, in spite of a certain callousness which comes of regarding everything in life, even love, as "lots of fun." I did not think that they, or the men either, had much natural sense of beauty. They admire beauty in a curious way through their intellect. Nearly every American girl has a cast of the Winged Victory of the Louvre in her room. She makes it a point of her education to admire it.

There! I am beginning to generalise—the very thing I made a resolution to avoid. How silly to generalise about a country which embraces such extremes of climate as the sharp winter winds of Boston and New York and the warm winter winds of Florida which blow through palms and orange groves!

NOTES TO CHAPTER X

1. *The First American Tour.* Abbey, the impresario who persuaded Irving to visit America for the first time in 1883, made a clear profit of £50,000 out of the enterprise. The profit Irving made is not mentioned by any of his biographers, not even by Bram Stoker who as his business-manager must have

known the figures. It is improbable that they were dazzling, for Irving's expenses were enormous. He brought with him to America all the scenery and properties of his productions, as well as the entire company and staff from the Lyceum. Such a princely method of touring could not have been very profitable, but it had the effect of giving Henry Irving and Ellen Terry a position in America which they might never have attained by their acting alone. Their position in England was by this time one of great eminence. Before they left for America a farewell banquet was given to Irving by representative Englishmen of distinction at the old St James's Hall, a building which has long since vanished from Piccadilly. In 1883, such banquets were for men only; but women were graciously permitted to listen to post-prandial speeches from a gallery set apart for them in banqueting halls. Round this gallery at the St James's Hall, Ellen Terry, strangely excluded, according to modern ideas, from the dinner, moved after it was over, to the sound of the loudest cheers and applause of the evening. "A fairer vision than Ellen Terry, then at the zenith of her loveliness, cannot be imagined. She shone with no shallow sparkle or glitter, but with a steady radiance that filled the room, and had the peculiar quality of making everybody else invisible." (Graham Robertson)

2. *Sandbagging*. Writing in 1906, Ellen Terry obviously thought her vague notion in 1883 that she might be sandbagged in the street in America, utterly ridiculous. In 1932 it does not strike us like that.

3. *Stanford White*. Before Ellen Terry had finished her book Stanford White was murdered. She was in New York at the time of the trial of Harry Thaw. (1906)

4. The procedure I have followed up to now of giving a list of the parts played by Ellen Terry during the period covered by each chapter, cannot be applied either to this chapter or to Chapter XI in which the American tours are described. It is resumed after Chapter XII. The only new part which Ellen Terry ever played in America was Yolande in Laurence Irving's "Godefroi and Yolande" in 1895.

CHAPTER XI

AMERICA (*Continued*)

§ 1

IT is only human to make comparison between American and English institutions, although they are likely to turn out as odious as the proverb says! The first institution in America that distressed me was the steam heat. It is far more manageable now than it was, both in hotels and theatres, because there are more individual heaters. But how I suffered from it at first I cannot describe! I used to feel dreadfully ill, and when we could not turn the heat off at the theatre, the plays always went badly. My voice was affected too. At Toledo once, it nearly went altogether. Then the next night, after a good fight for it, we got the theatre cooler, and the difference that it made to the play was extraordinary. I was in my best form, feeling well and jolly!

No wonder the Americans drink ice-water and wear very thin clothes indoors. Their rooms are hotter than ours ever are, even in the height of the summer—when we have a summer! But no wonder, either, that Americans in England shiver at our cold, draughty rooms. They are brought up in hot-houses.

If I did not like steam heat, I loved the ice which is such a feature at American meals. Everything is served on ice, and the ice-water, however pernicious the European may consider it as a drink, looks charming and cool in the hot rooms.

I liked the travelling; but then we travelled in a very princely fashion. The Lyceum company and the baggage occupied eight cars, and Henry's private parlour car was lovely. The only thing that we found was better understood in England, so far as railway travelling is concerned, was *privacy*. You may have a *private* car in America, but all the conductors on the train, and there is one to each car, can walk through it. So can any official, baggage man, or newsboy, who has the mind!

The "parlour car" in America is more luxurious than our first class, but you travel in it (if you have no "private" car) with thirty other people.

"What do you want to be private for?" asks an American, and you dont know how to answer, for you find that with them privacy means concealment. For this reason, I believe, they dont have hedges or walls round their estates and gardens. "Why should we? We have nothing to hide!"

In the cars, as in the rooms at one's hotel, the "cuspidor" is always with you as a thing of beauty! When I first went to America the "Ladies' Entrance" to the hotel was really necessary, because the ordinary entrance was impassable! Since then very severe laws against spitting in public places have been passed, and there is a *great* improvement. But the habit, I suppose due to the dryness of the climate, or to the very strong cigars smoked, or to chronic catarrh, or to a feeling of independence—"This is a free country and I can spit if I choose!"—remains sufficiently disgusting to a stranger visiting the country.

The American voice is the one thing in the country that I find unbearable; yet the worst variety does not exist in many states. The Southern voice is very low in tone and soothing, like the "darkey" voice. It is as different from Yankee as the Yorkshire burr is from the Cockney accent.

This question of accent is a very funny one. I had not been in America long when a friend said to me:

"We like your voice. You have so little English accent!"

This struck me as rather cool. Surely English should be spoken with an *English* accent, not with a French, German, or double-dutch one! Then I found that what they meant by an English accent was an English affectation of speech—a drawl with a tendency to "aw" and "ah" everything. They thought that every one in England, who did not miss out aspirates where they should be, and put them in where they should not be, talked of "the rivah," "ma brothar," and so on. Their conclusion was, after all, quite as well founded as ours about *their* accent. The American intonation, with its freedom from violent emphasis, is, I think, rather pretty when the quality of the voice is sweet.

Of course the Americans would have their jokes about Henry's method of speech. Ristori followed us once in New York, and a newspaper man said he was not sure whether she or Mr Irving was the more difficult for an American to understand.

"He pronounces the English tongue as it is pronounced by no other man, woman or child," wrote the critic, and proceeded to give a phonetically spelled version of Irving's delivery of Shylock's speech to Antonio.

> Wa thane, ett no eperes
> Ah! um! yo ned m'elp
> Ough! ough! Gaw too thane! Ha! um!
> Yo com'n say
> Ah! Shilok, um! ouch! we wode hev moanies!

I wonder if this American newspaper man stopped to think how *his* delivery of the same speech would look in print! As for the ejaculations, the interjections and grunts with which Henry interlarded the text, they often helped to reveal the meaning of Shakespeare to his audience—a meaning which many a perfect elocutionist has left perfectly obscure. The use of "m' " or "me" for "my" has often been hurled in my face as a reproach, but I never contracted "my" without good reason. I had a line in "Olivia" which I began by delivering as—

My sorrows and my shame are my own.

Then I saw that the "mys" sounded comic and abbreviated the two first ones into "me's."

§ 2

It has been said that the Americans did not like Irving as an actor, and that they only accepted him as a manager, that he triumphed in New York as he had done in London, through his lavish spectacular effects. This is all moonshine. Henry made his first appearance in "The Bells," his second in "Charles I," his third in "Louis XI." By that time he had conquered, and without the aid of anything at all notable in the mounting of the plays. It was not until we did "The Merchant of Venice" that he gave the Americans anything of a "production."

My first appearance in America in Shakespeare was as Portia, and I could not help feeling pleased by my success. A few weeks later I played Ophelia at Philadelphia. It is in Shakespeare that I have been best liked in America, and I consider that Beatrice was the part which met with most enthusiasm there.

During our first tour we visited in succession New York, Philadelphia, Boston, Baltimore, Brooklyn, Chicago, Cincinnati, St Louis, Detroit, and Toronto. To most of these places we paid return visits.

"To what do you attribute your success, Mr Irving?"

"To my acting," was the simple reply.

We never had poor houses except in Baltimore and St Louis. Our journey to Baltimore was made in a blizzard. They were clearing the snow before us all the way from New Jersey, and we took forty-two hours to reach Baltimore! The bells of trains before us and behind us sounded very alarming. We opened in Baltimore on Christmas Day. The audience was wretchedly small, but the poor things who were there had left their warm firesides to drive or tramp through the slush of melting snow, and each one who managed to reach the theatre was worth a hundred on an ordinary night.

At the hotel I put up holly and mistletoe, and produced from my trunks a real Christmas pudding that my mother had made. We had it for supper, and it was very good.

It never does to repeat an experiment. Next year at Pittsburgh my little son Teddy brought me out another pudding from England. For once we were in an uncomfortable hotel, and the Christmas dinner was deplorable. It began with *burned hare soup.*

"It seems to me," said Henry, "that we aren't going to get anything to eat, but we'll make up for it by drinking!"

He had brought his own wine out with him from England, and the company took him at his word and *did* make up for it!

"Never mind!" I said, as the soup was followed by worse and worse. "There's my pudding!"

It came on blazing, and looked superb. Henry tasted it.

"Very odd," he said, "but I think this is a camphor pudding."

He said it so politely, as if he might easily be mistaken!

My maid in England had packed the pudding with my furs! It simply reeked of camphor.

So we had to dine on Henry's wine and L. F. Austin's wit. This brilliant man, now dead, acted for many years as Henry's secretary, and one of his gifts was the happy knack of hitting off people's peculiarities in rhyme. This dreadful Christmas dinner at Pittsburgh was enlivened by a collection of such rhymes, which Mr. Austin called a "Lyceum Christmas Play."

Every one roared with laughter until it came to the verse of which he was the victim, when suddenly he found the fun rather poor!

The first verse was spoken by Loveday, who announces that the "Governor" has a new play which is *"Wonderful!"*, a great word of Loveday's.

George Alexander replies:

> But I say, Loveday, have I got a part in it,
> That I can wear a cloak in and look smart in it?
> Not that I care a fig for gaudy show, dear boy—
> But juveniles must *look* well, don't you know, dear boy.
> And shall I lordly hall and tuns of claret own?
> And may I murmur love in dulcet baritone?
> Tell me at least, this simple fact of it—
> Can I beat Terriss hollow in one act of it? [1]

[1] Alexander had just succeeded Terriss as our leading young man.

Photograph by Crook, Edinburgh

SIR HENRY IRVING

Norman Forbes:

Pooh for Wenman's bass![1] Why should he make a boast of it?
If he has a voice, I have got the ghost of it!
When I pitch it low, you may say how weak it is,
When I pitch it high, heavens! what a squeak it is!
But I never mind; for what does it signify?
See my graceful hands, they're the things that dignify;
All the rest is froth, and egotism's dizziness—
Have I not played with Phelps?
    (*To Wenman*)
    I'll teach you all the business!

T. Mead:

(Of whom much has already been written in these pages.)

"What's this about a voice? Surely you forget it, or
Wilfully conceal that *I* have no competitor!
I do not know the play, or even what the title is,
But safe to make success a charnel-house recital is!
So please to bear in mind, if I am not to fail in it,
That Hamlet's father's ghost must rob the Lyons Mail in it!
No! that's not correct! But you may spare your charity—
A good sepulchral groan's the thing for popularity!"

H. Howe:

(The "agricultural" actor, as Henry called him.)

Boys, take my advice, the stage is not the question,
But whether at three score you'll all have my digestion.
Why yearn for plays, to pose as Brutuses or Catos in,
When you may get a garden to grow the best potatoes in?
You see that at my age by Nature's shocks unharmed I am!
Tho' if I sneeze but thrice, good heavens, how alarmed I am!
But act your parts like men, and tho' you all great sinners are,
You're sure to act like men wherever Irving's dinners are!

J. H. Allen (our prompter):

Whatever be the play, *I* must have a hand in it,
For wont I teach the supers how to stalk and stand in it?
Tho' that blessed Shakespeare never gives a ray to them,
I explain the text, and then it's clear as day to them!
Plain as A B C is a plot historical,
When *I* overhaul allusions allegorical!
Shakespeare's not so bad; he'd have more pounds and pence in
    him,
If actors stood aside, and let me show the sense in him!

[1] Wenman had a rolling bass voice of which he was very proud. He was a valuable actor,
yet somehow never interesting. Young Norman Forbes-Robertson played Sir Andrew Ague-
cheek with us on our second American tour.

Once when Allen was rehearsing the supers in the Church Scene in "Much Ado about Nothing," we overheard him "show the sense" in Shakespeare like this:

"This 'Ero let me tell you is a perfect lady, a nice, innercent young thing, and when the feller she's engaged to calls 'er an 'approved wanton,' you naturally claps yer 'ands to yer swords. A wanton is a kind of —well, you know she ain't what she ought to be!"

Allen would then proceed to read the part of Claudio:

... not to knit my soul to an approved wanton.

Seven or eight times the supers clapped their " 'ands to their swords" without giving Allen satisfaction.

"No, no, no, that's not a bit like it, not a bit! If any of your sisters was 'ere and you 'eard me call 'er a ——, would yer stand gapin' at me as if this was a bloomin' tea party?"

Louis Austin's little "Lyceum Play" was presented to me with a silver tea-service, a souvenir from the gentlemen of the company, and ended up with the following pretty lines spoken by Katie Brown, a clever little girl who played all the small pages' parts at this time:

Although I'm but a little page,
    Who waits for Portia's kind behest,
Mine is the part upon this stage
    To tell the plot you have not guessed.

Dear lady, oft in Belmont's hall,
    Whose mistress is so sweet and fair,
Your humble slaves would gladly fall
    Upon their knees, and praise you there.

To offer you this little gift,
    Dear Portia, now we crave your leave,
And let it have the grace to lift
    Our hearts to yours this Christmas eve.

And so we pray that you may live
    Thro' many, many, happy years,
And feel what you so often give—
    The joy that is akin to tears!

How nice of Louis Austin! It quite made up for my mortification over the camphor pudding!

Pittsburgh has been called "hell with the lid off," and other insulting names. I have always thought it beautiful, especially at night when its furnaces make it look like a city of flame. The lovely park that the city has made on the heights that surround it is a lesson to Birmingham, Sheffield, and our other black towns. George Alexander said that Pittsburgh reminded him of his native town of Sheffield. "Had he said Birmingham, now instead of Sheffield," wrote a Pittsburgh newspaper man, "he would have touched our tender spot exactly. As it is, we can be as cheerful as the Chicago man was who boasted that his sweetheart 'came pretty near calling him "honey," ' when in fact she had called him 'old Beeswax!' "

When I played Ophelia for the first time in Chicago, I played the part better than I had ever played it before, and I don't believe I ever played it so well again. *Why*, it is almost impossible to say. I had heard a good deal of the crime of Chicago, that the people were a rough, murderous, sand-bagging crew. I ran on to the stage in the mad scene, and never have I felt such sympathy! This frail wraith, this poor demented thing, could hold them in the hollow of her hand...It was splendid! "How long can I hold them?" I thought: "For ever!" Then I laughed. That was the best Ophelia laugh of my life.

At the risk of being accused of indiscriminate flattery I must say that I liked *all* the American cities. Every one of them has a joke at the expense of the others. They talk in New York of a man who lost both his sons—"One died and the other went to live in Philadelphia." Pittsburgh is the subject of endless jibes, and Chicago is "the limit." To me, indeed, it seemed "the limit"—of the industry, energy, and enterprise of man. In 1812 this vast city was only a frontier post, Fort Dearborn. In 1871 the town that first rose on these great plains was burned to the ground. The growth of the present Chicago began when I was a grown woman. I have celebrated my jubilee. Chicago will not do that for another fifteen years!

I never visited the stock-yards. Somehow I had no curiosity to see a live pig turned in fifteen minutes into ham, sausages, hair-oil, and the binding for a Bible! I had some dread of being made sad by the spectacle of so much slaughter—of hating the Chicago of the "abattoir" as much as I had loved the Chicago of the Lake with the white buildings of the World's Fair shining on it, the Chicago built on piles in splendid isolation in the middle of the prairie, the Chicago of Marshall Field's beautiful palace of a store, the Chicago of my dear friends, the Chicago of my son's first appearance on the stage! Was it not a Chicago man who wrote of my boy, tending the roses in the stage garden in "Eugene Aram," that he was "a most beautiful lad"!

His eyes are full of sparkle, his smile is a ripple over his face, and his laugh is as cheery and natural as a bird's song. . . . This Joey is Miss Ellen Terry's son, and the apple of her eye. On this Wednesday night, January

14, 1885, he spoke his first lines upon the stage. His mother has high hopes of this child's dramatic future. He has the instinct and the soul of art in him. Already the theatre is his home. His postures and his playfulness with the gardener, his natural and graceful movement, had been the subject of much drilling, of study and practice. He acquitted himself beautifully and received the wise congratulations of his mother, of Mr. Irving, and of the company.

That is the nicest newspaper notice I have ever read!

At Chicago I made my first speech. The Haverley Theatre, at which we first appeared in 1884, was altered and rechristened the "Columbia" in 1885. I was called upon for a speech after the special performance in honour of the occasion, consisting of scenes from "Charles I," "Louis XI," "The Merchant of Venice," and "The Bells," had come to an end. I think it must be the shortest speech on record:

Ladies and Gentlemen, I have been asked to christen your beautiful theatre. "Hail Columbia!"

§ 3

When we acted in Brooklyn we used to stay in New York and drive over that wonderful bridge every night. There were no trolley cars on it then. I shall never forget how it looked in winter, with the snow and ice on it—a gigantic trellis of dazzling white, as incredible as a dream. The old stone bridges were works of *art*. This bridge, woven of iron and steel for a length of over 500 yards, and hung high in the air over the water so that great ships can pass beneath it, is the work of *science*. It looks as if it had been built by some power, not by men at all.

It was during our week at Brooklyn in 1885 that Henry was ill, too ill to act for four nights. Alexander played Benedick, and got through it wonderfully well. Then old Mr Mead did (*did* is the word) Shylock. There was no intention behind his words or what he did.

I had such a funny batch of letters on my birthday that year. "Dear, sweet Miss Terry, etc., etc. Will you give me a piano?" !! etc., etc. Another: "Dear Ellen. Come to Jesus. Mary." Another, a lovely letter of thanks from a poor woman in the most ghastly distress, and lastly an offer of a *two years'* engagement in America. There was a simple coming in for one woman acting at Brooklyn on her birthday!

Brooklyn is as sure of a laugh in New York as the mother-in-law in a London music hall. "All cities begin by being lonesome," a comedian explained, "and Brooklyn has never gotten over it."

My only complaint against Brooklyn was that they would not take Fussie in at the hotel there. Fussie, during these early American tours, was still *my* dog. Later on he became Henry's. He had his affections alienated by a course of chops, tomatoes, strawberries, asparagus, biscuits soaked in champagne, and a beautiful fur rug of his very own presented by the Baroness Burdett-Coutts!

How did I come by Fussie? I went to Newmarket with Rosa Corder, whom Whistler painted. She was one of those plain-beautiful women who are so far more attractive than some of the pretty ones. She had wonderful hair—like a fair, pale veil, a white, waxen face, and a very good figure; and she wore very odd clothes. She had a studio in Southampton Row, and another at Newmarket where she went to paint horses. I went to Cambridge once and drove back with her across the heath to her studio.

"How wonderfully different are the expressions on terriers' faces," I said to her, looking at a painting of hers of a fox-terrier pup. "That's the only sort of dog I should like to have."

"That one belonged to Fred Archer," Rosa Corder said. "I daresay he could get you one like it."

We went out to find Archer. Curiously enough I had known the famous jockey at Harpenden when he was a little boy, and I believe used to come round with vegetables.

"I'll send you a dog, Miss Terry, that wont be any trouble. He's got a very good head, a first-rate tail, stuck in splendidly, but his legs are too long. He'd follow you to America!"

Prophetic words! On one of our departures for America, Fussie was left behind by mistake at Southampton. He could not get across the Atlantic, but he did the next best thing. He found his way back from there to his own theatre in the Strand, London!

Fred Archer sent him originally to the stage-door at the Lyceum. The man who brought him out from there to my house in Earl's Court said:

"I'm afraid he gives tongue, Miss. He dont like music anyway. There was a band at the bottom of your road, and he started hollering."

We were at luncheon when Fussie made his first entry into the family circle, and I very quickly saw his *stomach* was his fault. He had a great dislike to "Charles I"; we could never make out why. Perhaps it was because Henry wore armour in one act—and Fussie may have barked his shins against it. Perhaps it was the firing off of the guns; but more probably it was because the play once got him into trouble. As a rule Fussie had the most wonderful sense of the stage, and at rehearsal would skirt the edge of it, but never cross it. But at Brooklyn one night when we were playing "Charles I"—the last act, and that most pathetic part of it where Charles is taking a last farewell of his wife and children— Fussie, perhaps excited by his run over the bridge from New York, sud-

217

denly bounded on to the stage! The good children who were playing Princess Mary and Prince Henry didn't even smile; the audience remained solemn, but Henry and I nearly went into hysterics. Fussie knew directly that he had done wrong. He lay down on his stomach, then rolled over on his back, whimpering an apology—while carpenters kept on whistling and calling to him from the wings. The children took him up to the window at the back of the scene, and he stayed there cowering between them until the end of the play.

America seems to have been always fatal to Fussie. Another time when Henry and I were playing in some charity performance in which John Drew and Maude Adams were also acting, he disgraced himself again. Henry having "done his bit" and put on hat and coat to leave the theatre, Fussie thought the end of the performance must have come; the stage had no further sanctity for him, and he ran across it to the stage door barking! John Drew and Maude Adams were playing "A Pair of Lunatics." Maude Adams, who was sitting looking into the fire at the moment, did not see Fussie, and was amazed to hear John Drew departing madly from the text:

> Is this a dog I see before me,
> His tail towards my hand?
> Come, let me clutch thee.

She began to think that he had really gone mad!

When Fussie first came, Charlie was still alive, and I have often gone into Henry's dressing-room and seen the two dogs curled up in both the available chairs, Henry *standing* while he made up, rather than disturb them!

When Charlie died, Fussie had Henry's idolatry all to himself. I have caught them often sitting quietly opposite each other at Grafton Street, just adoring each other! Occasionally Fussie would thump his tail on the ground to express his pleasure.

Wherever we went in America the hotel people wanted to get rid of the dog. In the paper they had it that Miss Terry asserted that Fussie was a little terrier, while the hotel people regarded him as a pointer, and funny caricatures were drawn of a very big me with a very tiny dog, and a very tiny me with a dog the size of an elephant! Henry often walked straight out of an hotel where an objection was made to Fussie. If he wanted to stay, he had recourse to strategy. At Detroit the manager of the hotel said that dogs were against the rules. Being very tired Henry let Fussie go to the stables for the night, and sent Walter to look after him. The next morning he sent for the manager.

"Yours is a very old-fashioned hotel, isnt it?"

"Yes, sir, very old and ancient."

"Got a good chef? I didnt think much of the supper last night; but still—the beds are comfortable enough. I am afraid you dont like animals?"

"Yes, sir, in their proper place."

"It's a pity," said Henry meditatively, "because you happen to be overrun by rats!"

"Sir, you must have made a mistake. Such a thing couldnt—"

"Well, I couldnt pass another night here without my dog," Henry interrupted. "But there are, I suppose, other hotels?"

"If it will be any comfort to you to have your dog with you, sir, do by all means, but I assure you he'll catch no rats here."

"I'll be on the safe side," said Henry calmly.

And so it was settled. That very night Fussie supped off, not rats, but terrapin and other delicacies in Henry's private sitting-room.

After that long separation, the year Fussie was left behind at Southampton, Henry naturally thought that the dog would go nearly mad with joy when he saw him again. He described the meeting in a letter to me.

My dear Fussie gave me a terrible shock on Sunday night. When we got in, J——, Hatton, and I dined at the Café Royal. I told Walter to bring Fussie there. He did, and Fussie burst into the room while the waiter was cutting some mutton, when, what d'ye think—one bound at me—another instantaneous bound at the mutton, and from the mutton nothing would get him until he'd got his plateful.

Oh, what a surprise it was indeed! He never now will leave my side, my legs, or my presence, but I cannot but think, alas, of that seductive piece of mutton!

Poor Fussie! He met his death through the same weakness. It was at Manchester, I think. A carpenter had thrown down his coat with a ham sandwich in the pocket, over an open trap on the stage. Fussie, nosing and nudging after the sandwich, fell through and was killed instantly. When they brought up the dog after the performance, every man took his hat off ... Henry was not told until the end of the play.

He took it so very quietly that I was frightened, and said to his son Laurence who was on that tour:

"Do let's go to his hotel and see how he is."

We drove there and found him sitting eating his supper with the poor dead Fussie, who would never eat supper any more, curled up in his rug on the sofa. Henry was talking to the dog exactly as if it were alive. The next day he took Fussie back in the train with him to London, covered with a coat. He is buried in the dogs' cemetery, Hyde Park.

His death made an enormous difference to Henry. Fussie was his constant companion. When he died, Henry was really alone. He never spoke of what he felt about it, but it was easy to know.

We used to get hints how to get this and that from watching Fussie! His look, his way of walking! He *sang*, whispered eloquently and low —then barked suddenly and whispered again! Such a lesson in the law of contrasts!

The first time that Henry went to the Lyceum after Fussie's death, every one was anxious and distressed, knowing how he would miss the dog in his dressing-room. Then an odd thing happened. The wardrobe cat, who had never been near the room in Fussie's lifetime, came down and sat on Fussie's cushion! No one knew how the "Governor" would take it. But when Walter was sent out to buy some meat for it, we saw that Henry was not going to resent it! From that night onwards the cat always sat night after night in the same place, and Henry liked its companionship. In 1902, when he left the theatre for good, he wrote to me:

The place is now given up to the rats—all light cut off, and only Barry [1] and a fireman left. Everything of mine I've moved away, including the Cat!

§ 4

I HAVE never been to America yet without going to Niagara. The first time I saw the great falls I thought it all more wonderful than beautiful. I got away by myself from my party, and looked and looked at it, and I listened—and at last it became dreadful and I was *frightened* at it. I wouldnt go alone again, for I felt queer and wanted to follow the great flow of it. But at twelve o'clock, with the "sun upon the topmost height of the day's journey," most of Nature's sights appear to me to be at their plainest. In the evening, when the shadows grow long and all hard lines are blurred, how soft, how different, everything is! It was noontide, that garish cruel time of day, when I first came in sight of the falls. I'm glad I went again in other lights—but one should live by the side of all this greatness to learn to love it. Only once did I catch Niagara in *beauty*, with pits of colour in its waters, no one colour definite. All was wonderment, allurement, fascination. The last time I was there it was wonderful, but not beautiful any more. The merely stupendous, the merely marvellous, has always repelled me. The great cañons give me unrest, just as the long low lines of my Sussex marshland near Winchelsea give me rest.

At Niagara William Terriss slipped and nearly lost his life. At night

_____
[1] The stage-door keeper.

when he appeared as Bassanio, he shrugged his shoulders, lowered his eyelids, and said to me—

"Nearly gone, dear,"—he would call everybody "dear"—"But Bill's luck! Tempus fugit!"

What tempus fugit had to do with it, I dont quite know!

When we were first in Canada I tobogganed at Rosedale. I should say it was like flying! The start! Amazing! "Farewell to this world," I thought, as I felt my breath go. Then I shut my mouth, opened my eyes, and found myself at the bottom of the hill in a jiffy—"over hill, over dale, thorough bush, thorough briar!" I rolled right out of the toboggan when we stopped. A very nice Canadian man was my escort, and he helped me up the hill afterwards. I didnt like *that* part of the affair quite so much.

Henry Irving would not come, much to my disappointment. He said that quick motion through the air always gave him the ear-ache. He had to give up swimming (his old Cornish Aunt Penberthy told me he delighted in swimming as a boy) because it gave him most violent pains in the ear.

§ 5

PHILADELPHIA, as I first knew it, was the most old-world place I saw in America, except perhaps Salem. Its red-brick side-walks, the trees in the streets, the low houses with their white marble cuffs and collars, the pretty design of the place, all give it a character of its own. The people, too, have a character of their own. They dress, or at least *did* dress, very quietly. This was the only sign of their Quaker origin, except a very fastidious taste—in plays as in other things.

Mrs Gillespie, the great-grandchild of Benjamin Franklin, was one of my earliest Philadelphia friends—a splendid type of the independent woman, a bit of a martinet, but immensely full of kindness and humour. She had a word to say in all Philadelphia matters. It would be difficult to imagine a greater contrast to Mrs Gillespie of Philadelphia than Mrs Fields of Boston, that other great American lady whom to know is a liberal education.

Mrs Fields reminded me of Lady Tennyson, Mrs Tom Taylor, and Miss Hogarth (Dickens's sister-in-law) all rolled into one. Her house is full of relics of the past. There is a portrait of Dickens as a young man with long hair. He had a feminine face in those days, for all its strength. Hard by is a sketch of Keats by Severn, with a lock of the poet's hair. Opposite is a head of Thackeray, with a note in his hand-writing fastened below. "Good-bye, Mrs Fields; good-bye, my dear Fields; good-bye to all. I go home."

Thackeray left Boston abruptly because a sudden desire to see his children had assailed him at Christmas time!

As you sit in Mrs Fields' spacious room overlooking the Bay, you realise suddenly that before you ever came into it, Dickens and Thackeray were both here, that this beautiful old lady who so kindly smiles on you has smiled on them and on many other great men of letters long since dead. It is here that they seem most alive. This is the house where the culture of Boston seems no fad to make a joke about, but a rare and delicate reality.

This—and Fen Court, the home of that wonderful woman Mrs Jack Gardiner, who represents the present worship of beauty in Boston as Mrs Fields represents its former worship of literary men. Fen Court is a house of enchantment, a palace, and Mrs Gardiner is like a great princess in it. She has "great possessions" indeed, but her most rare one, to my mind, is her beautiful voice, even though I remember her garden by moonlight with the fountain playing, her books and her pictures, the Sargent portrait of herself presiding over one of the most splendid of those splendid rooms, where everything great in old art and new art is represented. What a portrait it is! Some one once said of Sargent that "behind the individual he finds the real, and behind the real, a whole social order."

He has painted "Mrs Jack" in a tight-fitting black dress with no ornament but her world-famed pearl necklace round her waist, and on her shoes rubies like drops of blood. The daring, intellectual face seems to say: "I have acquired everything that is worth acquiring, through the energy and effort and labour of the country in which I was born."

Mrs Gardiner's house filled me with admiration, but if I want rest and peace I just think of the houses of Mrs James Fields and Oliver Wendell Holmes. He was another personage in Boston when I first went there. Oh, the visits I inflicted on him—yet he always seemed pleased to see me, the cheery, kind man. It was generally winter when I called on him. At once it was "four feet upon a fender!" Four feet upon a fender was his idea of happiness, he told me, during one of these lengthy visits of mine to his house in Beacon Street.

He came to see us in "Much Ado about Nothing" and, next day sent me some little volumes of his work with a lovely inscription on the front page. I miss him very much when I go to Boston now.

In New York, how much I miss Mrs Beecher I could never say. The Beechers were the most wonderful pair. What an actor he would have made! He read scenes from Shakespeare to Henry and me at luncheon one day. He sat next to his wife, and they held hands nearly all the while; I thought of that time when the great preacher was tried, and all through the trial his wife showed the world her faith in his innocence by sitting by his side and holding his hand.

He was indeed a great preacher. I have a little faded card in my possession now: "Mrs Henry W. Beecher." "Will ushers of Plymouth Church please seat the bearer in the Pastor's pew." And in the Pastor's pew I sat, listening to that magnificent bass-viol voice with its persuasive low accent, its torrential scorn! After the sermon I went to the Beechers' home. Mr Beecher sat with a saucer of uncut gems by him on the table. He ran his hand through them from time to time, held them up to the light, admiring them and speaking of their beauty and colour as eloquently as an hour before he had spoken of sin and death and redemption.

He asked me to choose a stone, and I selected an aquamarine. He had it splendidly mounted for me in Venetian style to wear in "The Merchant of Venice." Once when he was ill, he told me, his wife had some few score of his jewels set up in lead—a kind of small stained-glass window—and hung up opposite his bed. "It did me more good than the doctor's visits," he said.

Mrs Beecher was very remarkable. She had a way of lowering her head and looking at you with a strange intentness, gravely, kindly, and quietly. At her husband she looked a world of love, of faith, of undying devotion. She was fond of me, although I was told she disliked women generally and had been brought up to think all actresses children of Satan. Obedience to the iron rules which had always surrounded her had endowed her with extraordinary self-control. She would not allow herself ever to feel heat or cold, and could stand any pain or discomfort without a word of complaint.

She told me once that when she and her sister were children, a friend had given them some lovely bright blue silk, and as the material was so fine they thought they would have it made up a little more smartly than was usual in their sombre religious home. In spite of their father's hatred of gaudy clothes, they ventured on a little "V" at the neck, hardly showing more than the throat; but still, in a household where blue silk itself was a crime, it was a bold venture. They put on the dresses for the first time for five o'clock dinner, stole downstairs with trepidation, rather late, and took their seats as usual one on each side of their father. He was eating soup and never looked up. The little sisters were relieved. He was not going to say anything.

No, he was not going to say anything, but suddenly he took a ladleful of the hot soup and dashed it over the neck of one sister; another ladleful followed quickly on the neck of the other.

"Oh, father, you've burned my neck!"

"Oh, father, you've spoiled my dress!"

"Oh, father, why did you do that?"

"I thought you might be cold," said the severe father significantly and malevolently.

That a woman who had been brought up like this should form a friendship with me naturally caused a good deal of talk. But what did she care! She remained my true friend until her death, and wrote to me constantly when I was in England—such loving, wise letters, full of charity and simple faith. In 1889, after her husband's death, I wrote to her and sent my picture, and she replied:

MY DARLING NELLIE,—

You cannot know how it soothes my extreme heart-loneliness to receive a token of remembrance, and word of cheer from those I have faithfully loved, and who knew and reverenced my husband. . . . Ellen Terry is very sweet as Ellaline, but dearer far as my Nellie.

§ 6

THE Daly players were a revelation to me of the pitch of excellence which American acting had reached. My first night at Daly's was a night of enchantment. I wrote to Mr Daly and said: "You've got a girl in your company who is the most lovely, humourous darling I have ever seen on the stage." It was Ada Rehan! Now of course I didn't "discover" her or any rubbish of that kind; the public were already mad about her, but I did know her for what she was, even in that brilliant "all-star" company and before she had played in the classics and won enduring fame. The audacious, superb, quaint, Irish creature! Never have I seen such splendid high comedy! Then the charm of her voice—a little like Ethel Barrymore's when Miss Ethel is speaking very nicely—her smiles and dimples, and provocative, inviting coquetry. Her Rosalind, her Country Wife, her Helena, her performance in "The Railroad of Love"! And above all, her Katharine in "The Taming of the Shrew"! I can only exclaim, not explain! Directly she came on I knew how she was going to do the part. She had such shy, demure fun. She understood, like all great comedians, that you must not pretend to be serious so sincerely that no one in the audience sees through it!

As a woman off the stage Ada Rehan was even more wonderful than as a shrew on. She had a touch of dignity, of nobility, of beauty, rather like Eleonora Duse's. The mouth and the formation of the eye were lovely. Her guiltlessness of make-up off the stage was so attractive! She used to come in to a supper party with a lovely shining face which scorned a powder puff. The only thing one missed was the red hair which seemed such a part of her on the stage. Here is a dear letter from the dear, written in 1890:

My dear Miss Terry,—
Of course the first thing I was to do when I reached Paris was to write and thank you for your lovely red feathers. One week is gone. Today it rains and I am compelled to stay at home, and at last I write. I thought you had forgotten me and my feathers long ago. So imagine my delight when they came at the very end. I liked it so. It seemed as if I lived all the time in your mind: and they came as a good-bye.

I saw but little of you, but in that little I found no change. That was gratifying to me, for I am over-sensitive, and would never trouble you if you had forgotten me. How I shall prize those feathers—Henry Irving's, presented by Ellen Terry to me for my Rosalind Cap. I shall wear them once and then put them by as treasures. Thank you so much for the pretty words you wrote me about "As You Like It." I was hardly fit on that matinee. The great excitement I went through during the London season almost killed me. I am going to try and rest, but I fear my nerves and heart wont let me.

You must try and read between the lines all I feel. I am sure you can if any one ever did, but I cannot put into words my admiration for you—and that comes from deep down in my heart. Good-bye, with all good wishes for your health and success.

I remain

Yours most affectionately,

ADA REHAN.

I wish I could just once have played with Ada Rehan. When Mr Tree could not persuade Mrs Kendal to come and play in "The Merry Wives of Windsor" a second time, I hoped that Ada Rehan would come and rollick with me as Mrs Ford—but it was not to be.

Mr Daly himself interested me greatly. He was an excellent manager, a man in a million. But he had no artistic sense. His productions of Shakespeare at Daly's were really bad from the pictorial point of view. But what pace and ensemble he got from his company!

John Drew, the famous son of a famous mother, was another Daly player whom I loved. With what loyalty he supported Ada Rehan! He never played for his own hand but for the good of the piece. His mother, Mrs John Drew, had the same quiet methods as Mrs Alfred Wigan. Everything that she did told. I saw Mrs Drew play Mrs Malaprop, and it was a lesson to people who overact. Her daughter, Georgie Drew, Ethel Barrymore's mother, was also a charming actress. Maurice Barrymore was a brilliantly clever actor. Little Ethel, as I still call her, though she is a big "star," is carrying on the family traditions. She ought to play "Lady Teazle." She may take it from me that she would make a great success in it.

During my more recent tours in America Maude Adams is the actress of whom I have seen most, and "to see her is to love her!" In "The Little Minister" and in "Quality Street" I think she is at her best, but above all parts she herself is most adorable. She is just worshipped in America, and has an extraordinary effect—an *educational* effect upon all American girls.

I never saw Mary Anderson act. That seems a strange admission, but during her reign at the Lyceum Theatre, which she rented from Henry Irving, I was in America, and another time when I might have seen her act I was very ill and ordered abroad. I have, however, had the great pleasure of meeting her, and she has done me many little kindnesses. Hearing her praises sung on all sides, and her beauties spoken of everywhere, I was particularly struck by her modest evasion of publicity *off* the stage. I personally know her only as a most beautiful woman—as kind as beautiful—constantly working for her religion—*always* kind, a good daughter, a good wife, a good woman.

She cheered me before I first sailed for America by saying that her people would like me.

"Since seeing you in Portia and Letitia," she wrote, "I am convinced you will take America by storm." Certainly *she* took *England* by storm! But she abandoned her triumphs almost as soon as they were gained. They never made her happy, she once told me, and I could understand her better than most, since I had had success too, and knew that it did not mean happiness. I have a letter from her, written from St Raphael soon after her marriage. It is nice to think that she is just as happy now as she was then—that she made no mistake when she left the stage, where she had such a brief and brilliant career.

GRAND HOTEL DE VALESCURE,
ST RAPHAEL, FRANCE.

DEAR MISS TERRY,—

I am saying all kinds of fine things about your beautiful work in my book—which will appear shortly; but I cannot remember the name of the small part you made so attractive in the "Lyons' Mail." It was the first one I had seen you in, and I wish to write my delightful impression of it.

Will you be so very kind as to tell me the name of your character and the two Mr Irving acted so wonderfully in that play?

There is a brilliant blue sea before my windows, with purple mountains as a background and silver-topped olives and rich green pines in the middle distance. I wish you could drop down upon us in this golden land for a few days' holiday from your weary work.

226

I would like to tell you what a big darling my husband is, and how perfectly happy he makes my life—but there's no use trying.

The last time we met I promised you a photo—here it is! One of my latest! And wont you send me one of yours in private dress? DO!

Forgive me for troubling you, and believe me your admirer

MARY ANDERSON DE NAVARRO.

Henry and I were so fortunate as to gain the friendship and approval of Dr Horace Howard Furness, perhaps the finest Shakespearean scholar in America, and editor of the "Variorum Shakespeare," which Henry considered the best of all editions—"the one which counts." It was in Boston, I think, that I disgraced myself at one of Dr Furness's lectures. He was discussing "As You Like It" and Rosalind, and proving with much elaboration that English in Shakespeare's time was pronounced like a broad country dialect, and that Rosalind spoke Warwickshire! A little girl who was sitting in the row in front of me had lent me her copy of the play a moment before, and now, absorbed in Dr Furness's argument, I forgot the book wasn't mine and began scrawling controversial notes in it with my very thick and blotty fountain pen.

"Give me back my book! Give me my book!" screamed the little girl. "How dare you write in my book!" She began to cry with rage.

Her mother tried to hush her up: "Dont, darling. Be quiet! It's Miss Ellen Terry."

"I don't care! She's spoilt my book!"

I am glad to say that when the little girl understood, she forgave me; and the spoilt book is treasured very much by a tall Boston young lady of eighteen who has replaced the child of seven years ago!

§7

In November, 1901, I wrote in my diary: "*Philadelphia.*—Supper at Henry's. Jefferson there, sweeter and more interesting than ever—and younger."

Dear Joe Jefferson—actor, painter, courteous gentleman, *profound* student of Shakespeare! When the Bacon-Shakespeare controversy was raging in America (it really *did* rage there!) Jefferson wrote the most delicious doggerel about it. He ridiculed the Bacon fanatics, and his ridicule was the more effective because it was barbed with erudition.

He said that when I first came into the box to see him as "Rip" he thought I did not like him, because I fidgeted and rustled and moved my place, as is my wicked way. "But I'll get her, and I'll hold her," he said to himself. I was held indeed—enthralled.

In manner Jefferson was a little like Norman Forbes-Robertson. Perhaps that was why the two took such a fancy to each other. When Norman was walking with Jefferson one day, some one who met them said:

"Your son?"

"No," said Jefferson, "but I wish he were! The young man has such good manners!"

§ 8

OUR first American tours were in 1883 and 1884; the third in 1887-88, the year of the great blizzard. Henry fetched us at half-past ten in the morning! His hotel was near the theatre where we were to play at night. He said the weather was stormy, and we had better make for his hotel while there was time! The German actor Ludwig Barnay was to open in New York that night, but the blizzard affected his nerves to such an extent that he did not appear at all, and returned to Germany directly the weather improved!

Most of the theatres closed for three days, but ours remained open, although there was a famine in the town and the streets were impassable. The cold was intense. Henry sent Walter out to buy some violets for Barnay, and when he brought them in to the dressing room—he had only carried them a few yards—they were frozen so hard that they could have been chipped with a hammer!

We rang up on "Faust" three-quarters of an hour late! This was not bad considering our difficulties. Although the house was sold out, there was hardly any audience, and only a harp and two violins in the orchestra. Discipline was so strong in the Lyceum company that every member of it reached the theatre by eight o'clock, although some of them had had to walk from Brooklyn Bridge.

The Mayor of New York and his daughter managed to reach their box somehow. Then we thought it was time to begin. Some members of Daly's company, including John Drew, came in, and a few friends. It was the oddest, scantiest audience! But the enthusiasm was terrific!

§ 9

FIVE years went by before we visited America again. Five years in a country of rapid changes is a long time, long enough for friends to forget! But they didn't forget. This time we made new friends, too, in the Far West. We went to San Francisco, among other places. We attended part of a performance at the Chinese theatre. Oh, those rows of impenetrable faces gazing at the stage with their long, shining, inexpressive

228

eyes! What a look of the everlasting the Chinese have! "We have been before you—we shall be after you," they seem to say.

Just as we were getting interested in the play, the interpreter rose and hurried us out. Something that was not for the ears of women was being said, but we did not know it!

The chief incident of the fifth American tour was our production at Chicago of Laurence Irving's one-act play "Godefroi and Yolande." I regard that little play as an inspiration. By instinct the young author did everything right. The Chicago folk, in spite of the unpleasant theme of the play, recognised the genius of it, and received it splendidly.

In 1901 I was ill, and hated the parts I was playing in America. The Lyceum company was not what it had been. Everything was changed.

In 1907—only the other day—I toured in America for the first time on my own account—playing modern plays for the first time. I made new friends and found my old ones still faithful. This tour was a momentous one for me, because at Pittsburgh I was married for the third time, and married to an American. My marriage was my own affair, but very few people seemed to think so, and I was overwhelmed with enquiries, kind, and otherwise. Kindness and loyalty won the day.

NOTES TO CHAPTER XI

1. *Irving's Pronunciation.* The accusation that Irving could not speak English as it ought to be spoken was not confined to America. His pronunciation was criticised severely in England throughout his career, and was a stumbling block to some of his most devout admirers. There is an interesting defence of it in Gordon Craig's biographical study of Irving. Craig's case for Irving's English rests on its striking resemblance to Chaucer's English. "This is the old English speech, and Irving brought back to us something of the ripe old sounds."

2. *Dr Furness.* The son of this distinguished American scholar, Henry Howard Furness, who died only a short time ago, inherited, like many of the children of Ellen Terry's first friends and admirers in America, his father's enthusiastic appreciation of Henry Irving and Ellen Terry as interpreters of Shakespeare. During a visit to England after her death, the younger Furness learned from her daughter of the failure of efforts to rouse the interest of the survivors among her hosts of American friends in the proposed memorial to her at Smallhythe. Surprised, and rather shocked, he promised to do all he could on his return to get into touch with people to whom he knew Ellen Terry was still an enchanting memory. His first move was to write to some prominent men, who in their youth had, like him, been present at a luncheon party at Harvard, given by one of the college clubs in Ellen Terry's honour. The sequel to this appeal was that Mr J. Pierpont Morgan, who had not forgotten that joyous occasion, sent a cheque for £250 to the Ellen Terry

Memorial Fund. Mr Furness died soon after his happy thought had had this happy result.

3. *Godefroi and Yolande.* The American performances were the only public ones ever accorded to Laurence Irving's play, but in 1915 Edith Craig produced it in London under the auspices of the Pioneer Players, a Sunday play-producing Society, complimented by Bernard Shaw in a note in the Shaw-Terry correspondence on "having done more for the theatrical vanguard than any other of the coterie theatres."

Laurence Irving's gratitude to Ellen Terry for her keen interest in "Godefroi and Yolande" is expressed in a letter written shortly after he had read the play to her:

> I cannot tell you how deeply I felt all your generous enthusiasm over my play. Encouragement such as you give me will spur me on to renewed efforts, so that I may hope to merit it again. I will have another copy of the play got ready, and then I will send it to you for the comments you so kindly offered to make. That copy will then be more valuable for your comments than in itself it could ever hope to be. I do not know in what words to tell you how honoured I feel at such an offer from the first of English actresses.

After Laurence Irving gave up diplomacy for which he had been educated, and became an actor, his relations with his father which in his boyhood were distant, owing to the permanent estrangement of his parents, were changed. Laurence, as a member of the Lyceum Company, to which he was promoted after a brief training under Frank Benson, was brought into close contact with his father. One result of this was a friendship between Laurence and his father's "leading lady" which lasted until Laurence's untimely death in 1914. The promise of a great career in the theatre was broken when the *Empress of Ireland,* with Laurence Irving on board, sank in the River St Lawrence. Ellen Terry recognised his genius in its ugly duckling stage, and seems to have understood him better than his father. "My Irving boy," as she often called him, was very dear to her, and his presence in the Lyceum Company brought her happiness at an unhappy time in her life.

4. *Ellen Terry's Third Marriage.* The brief allusion to this event at the end of the chapter is amplified in Part II, Chapter I, when I take up the narrative of Ellen Terry's life at the point where she broke it off.

CHAPTER XII

THE MACBETH PERIOD

(1888–1892)

§ 1

B EFORE the production of "Macbeth" was definitely settled, Henry considered other plays. The prospects of "As You Like It" looked bright at one time, those of "The Tempest" at another. Henry was much attracted by the part of Caliban, but when I told him to go ahead and not to bother about there being no part in "The Tempest" which attracted *me,* he said: "It would never do. The young lovers are the thing in the play, and where are we going to find them?" During our "As You Like It" discussions, he told me he had no intention of playing Jacques. "I shall play Touchstone. He is in the vital part of the play." Henry put the objections to "As You Like It" so convincingly that although I was dying to play Rosalind, I believed he was right to give it up. Then we turned to other plays he was always being urged to add to his Shakespearean productions. There was talk about "King John," "Antony and Cleopatra," "Timon of Athens," "Richard II," and "Julius Cæsar," and all this talk "left me cold," even the talk about "Antony and Cleopatra," for I could not see myself as the serpent of old Nile. Besides, I knew Henry was not attracted by the part of Antony. He was intensely interested in Brutus in "Julius Cæsar." "That's the actor's part in the play," he said to me once, "because it needs acting. But the actor-manager's part is Antony, because Antony scores all along the line. Now when the claims of actor and actor-manager conflict in a play, and there is no part for *you* in it, I think it's wiser to leave that play alone." So "Julius Cæsar" was turned down, and Henry threw himself into the work of preparing the production of "Macbeth." In August 1887 we went to Scotland to get ideas for the scenes. I find an entry in my diary for that year describing a little incident in this quest for local colour. "Visited the 'Blasted Heath.' Behold a flourishing potato-field! A smooth softness everywhere. We must blast our own heath when we do Macbeth."

The rehearsals were very exhausting, but they were splendid to watch.

In this play Henry brought his manipulation of crowds to perfection. My acting edition of the play is riddled with rough sketches by him of different groups. Artists to whom I have shown them have been astonished at the spirited impressionism of these sketches. For his "purpose" Henry seems to have been able to do anything, even to draw and to compose music! Sir Arthur Sullivan's music at first did not quite please him. He walked up and down the stage humming, and showing the composer what he was going to do at certain situations. Sullivan, with wonderful quickness and open-mindedness, caught his meaning at once.

"Much better than mine, Irving—much better—I'll rough it out at once!"

When the orchestra played the new version, based on that humming of Henry's, it was exactly what he wanted!

Knowing what a task I had before me, I began to get anxious and worried about "Lady Mac." Henry wrote me such a nice letter about this:

Tonight, if possible, the last act. I want to get these great multitudinous scenes over and then we can attack *our* scenes.... Your sensitiveness is so acute that you must suffer sometimes. You are not like anybody else. You see things with such lightning quickness and unerring instinct that dull fools like myself grow irritable and impatient sometimes. I feel confused when I'm thinking of one thing, and disturbed by another. That's all. But I do feel very sorry afterwards when I don't seem to heed what I so much value....

I think things are going well, considering the time we've been at it, but I see so much that is wanting that it seems almost impossible to get through properly. "Tonight, commence, Mathias. If you sleep you are lost!" (A quotation from "The Bells")

Henry had played "Macbeth" before at the Lyceum in the days of the Bateman management; he told me that by intuition he had got the right idea of the character, and had since come to know from fresh study that it was *right*. His confidence in the rightness of his conception was not in the least shaken by criticisms of it, and he always maintained that as "Macbeth" he did his finest work. "And we know when we do our best," he would add. "We are the only people who do know." Perhaps he was right in putting his Macbeth before his Hamlet, yet I think his *performance* of "Hamlet" was the greater.

His conception of Macbeth attacked, and even derided, by the critics of 1888, seemed to me then, and seems to me now, as clear as daylight. But the carrying out of the conception was unequal. Henry's imagination was sometimes his worst enemy. It tempted him to try and do more than any actor can do.

One of his greatest moments was in the last act after the battle. He looked like a great famished wolf, weak with the weakness of an exhausted giant, spent with exertions ten times as great as those of giants of coarser fibre, and stouter build.

Of all men else I have avoided thee.

In that line, once more, he suggested as he only could suggest, the power of fate. He seemed to envisage a power against which no man can fight, to hear the beat of its inexorable wing. For Macbeth then, no hope, no mercy.

Henry's imagination was always stirred by the queer and the uncanny. This was a great advantage in "Macbeth" in which the atmosphere is charged with strange forces. How marvellously he could have played Lady Macbeth in the sleep-walking scene, which ought above all things to be uncanny! I am not surprised that he was dissatisfied with me in this scene. He knew so well how it ought to be done, and I never came near it.

Writing to me, I think after the dress-rehearsal—the letter has no date—he says:

You will be splendid in this part. The first time it has been *acted* for many years.

The sleeping scene will be beautiful too—the moment you are in it— *but* Lady M. should certainly have the appearance of having got out of bed, to which she is returning when she goes off. The hair to my mind should be wild and disturbed, and the whole appearance as distraught as possible, and disordered....

But the cause of my being all wrong in the scene lay deeper than my appearance, as I realise now. In other scenes, particularly in the banquet scene, I was not so wrong. There was much diversity of opinion about my Lady Macbeth. It was a satisfaction to me that some people saw what I was aiming at. Sargent saw it, and in his picture is all that I meant to do.

The dress in the picture was designed by Alice Comyns Carr, and made by Mrs Nettleship. It was one of "Mrs Nettle's" greatest triumphs. I am glad to think it is immortalised in the Sargent portrait. From the first I knew the portrait was going to be splendid. A letter I wrote to my daughter, who was in Germany at the time of the sittings, shows that I was enthusiastic about it all along.

The picture of me is nearly finished and I think it magnificent. The green and the blue of the dress is splendid, and the expression as Lady Macbeth holds the crown over her head quite wonderful.

I added that Mr Sargent was "painting a head of Henry—very good, but mean about the chin at present." How Henry hated that picture!

He would never allow it to be exhibited. But he greatly admired my portrait and was always willing to lend it for exhibition. It was talked of everywhere, and quarrelled about as much as my way of playing the part, as these further extracts from my letters to my daughter prove:

Sargent's "Lady Macbeth" in the New Gallery is a great success. The picture is the sensation of the year. Of course opinions differ about it, but there are dense crowds round it day after day. There is talk of putting it on exhibition by itself.

Since then it has gone over nearly the whole of Europe, and now is resting for life at the Tate Gallery.

Everybody hates Sargent's head of Henry. Henry, also. I like it, but not altogether. I think it perfectly wonderfully painted and like him, only not at his best by any means. There sat Henry and there by his side the picture, and I could scarce tell one from t'other. Henry looked white, with tired eyes, and holes in his cheeks and bored to death! And there was the picture with white face, tired eyes, holes in the cheeks and boredom in every line. Sargent tried to paint his smile and gave it up.

Sargent said to me, I remember, upon Henry's first visit to the studio to see the Macbeth picture of me: "What a Saint!" This to my mind promised well—that Sargent should see *that* side of Henry so swiftly. So then I never left off asking Henry to sit to Sargent, who wanted to paint him too, and said to me continually, "What a head!"

Sargent's picture is almost finished, and it is really splendid. Burne-Jones yesterday suggested two or three alterations about the colour which Sargent immediately adopted, but Burne-Jones raves about the picture.
It ("Macbeth") is a most tremendous success, and the last three days' advance booking has been greater than ever was known, even at the Lyceum. Yes, it is a success, and I am a success, which amazes me, for never did I think I should be let down so easily. Some people hate me in it; some, Henry among them, think it my best part, and the critics differ, and discuss it hotly, which in itself is my best success of all! Those who don't like me in it are those who don't want, and don't like to read it fresh from Shakespeare, and who hold by the "fiend" reading of the character.... Oh, dear! It is an exciting time! ... I wish you could see my dresses. They are superb, especially the first one: green beetles on it, and such a cloak! The photographs give no idea of it at all, for it is in colour that it is so splendid. The dark red hair is fine. The whole thing is Rossetti—rich stained-glass effects. I play some of it well, but, of course, I don't do what I want to do yet. Meanwhile I shall not budge an inch in the reading of it, for that I know is right. Oh, it's fun, but it's precious hard work for I by no means make her a "gentle, lovable woman" as some of 'em say. That's all pickles. She was nothing of the sort, although

234

she was *not* a fiend, and *did* love her husband. I have to what is vulgarly called "sweat at it," each night.

The few people who liked my Lady Macbeth, liked it ardently. My friend Lady Pollock was one of them.

... Burne-Jones has been with me this afternoon: he was at "Macbeth" last night, and you filled his whole soul with your beauty and your poetry. . . . He says you were a great Scandinavian queen; that your presence, your voice, your movement made a marvellously poetic harmony; that your dress was grandly imagined and grandly worn—and that he cannot criticise, he can only remember.

But Burne-Jones by this time had become one of our most ardent admirers, and was prejudiced in my favour because my acting appealed to his *eye*. Well, the drama is for the eye as well as for the ear and the mind.

§ 2

HERE I was in the very noonday of life, fresh from Lady Macbeth and still young enough to play Rosalind, suddenly called upon to play a rather uninteresting mother in "The Dead Heart." However, my son Teddy made his first appearance in it, and had such a big success that I soon forgot that for me the play was rather "small beer."

It was not a new play. It had been done before by Benjamin Webster and George Vining. Henry engaged Bancroft for the Abbé, a part of quite as much importance as his own. It was only a melodrama, but Henry could always invest a melodrama with life, beauty, interest, mystery, by his methods of production.

I'm full of French Revolution, he wrote to me when he was preparing the play for rehearsal, and could pass an examination in it. In our play, at the taking of the Bastille we must have a starving crowd—hungry, eager, cadaverous faces. If that can be well carried out, the effect will be very terrible, and the contrast to the other crowd (the red and fat crowd—the blood-gorged ones who look as if they'd been all drinking wine—*red* wine, as Dickens says) would be striking. . . . It's tiresome stuff to read, because it depends so much on situations. I have been touching the book up though, and improved it here and there, I think.

A letter this morning from the illustrious Blank offering me his prompt book to look at. . . . I think I shall borrow the treasure. Why not? Of course he will say that he has produced the play and all that sort of thing; but what does that matter, if one can only get one hint out of it?

The longer we live, the more we see that if we only do our own work thoroughly well, we can be independent of everything else or anything that may be said. . . .

235

I see in Landry a great deal of Manette—that same vacant gaze into years gone by when he crouched in his dungeon nursing his wrongs. . . .

I shall send you another book soon to put any of your alterations and additions in. I've added a lot of little things with a few lines for you—very good, I think, though I say it as shouldnt—I know you'll laugh! They are perhaps not startlingly original, but better than the original, anyhow! Here they are—last act!

"Ah, Robert, pity me. By the recollections of our youth, I implore you to save my boy!" (*Now* for 'em!)

"If my voice calls a tone that ever fell sweetly upon your ear, have pity on me! If the past is not a blank, if you once loved, have pity on me!" (Bravo!)

Now I call that very good, and if the "If" and the "pity" dont bring down the house, well it's a pity! I pity the pittites!

. . . I've just been copying out my part in an account book—a little more handy to put in one's pocket. It's really very short, but difficult to act, though, and so is ours. I like this "piling up" sort of acting, and I am sure you will, when you play the part. It's restful. "The Bells" is that sort of thing.

The crafty old Henry! All this was to put me in conceit with my part!

Many people at this time put me in conceit with my son, including dear Burne-Jones with his splendid gift of impulsive enthusiasm.

THE GRANGE,
WEST KENSINGTON, W.
Sunday.

MOST DEAR LADY,—

I thought all went wonderfully last night, and no sign could I see of hitch or difficulty; and as for your boy, he looked a lovely little gentleman— and in his cups was perfect, not overdoing by the least touch a part always perilously easy to overdo. I too had the impertinence to be a bit nervous for you about him, but not when he appeared—so altogether I was quite happy.

. . . Irving was very noble. I thought I had never seen his face so beauti-ful before—no, that isn't the word, and to hunt for the right one would be so like judicious criticism that I won't. Exalted and splendid it was—and you were you—YOU—and so all was well. I rather wanted more shouting and distant roar in the Bastille Scene—since the walls fell, like Jericho, by noise. A good dreadful growl always going on would have helped, I thought—and that was the only point where I missed anything.

And I was very glad you got your boy back again and that Mr Irving was ready to have his head cut off for you; so it had what I call a good end-ing, and I am in bright spirits today, and ever

Your real friend,
E. B.-J.

He was indeed one of my real friends, and his letters—he was a heaven-born letter-writer—were like no one else's; full of charm and humour and feeling. Once when I was starting for a long tour in America he sent me a picture with this particularly charming letter:

MY DEAR MISS TERRY,—

I never have the courage to throw you a huge bouquet as I should like to—so in default I send you a little sign of my homage and admiration. I made it purposely for you, which is its only excellence, and thought nothing but gold good enough to paint with for you—and now it's done, I am woefully disappointed. It looks such a poor wretch of a thing, and there is no time to make another before you go, so look mercifully upon it—it did mean so well—as you would upon a foolish friend, not holding it up to the iight, but putting it in a corner and never showing it.

As to what it is about, I think it's a little scene in Heaven (I am always pretending to know so much about that place!) a sort of patrol going to look to the battlements, some such thought as in Marlowe's lovely line: "Now walk the angels on the walls of Heaven." But I wanted it to be so different, and my old eyes cannot help me to finish it as I want—so forgive it and accept it with all its accompanying crowd of good wishes to you. They were always in my mind as I did it.

And come back soon from that America and stay here, and never go away again. Indeed I do wish you boundless happiness, and for our sake, such a length of life that you might shudder if I were to say how long.

Ever your poor artist,

E. B.-J.

If it is so faint that you can scarcely see it, let that stand for modest humility and shyness—as if I had only dared to whisper.

Another time, when I had sent him a trifle for some charity, he wrote:

This morning came the delightful crinkly paper that always means you! If anybody else ever used it, I think I should assault them! I certainly wouldnt read their letter or answer it.

And I know the cheque will be very useful. If I thought much about those wretched homes, or saw them often, I should do no more work, I know. There is but one thing to do—to help with a little money if you can manage it, and then try hard to forget. Yes, I am certain that I should never paint again if I saw much of those hopeless lives that have no remedy. I know of such a dear lad about my Phil's age who has felt this so sharply that he has given his happy, lucky, petted life to give himself wholly to share their squalor and unlovely lives—doing all he can, of evenings when his work is over, to amuse such as have the heart to be amused, reading to them and telling them about histories and what not—anything he knows that can entertain them. And this he has daily done for about a year, and if he carries it on for his life-time he shall have such a nimbus that he will look top-heavy with it.

No, you would always have been lovely and made some beauty about you if you had been born there—but I should have got drunk and beaten

237

my family and been altogether horrible! When everything goes just as I like, and painting prospers a bit, and the air is warm and friends well and everything perfectly comfortable, I can just manage to behave decently, and a spoilt fool I am—that's the truth. But wherever you were, some garden would grow.

Yes, I know Winchelsea and Rye and Lympne and Hythe—all bonny places, and Hythe has a church it may be proud of. Under the sea is another Winchelsea, a poor drowned city—about a mile out at sea, I think, always marked in old maps as "Winchelsea Dround." If ever the sea goes back on that changing coast there may be great fun when the spires and towers come up again. It's a pretty land to drive in.

I am growing downright stupid—I can't work at all nor think of anything. Will my wits ever come back to me?

And when are you coming back—when will the Lyceum be in its rightful hands again? I refuse to go there till you come back . . .

I have finished four pictures: come and tell me if they will do. I have worked so long at them that I know nothing about them, but I want you to see them—and like them if you can.

All Saturday and Sunday and Monday they are visible. Come any time you can that suits you best—only come.

I do hope you will like them. If you don't you must really pretend to, else I shall be heartbroken. And if I knew what time you would come and which day, I would get Margaret here.

I have had them about four years—long before I knew you, and now they are done and I can hardly believe it. But tell me pretty pacifying lies and say you like them, even if you find them rubbish.

Your devoted and affectionate
E. B.-J.

I went the next day to see the pictures with Edy. They were the "Briar Rose" series. They were *beautiful*. The lovely Lady Granby (now Duchess of Rutland) was there—reminding me, as always, of the reflection of something in water on a misty day. When she was Miss Violet Lindsay she did a drawing of me as Portia in the doctor's robes, which I think is very like me, as well as having all the charming qualities of her well-known pencil portraits.

§ 3

PLAYS adapted from novels are generally unsatisfactory. A whole story cannot be conveyed in three hours, and every reader of the story looks for something not in the play. Wills took from "The Vicar of Wakefield" an episode, and did it right well, but there was no *episode* in "The Bride of Lammermoor" for Merivale to take. He tried to traverse the whole ground, and failed. But he gave me some lovely things to do in

238

Lucy Ashton. I had to lose my poor wits, as in Ophelia, in the last act, and with hardly a word to say I was able to make an effect. The love scene at the well I did nicely too.

Seymour Lucas designed splendid dresses for this play. My "Ravenswood" riding dress set a fashion in ladies' coats for quite a long time. Mine was copied by Mr Lucas from a leather coat of Lord Mohun's. He is said to have had it on when he was killed. At any rate there was a large stab in the back of the coat, and a blood-stain. "Nance Oldfield" was my first speculation in play-buying! I saw it acted, and thought I could do something with it. Henry would not buy it, so I did! He let me do it first in front of a revival of "The Corsican Brothers" in 1891. It was a great success, although my son and I did not know a word on the first night and had our parts written out and pinned all over the furniture on the stage! Dear old Mr Howe wrote to me that Teddy's performance was "more than creditable; it was exceedingly good and full of character, and with your own charming performance the piece was a great success." Since 1891 I must have played "Nance Oldfield" hundreds of times, but I never had an Alexander Oldworthy so good as my son, although such talented actors as Marton Harvey, Laurence Irving and, more recently, Harcourt Williams and O. P. Heggie have all played the part.

§ 3

THE Lyceum production of "Henry VIII" (1892) was magnificent, but I was not keenly interested in it, or in my part.

Henry's pride as Cardinal Wolsey was the thing, not my pride as the Spanish Queen. How wonderful he looked (though not fat and self-indulgent like the pictures of the real Wolsey) in his flame-coloured robes! He had the silk dyed specially by the dyers to the Cardinal's College in Rome. Seymour Lucas designed the clothes. This letter from Burne-Jones about "Henry VIII" is a delightful tribute to Henry Irving's treatment of the play:

MY DEAR LADY,—

We went last night to the play (at my theatre) to see Henry VIII—Margaret and Mackail and I. It was delicious to go out again and see mankind, after such evil days. How kind they were to me no words can say—I went in at a private door and then into a cosy box and back the same way, swiftly, and am marvellously the better for the adventure. No you, alas!

I have written to Mr Irving just to thank him for his great kindness in making the path of pleasure so easy, for I go tremblingly at present. But I could not say to him what I thought of the Cardinal—a sort of shame keeps one from saying to an artist what one thinks of his work—but to you I can

239

say how nobly he warmed up the story of the old religion to my exacting mind in that impersonation. I shall think always of dying monarchy in his Charles—and always of dying hierarchy in his Wolsey. How Protestant and dull all grew when that noble type had gone!

I cant go to church till red cardinals come back (and may they be of exactly that red) nor to Court till trumpets and banners come back—nor to evening parties till the dances are like that dance. What a lovely young Queen has been found. But there was no you.... Perhaps it was as well. I couldnt have you slighted even in a play, and put aside. When I go back to see you, as I soon will, it will be easier. Mr Irving let me know you would not be acting, and proposed that I should go later on—wasnt that like him? So I sat with my children and was right happy; and, as usual, the streets looked dirty, and all the people muddy and black as we came away. Please not to answer this stuff.

Ever yours affectionately,
E. B.-J.

—I wish that Cardinal could have been made Pope, and sat with his foot on the Earl of Surrey's neck. Also I wish to be a Cardinal; but then I sometimes want to a pirate. We cant have all we want.

Your boy was very kind—I thought the race of young men who are polite and attentive to old fading ones had passed away with antique pageants —but it isnt so.

When the Duke and Duchess of Devonshire gave the famous fancy dress ball at Devonshire House, Henry attended it in the robes which had appealed so strongly to Burne-Jones's eye. I was told by one who was present at this ball that as the Cardinal swept up the staircase, his "cappa magna" trailing behind him at its full magnificent length, a sudden wave of reality seemed to sweep up with him, submerging the pretty make-believe of that aristocratic masquerade.

Many of my most effective dresses have been what I may call fakes. The splendid dress that I wore in the Trial Scene in "Henry VIII" is one example. There was great difficulty in finding a material at once rich and sombre enough for the effect desired. No one was ever cleverer in the pursuit of theatrically effective materials than Mrs Comyns Carr. She was never dazzled by the appearance of the stuff in the shop, never impressed by its price. If she was not sure it would look right on the stage she would have none of it. For Katharine she had to find me a brocade, all steely silver and bronzy gold; but all the brocades she saw were unsatisfactory because of their insignificant designs. If they had a silver design, it looked under the stage lights like a scratch in white cotton. At last Mrs Carr found a black satin, timorously and feebly decorated on the right side with a meandering rose and thistle pattern in silver thread. On the wrong side it was a sheet of silver, just the *right* steely silver, because it was the *wrong* side! Mrs Carr, having got the right silver, started on another quest for the right gold. She found it at last in some gold lace antimacassars at Whiteleys! From these base materials she and Mrs Nettleship constructed a magnificent dress fit for a Spanish Queen. Its only fault was that it was terribly heavy.

But the weight I can carry on the stage has often amazed me. I remember that for "King Arthur" Mrs Nettleship made me a splendid cloak embroidered all over with a pattern in jewels. At the dress-rehearsal when I made my entrance the cloak swept magnificently, and I daresay looked fine, but I knew at once that I should never be able to act in it. I called out to Mrs Nettleship and Alice Carr, who were in the stalls, and implored them to lighten it of some of the jewels.

"Oh, do keep it as it is," they answered, "it looks splendid."

"I cant breathe in it, much less act in it. Please send some one up to cut off a few stones."

I went on with my part, and then, during a wait, two of Mrs Nettleship's assistants came on to the stage and snipped off a jewel here and there. When they had filled a basket, I began to feel better!

But when they tried to lift that basket, their united efforts could not move it!

§4

DURING these great days at the Lyceum, Henry frequently gave suppers in the Beefsteak Room, once the meeting-place of the famous old Beefsteak Club. It was used as a lumber-room when Henry first became manager of the Lyceum; he restored it, hung pictures of actors and actresses on the panelled walls, put in a grill, a huge dining-table, and lighted it to perfection. It was a dignified and yet a cosy room, approached from the stage by a series of narrow and rather tortuous staircases. All the most famous and interesting people of the day climbed to the Beefsteak Room at Henry's invitation. I wish I had kept a record of the guests. Now when I conjure up a picture of the room, the faces are clear for a minute, then become dim and vanish. I recall an evening in 1891 when the Princess of Wales [1]—she was then Princess May of Teck—came to supper with her mother Princess Mary. It was her birthday, and she had chosen a visit to the Lyceum as a birthday treat, which was a great compliment to us. It was by no means the only time she and her mother were honoured "Beefsteak" guests.

Another face I see is that of Lady Dorothy Nevill, an old lady of the old aristocratic school. She was an ardent playgoer, and one of the most clever and amusing guests at the "Beefsteak" suppers. She dressed her

[1] Now Queen Mary.

241

hair to become her, irrespective of any fashion, and looked as original as she was. She was an ideal hostess as well as an ideal guest.

Then there was Lord Randolph Churchill, a great admirer of Henry's. He confessed once that he had never read a play of Shakespeare's until he saw Henry act! Then he thought "it was time to begin." His power to master any subject in an incredibly short time was shown by the fact that very soon after he began, he staggered Henry and me with his intimate knowledge of at least half a dozen of the plays. He was a delightful "Beefsteak" guest, brilliant yet strangely ingenuous at times. His beautiful wife often accompanied him. She came to supper one evening in a dress which inspired me with an idea for my Lady Macbeth dress. The bodice of her gown was embroidered with green beetles' wings. I told Mrs Comyns Carr of the effect produced, and she remembered it when she was designing the Macbeth dress. Often when I looked at Lady Randolph's mobile face, and listened to her most expressive voice, I thought: "What a good actress you would make!"

Famous singers were often among the guests in the Beefsteak Room, Patti, Melba, Calvé, Albani, Tamagno, Victor Maurel, and many others. The names of Calvé and Melba bring a crowd of delightful memories. "Salve Calvé!" was printed once in huge type in an American newspaper, and that's my greeting to her here. I am told that Grisi and Mario were fine dramatically as well as vocally. I saw them on the stage when I was a child, shortly before their retirement. Grisi had grown stout; she did not strike me as a fine actress; Mario impressed me more. In later days, when I was a better judge, I discovered that the marriage of the arts of singing and acting is seldom a happy one. Yet it was happy, and beautiful in Calvé's Carmen, and Maurel's performance as Iago in Verdi's "Otello" was superb. Another opera singer whose acting has roused my enthusiasm is Mary Garden. In "Griseldis" her singing was a perfect medium of sincere dramatic emotion.

Calvé, a great darling as well as a great artist, won my heart when we were staying in the same hotel in New York. I remember a wonderful Sunday evening when I dined with her, and she sang to me afterwards for hours! One song she said she had never sang as well before. She laughed in her delicious rapturous way and sang it all over again.

Her enthusiasm over any fellow-artist, singer or actor, who had given her pleasure, was delightful. Oh, what a generous, lovable woman! Such tender dark eyes, such pretty ways, such an enchanting mixture of nobility and *câlinerie*! She laughed and cried all in a moment like a child. That year we became friends in New York, she was raved about. She was pleased and amused, but not in the least spoiled by all the fuss.

I once watched Patti sing from behind scenes at the Metropolitan

Opera House, New York. My impression from that point of view was that she was actually a *bird!* She could not help singing! Her head, flattened on top, her nose tilted downwards like a lovely little beak, her throat swelling and swelling as it poured out that extraordinary volume of sound, all made me think that she must have been a nightingale before she was a human being!

The dear kind-hearted Melba has always been a good friend of mine. The first time I met her was in New York at a supper party, and she had a bad cold, and therefore a frightful *speaking* voice for the moment! I shall never forget the shock that it gave me. Thank goodness I very soon afterwards heard her again when she hadnt a cold!

Melba was one of the first to offer her services for my jubilee performance at Drury Lane, but unfortunately she was ill when the day came, and could not sing. She had her dresses in "Faust" copied from mine by Mrs Nettleship, and I came across a note from her the other day thanking me for having introduced her to a dressmaker who was "an angel." Another note sent round to me during a performance of "King Arthur" in Boston I shall always prize.

You are sublime, adorable *ce soir....* I wish I were a millionaire—I would throw *all* my millions at your feet. If there is another procession, tell the stage manager to see those imps of Satan *dont chew gum.* It looks awful.

Love, MELBA.

I think that time it was the solemn procession of mourners following the dead body of Elaine who were chewing gum; but we always had to be prepared for it among our American "supers," whether they were angels or devils or courtiers!

In "Faust" we "carried" about six leading witches for the Brocken Scene, and recruited the forty others from local talent in the different towns that we visited. Their general direction was to throw up their arms and look fierce at certain music cues. One night I noticed a girl going through the most terrible contortions with her jaw, and thought I must say something.

"That's right, dear. Very good, but dont exaggerate."

"How?" was all the answer that I got in the choicest nasal twang, and the girl continued to make faces as before.

I was contemplating a second attempt, when Templeton, the limelight man, who had heard me speak to her, touched me on the shoulder.

"Beg pardon, miss, she dont mean it. She's only *chewing gum!*"

I seem to have travelled a long way from the Beefsteak Room! In the 'nineties there were many new faces at Henry's suppers. One, very dear to me, was the face of the young novelist who wrote under the name of

243

John Oliver Hobbes. In private life she was Mrs Craigie. She sent me a little one-act play she had written in collaboration with George Moore. It was but a trifle yet it convinced me she had great talent as a dramatist. From the time (1894) I acted in this play ("Journeys End in Lovers' Meeting") with Terriss and Forbes-Robertson at a charity matinée, we became great friends, and the friendship was unbroken when she died. "She should have died hereafter." The great play of which I know she was capable had not been written.

Pearl Craigie had a man's intellect, a woman's wit and swiftness of apprehension. Brilliant she always managed to be, even in the dullest company, and well as she talked, she was never guilty of monopolising conversation. She would be silent at times to give "the other fellow" a chance. Wonderfully tolerant, she could all the same not easily forgive any meanness or injustice that seemed to her deliberate. Hers was a splendid spirit.

I shall always bless that little play of hers which first brought me near to so fine a creature. I rather think that I never met any one who *gave out* so much as she did. To me, at least, she *gave, gave* all the time. I hope she was not exhausted after our long "confabs." *I* was most certainly refreshed and replenished.

The first performance of "Journeys End in Lovers' Meeting" she watched from a private box with the Princess of Wales (our present Queen)[1] and Henry Irving. She came round afterwards just blazing with enthusiasm and praising me for work which was really not good.

Her best play was, I think, "The Ambassador," in which Violet Vanbrugh played a pathetic part very beautifully, and made a great advance in her profession.

There was some idea of Pearl Craigie writing a play for Henry Irving and me, but it never came to anything. There was a play of hers on the same subject as her novel, "The School for Saints," and another about Guizot.

February 11, 1898.

My very dear Nell,—

I have an idea for a real four-act comedy (in these matters nothing daunts me!) founded on a charming little episode in the private lives of Princess Lieven (the famous Russian ambassadress) and the celebrated Guizot, the French Prime Minister and historian. I should have to veil the identity *slightly,* and also make the story a husband and wife story—it would be more amusing this way. It is comedy from beginning to end. Sir Henry would make a splendid Guizot, and you the ideal Madame de Lieven. Do let me talk it over

[1] Queen Alexandra.

244

with you. "The School for Saints" was, as it were, a born biography. But the Lieven-Guizot idea is a play.

Yours ever affectionately,
PEARL MARY THERESA CRAIGIE.

In another letter she writes (how tersely!): "I am changing all my views about so-called 'literary' dialogue. It means pedantry. The great thing is to be natural."

My portrait as Lady Macbeth by Sargent used to hang in the alcove in the Beefsteak Room when it was not away at some exhibition, and the artist and I have often supped under it. I have always loved the picture, and think it is far more like me than any other. Mr Sargent first of all thought that he would paint me at the moment when Lady Macbeth comes out of the castle to welcome Duncan. He liked the swirl of the dress, and the torches, and the women bowing down on either side. He used to make me walk up and down his studio until I nearly dropped in my heavy dress, saying suddenly as I got the swirl:—"That's it, that's it!" and rushing off to his canvas to throw on some paint in his wonderful inimitable fashion!

But he had to give up *that* idea of the Lady Macbeth picture all the same. I was the gainer, for he gave me the unfinished sketch, and it is certainly very beautiful.

By this sketch hangs a tale of Mr Sargent's great-heartedness. When the details of my jubilee performance at Drury Lane were being arranged, the Committee decided to ask certain distinguished artists to contribute to the programme. They were all delighted about it, and such busy men as Sir Laurence Alma-Tadema, Mr Abbey, Mr Byam Shaw, Mr Walter Crane, Mr Bernard Partridge, Mr James Pryde, Mr Orpen, and Mr William Nicholson all gave some of their work to me. Mr Sargent was asked if he would allow the first Lady Macbeth study to be reproduced. He found that it would not reproduce well, so in the height of the season and of his work with fashionable sitters, he did an entirely new black and white painting of the same subject, which *would* reproduce! This act of friendship I could never forget even if the picture were not in front of me at this minute to remind me of it. "You must think of me as one of the people bowing down to you in the picture," he wrote to me when he sent the new version for the programme. Nothing during my jubilee celebrations touched me more than this wonderful kindness of Mr Sargent's.

Henry never cared much about "going into society," but as the host of "Society" in the Beefsteak Room, he thoroughly enjoyed himself. His face at those suppers was alive with raffish humour, and mischief. Very

245

mischievous he could be about some of his guests. I remember some one saying to him after the first night of "Ravenswood": "I dont fancy that your hopes will be quite fulfilled about the play. I heard one or two in the Beefsteak Room on Saturday night——"

"Ah, yes!" Henry interrupted in his most gentle voice. "But they were *friends!* One must not expect too much from friends. The paying public will, I think, decide favourably."

This is the Irving, the Irving at play, you can see in the Bastien-Lepage portrait. The artist was enchanted with Henry's face and expressed a strong desire to paint him. The portrait originated at a supper in the Beefsteak Room at which both Bastien-Lepage and Sarah Bernhardt were guests. The artist did a sketch of Henry on a sheet of notepaper, then another of Sarah, and gave them to me. They are among my most precious relics. Henry gave Bastien-Lepage two sittings for the portrait afterwards at Grafton Street, but it is a "Beefsteak" portrait all the same.

How brilliantly, delightfully and whimsically Alfred Gilbert talked to me the other day, when I met him again in Bruges, of Beefsteak suppers at which he had been present! He is the man who can make you live them, and first nights at the Lyceum, over again! I think it was after one of these suppers that he took the whole party to drink at the fountain in Piccadilly Circus the night before his statue of Eros was unveiled. Years later, another sculptor, George Frampton, told me of his certainty that the statue would stand the test of time, and hold its own with the finest work of the same kind done by the great masters of the Renaissance period. "I have no patience with people who criticise it as inappropriate to its surroundings. That is the fault of the surroundings. In a more enlightened age than this, Piccadilly Circus will be destroyed and rebuilt merely to provide a finer setting for Gilbert's jewel."

We were, as he spoke, looking at Henry's death-mask, which Frampton had taken, and the dead face dissolved into that living one with the quizzed expression which it wore at the Beefsteak suppers. Then came a vision of Alfred Gilbert's Beethoven-like head with its lion-like mane of tawny hair, and I began to cry. Henry dead, and Gilbert in exile. Neither appreciated in this age as they should be. The Beefsteak Room a lumber-room again, if it exists at all in the rebuilt Lyceum!

NOTES TO CHAPTER XII

1. *The Lyceum Problem.* When Henry Irving in the year 1878 engaged Ellen Terry as his "leading lady," it is improbable, as he had no personal knowledge of her remarkable powers, that he foresaw the problem which was to arise out of the engagement. This was, briefly stated, to find plays with

parts for both, commensurate not only with their ambitions and talents, but with their attractiveness to the public. It is clear from what Ellen Terry says at the beginning of this chapter that Irving was conscious of the problem, and devoted much time and thought to its solution. It was not to his interest as a manager to keep Ellen Terry in the background in his theatre. Even if he had been indifferent himself to the waste of her talent in parts which did not require a great performer, he would have had to consider whether the waste would be good policy. There was the possibility of its being resented by the large section of the public drawn to the Lyceum by Ellen Terry. They did not go there to see Irving carry a play on his back, with merely ornamental assistance from her. It was probably because Irving realised this, although he may also have been influenced by his admiration for Ellen Terry's gifts and a genuine desire that they should have opportunity, that his solution of the Lyceum problem was not, at any rate in the early years of his management, wholly egotistical. It was not for the sake of his own part that he produced "The Cup," or "The Belle's Stratagem," "Romeo and Juliet" or "Much Ado About Nothing," "Twelfth Night" or "Olivia." The disparity between the chances he gave himself, and the chances he gave Ellen Terry at the Lyceum has been much exaggerated. There is no proof that he sterilized her greatest possibilities. It is pure speculation that she would have developed into a finer actress, with less restricted opportunities than her partnership with Irving afforded. They at any rate sufficed for her to win an enduring fame as an interpreter of Shakespeare.

2. *The Sargent Portrait.* Sir Joseph Duveen bought Sargent's portrait of Ellen Terry as Lady Macbeth at the sale of Irving's possessions at Christie's in December 1905. In January 1906 he presented it to the nation. In reply to a letter from Ellen Terry, expressing her appreciation of his action, and the joy that it had given her, Sir Joseph wrote: "It was very nice of you to write me such a kind letter, and I assure you I appreciate its contents very much. I was largely actuated in my desire to present your picture to the nation by the great admiration which, I hope you will allow me to say, I have always entertained for you: you have given me so much pleasure in life. When the opportunity presented itself of obtaining the 'Lady Macbeth' I can assure you I was as much influenced by the desire of letting the nation possess for ever a portrait of a famous actress, as by a wish to preserve in a National Gallery one of our great painter's masterpieces. That you are pleased and satisfied with the home which has been given to the 'Lady Macbeth' is at once a pleasure and a satisfaction to me.

"I think you will like the position which Sir Charles Holroyd has selected for the picture in the Tate Gallery. I am informed that thousands of people have already paid a visit to the Gallery in order to look at it; and although you are accustomed to such large audiences, it probably will be a source of pride and gratification to you to think that thousands of unknown friends throughout future generations will have an opportunity of looking upon your likeness in a national gallery."

Sargent's masterpiece has not suffered in reputation with the passage of

247

time, but stands rather higher in the esteem of connoisseurs now than it did in 1906. Ellen Terry's high opinion of it in 1888, expressed long before its merits had been proclaimed, has been abundantly vindicated.

3. *Lady Macbeth's Dress.* Graham Robertson recalls that Oscar Wilde remarked apropos of the dress immortalised in Sargent's picture: "Judging from the banquet, Lady Macbeth seems an economical housekeeper, and evidently patronises local industries for her husband's clothes and the servants' liveries; but she takes care to do all her own shopping in Byzantium."

4. *The Sargent Sketches.* The oil sketch in black and white Sargent made for reproduction in Ellen Terry's Jubilee Programme was sold at Christie's after her death, and is now in the National Portrait Gallery. The coloured sketch is still in the possession of Edith Craig, who has lent it to the Ellen Terry Memorial Museum at Smallhythe.

5. *Irving's Wolsey Dress.* Ellen Terry was mistaken in thinking that the silk for this dress was dyed in Rome. It was woven and dyed in her own birthplace of Coventry. "This is one of the wrong little things that must be made right little things when the book is reprinted" she wrote on the margin of the first edition.

6. *Alfred Gilbert.* This gifted sculptor returned from his exile in Bruges, not long after Ellen Terry's death, to work in London on a memorial monument to Queen Alexandra, which was opened in June 1932. His breach with the Royal Academy has been healed, and he is once more R. A. He was knighted after the opening of the Memorial. Frampton's prophecy about Gilbert's Eros has been partly fulfilled. Piccadilly Circus has been rebuilt, and if the motive was not to provide "a finer setting for Gilbert's jewel," the jewel certainly shines more bright in the new Circus than in the old.

7. The parts played by Ellen Terry during the period covered by Chapter XII were: Lady Macbeth ("Macbeth," 1887); Catharine Duval ("The Dead Heart," 1889); Lucy Ashton ("Ravenswood," 1890); Nance Oldfield ("Nance Oldfield," 1891); Katharine ("Henry VIII," 1891).

Chapter XIII

THE END OF THE LYCEUM

(1892–1902)

§ 1

I REMAINED exactly ten years more with Henry Irving after the production of "Henry VIII." During that time the vogue of the Lyceum declined, very gradually, and not always perceptibly to us, for we had ups as well as downs, and the ups created an illusion that nothing was changed. I know I did not realise at the time that the position of the theatre as an unique institution was changed by the opening of Her Majesty's Theatre in 1897. Mr Beerbohm Tree (now Sir Herbert Tree) shortly afterwards began a series of sumptuous productions of Shakespeare's plays which eventually became as fashionable as Henry's had been in the 'eighties and early 'nineties.

Of the productions at the Lyceum in its "twilight of the gods" period, "Cymbeline" was the most notable for me. I think as Imogen I gave the *only* inspired performance of these last rather sad years, when Henry had to fight ill-health as well as ill-luck. Yet I felt far from inspired on the first night. I wrote in my diary the next day (September 23, 1896): "Nothing seemed right. Everything was so slow, so slow. I didnt feel a bit inspired, only dull and hide-bound." Sir Laurence Alma-Tadema did the designs for the scenery and dresses in "Cymbeline," and I have to thank him for one of the loveliest dresses I ever wore.

Somehow these productions seem too near for me to see them properly. "King Lear," "King Arthur," "Becket," "Madame Sans-Gêne," "Peter the Great," "The Medicine Man"—they are all still in the foreground of my memory; I feel I could write about them more easily if they were further off. Before "King Lear" I wrote in my diary (January 18, 1892): "H. I. is hard at work, studying Lear. This is what only a great man would do at such a moment in the hottest blush of success" (I was referring to his triumph as Wolsey in "Henry VIII" which was still running then). "No swelled head—only fervent endeavour to do better work. The fools hardly conceive what he is." Later after the first night of "Lear" I wrote: "H. was just marvellous, but indistinct from

249

nervousness. T. spoke out, but who cared! Haviland was very good, and my Ted splendid in the little bit he had to do as Oswald. I was rather good tonight. Cordelia *is* a wee part, but a fine one all the same."

"King Lear" was one of our rare failures. "H. I. not well," I wrote in December, 1892. "Business by no means up to the proper point. A death in the Royal Family. Depression—depression!"

We had an "up" the following year when Henry put on "Madame Sans-Gêne." "A wonderful first-night audience," I wrote in my diary in April. "I acted *courageously*, and fairly well too. Extraordinary success." I remember that the old Duke of Cambridge patted, or rather *thumped* me on the back, and said enthusiastically: "Ah, my dear, *you* can act!"

I hate to think of "The Medicine Man." It was, in my opinion, the only production at the Lyceum *quite* unworthy of us. "Poor Taber," I wrote in my diary after the first night, "has an awful part, and mine is even worse. It is short enough, yet I feel I cant cut too much of it.... The gem of the whole play is my hair! Not waved at all, and very filmy and pale. Henry, I admit, is splendid; but oh, it is all such rubbish! ... If Manfred, and a few such plays are to succeed this, I simply *must* do something else."

But I did not! I stayed on, as every one knows, when the Lyceum, as a personal enterprise of Henry's, was no more. After the farcical Lyceum syndicate took over the theatre, I stayed on, and played a wretched part in "Robespierre." The idea that I deserted the sinking ship is rubbish. I think I did Henry a real service by refusing to play in his last new production, "Dante." It was a service which cost me £12,000, the sum I was offered to accompany him to America in "Dante," after its production at Drury Lane.

Henry was a changed man from the time he sold his rights in the theatre to a Company. He became less autocratic both as producer and manager, and left things to other people. As an actor he worked as conscientiously as ever, but his increasing physical weakness was a serious disadvantage. If I could tell here the whole story of the end of our long partnership, it would show that the accusation that he treated me badly is as silly as the accusation that I treated him badly. But I have decided that the time for that story has not come yet. I can say only that we never quarrelled, and that our separation could not be avoided.

In this last phase Henry was reproached more than ever for neglecting modern English dramatists. It should be remembered in his defence that the best of them were not writing plays of the type with which the Lyceum was associated. He was really anxious to produce J. M. Barrie's "The Professor's Love Story," and was delighted with the first act. When he had read the rest, he came to the conclusion that the play was on

250

much too small a scale for the Lyceum. This was his objection to most of the modern plays offered him.

In Mr Shaw's play "A Man of Destiny" there were two good parts, and Henry, at my request, considered it, although it was always difficult to fit a one-act play into the Lyceum bill. For reasons of his own Henry never produced it, and this caused a good deal of fuss at the time (1897). Ten years ago Mr Shaw was not as well known as he is now, and the fuss was probably of use to him as an advertisement. "A Man of Destiny" has been produced since, but without any great success. I have often wondered whether Henry and I could have done more with it.

At this time Mr Shaw and I frequently corresponded. It began by my writing to ask him, as musical critic of *The Saturday Review* to tell me frankly what he thought of the chances of a composer-singer friend of mine. He answered characteristically, and we developed a perfect fury for writing to each other. Sometimes the letters were on business, sometimes they were not, but always his were entertaining, and mine must have been "good copy," for he drew the character of Lady Cecily Wayn-flete in "Captain Brassbound's Conversion" entirely from my letters. He never met me until after the play was written. In 1902 he sent me this ultimatum:

April 3, 1902.

Mr Bernard Shaw's compliments to Miss Ellen Terry.

Mr Bernard Shaw has been approached by Mrs Langtry with a view to the immediate and splendid production of "Captain Brassbound's Conversion."

Mr Bernard Shaw, with the last flash of a trampled-out love, has repulsed Mrs Langtry with a petulance bordering on brutality.

Mr Bernard Shaw has been actuated in this ungentlemanly and unbusi-nesslike course by an angry desire to seize Miss Ellen Terry by the hair and make her play Lady Cicely.

Mr Bernard Shaw would be glad to know whether Miss Ellen Terry wishes to play Martha at the Lyceum instead.

Mr Bernard Shaw will go to the length of keeping a minor part open for Sir Henry Irving when "Faust" fails, if Miss Ellen Terry desires it.

Mr Bernard Shaw lives in daily fear of Mrs Langtry recovering suffi-ciently from her natural resentment of his ill manners to reopen the subject.

Mr Bernard Shaw begs Miss Ellen Terry to answer this letter.

Mr Bernard Shaw is looking for a new cottage or house in the coun-try, and wants advice on the subject.

Mr Bernard Shaw craves for the sight of Miss Ellen Terry's once familiar handwriting.

The first time he came to my house I was not present, but a young American lady who had long adored him from the other side of the

Atlantic took my place as hostess (I was at the theatre as usual); and I took great pains to have everything looking nice! I spent a long time putting out my best blue china, and ordered a splendid dinner, quite forgetting the honoured guest generally dined off a Plasmon biscuit and a bean!

Mr Shaw read "Arms and the Man" to my young American friend (Miss Satty Fairchild) without even going into the dining-room where the blue china was spread out to delight his eye. My daughter Edy was present at the reading, and appeared so much absorbed in some embroidery, and paid the author so few compliments about his play, that he expressed the opinion afterwards that she behaved as if she had been married to him for twenty years!

§ 2

On Whit Monday, 1902, I received a telegram from Mr Tree saying that he was coming down to Winchelsea to see me on "an important matter of business." I was at the time suffering from considerable depression about the future.

At Stratford-on-Avon a few weeks earlier I had played Queen Katharine with Mr Benson's company during the Shakespeare Birthday Festival, and that had inspired me with a feeling that there was life in this old 'un yet, that she need not retire from the stage because she was being forced into retirement from the Lyceum. Henry had just revived "Faust," a wise move, as it had been one of his biggest money-makers, and had engaged Cissy Loftus for Margaret. It was out of the question for me to play the part. There are some young parts that an actress can play when she is no longer young. Beatrice and Portia, and many others, come to mind. But there are some impossible for her. The part of a young girl, from whose childlike innocence the poignancy of the dramatic situation when she is betrayed arises, is one of these. No amount of skill on the part of the actress can make up for the loss of youth. It was suggested to me (not by Henry) that as I was too old for Margaret, I might play Martha! Well! Well! I didnt quite see *that!* So I kept a promise made in jest to Frank Benson at the Lyceum twenty years earlier, and went off to Stratford.

Mr Benson was wonderful to work with. "I am proud to think," he wrote me just before our few rehearsals of "Henry VIII" began, "that I have trained my folk (as I was taught by my elders and betters at the Lyceum) to be pretty quick at adapting themselves to anything that may be required of them, so that you need not be uneasy as to their not fitting in with your business."

Mr Benson's "folk" were excellent, especially young Harcourt Williams as Surrey, Matheson Lang as Norfolk, and H. O. Nicholson (a wonderful actor in Shakespeare) as Griffith. I played Katharine on Shakespeare's birthday—such a lovely day it was, bright and sunny and warm. The performance went finely; my reception cheered my heart. I was presented with the Certificate of Governorship of the Memorial Theatre, and left Stratford happy and invigorated. But there was nothing ahead except two matinées a week at the Lyceum, to be followed by a provincial tour in which I was only to play twice weekly, as the chief attraction was to be "Faust." This "dowager" engagement did not tempt me. I disliked the idea of it all the more because I was to be paid a large salary for doing next to no work.

It was while I was in this mood, finding my position almost unbearable, that I heard from Mr Tree. His proposal was that I should play Mrs Page (Mrs Kendal being Mrs Ford) in "The Merry Wives of Windsor" at His Majesty's. Before I accepted it, I telegraphed to Henry Irving, asking him if he had any objection to my playing at His Majesty's. He answered "Quite willing if proposed arrangements about matinées are adhered to."

I have thought it worth while to give the facts about this engagement, because so many people at the time seemed to think it was disloyal of me to desert the Lyceum for another theatre, and that theatre one where a certain rivalry with the Lyceum as regards Shakespearean productions had grown up. There is absolutely no foundation for the story that my "desertion" caused further estrangement between Henry Irving and me.

"Heaven give you many, many merry days and nights," he telegraphed to me on the first night; and after that first night (the jolliest I ever saw), he wrote, delighting in my success.

It *was* a success. There was no doubt about it! Some people accused the Merry Wives of rollicking overmuch, but these were the people who forgot that we were acting in a farce, and that farces will be farces, even when Shakespeare is their author.

All that summer I enjoyed myself thoroughly. It was all such good fun. Mrs Kendal was so clever and delightful to play with, Mr Tree so indefatigable in discovering new funny "business."

After the dress-rehearsal I wrote in my diary: "Edy has real genius for dresses for the stage." The dress she made me for Mrs Page, which Percy Anderson had to confess was a great improvement on his original design for it, was such a *real* thing! It helped me enormously to be a real merry wife. During the first week of the run there was a fire in my dressing-room, an odd fire which was never accounted for. In the morning they found my merry pink dress burnt to a cinder. A messenger from the theatre was despatched to my daughter who at the time had a theatrical costumier's "atelier" in Covent Garden to ask her what could be done. "Miss Terry will, I suppose, have to wear one of our dresses tonight. Perhaps you could replace hers by the end of the week?"

"Oh, dont worry," said Edy, bluffing. "I'll make her another dress by tonight." She has since told me that she did not really think it possible, but meant to have a try.

All hands in her workshop were put on the job, and every one who drifted in during the day was pressed into the service. The new dress, begun at 10.30 A.M. was in my dressing room at His Majesty's by 7 P.M. And, more wonderful still, it was better than the dress that had been burned! It stood the wear and tear of the long first run, and of all the revivals, and is now as fresh and pink and merry as ever!

It was an admirable all-round cast—almost a "star" cast: Oscar Asche as Ford, Henry Kemble (since dead) as Dr Caius, Courtice Pounds as Sir Hugh Evans, and Mrs Tree as sweet Anne Page all rowed in the boat with precisely the right swing. There were no "passengers" in the cast. The audience at first used to seem rather amazed! This thwacking rough-and-tumble, Rabelaisian horse-play, Shakespeare! Impossible! But as the evening went on we used to capture even the most sophisticated and force them to return to a simple Elizabethan frame of mind.

In my later career I think I have had no success equal to this! Letters rained on me, yes, even love-letters, as if, to quote Mrs Page, I were still in "the holiday-time of my beauty." As I would always rather make people laugh than see them weep, it may be guessed how much I enjoyed the hearty laughter at His Majesty's during the run of "The Merry Wives of Windsor."

All the time I was at His Majesty's I continued to play in matinées of "Charles I" and "The Merchant of Venice" at the Lyceum with Henry Irving. We went on negotiating, too, about the possibility of my appearing in "Dante," which Sardou had written specially for Henry, and on which he was relying for his next tour in America.

On the 19th of July, 1902, I acted at the Lyceum for the very last time, although I did not know it then. These last Lyceum days were very sad. The reception given by Henry to the Indian Princes, who were in England for the Coronation, was the last flash of the splendid hospitality which had for so many years been one of the glories of the theatre.

During my provincial tour with Henry in the autumn of this year, I thought long and anxiously over the proposition that I should play in "Dante." I heard the play read, and saw no possible part for me in it.

As I have already related, I refused a large sum of money to go to America on Henry's "Dante" tour.

Having made the decision not to go, I began to wonder what I should do. My partnership with Henry was definitely broken. There were many roads open to me. I chose one which, from a financial point of view, was unsafe.

I decided to take a theatre with my son, and produce plays in conjunction with him.

§ 3

I HAD several plays in view—an English translation of a French play about the patient Griselda, and a comedy by Miss Clo Graves among them. Finally, I decided upon Ibsen's "Vikings."

We read it aloud on Christmas Day, and it seemed *tremendous*. Not in my most wildly optimistic moments did I think Hiordis, the chief female character—a primitive, fighting, free, open-air person—suited to me, but I saw a way of playing her more *brilliantly* and less *weightily* than the text suggested, and anyhow I was not thinking so much of the play's suitability for me, as of its suitability for my son. He had just produced Mr Laurence Housman's Nativity play "Bethlehem" in the hall of the Imperial Institute, and every one had spoken enthusiastically of the beauty of his work. He had previously applied the same principles to the mounting of operas by Handel and Purcell.

It had been a great grief to me when I lost my son as an actor. I have never known any one with so much natural gift for the stage. Unconsciously he did everything right from the first—I mean all the technical things over which some of us have to labour for years. The first part that he played at the Lyceum, Arthur St Valery in "The Dead Heart," was good, and he went on steadily improving. The last part that he played at the Lyceum—Edward IV in "Richard III"—was a really great performance.

Later on he played Hamlet, Macbeth and Romeo on a small provincial tour. His future as an actor seemed assured, but it wasnt! One day when he was with William Nicholson, best known then as one of the Beggarstaff Brothers of poster fame, he began chipping at a woodblock in imitation of Nicholson, and produced in a few hours an admirable woodcut of Walt Whitman. From that moment he had the "black and white" fever badly. Acting for a time seemed hardly to interest him at all. When his interest in the theatre revived, it was not as an actor but as a stage director that he wanted to work.

What more natural than that I should be anxious to co-operate with him in exploiting his ideas in London? Ideas he had in plenty. "Unpractical" ideas people called them; but what else should *ideas* be?

At the Imperial Theatre, where I made my first venture into management in April, 1903, I gave my son a free hand. I hope it will be remembered, when I am spoken of by young critics after my death as a "Victorian" actress, an actress belonging to the "old school," that I produced a spectacular play of Ibsen's in a manner which possibly anticipated the scenic ideas of the future by a century.

Naturally I am not inclined to criticise my son's methods. I think there is a great deal to be said for the views that he has expressed in his book on "The Art of the Theatre," and when I worked with him I found him far from unpractical. It was the modern theatre which was unpractical when he was in it! It was wrongly designed, wrongly built. We had to disembowel the Imperial behind scenes before he could even make a start, and then the great height of the proscenium made his lighting lose all its value. He always considered the pictorial side of the scene before its dramatic significance, arguing that this significance lay in the picture and in movement, the drama having originated not with the poet but with the dancer.

When his idea of dramatic significance clashed with Ibsen's, strange things would happen.

Mr Bernard Shaw, though impressed by my son's work and the beauty that he brought on to the stage of the Imperial, wrote to me that the atmosphere of the first act according to Ibsen should be dawn, youth rising with the morning sun, reconciliation, rich gifts, brightness, lightness, pleasant feelings, peace. On to this sunlit scene stalks Hiordis, a figure symbolic of gloom, revenge, eternal feud, of relentless hatred and uncompromising unforgetfulness of wrong. At the Imperial, said Mr Shaw, the curtain rose on profound gloom. When you *could* see anything you saw eld and severity—old men with white hair substituted for the gallant young sons of Ornulf—everywhere murky cliffs and shadowy spears, melancholy, and—darkness!

Into this symbolic night enter, in a blaze of limelight, a fair figure robed in complete fluffy white fur, a gay and bright Hiordis with a timid manner and a hesitating utterance.

For the last items in this list of incongruities my son was not responsible. They were my fault!

His beautiful production was received with such enthusiasm on the first night that I was sanguine of a success. But people did not come to the Imperial in sufficient numbers to make it possible for me to keep it on long. The running expenses were a terrible drain on my purse. "The Vikings" had to be withdrawn before our second production, "Much

Photograph by Steichen

GORDON CRAIG

Ado About Nothing," was ready. Like "The Vikings" "Much Ado" had a splendid first night, and the distinction of my son's work in it was generally recognised, but it did not draw the public. In June I was compelled to give in, and close the theatre.

§ 4

DURING one of the provincial tours which followed this London season, I produced "The Good Hope," a play by the Dutch dramatist, Heijermans, dealing with life in a small port on the North Sea. Done into simple and vigorous English by Christopher St John, the play proved a great success in the provinces. This was almost as new a departure for me as my season at the Imperial. The play was essentially modern in construction and development—full of action, but the action of incident rather than the action of stage situation. It had no "star" parts, but every part was good, and the tragedy of the story was made bearable by the beauty of the atmosphere—of the *sea,* which plays a bigger part in it than any of the characters.

For the first time in my career I played an old woman, a very homely old peasant woman too. It was not a big part, but it was interesting, and in the last act I had a little scene in which I was able to make the same kind of effect that I had made years before in the last act of "Ravenswood"—an effect of *quiet* and stillness.

I flattered myself that I was able to assume a certain roughness and stolidity in "The Good Hope," but although I stumped about heavily in large sabots, I was told by the critics that I walked like a fairy, and was far too graceful for a Dutch fisherwoman! Give a dog a bad name, and hang him! I have a "name" as an actress for being graceful and charming, so nothing will persuade some people that I have been neither in some parts! It does not seem to occur to them that if I convey the impression of fairy-like grace when I am representing a fisherwoman or a washerwoman I must be a very bad actress.

§ 5

IN 1905, the year of Henry Irving's death, I had the privilege of "creating" a new part in a play by Mr Barrie, which he wrote specially for me. When he came down to my old farm at Smallhythe with Mr Frohman, and told me the story of "Alice-Sit-By-The-Fire," I was enchanted with it; I believe he told it better than he wrote it. He thought he had got a lot of *me* into the part, and Alice was certainly endowed with many of my ways, my way of carrying a large bag, crammed full of letters and

257

odds and ends, about with me everywhere, for example. I knew how many personal friends of mine were in the audience, when I played this part, by the amount of laughter there was at the line: "If you dont know what is in that bag, you dont know your mother!" Irene Vanbrugh was my daughter in the play, and gave a delightful performance. I was never happy in my part, perhaps because although it had been made to measure, it didnt fit me. I sometimes felt that I was bursting the seams! I was accustomed to broader work in a larger theatre.

It was a joy to be brought in contact with Mr Barrie again. I had been an ardent lover of his ever since the publication of "Sentimental Tommy." I simply had to write and tell him how hugely I had enjoyed it, and my letter got a reply from Tommy himself!

DEAR MISS ELLEN TERRY,—

I just wondered at you. I noticed that Mr Barrie the author (so-called) and his masterful wife had a letter they wanted to conceal from me, so I got hold of it, and it turned out to be from you, and *not a line to me in it!* If you like the book, it is *me* you like, not him, and it is to me you should send your love, not to him. Corp thinks, however, that you did not like to make the first overtures, and if that is the explanation, I beg herewith to send you my warm love (dont mention this to Elspeth) and to say that I wish you would come and have a game with us in the Den (dont let on to Grizel that I invited you). The first moment I saw you, I said to myself, "This is the kind I like," and while the people round about me were only thinking of your acting, I was wondering which would be the best way of making you my willing slave, and I beg to say that I believe I have "found a way," for most happily the very ones I want most to lord it over, are the ones who are least able to resist me.

We should have ripping fun. You would be Jean MacGregor, captive in the Queen's Bower, but I would climb up at the peril of my neck to rescue you, and you would faint in my strong arms, and wouldn't Grizel get a turn when she came upon you and me whispering sweet nothings in the Lovers' Walk? I think it advisable to say *in writing* that I would only mean them as nothings (because Grizel is really my one), but so long as they were sweet, what does that matter (at the time); and besides, *you* could *love me* genuinely, and I would carelessly kiss your burning tears away.

Corp is a bit fidgety about it, because he says I have two to love me already, but I feel confident that I can manage more than two.

Trusting to see you at the Cuttle Well on Saturday when the eight o'clock bell is ringing,

I am,

Your indulgent Commander,

T. SANDYS.

P.S. Can you bring some of the Lyceum armor with you, and two hard-boiled eggs?

IT is now common knowledge that Henry Irving's health began to fail in the year 1896, but for years few outside the small circle of his fellow-workers and intimate friends were aware that he was constantly ill. He fought valiantly against the physical weakness each illness increased, and seldom betrayed in his acting that he had to be careful how he exerted himself.

He was never as active again after the first night of the revival of "Richard III," which followed "Cymbeline." It was as Richard that he had achieved one of his greatest successes before he became manager of the Lyceum, and now after the lapse of twenty years, he had done it again. I had gone abroad for a holiday after "Cymbeline," and was not present at that wonderful first night which had such a disastrous sequel. Henry after sitting up till dawn with his crony Professor Dewar, first at the Garrick Club, then at Professor Dewar's rooms in Albemarle Street, then at Henry's rooms in Grafton Street, slipped on the steep dark staircase leading to his bedroom, and injured his knee. He struggled to his feet, and walked to his room. This made the consequences of the accident more serious, and ten weeks passed before he was able to act again. It was a bad year at the Lyceum. Instead of the prosperous season which the success of "Richard III" on the first night augured, we had one which ended with a loss of six thousand pounds. The only "up" was the success of a revival of "Olivia," in which I hurried back from my holiday to play. Herman Vezin, who had played Dr Primrose with me at the Court Theatre, took Henry's place.

A slip of the foot destroyed Henry's activity. Getting his feet wet, walking to the station at Edinburgh, during our provincial tour in 1898, destroyed his health. He arrived in Glasgow suffering from a chill. Pleurisy, bronchitis and pneumonia developed. He was near death.

"I am still fearfully anxious about H.," I wrote to my daughter, at the time of this serious illness: "It will be a long time at best before he regains strength.... All he wants is for me to keep my health—not my head! He knows I'm doing that! Last night I did three acts of 'Sans-Gêne,' with 'Nance Oldfield' thrown in! That is a bit too much—awful work—and I cant risk it again.... A telegram just come: 'Steadily improving.' ... You should have seen Norman as Shylock! It was not a bare 'get-through.' An admirable performance as well as a plucky one. H. is more seriously ill than any one dreams. His look! Like the last act of Louis XI."

When I think of Henry's work during the next seven years, I could weep! Never was there a more admirable, extraordinary worker; never had any one more courage and patience. Blow after blow; that accident which crippled him and the Lyceum; that illness which made him suddenly an old man; that fire which destroyed the scenery of some of his finest productions; yet he never complained, never spoke bitterly of his ill-luck.

In 1902, on the last provincial tour that we ever went together, he was ill again, but he did not give in. One night when his cough was rending him, and he could hardly stand up from weakness, he acted so brilliantly and powerfully that it was easy to believe in the triumph of mind over matter. Strange to say, a newspaper man noticed the splendid force of his performance that night, and wrote about it with uncommon discernment.

In London at this time he was still being urged to produce new plays. But in the face of the failure of his last new Shakespearean venture, "Coriolanus," of his departing strength, and of the extraordinary support given him in the old plays (during this 1902 tour we took £4,000 at Glasgow in one week) he would have been wiser to rely on them to the end of the chapter. His experience when he produced "Dante" proves this. Both in England and America, "Dante" was far less successful than the old plays put on at the same time.

I realised how near, not only the end of the chapter, but the end of the book was when he was taken ill at Wolverhampton in the spring of 1905.

We had not acted together for over two years then, and times were changed indeed.

I went down to Wolverhampton immediately after the news of the illness, and the abandonment of his tour, had reached London. I arrived late and went to an hotel for the night. The next morning I got up early and went out with the intention of buying Henry some flowers. I wanted some bright-coloured ones for him—he had always liked bright flowers—but the Wolverhampton florist dealt chiefly in white flowers—*funeral* flowers.

At last I found some daffodils—my favourite flower. I bought a bunch, and the kind florist found me a nice simple glass to put it in. I knew the sort of vase that I should find at Henry's hotel.

I remembered, on my way to the doctor's—for I had decided to see the doctor first—that in 1892 when my dear mother died, and I did not act for a few nights, I came back to the Lyceum and found my room filled with daffodils. "To make it look like sunshine," Henry said.

The doctor talked to me quite frankly.

"His heart is dangerously weak," he said.

"Have you told him?" I asked.

"I had to, because the heart being in that condition he must be careful."

"Did he understand *really?*"

"Oh, yes. He said he quite understood."

Yet a few minutes later when I saw Henry, and begged him to remember what the doctor had said about his heart, he exclaimed: "Fiddle! It's not my heart at all! It's my *breath!*" (Oh, the ignorance of great men about themselves!)

"I also told him," the Wolverhampton doctor went on, "that he must not work so hard in future."

I said: "He will, though—and he's stronger than any of us."

Then I went round to the hotel.

I found him sitting up in bed, drinking his coffee.

He looked like some beautiful grey tree that I have seen in Savannah. His old dressing-gown hung about his frail yet majestic figure like some mysterious grey drapery.

We were both very much moved, and said little.

"I'm glad you've come. Two Queens have been kind to me this morning. Queen Alexandra telegraphed to say how sorry she was I was ill, and now you—"

He showed me the Queen's gracious message.

I told him he looked thin and ill, but *rested.*

"Rested! I should think so. I have plenty of time to rest. They tell me I shall be here eight weeks. Of course I shant, but still—. It was that rug in front of the door. I tripped over it. A commercial traveller picked me up—a kind fellow, but damn him, he wouldnt leave me afterwards. He wanted to talk to me all night."

I remembered his having said this, when I was told by his servant, Walter Collinson, that on the night of his death at Bradford, he had stumbled over the rug when he walked into the corridor.

We fell to talking about work. He said he hoped that I had a good manager...agreed very heartily with me about Frohman, saying he was always so fair—more than fair.

"What a wonderful life you've had, havent you?" I exclaimed, thinking of it all in a flash.

"Oh, yes," he said quietly..."a wonderful life—of work."

"And there's nothing better, after all, is there?"

"Nothing."

"What have you got out of it all?...You and I are 'getting on,' as they say. Do you ever think, as I do sometimes, what you have got out of life?"

"What have I got out of it?" said Henry, stroking his chin and smiling slightly. "Let me see.... Well, a good cigar, a good glass of wine—good friends." Here he kissed my hand with courtesy. Always he was so courteous; always his actions, like this little one of kissing my hand, were so beautifully timed. They came just before the spoken words, and gave them peculiar value.

"That's not a bad summing-up of it all," I said. "And the end.... How would you like that to come?"

"How would I like that to come?" He repeated my question lightly, yet meditatively too. Then he was silent for some thirty seconds before he snapped his fingers—the action again before the words.

"Like that!"

I thought of the definition of inspiration—"A calculation rapidly made." Perhaps he had never thought of the manner of his death before. Now he had an inspiration as to how it would come.

We were silent a long time. I thought how like some splendid Doge of Venice he looked, sitting up in bed, his beautiful mobile hand stroking his chin.

I agreed, when I could speak, that to be snuffed out like a candle would save a lot of trouble.

After Henry Irving's sudden death in October of the same year, some of his friends protested against the statement that it was the kind of death that he desired—that they knew, on the contrary, that he thought sudden death inexpressibly sad.

I can only say what he told me.

I stayed with him about three hours at Wolverhampton. Before I left, I went back to see the doctor again—a very nice man by the way, and clever.

He told me that Henry ought never to play "The Bells" again, even if he acted again, which he said ought not to be.

It was clever of the doctor to see what a terrible emotional strain "The Bells" put upon Henry—how he never could play Mathias with ease as he could Louis XI, for example.

Every time he heard the sound of the bells, the throbbing of his heart must have nearly killed him. He used always to turn quite white—there was no trick about it. It was imagination acting physically on the body.

His death as Mathias—the death of a strong, robust man—was different from all his other stage deaths. He did really almost die—he imagined death with such horrible intensity. His eyes would disappear upwards, his face grow grey, his limbs cold.

No wonder, then, that the first time that the Wolverhampton doctor's warning was disregarded, and Henry played "The Bells" at Bradford, his heart could not stand the strain. Within twenty-four hours of his last death as Mathias, he was dead.

What a heroic thing was that last performance of Becket which came between! I am told by those who were in the company at the time that he was obviously suffering and dazed, this last night of life. But he went through it all as usual. The courteous little speech to the audience, the signing of a worrying boy's drawing at the stage-door—all that he had done for years, he did faithfully for the last time.

I know it seems sad to some that he should have died in the entrance to an hotel in a provincial town with no friend, no relation near him. Only his faithful and devoted servant Walter (whom, as was not his usual custom, he had asked to drive back to the hotel with him that night) was there. Yet I feel that such a deathbed was more fitting for such a man than one where friends and relations weep.

Henry Irving belonged to England, not to a family. England showed that she knew it when she buried him in Westminster Abbey.

Years before I had discussed, half in joke, the possibility of this honour. I remember his saying to me with great simplicity, when I asked him what he expected of the public after his death: "I should like them to do their duty by me. And they will—they will!"

There was not a touch of arrogance in this. I hope there was not a touch of heartlessness in me because my chief thought during the funeral in Westminster Abbey: "How Henry would have liked it!" The right note was struck, as I think it was not at Tennyson's funeral thirteen years earlier.

Tennyson is buried today in Westminster Abbey, I wrote in my diary, October 12, 1892. His majestic life and death spoke of him better than the service ... The music was poor and dull and weak, while he was *strong*. The triumphant should have been the sentiment expressed ... No face there, looked anything by the side of Henry's ... He looked very pale and slim and wonderful.

How terribly I missed that face at Henry's own funeral! I kept on expecting to see it, for indeed it seemed to me that he was directing the whole most moving and impressive ceremony. I could almost hear him saying, "Get on! get on!" in the parts of the service that dragged. When the sun—such a splendid, tawny sun—burst across the solemn misty grey of the Abbey, at the very moment when the coffin, under its superb pall of laurel leaves [1] was carried up the choir, I felt that it was an effect which he would have loved.

[1] Every lover of beauty and every lover of Henry Irving must have breathed a silent thanksgiving that day to the friend who had that inspiration and made the pall with her own hands.

263

I can understand any one who was present at Henry Irving's funeral thinking that this was his best memorial, and that any attempt to honour him afterwards would be superfluous and inadequate.

Yet when some further memorial was discussed, it was not always easy to sympathise with those who said: "We got him buried in Westminster Abbey. What more do you want?"

After all it was Henry Irving's commanding genius, and his devotion of it to high objects, his personal influence on the English people, which secured him burial among England's great dead. The petition for the burial presented to the Dean and Chapter, and signed, on the initiative of Henry Irving's leading fellow-actors, by representative personages of influence, succeeded only because of Henry's unique position.

"We worked very hard to get it done," I heard said—more than once. And I often longed to answer: "Yes, and all honour to your efforts, but you worked for it between Henry's death and his funeral. *He* worked for it all his life!"

I have always desired some other memorial to Henry Irving than his honoured grave, not so much for *his* sake as for the sake of those who loved him and would gladly welcome the opportunity of some great test of their devotion.

Henry Irving's profession decided last year, after much belated discussion, to put up a statue to him in the streets of London. I believe that it is to take the form of a portrait statue in academic robes. A statue can never at any time be a very happy memorial to an actor, who does not do his work in his own person, but through his imagination of many different persons. If statue it had to be, the work should have had a symbolic character. My dear friend Alfred Gilbert, one of the most gifted sculptors of this or any age, expressed a similar opinion to the committee of the memorial, and later on wrote to me as follows:

I should never have attempted the representation of Irving as a mummer, nor literally as Irving, disguised as this one or that one, but as *Irving*—the artistic exponent of other great artists' conceptions—*Irving*, the greatest illustrator of the greatest men's creations—he himself being a creator.

I had no idea of making use of Irving's facial and physical peculiarities as a means to perpetuate his life's work. The spirit of this work was worship of an ideal, and it was no fault of his that his strong personality dominated the honest conviction of his critics. These judged Irving as the man masquerading, not as the artist interpreting, for the single reason that they were themselves overcome by the magic personality of a man above their comprehension.

I am convinced that Irving, when playing the rôle of whatever character he undertook to represent, lived in that character, and not as the actor playing the part for the applause of those in front. Charles I was a masterpiece of conception as to the representation of a great gentleman. His Cardinal Wolsey was the most perfect presentation of greatness, of self-abnegation, and of power to suffer I can realise ... Jingle and Mathias were, in Comedy and Tragedy combined, masterpieces of histrionic art. I could write volumes upon Irving as an actor, but to write of him as a *man,* and as a very great Artist, I should require more time than is still allotted to me of man's brief span of life, and far, far more power than that which was given to those who wrote of him in a hurry during his lifetime.... Do you wonder, then, that I should rather elect to regard Irving in the abstract, when called upon to suggest a fitting monument, than to promise a faithful portrait? ... Let us be grateful, however, that a great artist is to be commemorated at all, side by side with the effigies of great butchers of mankind, and ephemeral statesmen, the instigators of useless bloodshed....

NOTES TO CHAPTER XIII

1. 1892-1902. The "undeniable scrappiness" of the last chapters of Ellen Terry's autobiography is explained in the preface to this new edition. The explanation accounts for my having made many revisions. The most important are not in the text itself, but in its arrangment. The narrative of the last years at the Lyceum, of the end of Ellen Terry's partnership with Irving, of her venture into management, and of Irving's death has been reconstructed, and is now given in a single chapter. I have interpolated some of the extracts from her diaries, which were given *apropos des bottes* at the end of the book in the old edition. Those who are able to compare that edition with the new one will find that after the chapter on "The Macbeth Period" (numbered XIII in the old, and XII in the new) there are many differences between the two. The narrative takes a less rambling course in the new edition, and so can be more easily followed. I might have hesitated to revise these last pages so drastically if I had not known that Ellen Terry, after their publication, was dissatisfied with them. They are annotated in her copy with many unflattering remarks. The passages she disliked most have been omitted altogether, for example one after the letter from Bernard Shaw on page 251. "This is jolly poor of 'such a man as Orlando' " she wrote in the margin about a somewhat superficial character-sketch of her distinguished correspondent. Another character-sketch, scored through, with the note: "This is unfair and inadequate," I have also felt it my duty to cut.

2. *Ellen Terry's "Cymbeline" dress.* The photograph taken of Ellen Terry in this dress by her official photographers, Window and Grove, was a special favourite of hers. On the back of a copy she kept at Smallhythe she wrote: "Imogen, 1896. Think of me like this. Good-bye, everybody, at the farm, 192-". The inscription, with the blank in the last date, shows that Ellen Terry had a prescience when and where she would die. She died in 1928 at her farm at Smallhythe.

3. *The correspondence with Bernard Shaw.* Various inferences will no

doubt be drawn from the rather surprising fact that although Ellen Terry had over a hundred letters from Shaw in her possession in 1906, she published only one in her memoirs. I have already stated in the editorial note preceding this letter in "Ellen Terry and Bernard Shaw: A Correspondence," published in 1931, that when we were working together on her book, I urged her, after she had told me she had heaps of other letters from Shaw, to select some for inclusion, and submit them to him for the necessary permission, and that she put me off with the plea that she could not find them. I have no doubt this was true. She often could not find things she cherished, not because she had carelessly mislaid them, but because she had carefully put them away in some "safe place," the whereabouts of which she had forgotten. But she gave me the impression that she did not want to find these letters. After one rather cursory search, she said her inability to find them didn't matter, as there were "things in them about Henry which ought not to be published so soon after his death." She may have had other objections to their being published at that time, or at any time while she was alive, but I am convinced she foresaw the possibility of their being published in a remote future, and was not horrified at the possibility. The chief reason for this conviction is that she destroyed all letters of a very intimate nature. Of the thousands of love-letters she must have received, very few were found in her archives after her death, and these few seem to have been kept for a definite purpose. She was not one of those people who are averse to all thought of what will happen after they are dead, and would, I believe, have made careful provision for the destruction by her executors of those letters, diaries and note-books which she had refrained from destroying herself, if she had been anxious that they should not survive her. It is a reasonable conjecture that she knew their value, and foresaw their future interest.

The account given in this chapter of the origin of the correspondence with Bernard Shaw is in all essentials accurate. There are slips in details, which have already been corrected in the first editorial note in "Ellen Terry and Bernard Shaw: A Correspondence." Ellen Terry's first letter about her "composer-singer friend" was addressed not to Shaw, but to Edmund Yates, and Shaw was writing musical criticism for Yates's weekly "The World" at the time, not for "The Saturday Review." The brevity of Ellen Terry's allusion to a correspondence, now famous, is quite natural when one considers that it was made at a period when Shaw was not, although she was playing in "Captain Brassbound's Conversion," of great importance in her life. The time when they wrote to one another every day was over. As correspondents, who never met, they were on terms of much greater intimacy than as author and actress, who met every day at rehearsals. It is possible that this might not have been so, if during these rehearsals Ellen Terry had been fancy-free. But she was in the toils of one of those strange infatuations which seem to us stranger when women of strong character and great talent are their victims. A young American actor in the cast of "Brassbound" had the embarrassing privilege of putting Bernard Shaw's nose out of joint. The reader who is surprised at the insignificant place occupied by Shaw in Ellen Terry's memoirs should remember that at this stage in them she had just been married to the young actor. That Shaw-Irving controversy over "A Man of Destiny" which had once concerned her so deeply, and been the theme of scores of the letters in her long correspondence with Shaw, now seems to her a lot of fuss about nothing.

In this Shaw-detached state of mind, it is perhaps natural that Ellen Terry should not have bothered to verify her references to him. It was not "Arms and the Man" he read at her house to Satty Fairchild and Edy, but "You Never Can Tell."

4. *The Vikings.* Some idea of the impression made by Ellen Terry's enterprise at the Imperial Theatre, which her son, to judge from his account of it in "Ellen Terry and Her Secret Self," now thinks would have been far more successful if she had had co-adjutors of his choosing, can be gained from a letter from Mr (now Sir William) Rothenstein dated May 8, 1903.

DEAR MISS TERRY: We all owe you a double debt of gratitude. First of all you have given Teddie the chance of showing us how far he could surpass even his best friends' and admirers' expectations of his powers, and secondly because you yourself have helped him by interpreting the principal part in the play in a magnificent, profoundly imaginative manner....

Will you tell Teddie I have never before been so actually excited by any production as by this. I only wish people could distinguish more innocently and frankly between the highest and best work, and more or less intelligent or skillful, or modern-archaistical experiments. Teddie has the *right* conception, and simple as it sounds, we all know how difficult it is to be right, not merely nearly right. It seemed to me, indeed, to all of us (my wife and the Protheros were equally moved by acting and scenery) that never before had we seen such perfect marriage of dramatic suggestion in the foreground, background and grouping of the figures, and the actual delivery and gesture, which resulted in a perfectly noble expression of the tragedy of men's and women's lives. Nothing seemed to lag behind, or to hurry in front. Everything seemed terribly but simply inevitable, from the black sky, to the checked gowns of the heroes, from your laugh at the bending of your bow, to the burning of the house. I feel I owe you and Teddie much; I wish I could prove my gratitude.... You have been so brave and good to Teddie. I am so delighted he has been able to show you how wise you have been; I am sure that in a very short time he will have won that foremost place in the modern theatre he already has shown his right to.

It is interesting to compare Rothenstein's impression with Shaw's, derived by Ellen Terry from a letter which is not included in the published correspondence. Shaw may have been right about the timid entrance of Hiordis—Ellen Terry had to descend a precipitous slope, and was half-blinded at the start by the battery of arcs from the bridge—but he was wrong about Craig's scene being the exact opposite of Ibsen's intentions. Ibsen states that "it is a stormy snow-grey winter day." There is nothing about sunshine until after Hiordis's entrance, and then the sun is described as "a red disc low upon the rim of the sea."

Craig, like Shaw, suffers in this chapter from Ellen Terry's pre-occupation at the time it was written with other things than her memories of the past. She was quite sensible, at a later period, that she had not done her son's work for her justice.

5. *The Good Hope.* Ellen Terry's enterprise in producing this play was

267

very inadequately recognised. She must have been cheered by a letter from Laurence Irving in which he congratulates her on her pluck in doing a play "that deals with lives as they are lived," adding that it is a proof "you are not going to let the times leave you behind them."

6. *The separation from Irving.* The passage in which Ellen Terry says the time for the story of this separation "has not come yet," implies that she was not averse to its being told later. It is simply not possible for a biography written shortly after a man's death by one of his intimates to be entirely honest. This impossibility was felt by Ellen Terry, whenever she wrote about Henry Irving in this book, begun within a year of his death. She therefore made no use of a frank and honest study of him, compiled at various dates during the Lyceum partnership. It was found in a shabby little account book, and both Edith Craig and I felt after reading it that it threw a light on Irving which ought not to be hidden under a bushel. We have decided to publish it in the form of an appendix to this chapter, and believe it will enormously increase respect both for the genius of its writer, and the character of her subject.

7. The parts played by Ellen Terry during the period covered by Chapter XIII were: Cordelia ("King Lear," 1892): Rosamund ("Becket," 1892): Lady Soupire ("Journeys End in Lovers' Meeting," 1894): Guinevere ("King Arthur," 1895): Yolande ("Godefroi and Yolande," 1895): Imogen ("Cymbeline," 1895): Catharine ("Madame Sans-Gêne," 1897): Catharine ("Peter the Great," 1898): Sylvia Wynford ("The Medicine Man," 1898): Clarice ("Robespierre," 1899): Mrs Tresilian ("Variations," 1899): Volumnia ("Coriolanus," 1901): Mrs Page ("Merry Wives of Windsor," 1902): Hiordis ("The Vikings," 1903): Evodia ("The Mistress of the Robes," 1903): Kniertje ("The Good Hope," 1904): Brita ("Eriksson's Wife," 1904): Alice Grey ("Alice Sit by the Fire," 1905): Lady Cecily Waynflete ("Captain Brassbound's Conversion," 1906): Francisca ("Measure for Measure," 1906): Hermione ("A Winter's Tale," 1906).

APPENDIX TO CHAPTER XIII

"ABOUT H. I." (BY ELLEN TERRY)

December, 1894. He is the first to be perfect in his words at rehearsal of any new play. For "a good poet (and actor) is *made* as well as born"—as old Ben Jonson wrote.

He sees things at a flash, *after* pondering upon them for weeks! He studies, and studies, and then *has inspiration.*

He is always punctual and never in a hurry. Will not read his parts, nor think of it last thing at night. *Clever.*

He believes in "2 or 3 dress-rehearsals." *Clever.*

1895. He very seldom will rehearse his part *quite* as he is going to do it at night, but he maps it all out, and scientifically goes through it with the others so that they may see what he intends to do, but he reserves all passion of the part until the evening performance.

He dines between 2 and 3, and takes a cup of coffee only, *just* before starting for the theatre. *Clever.*

He is so careful and cautious. I wish he were more ingenuous and more direct.

A thousand little things prove he has no idea of his own beauty—personal beauty. He uses his very fine hands unconsciously, except in what are called "character" parts. One day he said: "Physical gifts of voice, beauty, etc. are the best equipment for an actor, and I believe I am the only actor on record who has succeeded in spite of having none of these gifts." He said it very earnestly, almost triumphantly, quite believing it. I grant his intellectuality dominates his other powers and gifts, but I have never seen in living man, or picture, such distinction of bearing. A splendid figure, and his face very noble. A superb brow; rather small dark eyes which can at moments become immense, and hang like a bowl of dark liquid with light shining through; a most refined curving Roman nose, strong and delicate in line, and *cut clean* (as all his features); a smallish mouth, and full of the most wonderful teeth, even at 55; lips most delicate and refined—firm, firm, firm—and with a rare smile of the most exquisite beauty, and quite-not-to-be described kind. (He seems always ashamed of his smile, even in very private life, and will withdraw it at once in public.) His chin, and the line from the ear to chin is firm, extremely delicate, and very strong and clean defined. He has an ugly ear! Large, flabby, ill-cut, and pasty-looking, pale and lumpy. His hair is superb; beautiful in 1867, when I first met him, when it was blue-black like a raven's wing, it is even more splendid now (1895) when it is liberally streaked with white. It is rather long, and hangs in lumps on his neck, which is now like the neck of a youth of 20! His skin is very pale, delicate, refined, and stretched tightly over his features. Under the influence of strong emotion, it contracts more, and turning somewhat paler, a grey look comes into his face, and the hollows of his cheeks and eyes show up clearly.

Never have I seen such hands, "in form and moving how *express* and admirable." He always makes them up for the stage very brown.

May, 1895. The Queen has made him a Knight, the first actor who has ever received that honour. Better late than never. The dear fellow deserves any honour, all honours. He is just as pleased about it as he should be, and I'm much pleased too.

He has a strange desire to hide some things—to be sly! He is not oversuccessful at all times. He and A and B will be sitting together, and he will say something to A covertly about himself (A) and *touch* B! All as transparent as possible, and those who know H. I. will understand perfectly.

But I must keep to *his work*.

August, 1895. At Winchelsea he read out loud in the evening the play of "Coriolanus" as he had prepared it for the stage. He had announced it the last night of the season, and for a fortnight had been working on it all day and a good part of the night. It was now quite ship-shape, and he read it to us—Joe Evans of New York, Anna Evans, Edy and me. As it went on and on, we thought it duller and duller, and at the end I felt convinced it was no good as an acting play, and said so. The rest were—polite. I said nothing could make me believe Shakespeare ever wrote it. Henry, for contradiction, said it was very fine, and he'd cut it more! But the next morning he called out to me from his bedroom to mine: "I shant do that play." Joy! Joy! He had *thought* about it in the night, and after thinking, decided quickly. He said: "I'll do 'Julius Cæsar' instead." I am *very* glad, because J. C. is such a living play. I've nothing of a part in it, but it's a fine play.

August 25, 1895. Very hot in London. Back, snatching a few rehearsals of our old plays with our new people. H. I. sticks on at it through the heat, for there's only a week before we start for America.

August 31, 1895. Off we go by the *New York,* a huge boat, 400 passengers. No identity for any one. Yes, a little perhaps for H. I., but on a boat he does not shine at his best! A bad passage. H. I. very patient.

September 12, 1895. Montreal, and meeting the company (who came from England by another ship). We rehearse "Faust." H. I. is odd when he says he hates meeting the company, and "shaking their greasy paws." I think it is not quite right in him that he does not care for anybody much. (I think he has always cared for me a little, very little, and has had passing fancies, but he really *cares* for scarcely any one.)

Quiet, patient, tolerant, impersonal, gentle, *close,* crafty! Crafty sounds unkind, but it is H. I. "Crafty" fits him.

1896. H. I. appears to me to be getting impatient as other actors come on. He is tired.

His work, his work! He has always held his life, and his death, second to his work. When he dies, it will be because he is tired out. Now, double performances (Saturday mornings and evenings) oblige him to stimulate himself with wine, and at about midnight he looks like a corpse.

I have a quick ear for different people's *step,* and a familiar step I generally hear before I see the stepper, but though I have listened for many years for Henry Irving's step, *I have never heard it!*

I consider I have been of a good deal of use to him as a buffer between him and his company.

H. I. is much handsomer now than when I first knew him in 1867. Handsomer, but somehow more furtive-looking. Is his dominant note intellectuality? Yes, I think so. He has so much character.

The best in him is his patience, his caution, his strong, practical will, and his gentle courtesy. His worst is his being incapable of caring for people, sons, friends, any one, and his lack of enthusiasm for other people's work, or indeed for anything outside *his own* work. It has caused him, I should say, a great loss of happiness, yet the *concentration* has achieved results.

He is a wonderful man.

If it could be possible for him to take this infinite pains for *another,* he would be a perfect being, but self-concentration spoils the porridge.

Indifference is personified in H. I.

He has faults, but still such an over-balancing amount of virtues, that he is quite one of the best and most remarkable men of his time.

270

He is a very *gentle* man, though not in the least a *tender* man.

1897. Very odd. He is not improving with age.

I was at Tewkesbury yesterday, and felt how like he *really* is to the great Abbey there, but his admiration is for something of quite another sort. He tries to be like Milan Cathedral. He never admires the right thing. (This tells against myself since I know he has always "admired" me! Perhaps though, he has only "admired" my usefulness to him!)

February, 1898. For years he has accepted favours, obligations to, etc., *through* Bram Stoker! Never will he acknowledge them himself, either by business-like receipt or by any word or sign. He "lays low" like Brer Rabbit better than any one I have ever met. His hold upon *me* is that he is INTERESTING no matter how he behaves. I think he must be put down among the "Greats," and that *that* is his only fault. He is Great. Constantine, Nero, Cæsar, Charlemagne, Peter, Napoleon, all "Great," all selfish, all, but all INTERESTING. Interesting, but terrors in the family.

January, 1899. Poor old King H. is at his downest, and I'm amazed at the few in number of his useful friends. After a dreadful illness (the first in all his life!) he has to lie up for months, and is at Bournemouth, twiddling his poor thumbs, and thinking out the best way to get to work again. He is ruined in pocket, heavily in debt, and I doubt not, will, in spite of all and everybody, rise from his ashes like *the* Bird! We have all (his friends) helped him a little. No word from him, however! Is it shyness? Indifference? Anger? *What?* I rather think self-consciousness by indifference out of conceit! It sounds hard, but I think this is just true.

I wonder how his other friends and lovers feel to him. I have contempt and affection and admiration. What a mixture!

His illness has made him look queer. He is stouter, very grey, sly-looking, and more cautious than ever. Bother!

He evidently doesn't like taking favours from any of his friends (which he is obliged to do at present). I don't think it *gracious* to be unable to take favours sweetly. He will take them, but will *not* acknowledge them.

He wrote and asked me to go down and see him at Bournemouth. I went, and found him looking much better. He wanted to tell me that not only was he broken in health but he was what is called "ruined." At which word I refused to shed tears, for, said I: "As long as you and I have health, we have means of wealth. We can pack a bag, each of us, and trot round the Provinces. Yes, and go to America, Australia, India, Japan, and pick up money by the bushel, even were we to take just the magic book of Shakespeare alone with us." I then asked his plans, and he astonished me by saying: "That's why I asked you to come down to Bournemouth. (He might have written, but no; he'd not *write* that.) I propose—have in fact written to the managers—going round the English provinces with a very small company, and playing 'The Bells,' 'Louis XI,' 'Waterloo,' and perhaps another play." Long pause. I didn't think it *possible* I heard aright. "*What* plays?" said I. "Bells, Louis, Waterloo," he said irritably. "Well, and where do *I* come in?" said I. "Oh well, for the present, at all events, there's no chance of acting at the

Lyceum." (He looked exceedingly silly.) "For the present, you can, of course, er, *do as you like!*"

I felt—a good many feelings! At top of all came amusement to save the situation. "Then," said I, "I have in plain terms what Ted would call 'the dirty kick out'?"

"Well—er—for the present I don't see what can be done, and I daresay you—" I cut him short. "Oh, I daresay I shall get along somehow. Have I your permission to shift for myself, and make up a tour for myself?" "Yes." "For how long?" "Well, I can scarcely say." "Until Christmas next?" "Yes."

That was enough. I went up to London next day, and asked Griffiths to make me up a tour. He was delighted, and within a week had signed and sealed for 9 weeks, and pencilled in dates up to next Christmas.

Soon after I left Bournemouth, free to think H. a Donkey, and make my own plans, he wrote me: "Joe Carr will call and propose new plan."

J. Carr *did* call, and told me (January 10) that a Syndicate could be formed to help H. I. out of all his difficulties. They would produce "Robespierre," and I was to make no new plans for my own tour! I said I had already settled for 9 weeks, to begin January 30, but would cancel the other engagements up to Christmas. No thanks from Henry! All taken as a matter of course from me!

No acknowledgement that *I* had advised the Carr plan at Bournemouth: "You are down for the moment, but the thing to do *directly* you are strong again is to come out bang with a new play at the Lyceum." "All very well" (testily and ironically) "but there's no money, and there's no play." I told him he could get the money, and had 3 or 4 plays. I mentioned "Robespierre." "It's only half written." "Then, hurry up Mr. Sardou, and make him finish it!" I said.

H. I.'s arrangement with Syndicate: £11,000 for the remainder of Lyceum lease. (£5,000 on mortagage still leaves £6,000 to go on with.) Then another £1,000 for "Robespierre." Every season *both of us* to play at Lyceum from April to July. H. I.'s share, 60 per cent. Then tours in America and the Provinces, also on sharing terms.

J. Carr asked me to write a letter to Henry, saying I would stay on at the Lyceum and go to America afterwards, as *the Syndicate would not sign until they knew I was to be part of the Show!* I would not write to H. since he had done the business through J. Carr, but I wrote J. C. a note he could show to the Syndicate.

And so *that* was how it was all settled about the "future plans of Henry Irving."

April, 1899. He is afloat again! "Robespierre" was a grand success last night. It's a bad play, but a wonderfully showy one. Much variety in scene, no development of character. A one-man piece. Henry, and over 250 supers. He acts the 3rd Act splendidly.

May 15, 1899. Henry too ill to act, and Laurence plays his part. L. plays ghost scene better than his father, but none of the rest to compare with H.'s.

May 25, 1899. H. back in "Robespierre." All the company asking my advice about their going to America. I will have nothing to do with it. I dont believe any of 'em will go, except me, and I am a fool to do it, but after all these years ...

June 25, 1899. All the time good business in "Robespierre," but not crammed as at first. H. seeming generally well, but now and again I have grave doubts of him for the American tour. He coughs badly.

June 30, 1899. He said last night he was losing money on Robespierre! Pray God the tours will bring him better luck. A play with one big part, and hundreds of supers should not cost so much as a good company of artists, but it does, it appears. The supers run away with the receipts. The public has never ceased to support him.

July, 1899. End of the London season, and H. tells me he has lost £4,000!

After describing the success of the provincial tour of "Robespierre," Ellen Terry writes:

New York. October, 1899. Henry much improved in health, and he is very much afloat. Money pouring in. Public here support him more and more, and the tide is all in his favour, thank the Lord. He is pleased. Looks very old. Is just the same in his self-centring. Laurence is with us. H. scarcely takes any notice of him. Doesn't believe in him much—*not at all* as an actor, and doesnt help him a bit. A quite common young fellow in the company plays all the good parts which might benefit Laurence, but H. I., thinking only of H. I., fancies L. an inch or so too tall to act with, so down goes L., and up goes himself!

Baltimore. January 1, 1900. A new year. H. still prospers, and talks, as Chatterton of Drury Lane talked, of Shakespeare "spelling ruin." Shame! Shame! He has always laughed at Chatterton for saying that, and now to agree with him! Shame! He is able to pay all his debts now, and is doing so. He seems fairly well. Not tired, but *old.*

Brooklyn, January 14, 1900. Went last night to see "The Bells." First time for a long while. He is strangely altered in his acting of Mathias. Acts weakly, effeminately. He used to assume a rough, masculine vigour, but now he does odd things. Puts out a leg, elevates his chin. Goes for pathos of a *very* weak kind! As wrong as wrong can be, all of it, until he comes to the last act. He acted the Dream Scene *perfectly* last night.

He is more than ever given over to *details,* instead of getting great emotional effects. He is the wonderfullest man, for he is *not* richly gifted, except in *constructive* brains.

Cleveland. January 22, 1900. I have offered through Bram to play seven times a week for him, and to cut out the last act of "Merchant of Venice" in order to be able to do it. No word of thanks from H. although he thinks it an admirable plan. Of course I hate cutting out my best act, and mangling the play, and tiring myself to death.

April, 1900. H. has sciatica badly. Really he has a very dull time of it, it seems to me, and I believe for the first time begins to appreciate my very long service, to know I am valuable.

May, 1900. The last seven places we have visited H. has had seven different doctors, and followed the different advice of each! He is singularly simple, or singularly stupid in the matter of his health. I think the latter!

June, 1900. Back in London. "Olivia." Too bad! Every one, but H., is about half my age. I'm angry at having to do it, but patience!

October, 1900. A wonderfully successful tour. "Olivia" is a tremendous attraction in the provinces. H. is very ill, and is ordered to give up the tour in the spring, and also the Lyceum season. . . . He has terrified me once or twice by his exhaustion and feebleness. Then he appears grateful to us all, for we *all* give him *all*. But when he gets a little better, anything so icy, indifferent, and almost contemptuous, I never saw.

We are all to go on tour in February and March without him.

(The note "About H. I." breaks off here. It makes perfectly clear that Ellen Terry loyally continued to serve Henry Irving, against her own interests, until she was finally convinced she could no longer be of use to him. The note has the further interest of having been compiled during the years when Ellen Terry was corresponding with Shaw. He claims [in his preface to the published correspondence] that he "destroyed Ellen Terry's belief in Irving." The note hardly confirms this, but it suggests the probability that Shaw gave shape and consciousness to Ellen Terry's disillusionment. She had however never been blind to the fact that there were flaws in the diamond.)

CHAPTER XIV

JUBILEE

1906

§ 1

THE celebration of my stage jubilee in 1906 came to me as a surprise. Henry had told me not long before his death in 1905 that the theatrical profession intended to "celebrate our jubilee." (If he had lived, he would have completed his fifty years on the stage in the autumn of 1906.) He said that there was going to be a commemoration performance at Drury Lane, and that a committee had been formed to discuss the programme. After his death I thought no more of the matter. It would not have surprised me if I had *heard* no more of it, for any recognition of my jubilee which did not include his seemed to me very unnecessary.

Of course I was pleased when I found that this was not the opinion of my profession or the public. I enjoyed all the demonstrations of homage and affection. But I never forgot for a moment that they were not for me alone, and that many were anxious to show me honour because I had worked with Henry Irving for a quarter-of-a-century. I represented a chapter in the history of the English theatre, of which they were proud.

The matinée given at Drury Lane in honour of my jubilee began before noon and was not over until long past six! A wonderful programme and a wonderful audience. In the first act of "Much Ado About Nothing," there was quite a big family party, with my brother Fred as Don Pedro, my sister Marion as Hero, my sister Kate as Ursula, and my niece Minnie as Margaret. It was a joyful occasion for me, and I believe I played Beatrice as joyfully as at any time in my life. "Out of question you were born in a merry hour!" I felt that this was true of me, and that there was something appropriate in there being no sadness of farewell in this commemoration of my jubilee. I was being fêted not as a veteran on the retired list, but as an actress still able to serve the public. The mammoth matinée at Drury Lane over, I went to the Court Theatre as usual to appear in "Captain Brassbound's Conversion."

The two things which touched me most during that exciting day were

275

my reception from the crowd waiting to get into the gallery, when I visited them at about two in the morning, and the presence of Eleonora Duse, who had come all the way from Florence just to honour me. She told me afterwards that she would have come farther, from South America or from heaven! I appreciated very deeply too the kindness of Caruso in singing at the matinée. I did not know him at all; he was inspired by the impersonal motive of an artist, desiring to pay a tribute to a fellow-artist.

There are some stories which seem almost too good to be true. Here is one about an incident after my jubilee matinée. The cars and carriages with their rich cargo of "stars" had long since rolled away from the stage-door; the crowd, waiting to see me come out, had thinned, when the stage-door keeper hailed a rather shabby "four-wheeler" for me. My daughter and I drove off to Berkeley Square to leave some flowers for Lady Bancroft. While I was within, the cabman told my daughter that in old days he had often driven Charles Kean home from the Princess's Theatre, and that sometimes Mrs Kean had given the little Miss Terrys a lift! That this cabman should have come to Drury Lane by chance on my jubilee day was indeed an extraordinary coincidence. My daughter took his address, and promised he should have a photograph of me to commemorate the day he had met me again. Unfortunately I lost the address, and all my efforts to trace the old cabman failed. I should think he must be a dream, if Edy were not so sure of his reality.

§ 2

Now that I have finished the story of sixty years of my life, I am conscious that through want of skill in selection, I have included some things which ought to have been omitted, and omitted others which ought to have been included, but I have tried my best to tell all things that are here, faithfully. It is not easy to be both honest and discreet, so it is possible that I have given offence where offence was not dreamed of. One reader may think I ought not to have said "this," while another who sees no harm in "this," may strongly object to "that." But neither this nor that, nor aught in this story has been "set down in malice."

If I have not revealed myself, (Myself? Why even I, I often think, know little of myself!) I hope I have given a true picture of my life as an actress, and shown what years of labour and practice are needed for the attainment of a permanent position on the stage. To quote Mrs Nance Oldfield:

"Art needs all that we can bring to her, I assure you."

PART II

BIOGRAPHY

BY CHRISTOPHER ST JOHN

(1906–1928)

CHAPTER I

LAST DAYS IN THE THEATRE

(1906–1914)

§ 1

IN the Ellen Terry Memorial Museum at Smallhythe Place, the unpretentious old timbered farm-house about which there still seems to hang some of the shimmering iridescence that was Ellen Terry, one of the exhibits is an imposing folio, massively bound in oak boards, the top one massively decorated with a bronze shield, the shield massively embossed with the name Ellen Terry, a classical mask, and a romantic star. The interior of the volume is less massive than the exterior; the thousands of newspaper-cuttings pasted on its pages are more flimsy and perishable stuff than oak or bronze. But here, for such time as pulp-paper and printer's ink endure, is an almost complete record of Ellen Terry's Jubilee, drawn from English, American and Continental journals during the year 1906. It was presented to Ellen Terry by Mr Franklyn Thomasson, the managing-director of *The Tribune,* a new daily organ of the Liberal party. The chief event of this newspaper's short life was its inauguration of the Ellen Terry Jubilee Celebration Fund. It was a shilling fund, which enabled the financially poorest of Ellen Terry's admirers to become subscribers. The shillings poured in singly and in thousands, and eventually the fund reached a total of £3,000. It is possible that if the appeal to the nation to show its appreciation of Ellen Terry in this practical way had been made jointly by an united press, not by one journal, whose enterprise was suspect as a scoop, the result would have been more dazzling. The figures of the *Tribune* total, amassed slowly during weeks, were doubled in one day at Drury Lane. The Jubilee Commemoration performance there added nearly £6,000 to Ellen Terry's testimonial.

All this is on record in the oak-bound book, but there is not a word about it in Ellen Terry's autobiography. By the time she came to the Jubilee period, the subject of the last brief chapter, she was no longer Ellen Terry. She was Mrs James Carew, a different person from Ellen Terry, the veteran actress who had just celebrated her stage jubilee. Mrs

Carew was rather bored by Ellen Terry. She was anxious to finish the story of her life as soon as possible, and be done with her. To Mrs Carew, the tributes paid to Ellen Terry by her professional comrades in all parts of the world, her matinée at Drury Lane, her banquet at the Hotel Cecil, the *Tribune* fund, royal presents, and other demonstrations of admiration and affection, were not of much interest or importance. So she polished off the story of Ellen Terry's jubilee, which, told in full, occupies a stout folio volume, in a few astonishingly casual lines.

I am debarred by the amount of ground I have to cover in this narrative of Ellen Terry's last years from making adequate reparation to her for Mrs Carew's perfunctory account of the jubilee. But I could produce more from that folio than a patchwork of faded raptures. There is much of historical interest, much that shows what a great part Ellen Terry played in the life of her time. She had as great a reputation on the Continent, where she never acted, as in Great Britain and America, where she was a familiar figure on the stage. The messages, expressing enthusiasm for the project of commemorating her jubilee, sent by people eminent in the theatres of Europe, are a good proof that they were aware that her genius had glorified their calling. Her compatriots, ever more inclined to claim her as "a great dear" than as a great actress, must have been astounded when they read some of these messages. Neither Italy (Duse and Ristori) nor Germany (Agnes Sorma and Max Reinhardt) nor France (Bernhardt, Réjane, Judic, Coquelin, Sardou, Claretie, Hervieu, Capus) wished to join in tributes to a "great dear." Their homage was given to the great interpreter of Shakespeare. A message from the actors and actresses of America, sent through Charles Frohman, signed by names still famous, Richard Mansfield, John Drew, Eleanor Robson and Julia Marlowe among them, was not in the "great dear" vein either, but emphasised the admiration due to Ellen Terry for having upheld "the noblest traditions of the stage."

In the oak-bound book there is a report of a speech made by Mr Winston Churchill, who presided at the jubilee banquet to Ellen Terry. The word charm does not occur in the speech. This is such a rare thing in any English tribute to Ellen Terry that I think it worth mentioning. Mr Churchill appears to have been convinced that Ellen Terry's jubilee was being honoured, not on account of her charm, but because she was a great actress, who by her gifts and powers had "elevated and sustained the quality and distinction of theatrical art in England during long years when it had been discreditably neglected by the state." And, which may seem strange to those who regard Mr Churchill as a militarist and imperialist, he added that "if we could only divert the often senseless process of territorial expansion, and the ugly apparatus of war to those more graceful and gentle flights of fancy associated with the drama, we should more securely vindicate our claim to be a civilised people."

Some guests at the banquet who no doubt applauded this remark proceeded to refute our claim to be "a civilised people," or at any rate a highly cultured one, by throwing away the delightful souvenir designed by William Nicholson with which they had been presented. The floor, when the company dispersed, was strewn with copies of a genuine work of art, a long roll depicting Ellen Terry in various parts, from Mamillius to Lady Cecily Waynflete.

There is no reference to this incident in the oak-bound book; it was one of many incidents which did not get into the papers from which Mr Thomasson's history of the jubilee was compiled. The press in 1906 made no comment on the extraordinary fact that not a single woman was invited to join either the General or Executive Committee constituted to organise the Commemoration performance at Drury Lane. One interesting result was that the Executive arranged a programme, as nearly as possible all-male. Actresses, with the exception of those belonging to the Terry family, who had parts in "Much Ado About Nothing," were to be represented on the stage only in Gilbert's "Trial by Jury." Theirs not to reason why, theirs but to serve as programme sellers. When the draft programme was submitted to Ellen Terry she could at first hardly believe her eyes! "No, no! It's not possible!" she gasped, and then, assured that it was, could not speak for some time for laughter. An actress-less programme in honour of an actress! What a joke! Ellen Terry could not help relishing it, but to the consternation of the committee she said that she didnt want to spoil the joke by appearing herself! This threat led to the eleventh-hour addition to the programme of a series of tableaux in which the leading actresses in the London Theatre could at least be seen. How ungrateful and tiresome of Ellen Terry not to be satisfied by this concession! She despatched a letter to Mr Arthur (now Sir Arthur) Pinero, the chairman of the Executive: "Dear Pinny, An amusing notion this, of women of talent appearing in *tableaux* only, but if that has been decided upon by the Committee, I elect, if you please, to appear only in a tableau myself. I couldnt, I couldnt, I *couldnt* do anything else!"

I dont know who or what induced Ellen Terry to change her mind. Possibly it was the evidence that in one number at least, actresses predominated. This was a scene from "The Beauty of Bath," presented by "Mr Seymour Hicks and *all* the Bath Buns."

§ 2

MISS LAURENCE ALMA-TADEMA, daughter of the distinguished painter to whom Ellen Terry refers in her memoirs in connection with his designs

for "Cymbeline," once applied her astrological lore to casting the horoscopes of Henry Irving and Ellen Terry, her idols in the theatre, her dear
friends outside it, from girlhood. She saw that the planets are favourable
to both horoscopes up to the time of the end of the Lyceum partnership. Then they begin to show a contrary disposition, and are never
again propitious. Henry Irving's career after the separation does seem
to have been ill-starred. He lost his health, his theatre, his money,
and to a certain extent his position. The King of the London stage was
banished from the capital, and forced to exploit his reputation in the
provinces. He died, a poor, afflicted and disappointed man, one who in his
last days could get through his performances on these arduous tours only
by a supreme exertion of his indomitable will. Yet an observer of the
heavens must surely have noted some improvement in the disposition of
his stars on the day he was buried in Westminster Abbey. Then at least
he regained his throne.

Turning to Ellen Terry's career after December 1902, the date of
her final rupture with Irving (she acted with him only once after it in
a special performance of "The Merchant of Venice" given at Drury Lane,
in July 1903 in aid of the Actors' Association) we find evidence that both
confirms and contradicts the horoscope. Ellen Terry's first venture into
the uncharted seas of management after she left the Lyceum harbour
(a harbour, it should be remembered, which had become unsafe) was a
disaster. But her first engagement at another theatre was a triumphant
success. (The engagement with Tree in "The Merry Wives of Windsor.")
Her first tours in the provinces without Irving showed no decline in
prosperity. In 1905 and 1906 she continued to prosper, appearing in plays
written for her by two of the most eminent dramatists of the time (J. M.
Barrie and Bernard Shaw). Having climbed to the highest summit it was
possible to climb in classical poetic drama, she now, at the age of 58,
started a new career in contemporary prose drama. Max Beerbohm may
say that the quality of exuberance that was right for Beatrice and Portia
is wrong for Barrie's Alice and Shaw's Lady Cecily, and that she needs a
Shakespeare to stand up to her, but the public, exhilarated by her beautiful
boisterousness, ignore that it is making havoc of "Alice-Sit-By-the-Fire"
and "Captain Brassbound's Conversion." Then comes the jubilee celebration, Ellen Terry's apotheosis. Her exchequer, emptied during her enterprise at the Imperial Theatre in 1904, is replenished by the testimonial.
It would seem as if her stock had declined at the beginning of the century, only because the stock of the Lyceum had declined. There is now a
sharp rise. Ellen Terry is the acknowledged queen of the English theatre.
Despite greying hair, and a more ample figure, she is still beautiful.
Grace still "pervades the hussy." There is still magic in the voice; "the

nervous athleticism behind the voice" (Shaw's phrase) "is still of championship quality. In new parts there may be a deterioration in pace. Ellen Terry finds it increasingly difficult to memorise words, especially the informal dialogue of the modern playwright, and this forces her to slow up her delivery against her will. But she is not compelled to slow up her movement and gesture. Her swiftness and agility are marvellous. She still skims over the ground on winged feet. She still has that peculiar quality of diffusing light and warmth directly she makes her entrance.

Yet, according to Miss Alma-Tadema, her stars are not lucky in 1906. This is perhaps not so strange as it seems.

§ 3

IN April 1905 Miss Maxine Elliott came to London for a season at the Lyric Theatre. The visit had important consequences for Ellen Terry, because James Carew was a member of the company Miss Elliott brought with her from America. Ten years earlier, Carew, who had not then adopted this name, and was living with his family in Chicago, had seen a performance there by the Lyceum Company. Henry Irving stirred the callow youth with the ambition to become an actor as great as Irving. This ambition was not to be realised, but at any rate Carew had the privilege in later years of occupying Irving's position as Ellen Terry's partner. His tenacity had got him on to the stage within two years of the night he had determined to make it his profession, and by 1905 when he made his first appearance in London with Maxine Elliott in "Her Own Way" he was an efficient actor in parts which suited him. He was then about thirty years of age, a tall strongly-built, rough-hewn, rather burly fellow of the type which became known later as the "he-man." He had a "he-man" part in "Her Own Way," and made a great success in it. Sam Coast's catch-line, "I mean to get it" might have been written for James Carew, with his stolid, determined demeanour, and stolid monotonous voice.

A young actress in the company at the Duke of York's theatre, where "Alice-Sit-By-the-Fire" was being played, came back from a matinée at the Lyric, raving about the he-man. She was chaffed by every one, Ellen Terry included. This, I think, must have been the first time Ellen Terry heard the name of James Carew, and it meant nothing to her. The name of Ellen Terry meant something to James Carew. The first stall he ever bought in England was one at the Duke of York's theatre, to see her act.

He was engaged in the following year to play Captain Kearney in "Captain Brassbound's Conversion." "Who is that?" said Ellen Terry to Bernard Shaw, when Carew first entered the rehearsal-room at the

283

Court Theatre. The rest of the story can be read in Shaw's preface to "Ellen Terry and Bernard Shaw: A Correspondence." Rather incredulous of Shaw's version of what happened, I recently asked Carew if it was really to be relied on. Was it really true, for example, that Ellen Terry put him in her pocket (so to speak) and bore him off before he had time to realise who she was? Now Carew, although a simple fellow, is incapable of answering a simple question simply. His conversation abounds in circumlocutions. But as I threaded the verbal maze, I became convinced that things must have happened exactly as Shaw relates. "But why, why did she marry you?" I asked, bothered by a problem I had never been able to solve, for I knew perfectly well that Ellen Terry had had other infatuations in her life which had not ended this way. He did not take offence, which I think is greatly to his credit, and for once, speaking simply and directly, replied: "I suppose because she was mad about me."

Well this lunacy, if lunacy it was, fully accounts for the distrait air some of us found so irritating in Ellen Terry during her jubilee celebrations. Her diary for 1906 contains more allusions to her "Jimmy" than to her jubilee. She spent the summer at Smallhythe, with "Jimmy" as her guest. When they were not careering over the countryside in her pony-cart, they were busy with preparations for the tour in America, which was to begin in New York in January 1907. "There is always work," as Ellen Terry remarks in her autobiography, and never in her life, not even when midsummer mad, did she neglect her work. She was studying Hermione at this time, Tree having engaged her to play it for a few weeks at His Majesty's before she left for America, and it was one of Jimmy's duties to hear her in her part. He perhaps can claim some of the credit for her being word-perfect on the first night (September 1, 1906). This production of "The Winter's Tale" was not one of Tree's best. The effect of the Trial Scene, I remember, was marred by the behaviour of the crowd who showed their sympathy with the accused by mechanically repeating "O pore 'Ermione" at certain cues. Ellen Terry herself gave a beautiful performance in the profoundly human first Act, but was not so good in the more rhetorical second. Her acting in the Trial Scene was admirably expressive of spiritual strength overcoming physical weakness, but some of Hermione's grandiloquent retorts to Leontes may have been better delivered by Mrs Charles Kean.

"All went well," Ellen Terry writes in her diary. "First act splendidly. Edy delighted." (Good, for Edy was a stern critic of her mother's acting.) "Viola" (Viola Tree played Perdita) "was very sweet-looking, very pretty, and danced delightfully. Her tears and mine mingled in the last Act."

"Miss Viola Tree need not fear," said one critic, "that we shall accuse her of superstition when she kneels and implores Hermione's blessing, for we see Ellen Terry now not only as a great actress, and a great personality, but as a great religion."

"My marriage was my own affair," Ellen Terry writes in her memoirs at the end of the second of the two chapters devoted to America. This was the opinion of Mrs Carew. Ellen Terry would have allowed that it was to a certain extent the affair also of the nation to which she was "a great religion," and of her children, both some years older than her third husband, whose lives might be affected by the change in her state. It is true that these lives were no longer bound up with hers. Her son was not even living in the same country. He had a home and a family abroad. The family he had left in England, when his first marriage came to grief, had long been Ellen Terry's responsibility and care; she had been a good "father" to her grandchildren, and a good friend to their mother, but it cannot be said that they occupied an important place in her life or in her heart. During one of her long American tours at the beginning of the century her daughter had left home and set up house with me, a step which provoked hostile criticism from people who are quite unable to understand that daughters, like sons, may wish to leave the parental nest without wishing to marry. Had Ellen Terry objected to Edy's deserting the nest when she grew up, the objection must have been based either on sentiment, or on respect for convention, for she was too often absent from the nest herself to suffer from the desertion. But she did not object, and the relations between mother and daughter became more, rather than less, intimate after the daughter had made a nest of her own. They even saw more of one another. "How wise Edy was," James Carew said to me after Ellen Terry's death. "If I had had a place of my own, I should never have quarrelled with Nell. The only way to get on with her was not to live in the same house."

That may be true, but it is not to the point. I want to make clear that Ellen Terry had no family life to hinder her from marrying again at the age of 59, and that her children did not supply the need she imagined she had (for, as subsequent events proved, it was not a real need) to be "the one" in another's life and affections. It was this need she gave me as an explanation of her marriage when it was first made public. We were crossing the Atlantic at the time on our way back to England after the American tour. There was no storm except in Ellen Terry's cabin, where I frankly confess I was expressing intemperately the indignation I felt at the marriage, which had taken place in March, having been kept a secret from Edy until June. I could not understand the

285

mother's want of confidence in the daughter so dear to her, and was shocked that she should have let the news reach Edy first through a wireless message to the ship. It was a painful interview. Ellen Terry resented my resentment. The breach between us was not healed for some years.

Gordon Craig, who in his biography of his mother portrays his sister as a self-righteous and disagreeable prig, derides her for her "silly disapproval" of the marriage. It was not of the marriage that Edith Craig disapproved, but of the husband. She did not think that he, good fellow as he might be, was worthy of her mother, and distrusted his ability to make her happy. "I give it two years," said Edy soon after she heard of the marriage, and that was exactly the time it lasted. Yet as it brought Ellen Terry a few golden days it is not to be regretted. Her own description of how it came about I found in a note-book, recording "golden days." One, when "I first saw deep in a wood splashes of colour! Bluebells, sheets and sheets of bluebells." Another, "when I was taken into the manuscript room at the British Museum, and shown Queen Mary's Psalter." Another, "when I was first married, and driving away in the carriage, thought how queer it was that everything in the streets seemed to be going on just as usual—people looking dull, whilst I felt so elated, so different, and I had no idea *why,* unless it was because I was very fond of somebody, and was going to stay with him always among the pictures." Another, "when my girl was born, the goldenest day of all." Another, "the night I played Portia at the Prince of Wales's." Another, "the evening I saw H. I. play Hamlet at Birmingham." Another, "the first time I acted in Chicago. I had been told so much of the roughness of the people, and now I found out for myself, as I played Ophelia, their sensitiveness to the appeal of art." Another, "the scene in Westminster Abbey when Irving was laid to rest. (This may be thought a doubtful *golden* day, but it was.)" Another, "January 1907 when New York settled for me by its cordial welcome the question as to whether or no I would marry James Carew. It depended on that. In fact the audiences and the press of America married us. If I was coldly received, in other words plainly told I was too old and ugly to remain upon the stage, I had determined to give up all thoughts of the marriage, to put away 'all foolish fond records,' and leave the stage quietly at the end of the tour. But they opened their arms to me, flattered and spoiled me delightfully to the top of my bent, and I was married in America on the 22nd of March, 1907."

Later, when this golden day was further off, Ellen Terry added: "I felt I could not live alone. Afterwards I thought it better to live alone, apart from Jim, for we do not suit each other. We are better, and happier apart, and now we *like* each other very much."

286

Among the "character-sketches," which Ellen Terry frequently jotted down in note-books, is one of Carew, which in its way is as penetrating as her study of Irving.

J. AN INTERESTING STUDY

I love him. He is a child, but the child is father to the man, and the child, J., makes me wish I were twenty years younger and could grow to him. As it is, he shows promise of being a spoiled child, and that is a difficult thing to be husbanded by! Off the stage I am sure he may be great, if he will, in the near future. On the stage he cannot make progress, unless he gives more, *serves* more. Small people are doing that, and are making progress, simply because of it. He has fine gifts for the stage, gifts of nature, and the gift of fiery determination and sincerity.

But he has jealousy, and *sloth* seizes him now and again when he is impatient, which is very often. When he can lesson himself to do things for others, then, without knowing it, he will be developing.

A mixture. He is a half-wild thing, but that part of him I like best. The rather violent explosions are temporary, and at times merely amusing. But the wild thing gives itself up to over-heated rooms, first-class railway carriages, hot water bottles, and eiderdown quilts! And the wild thing's appetite runs to more elaborate food than nuts and fruit. I fear I dont influence him towards quiet, and he needs that, for violence means heaven and earth made hell, if no attempt is made to control it. When the fits are past it is hard to realise they have been, but their daily recurrence means more than ordinary wear and tear of one's body and spirit. I only ask for the *attempt* for control. ... A call to the telephone, and all stress is over for the moment, to be immediately resumed, when the message has been received, and answered *humorously!*

Six months after. A grand upheaval on *both* sides! More reasonable, quieter, much better manners.

To me the word "great," of oneself, is surely absurd, and to object to people who dont use that particular word when referring to one—absurd!

§5

THERE are many indications both in Ellen Terry's memoirs and in her letters to Bernard Shaw that she was not convinced that her long service at the Lyceum was a waste of her talent. She was chagrined at times at having to play poor parts, but she knew quite well that it might not be to her advantage to leave Irving. She did not value herself enough to be ambitious; and there is no evidence that when his yoke chafed her most, she looked forward to a day when she would be her own mistress, and do what she wished in the theatre. It may be argued that if she had left Irving earlier, before the loss of youth had restricted her range of parts, her subsequent career would have been more distinguished, but the use which she made of her belated enfranchisement does not support the argument. She soon drifted back into her familiar occupation of serving some one else's interests. Unfortunately the occupation grew more precarious each year, and Ellen Terry's new masters got more out of her than they gave in return. Her devotion of her talents to the support of Irving, deplored by Bernard Shaw, had some result, the national homage at her jubilee for instance, but her appearance at Shaw's little Lyceum, the Court Theatre, in "Captain Brassbound's Conversion" led to nothing. Shaw, having achieved his ambition of making Irving's leading lady serve him and the new drama, did no more for her. Her son, Gordon Craig, went abroad after "The Vikings" to reap what advantage he could from the service Ellen Terry had rendered him by its production. Her service of James Carew was even more poorly rewarded. As the leading lady of her husband, Ellen Terry humbled herself to the extent of supporting him in a part far worse than any Irving had ever demanded she should play. I went to the first night of the production of Gladys Unger's historical drama "Henry of Lancaster" at Nottingham. It was the only time I ever saw Ellen Terry on the stage without experiencing any pleasure at all. She had a colourless ingénue sort of part, and played it in a timid, apologetic way, which suggested that she had an uneasy conscience about trifling with her reputation to give her James a chance. That he should have imagined it was a chance proves the truth of Ellen Terry's remark in Chapter VI, that actors are often blind to their true interests. The he-man was ill-suited to the part of a romantic prince babbling of his lady's rosy lips. The failure of "Henry of Lancaster" fortunately limited the babbling to a few nights, and prevented the sad spectacle of Ellen Terry's immolation of her art from being witnessed in London.

She played few new parts after Princess Elizabeth of the rosy lips. In the autumn of 1908 she appeared as Aunt Imogen in Graham Robertson's "Pinkie of the Fairies" at His Majesty's. A service again, but her dear friend Graham never asked it of her. She volunteered it, writing from Smallhythe that "I really would like to play Aunt Imogen for I think I might be very funny in that very funny part. I wonder would Tree think it worth while?" Tree, when he was convinced that this letter to Graham Robertson was not a hoax, showed that he thought it worth while by telegraphing to Ellen Terry to clinch the bargain. It is one of the few letters of Ellen Terry's at this period in which James Carew is not mentioned. When they were living together at Smallhythe she spent much of her time in writing letters, beseeching authors and managers to give her husband some work. "Do, do remember," she writes to Bernard Shaw in March 1909, "to put in a word for Jim, or more, put in a whole recommendation for him. It would give me so much happiness." This letter is not published in "Ellen Terry and Bernard Shaw: A Correspondence." When the necessity for sacrificing some of the letters to Shaw arose, it was easy to select the victims. The book would have had some dull pages if the letters written at this period had been included, for Ellen Terry was often bored now, for the first time in her life. "Kindness and loyalty won the day," she writes in her memoirs, apropos of the consternation caused by the news of her marriage, but nevertheless her relations with many of her friends were affected by it. They had nothing in common with Carew. I felt a certain sympathy with him, of which he could not have been aware, as we seldom met. He was so obviously a fish out of water in Ellen Terry's milieu. The position of the obscure husband of a famous woman is never enviable, and Carew's was the less enviable because he "did not belong." I surmise that he welcomed rather than resented Ellen Terry's decision that they would be happier apart.

Before this amicable separation, Ellen Terry had made changes in her mode of life which, I believe, were a factor in that abnormally swift deterioration in her health, which surprised every one in her last years. For the sake of her work she had hitherto rested in the afternoon, abstained from social diversions, luncheons, dinners, and parties of all kinds, paid visits only to intimate friends who knew her ways, wore the clothes she liked and felt comfortable in, irrespective of fashion, lived simply, and well within her means, denying herself all luxuries except that of sending cheques secretly to help needy individuals and charitable institutions. The last habit was about the only one which was not altered by her third marriage. She began to squander her strength and her money recklessly, went out more, in her husband's interests, lived more conventionally, and dressed more conventionally too. The disparity in age between her and her husband made her draw too heavily on the large balance of youth and vigour she had in her favour in her sixtieth year. The costliness of these "golden days" was not however realised by any one at the time.

§ 6

ELLEN TERRY did not retire from the theatre. The theatre retired from her. Perhaps this was the penalty of her infidelities to it in the past. The more coldly it now received her advances ("Too late, Ellen Terry"), the more her ardour increased. She was passionately anxious to act again, but Bernard Shaw's objection, when she asked him to find her work, that a battleship in the part of a canal-barge may ruin a play, appears to have been shared by many authors and managers. She had to content herself with playing one of her old battleship parts now and again in special performances. According to the records, she played Portia during the Shakespeare Festival at Stratford-on-Avon in 1910. The same year the public were given a chance of seeing her again at her most enchanting best in "The Merry Wives of Windsor" at His Majesty's. In 1914 she played the Abbess in "Paphnutius" for the Pioneer Players. She was keenly interested in this production by her daughter, the first in modern times of a play by the 10th century nun-dramatist, Roswitha, and studied her small part with a devotion which I, the author of the translation, treasure among my dearest memories of her. She asked me, as a person acquainted with monastic forms and ceremonies, to instruct her how to walk with her crozier, and how to conduct herself during Thaïs's incarceration in the penitent's cell. "I feel so terribly sorry for her," she said, "and am afraid of crying. Now be sure and tell me if I am not stern enough. Perhaps the Abbess ought to show no more sympathy than a nurse while a surgeon is operating."

In 1919 she played the Nurse in "Romeo and Juliet," the last addition to her long list of Shakespearean parts. In this wonderful study of the "Ancient damnation," Ellen Terry's genius flamed up for the last time. How high it flamed is known only to those who were present on the first night of the Basil Sydney-Doris Keane production at the Lyric Theatre. Then Ellen Terry, besides giving the audience a feast of rich, highly-spiced comedy (her Nurse was a sly, coarse old baggage, if an alluring one), thrilled them with an exhibition of tragic force in the scene in which the Nurse tries to wake Juliet on her wedding morning. There was the old nervous athleticism behind the voice in that whisper which reached the remotest listener in the theatre: "She's dead." Miss Doris Keane decided to cut out the scene after the first night. There may not have been any connection between this decision and Ellen Terry's triumph, but if there was, Miss Keane's provocation is her excuse. Juliet ought not to be played off the stage by the Nurse. The Nurse ought not to be first, and the rest nowhere, in press notices of a production of "Romeo and Juliet." Here was some justification of Shaw's objection to casting a battleship for the part of a canal-barge.

The behaviour of the "battleship" when she heard, just before the second performance, that her best scene had been cut, was exemplary. The beautiful face, radiant from the embrace of the audience the night before, saddened for a moment. I believe it was one of the cruellest disappointments of Ellen Terry's life. Then she smiled, and said quietly, and without a touch of irony: "Well, I suppose they know what they are about."

From a photograph by E. O. Hoppé

ELLEN TERRY
As the Nurse in "Romeo and Juliet"
(Her Last Shakespearean Part)

1. After studying a mass of documents, some of which I found after I had completed this chapter, I have come to the conclusion that Ellen Terry never "left" Irving. She does not seem, from the correspondence between her and Irving's manager, Bram Stoker, to have viewed her refusal to accompany Irving on the American tour of "Dante" as tantamount to "leaving" him for good. She broaches plans in her letters for appearing with him again in "The Merchant of Venice," and other old Lyceum successes, after that tour. It was not until Stoker made quite clear that these plans were unrealisable that she went into management at the Imperial, and arranged provincial tours ahead as an independent "star."

2. The parts played by Ellen Terry during the period covered by this chapter were: Elizabeth of York ("Henry of Lancaster," 1908); Aunt Imogen ("Pinkie and the Fairies," 1908); Alexia Vane ("At a Junction," 1909); Nance Oldfield ("A Pageant of Famous Women," 1909); Nell Gwynne ("The First Actress," 1911); The Abbess ("Paphnutius," 1914).

CHAPTER II

WAR

(1914–1921)

§ 1

ELLEN TERRY's private war began at an earlier date than 1914. She despatched her ultimatum to the enemy in 1907 on that "golden day" in New York when she decided to marry again. Her soul "in arms, all eager for the fray," put old Time on the defensive. He knew the inevitable issue of the combat. Visualising Time incarnate, I see him reading with a cynical smile the tales of Ellen Terry's victories. "Eternal youth! Rubbish! She will grow old, as all who do not cheat me by dying young, grow old. She has beaten off the first attack, true. I have returned, but there will be another assault, and another. Why do these mortals fight me?" And as Time cannot possibly think of Ellen Terry without being reminded of Shakespeare, he snarls:

> Golden lads and lasses must
> Like chimney-sweepers come to dust, ˙

and vanishes, no doubt to sharpen his scythe.

§ 2

THE marriage action, the first in Ellen Terry's war, appeared to be a victory for her, but really, as I suggested in the last chapter, it reduced her strength and hastened the day of her surrender. Her next action was fought not as a woman but as an artist. It may be remembered by those who have read her memoirs attentively that she mentions a lecture on "The Letters in Shakespeare's Plays" which she first gave in 1903. I, then a young woman, who had been trying to make a living with my pen since I left Oxford, sometimes finding no better-paid occupation for it than that of addressing envelopes in a City office, had, through the influence of my friend, Edith Craig, been engaged as a "super" in Ellen Terry's company at the Imperial Theatre. I believe I justified the engagement by quickly becoming a first-rate super. Gordon Craig's precipitous slope in

"The Vikings" had no terrors for me, because at Oxford I had devoted as much time to athletic sports as to history. It was the ease with which I kept my feet on the slope that led to my being singled out by Gordon Craig from the crowd of Kari's followers, and given the part of Kari's wife. Ibsen does not mention Mrs Kari, but Craig must have been convinced of her existence, for he had designed a dress for her. She had nothing to say, but a good deal to shout, and as I was not hindered by self-consciousness from giving tongue on the stage, I had another qualification besides my agility for playing the part. Besides serving Ellen Terry as a super in the theatre, I did jobs for her outside it, the jobs of a literary henchman. One of these jobs was to help her compile the lecture on "The Letters in Shakespeare's Plays." We also drafted one on "The Children in the Plays," which was completed later on.

Either in 1908, or 1909, Mr Hughes Massie, then a partner in the famous firm of Curtis Brown, literary agents, approached Ellen Terry about giving some Shakespeare lectures in America. It was suggested that the heroines would be a popular subject. The "literary henchman," who had been banished from Ellen Terry's society "like one infectious" since her marriage, was recalled from exile (the exile was not merely figurative as I was in Italy at the time) and reinstated in her old job. I have described the nature of my work for Ellen Terry in the preface to the lectures which were published for the first time in 1931. ("Four Lectures on Shakespeare" by Ellen Terry. Edited by Christopher St John. Martin Hopkinson.) The two on the heroines became in time, as more and more scenes were introduced, an epitome of Ellen Terry's Shakespearean impersonations. The preference, particularly common in England, for acting which creates the illusion that it is not acting at all, an illusion which an actress no longer young, cannot create in a young part, would alone have prevented Ellen Terry, at sixty-two, from giving these impersonations on the stage. Debarred from representing a Juliet, a Desdemona, a Beatrice, an Imogen to the life, she found scope in these so-called "lectures," for giving compelling presentations of the characters with which at the Lyceum she had been identified, and adding to them glimpses of others she had studied but never played.

"If you amount to nothing, your art in the end amounts to nothing; that is a fact almost biological in its brutal certainty." (Stark Young in "Theatre Practice.") Now Ellen Terry perhaps amounted to more in her sixties than at any time in her life. She was rich in experience of humanity, and had, stored up in her mind, a great treasure, accumulated during years of study of Shakespeare. She had developed into a philosopher, who had ceased to fear age, and had set about inventing a new beauty to take the place of the old beauty of her youth. It was unnecessary for her to invent a new method of charming people. The old method, if the effortless and generous use of a natural endowment can be called a method, had not been affected by age. The eloquent magnetism of Ellen Terry's personality owed little to the sexual allurement to which time is merciless. She was not a vain woman or a vain artist, yet she felt that, still amounting to so much, it was hard to be denied opportunity in the theatre for showing to what she amounted. The proposal that she should lecture on Shakespeare came at a moment when she was puzzled, disheartened and disappointed at her failure to maintain her position. Time was pushing her into retirement. Her war with Time was going badly when she signed the contract with the Civic Forum Lecture Bureau for a three months' tour on the Continent of America with the lectures. The tour opened in New York at a matinée at the Hudson Theatre on November 3, 1910. The lecture chosen for the occasion was the one which was afterwards to prove most popular: "The Triumphant Heroines." Ellen Terry had given it in London before she sailed, and had had a triumph herself, which was repeated in New York. But it was not until she returned to England in 1911 that any one had the enterprise to arrange a lecture-tour for her there. America must have the credit for having initiated the tours which went on almost continuously until 1915.

Writing of the two lectures on Shakespeare's women after they were published, *The Times* reviewer says that "in reading them it is difficult to shake off a queer impression that she who is speaking was herself one of Shakespeare's women, and that in the native country of them all, his creative mind, she had met, and talked with, and lived with them all." That "queer impression" was naturally much stronger in Ellen Terry's living presence. You felt that she was just as lovely, as high-mettled, as gallant, as humorous, as sensible, as Shakespeare's favourite type of heroine. These lectures, with their wealth of shrewd and penetrating comment on the characteristics, not only of the women but of the men presented in the scenes that Ellen Terry read or acted, ought to have dispelled for ever the silly notion, sedulously encouraged by the "great dear" party of her admirers, that she was not a great actress with a great insight into character, and a great power of expressing it. Yet it still survives. I recall that when Marion Terry died in 1930, the obituary notices all emphasised her intellectual superiority to her more famous and popular sister. Marion was a well-graced and very charming actress, capable of expressing the simpler human emotions with appealing sincerity, but if there was one thing more than another which prevented her from reaching the peaks to which Ellen climbed it was a lack of this very faculty she was supposed to possess. Her mental powers were not of the same calibre as Ellen's, as ought to have been clear from their performances on the stage. But because on the stage these powers of Ellen Terry's ran on the lightest of feet ("all divine things run on light feet," says Nietzsche) their strength and profundity were seldom recognised. Hence the general notion that she was a charming actress, but not a particularly thoughtful or intellectual one. In her lifetime, even the evidence supplied by her autobiography and the lectures that she had a first-rate brain, of quite as rare a quality as her imagination and her heart, could not upset the notion. It was not until she was dead, and her letters to Shaw were published, that it was even disturbed. The surprise expressed that *Ellen Terry* could hold her own in a correspondence with Shaw indicates how firmly rooted a false Ellen Terry legend was in the public mind.

Many incidents during the 1910-1911 American lecture-tour proved that Ellen Terry was still held in great honour in a country where memories are supposed to be shorter than elsewhere, and reputations are built and destroyed even more quickly than hotels. One of these happy incidents was the presentation of a medal by the Founders of the New Theatre, New York, of which Mr Winthrop Ames was the ambitious director. I believe he aspired to making this theatre a national temple of dramatic art, but it was described at this time as "the rich men's new plaything." The rich men appear to have played with the idea of an Order of Dramatic Merit. Its medal was first conferred on the distinguished Shakespearean scholar, Dr Furness of Philadelphia; the second recipient was Ellen Terry. Another medal, inscribed with a poem, was presented to her at Columbus. North, South, West, back East again she travelled, rejuvenated, in spite of the fatigue of the long journeys, by work, always her best tonic. The war against Time and Age was going very well now.

She returned to England in the spring of 1911, and now England wanted the lectures, that is if it could be made clear that they were not lectures in the ordinary sense of the word. It was feared that even the magic of Ellen Terry's name would not draw the British public to a "lecture," with its academic, dry-as-dust associations. So when Ellen Terry visited English towns, she was billed as appearing in "A Shakespearean Discourse With Illustrative Acting" or in "A Shakespearean Recital." She had never neglected the appeal to the eye in her stage performances —it was this which made Graham Robertson describe her as "The Painter's Actress"—and she now took great pains to present herself in the rôle of lecturer with beauty and dignity. Aided by her daughter, she created "scene" on the platform with dark green curtains, bunches of flowers and ingenious lighting. She wore flowing robes of crimson, or white or grey, the colour being determined by the mood of the discourses in her repertory and of the scenes she read, or acted, to illustrate them.

For a lectern, she used one of the decorative desks, made for Irving and her in the year 1889 when they gave readings of "Macbeth." She had several copies of each lecture printed in a type large and bold enough for her to read the text without spectacles, and these folios were finely and solidly bound. The text, by the way, was constantly being altered. By the spring of 1914 when she sailed for Australia, to give the lectures there, the original versions had been completely transformed by cuts, transpositions, and the addition of "gags," which on their first spontaneous utterance had justified their preservation. The critic of *The Times* who wrote after hearing one of the lectures at the Haymarket Theatre in 1911 that "wherever and whenever Ellen Terry speaks, it will always be different and always fresh" may not have meant that she would never give the same lecture, but this is what actually happened.

It was not until the publication of my blend of the various texts of what was at best a kind of scenario which Ellen Terry filled in as she went along, that the importance of the lectures as a contribution to the study of Shakespeare's characters was fully realised. Naturally those who heard them were more interested in Ellen Terry's "how" than in her "what." In the atmosphere of the theatre, the "how" burgeoned. The lecture became a performance, but it was not a performance which could fill the bill and attract an audience into the theatre nightly. This objection to putting on the lectures like a play, for a run, was overcome at the Savoy Theatre in 1912 by the collaboration of Albert Chevalier, a genius of the music-hall. One of Ellen Terry's lectures was sandwiched between two plays, Gloriel's "The House," and J. M. Barrie's "Pantaloon," in which Chevalier appeared. The Savoy season lasted about three weeks. Very happy weeks they were for Ellen Terry. She had never found compensation for her estrangement from the theatre in giving her lecture-performance in halls, assembly-rooms, pavilions, clubs, colleges and schools.

§ 3

"This discoursing is exhausting work, far more exhausting than playing a part, for I have to sustain the burden of the whole entertainment for nearly two hours. And then there is the travelling." This note by Ellen Terry on a letter, suggesting a world-tour of her lectures, to begin in Australia in 1914, shows that Time had started a new offensive. With great gallantry she held her ground. Her courage in accepting the Australian offer will be better appreciated if some of the reasons she had for refusing it are considered. A doctor, for whom she had a great respect, had told her that her heart was in such a condition that she ought never to walk upstairs, and that any exertion or excitement might be fatal. It was pointed out by her business manager that the Australians who had never seen her act would be attracted to her lectures only by her reputation, and might think that in them she hardly lived up to it. "Why risk your prestige in a strange land at your time of life?" This gentleman also doubted the stability of the syndicate, whose representative believed that Australia would give Ellen Terry a warm welcome. Better Ellen Terry late than Ellen Terry never, he thought, and offered her fairly good terms. So, making light of the warnings that she was risking her life and her reputation, she told her croaking counsellors that it was her duty to accept them. It was important for her to make money. A third croaker, her lawyer, then intervened. In his view it was quite unnecessary for Ellen Terry to go on working, that is if she took his advice. This was to reduce her allowances to certain dependents (these allowances account in part for Ellen Terry's comparative poverty in her old age), to sell her securities, and purchase an annuity. The advice was conveyed to Ellen Terry through her business manager, who thought it excellent. He urged her to take it on the ground that she had done all that could be expected of her, and a great deal more, for her children, and that she ought not to go on working merely to enable her to leave them an income at her death.

It was lucky for Ellen Terry's children that, on reading this letter, she did not show any of that "curious hesitancy before she could bring herself to decisions" which her son says was characteristic of her. I fancy that a deal of scorn looked beautiful in the contempt and anger of her lip as she took up her pen to reply. It looks beautiful now in the note, in her firmest and boldest writing, with which the last sheet of the letter is inscribed: "Answered: Go ahead, and settle everything about tour *at once.*" The note is dated, and the date proves that she must have made her decision to go to Australia directly the letter, urging her not to go, was received.

In spite of that troublesome heart, which in one of her letters from Australia to her daughter she likens to "a kicking donkey," Ellen Terry survived the exertion and excitement and eventual disappointment of the tour. She had an enthusiastic welcome from Melbourne on her belated Australian début in May, 1914. The press and public found her all that they had expected her to be, a total of rare talent, beauty and fascination, which had been accumulating for years. At the age of sixty-six she is described in the Melbourne journal, *The Age,* as "tall, graceful and fair-featured. With a chaplet round her head, and a flowing robe, such as she wore last night, she looked the queen of tears and laughter that audiences in England and America have acclaimed any time these past thirty years. The beauty that helped to make her what she is has not gone with her youth. It is a beauty of mind and expression as well as of feature. It is something that youth might even envy. Her voice, which was one of her greatest charms, will not carry as easily as it did, but still it carries. Its changes, its modulations, which have illustrated every mood that Shakespeare knew, stand by their owner still."

The writer then adds an account of an unfortunate incident which might have made the début of any one less capable than Ellen Terry of immediately impressing herself on a strange audience, a fiasco. That "kicking donkey" had a way of kicking her to pieces during Juliet's potion scene. It had been her custom in England and America to retire from the platform at its conclusion for a five minutes' rest, and then return for the second part of the lecture on the heroines of the tragedies. At Melbourne Town Hall on the first night, through some misunderstanding, it was assumed that the end of the potion scene was the end of the programme. After numerous calls, which must have still further exhausted the actress, already exhausted by the expenditure of force needed to sustain the "horror on horror's head" accumulating in Juliet's distraught monologue, the length of the interval perplexed the audience. They began to leave the hall, and any doubt they might have been in that the lecture was really over was settled when the National Anthem was played. Only a few people remained to hear the apology of Ellen Terry's agent for the blunder.

Poor Ellen Terry! This compassionate way of referring to her is for once justified. She really seems to have imagined that the dunderhead struck up the National Anthem because the audience had had enough of her. She writes in her diary: "First lecture in Australia. Very ill, very nervous, but I let myself go! I dont think they liked it much, however. After the Juliet scene, a lot of floral tributes and applause, but also God Save the King, and every one went out before I had nearly finished!"

The tour went fairly well—"houses good, notices splendid," Ellen Terry writes to her daughter in June—but might have gone better if the agent had not charged prices for admission to the lecture, higher than any ever known in Australia, "except for Harry Lauder." Ellen Terry had nothing to do with this, but writes that she considers it "unwise." However, B. (who had brought her to Australia) "declares he has done very well." She always writes affectionately of this "good fellow," and her sorrow when the outbreak of the war in August put an end to the ambitious scheme of a "world-tour" is all on his account. Before this fateful August came, she had had a serious illness. "My blessed old Edy," she writes from New Zealand at the end of June, "how hard I've been trying to keep going at my work, you'll never know, but it was no use trying, and on the conclusion of my last performance in Sydney, the

298

doctor flatly told me I must not appear for a fortnight at least. I had to give in, and then we went over the water to Auckland, twelve hundred miles or so. I was worse than ever when I got there, but I landed in a dear little hotel, and was just nursed through my great weakness by the kind landlady, and now I think I'll get through the rest of the lectures easily."

After August 4, 1914, the rest dwindled. "All engagements are being cancelled." (This was written from Melba's country home in Victoria in September.) "Yet all professional folk are acting 'for the War,' or for various charities, 'for love.'" Ellen Terry did her bit. "Melba is ever-lastingly promising to come and sing at this, that and the other little village round about fifty miles of her home, and I shall go with her to some of the affairs. So I call myself 'touring with Madame Melba.'... This (Melba's cottage at Coldstream) is an ideal spot, and Melba makes it an ideal home. She is so strong in body and character—a *splendid* woman, a magnetic one. She is thinking out kindnesses every hour of the day. I just love her now." Looking over the hedges of myrtle in bloom at the distant hills yellow with wattle ("it is like mimosa, of a very large kind, very softly, beautifully golden, with strange dreamy silver leaves") Ellen Terry thinks of the Germans raging through "little Bruges," a place she had loved in the past. "Maybe they are in Kent by now, perhaps inhabiting *our cottages!* And perhaps you may be giving them some tea! Or toko! The horrors of this war for a few minutes now and again make me crazy, when I dare think, but I *darent,* and only pray that no harm comes near you, and that somehow or another we meet at home before Christmas."

The meeting was delayed until May, 1915. "I am strongly advised to go home via America, as it will not be safe in the Mediterranean, so I've written to Tyler (who offered me a big engagement when I was last there) to find out whether America would stand a few more Shake-spearean discourses, so as to pay my way along. It is of no use trying to stay on here with the lectures. Every one in the 'entertaining' line is shutting up shop, except a few theatres with musical comedy....I should hate to be blown up by a mine."

Ellen Terry came very near being blown up, not by a mine, but by a torpedo on her supposedly safer way home. At the conclusion of the American lecture tour in April, 1915, she booked her passage back to England on an American liner, the *New York*. Charles Frohman, who was returning by the swifter and the more luxurious *Lusitania* on May 1, told Ellen Terry that a rich friend of his was anxious to put a suite on the boat at her disposal and urged her to let him make the arrangements. But she had promised her daughter not to come home on an English boat, and Frohman's assurance that the rumours current about the Germans and the *Lusitania* were absurd could not persuade her to cancel the booking on the *New York*. It was not indeed until the morning of the first of May that the official German warning to travellers intending to embark on the *Lusitania* was issued. By that time Ellen Terry had sailed. "C. F. told me I should be uncomfortable," she writes in her diary during the voyage, "but that is a tame word for it. However, this experience is only the beginning of favours to come! I suppose on the whole I prefer *this* bed to the Ocean Bed!" On May 8: "We are now in the war zone. Wireless that a submarine is off the Irish coast. We alter our course at once." She continued to wear the woollen "drowning" suit she had bought in New York until she was safe at Liverpool, where she was met by Edy. Just before she landed, a message reached the *New York* that the *Lusitania* had been sunk.

It had been a real grief, as well as a great inconvenience to her to part with her brisk clever maid Bertha in New York. Of all the personal attendants who went in and out of Ellen Terry's service in my time (the intervals between arrival and departure became shorter and shorter with the years), this German girl was the most intelligent, and consequently the most sympathetic, for it was quite impossible for a dense person, however good-hearted, to serve Ellen Terry sympathetically. Bertha was too well educated not to have heard the saying that no man is a hero to his valet. She did not expect "Mistress" (Ellen Terry always insisted on being addressed in this old-fashioned way) to be a heroine to her, and took any bricks that might be thrown, when "Mistress" was in one of her nervous, irritable moods, without complaining, as many of her more sentimental English successors complained, that she was "hurt." The separation from Bertha was one of the hardships that the War brought to Ellen Terry. She would have felt it more on the way home, if there had not been on board the *New York* a young pupil of Isadora Duncan's, who did not value her position as the belle of the ship, nearly as much as the privilege of rendering Ellen Terry all sorts of little services. "D. (Diana Wilson) read to me for two hours." "D. packed for me like the kind thing she is." "D.'s quiet gravity and her beauty gain every one." No doubt there were many conversations between "D." and Ellen Terry about Isadora, whom they had left in New York. Ellen Terry had a great affection as well as admiration for this wayward genius, not her daughter-in-law but her daughter-in-love, the mother of her fairest grandchild, Deirdre. Little Deirdre's untimely death that dreadful day when a car, with its precious freight of Isadora's adored children, swerved into the Seine, was one of the tragedies of which Ellen Terry could not speak. Another was Laurence Irving's death in the wreck of the *Empress of Ireland.* Her reticence about the things which moved her most deeply was sometimes misconstrued as insensitiveness. I remember hearing surprise expressed that she, who wept easily, did not shed a tear when she heard that Henry Irving had died suddenly at Bradford. She was reckoned emotional, even hysterically emotional in her younger days by Charles Reade, yet she was better able than most of us to refrain from a display of emotion which travesties a feeling beyond words and tears. We may perhaps attribute to this fine sense of the situation in which both are idle Ellen Terry's unemotional attitude during the War. She kept her head, and never joined in those emotional orgies of hatred and blood-lust in which old men, women and even children found solace for their non-combatant fate and their bereavements. At a time when the word "peace" was abhorrent Ellen Terry writes in her diary, "Glory to God in the highest. *Peace* on earth to men of good-will." There are many references in it to the "madness" of the war. "What madness! Thousands of lives lost today to gain ten yards in a little field." She had the common sense to appreciate Shaw's "Common Sense About the War." I am not trying to make her out a pacifist. She was no more a pacifist than she was a suffragist or a socialist, or any other " 'ist." "I cant help seeing this way, and that," she would say sooner or later during any argument. "I'm a wobbler."

This, I think, was true, and accounts for the fact that while in letters to her daughter, a doughty fighter in the cause of sex-equality, she appears to be of her feminist mind, in letters to her son she appears to be of his anti-feminist mind. But during the war she never wobbled far from a conviction that the civilised world had gone mad.

§ 4

"NEVER was any one less actually ill than she," Gordon Craig writes of his mother, and attributes her constant references to "feeling ill" in her letters to Shaw to her habit of taking refuge in the Victorian excuse of ill-health when she was disinclined to see some one, or do something, and equally disinclined to give pain or offence by telling the truth. Gordon Craig's illusion that Ellen Terry was always as fit as a fiddle, even in her old age, is quite natural as her health was on the whole very good up to the time of his departure from England. Yet even before that date (1904) the trouble with her eyes, which often caused her excruciating pain, may have made the plea of "feeling ill" more genuine than her fine constitution and immense vitality let people believe. The trouble had become so serious in Australia, that when she reached America she felt that she ought not to wait until her return home to consult an "eye-smith," her good old Saxon term for oculist. The New York eye-smith found that cataract had taken such a hold of the left eye that an immediate operation was necessary. It took place shortly before her sixty-seventh birthday (February 27, 1915). By the 16th of March she had almost recovered, and writes in her diary that "the tons of depression that have weighed on me, and anguished me, since the operation, are rolling away. New life and joy!" She did not fear now that she was going to be cut off for ever from the visible world. To her, one of the people for whom that world, as Baudelaire says, "exists," blindness would have been a more than ordinarily cruel affliction. Yet henceforth, one of the eyes which saw this world with a genius rare in any one but a painter, the genius for seeing swiftly, precisely and imaginatively, was to be useless without the aid of a lens. The difficulty she had in focussing accurately with it made her impatient. She would take off the spectacles, and depend on the eye which could still see. This put an intolerable strain on it.

"The operation was—informing! I asked if it would hurt, and was answered 'very little,' but, as I told the doctor while it was going on, it hurt like hell. But there I was, and I knew if I moved, it would cost me my eye. The pains taken were exactly like the pains a doctor takes during a confinement! I was watching all the time, and was much interested. First he cut (as at a corn) round and round. Then he prized up something, and then he cut, and my eye was all wet, and then my head seemed to be cut open at the top of my spine, and then torture for a *month*, it seemed, and then to bed, but no sleep. Always groping about in a muddy cave tumbling into great holes. All murky and filthy, and grotesque *faces!* All these horrors lasted until the Friday morning" (the operation was on a Tuesday) "and then more vitality came; I slept a little without hallucinations. My old birthday cheered me up, but it was awful not to see. I had to have a letter from Edy read to me."

This was written on March the 2nd. On the 4th the gallant fighter writes: "Oh, I do feel mighty well, but I am not allowed to get out of bed yet—nor write!"

There was another gallant fighter against Time that February. Ellen Terry was going on with the struggle, crippled by failing eye-sight: the indomitable Sarah Bernhardt had henceforth to hold her ground on one leg. The news of the amputation of the other leg first reached Ellen Terry through the papers on February 17. An entry in her diary shows that at first she could not believe it.

The newspapers say Sarah has lost a leg. I daresay she hasnt. The mere idea seems grotesque when a reporter asks you to say *"what you think of it"!* Wants an appreciation of the Leg in fact, or the rest of her. Well if any bit of her is left, it is precious, and after all we lose our hair, and our teeth, and our temper often, and shame to us! It is—it is *grotesque*, though. One thing I swear: Sarah *has not lost her soul,* and I love every bit of her that is left. I suppose it really is loss of rhythm, of balance, that makes *grotesque*. War is grotesque.... I see D'Annunzio opens a verse campaign to speed the War. Well, the pen is mightier than the sword, and so the verse may cut deeper, and live on and cut for ever.

Sarah's courage was an inspiration to Ellen. Never did she commune with herself in her diary more brilliantly and powerfully than in these days of Sarah's affliction. She was still in bed, recovering from the effects of the eye-smith's operation, when the bad news about Sarah was confirmed, but her own trial did not make her forget Sarah's. She cabled to Paris: "Fine little Queen. Beloved woman. You frightened me, but you are ever young and ever triumphant. Congratulations. Devotedly, E. T."

It was on Shakespeare's birthday (April 23, 1915) that a New York audience acclaimed Ellen Terry for the last time. She went to the Neighbourhood Theatre to give extracts from her Shakespeare lectures. "Nervous and weak at first. Soon inspired by the warmth of the audience." Her own brief account of this last appearance in a city where she had been loved for thirty-two years ought to be amplified. I have before me a copy of "An Appreciation" which was printed, and very beautifully printed too, on handmade paper, to commemorate the occasion. It was not realised that it was Ellen Terry's farewell to New York and to America, so the appreciation is in a joyful vein. The writer is full of the joy radiated by Ellen Terry, who "looked beautiful, dressed in a red gown with long flowing sleeves," but finds the joy impossible to describe. "One little interpolation that she brought into her lecture seemed particularly to bring the audience very close to her. After the short intermission when she came back to speak of the joyous women of Shakespeare, it was noticed that she had put on a long string of amber beads. She talked for a few moments, then suddenly took them off, and turning to the audience in a slightly apologetic way said: 'The weight of them is too much for me,' adding, with that laugh, and in that way, which are only hers: 'The burden of my riches hangs heavy on me.' It sounds so simple, and yet those who heard her will never forget it."

The writer goes on to describe the scene in Ellen Terry's dressing-room after the lecture. Some valuable editions of Shakespeare, including a copy of the First Folio 1623, had been lent by Mr J. P. Morgan for exhibition in the foyer of the theatre that evening, and they had been brought to Ellen Terry's room for her to examine them more closely. "Her charm was now even greater.... To see her reverently handle these books, to hear her talk about them, and other famous editions she had seen, held us fascinated."

Ellen Terry was never known to blunder over an exit. She even made her exit from this world at the right time, in the right place, leaving no dreadful memory of a prolonged last agony. Unconsciously she made a perfect exit from New York. How better could she be last seen by playgoers there than turning over leaves of the works of a dead author, whom she loved more faithfully and whole-heartedly than any living man, that Shakespeare whom she described in a pregnant message at the time of the celebration of his Tercentenary in 1916 as: "My friend, my sorrow's cure, my teacher, my companion, the very eyes of me."

§ 5

BEFORE Ellen Terry left England in 1914 for the tour which was to be her last abroad, she had begun a new family life with her grandchildren who had been brought over from Italy by their father, and dumped with their mother, Elena, in a flat in the Adelphi. They were a little older than Ellen Terry's boy and girl in the days of the Harpenden idyll, but they took the place of those dream-children, and had the felicity of being twice loved, as young Ellen Terry's little Edy and little Teddy of the past, and as old Ellen Terry's grandchildren of the present. When Ellen Terry was thinking of the dream-children, she would call the elder grandchild "Edy," although her name was Nellie. The younger had the same name as his father, and could be little Teddy any time. They arrived in England soon after James Carew had, with unspoiled good will on both sides, walked out of Ellen Terry's home, although not out of her life. The English custom of taxing the incomes of husband and wife together would alone have sufficed to remind Ellen Terry of James Carew's existence, but there were other reminders. Those fine country boots he had left at Smallhythe, which she wore after his departure. The name "Ellen Carew" in all legal documents. The great pleasure all really respectable people took in addressing her as "Mrs Carew." Occasional visits from a friend, who, when Ellen Terry was in her seventies, she had some difficulty in remembering was her husband. The place he had left vacant in the Tudor timbered house at Smallhythe, and in the Georgian panelled house in King's Road, Chelsea, was soon filled to overflowing by Elena and the children. The flat in the Adelphi, which also served as the London Office of the School of the Theatre Gordon Craig had started in Florence, was given up, I think, before Ellen Terry's tour. She writes in a note-book, which, from its contents, appears to belong to the year 1914, of her new family having "lived with" her for four years, but the

304

note may refer only to their life with her at Smallhythe which began in 1909. "For the last four years Elena and her two wonderful children, my most beloved grandchildren, have lived with me, and I am most happy, and not alone. Ted comes and goes from his work in Italy, and this must soon fix them all there. Meanwhile, they are my joys."

Ellen Terry had not been a foolish-fond mother, and in these days she was not a foolish-fond grandmother. She was indeed far more daft about Elena, whose single-hearted devotion to her son and his work won her heart, than about Elena's offspring. The "wonderful children" were not spoiled by flattery. Their grandmother was a stern critic of their first attempts to act and draw; she taught them early that art is something more than a game, and that they must work, not play at it. She soon recognised that although the boy at this time had the greatest desire to act, and was more teachable, the girl had more natural talent for the stage. Ellen Terry's conviction that "poor old Nenny," as she often called her backward pupil, was a born actress, did not seem strange to those who noticed how completely the dull, rather apathetic child, less graceful and charming than little Teddy in real life, was transformed in the theatre. The few appearances on the stage she made in early youth justified Ellen Terry's belief in her vocation. She was never to follow it however. In 1907 both children returned to Italy with their mother, and any chance Nellie had of wearing her grandmother's mantle was destroyed. Teddy suffered less from the change of environment. He developed, under his father's guidance, into an expert wood-engraver, and now promises to have a distinguished career as an artist. It is as an artist, not as an actor, that he will be associated with the theatre. His talent for scene-design has hitherto been chiefly employed in film-studios.

Ellen Terry records in her diary little Teddy's first appearance on the stage "as an *Actor,* speaking words." It was at a matinée given by Jean Sterling Mackinlay, who had recently begun those holiday performances for children which are now a firmly established institution. Teddy played the Bear-prince in "Snow White and Red Rose," not to the complete satisfaction of his critical granny. "He was good, but not so good as at rehearsal. He wrestled to get his bearskin off at the moment the bear turns into a prince, and was too rough. He looked more like a dear little ploughboy than a prince, when he had got rid of the skin! It was a case of 'trop de zèle.' He was too anxious to be in time." Earlier this year (1915) both grandchildren had "walked on" in "The Princess and the Pea," a ballet-pantomime in which Ellen Terry appeared with Adeline Genée at the Haymarket in aid of "The Invalid Kitchens of London," which not being a war charity, was in urgent need of funds. She took the last call with Teddy and Nellie. To some present this was the most enchanting moment of the entertainment. The three were seen together again in the Chelsea Revue in 1917. Then they were heard as well as seen. E. V. Lucas, the author, fitted them with speaking parts. In reply to a reporter, who asked him before the performance (given in aid of Lena Ashwell's "Concerts at the Front"), what was the greatest novelty he could promise, Mr Lucas answered: "A 'jeune premier' of superb genius and charm we have discovered. Of the part he is going to play I must say nothing, but I can say that as a man he is rendered unique by a peculiar and enviable distinction.... It is his great good fortune to possess the sweetest grandmother in the world." The "sweetest grandmother" appeared as the Spirit of Chelsea.

§ 6

THE departure of the children, who had given Ellen Terry's life a new zest, weakened her resistance to the advance of Time. From 1917 she began to lose ground. Allusions in diaries and letters to feeling old and tired show that she was conscious of defeat, and often tempted to capitulate. She seldom refused an appeal to help some war charity by appearing on the stage, but before every appearance she was now nervous and distressed. The fear that she would not remember her words, even the words of the Trial Scene in "The Merchant of Venice," which she was called upon to do over and over again in these war days, caused her real torture. It was probably the intermittence of these performances "for love" which strained her nerves, for she became more calm and confident about her powers during her engagement at the Coliseum in November 1917, and stood the subsequent tour of the Stoll music-halls in the provinces with much of her old robustness and energy. The success of the scenes from "The Merry Wives of Windsor" on the halls pleased and exhilarated her. "Yesterday a Success!" she writes after the first performance at the Coliseum. "What a blessing (from Whom all blessings flow)." She had, on her daughter's recommendation, chosen a young actress, then unknown to fame, for the part of Mrs Ford. Edith Evans, who is now reckoned the most brilliant comedy actress on the English stage, justified the choice by a performance which was not eclipsed by Ellen Terry's, but shone with the same kind of lustre. Mrs Page was enthusiastic about Mrs Ford, and generously acknowledged her share in the success of the merry wives. They were lucky in their Falstaff, played by Roy Byford, who had other qualifications for the part of the Fat Knight than that of a figure which made it unnecessary for him to wear a false stomach. The success made Mr Stoll (now Sir Oswald Stoll) re-engage Ellen Terry to appear in the Trial Scene in "The Merchant of Venice" in 1918. One night while

306

it was in the bill at the Coliseum there was an air-raid. The coolness of Ellen Terry while the German bombs were raining from the heavens was not shown by many younger artists who were giving turns in the same programme. "You ought to be ashamed," the manager said to two who were screaming with terror in their dressing-room, and far too panic-stricken to appear. "Think of Ellen Terry! She's an old woman, and she's as cool as a cucumber. If she dont mind the bombs, why on earth should you?" At the moment Ellen Terry was on the stage, infecting the audience with her own calm courage as she proceeded with the "Mercy" speech:

The quality of mercy is not strained: (*Bang went a bomb*)
It droppeth as the gentle rain from heaven (*A louder bang*)

The audience could not help seeing the joke! They laughed, although they could hear the wings of death as well as the vibrant tones of Ellen Terry's voice, and she enjoyed the laughter, controlled it, and held them to the end of the scene, when the cheering made the noise of the infernal machines overhead inaudible.

In 1916 Ellen Terry made her first appearance on the screen. She accepted an offer from the Ideal Film Company to act in a film specially written for her. It was called "Her Greatest Performance," a title which proved to have a touch of irony, for, considered in relation to Ellen Terry's stage performances in the past, her screen performance did not amount to much. It might have amounted to more, for Ellen Terry · showed in flashes that she was quite capable of adapting her flexible and fluid talent to a new medium, if she had been more intelligently directed. However well the method of instructing players before the camera to feel this and do that, without enlightening them about the motive, may work with some who can show the effect of an emotion without probing deeply into its cause, it did not work with Ellen Terry. She was hampered too by the film practice, of which she knew nothing, of concentrating attention on one person at a time. For example she saw in the trial scene in "Her Greatest Performance," when a mother has the terrible experience of seeing her son of whose innocence she is certain, made to appear guilty through a weight of incriminating evidence, her best opportunity for acting. But throughout the scene, the camera was picking out the prisoner, the witnesses, the judge, and members of the jury as well as the distraught mother. The scene was not moving in the same way or at the same pace as it was in Ellen Terry's imagination, with the result that when she was "shot," she was often expressing an emotion inappropriate at the particular moment. In other films in which she took part, "The Pillars of Society" (1920) and "The Bohemian Girl" (1921) she had less to do, but profiting by her first experience of the strange ways of film directors, she did that less more effectively. If films were made of less perishable stuff, there would be in the prologue to "The Pillars of Society" a lasting, if all too cursory, record of Ellen Terry's emotional powers.

NOTES TO CHAPTER II

1. The parts played by Ellen Terry during the period covered by this chapter were: The Queen ("The Princess and the Pea," 1915); Darling ("The Admirable Crichton," 1915); The Lady of the Manor ("The Home-coming," 1916); "The Sybil Sage" (Nativity Play, 1917); Gran'mère ("Ellen Terry's Bouquet," 1917); The Nurse ("Romeo and Juliet," 1919); Mrs. Long ("Pride and Prejudice," 1922); The Old Woman ("The Shoe," 1922); Ellen Terry ("The Street," 1922); Susan Wildersham ("Crossings," 1925). She also appeared in four films: "Her Greatest Performance," "Pillars of Society," "The Bohemian Girl," and "Potter's Clay." The part of "Darling," an old housekeeper, was introduced into "The Admirable Crichton" for her by Barrie, when the play was revived with a star cast at a matinée in aid of a war charity. I was not present at the performance of Walter de la Mare's "Crossings" in which Ellen made her final appearance on the stage, but I remember the dress-rehearsal. I was standing in the stalls at the Lyric Theatre, Hammersmith, when Ellen Terry made her first entrance. The vision of this fragile creature, far advanced in years, yet somehow not old, tremulously gliding across the stage with loving arms outstretched, all earthiness purged away by time, the spirit of beauty, rather than beauty itself, filled the spectators with a strange awe. A long sighing "Oh!" arose from them all, and the sound was a more wonderful tribute than any applause I have ever heard.

Chapter III

OLD AGE: ARIEL IMPRISONED

(1921–1928)

§ 1

WHATEVER may be said of the twentieth century in times to come, it seems improbable that any one will accuse those who lived in it of self-depreciation. Our use of the word "modern" in a highly complimentary sense will alone be evidence that we had a jolly good opinion of ourselves. "To the modern mind this seems absurd." "According to modern ideas, that is incredible." "A very brilliant novel, so modern." "A modern audience cannot be expected to swallow the kind of thing which went down with the simple playgoers of the past." (Probably "The Merchant of Venice.") Then, the historian of the future, who, viewing our age in perspective, may not share our impression of its importance, will be struck by our habit of boasting. "Always boasting of something: the conquest of the air, the conquest of the sea, the conquest of time, and a lot of other unconquerable things."

The boast I was thinking of when I began this chapter about Ellen Terry's old age was that of having prolonged the average span of human life. There appears to be some foundation for it. Statistics show that in the twentieth century the middle-aged have a greater expectation of life than they had in the nineteenth. But I have never read or heard or experienced anything which refuted the accuracy of the Psalmist's estimate of the limit to our time on earth. Surely he is quite right too about what happens when the limit is exceeded. We are sometimes tempted by an appearance of mental and physical vigour in people who have reached four-score to pooh-pooh the saying: "Then is their strength but labour and sorrow." We begin to think that there may be something in Shaw's "Back to Methuselah." Then comes the news that this hearty octogenarian, who last year was still riding to hounds, or that other, who two years ago was still in practice as a doctor, or a third who only the other day published a new book, has suddenly gone the way of all flesh. The Psalmist, even "according to modern ideas," was no fool. We must admit that he is not discredited by portraits of centenarians.

A man's strength may have been giving way for some time, but he still bears up and stands firm. Then suddenly a last blow is dealt him out of the blue. It is very difficult to foresee the blow and to understand that it is inevitable. We know nothing about it in fact, for no one has ever been able to speak of it from experience. The victim is silent, for it is the blow which instantly and irrevocably turns an active and energetic person into a complete wreck.

Perhaps there is nothing more marvellous to be recorded of Ellen Terry than that she knew she had received such a blow in 1921. She was then seventy-three, which "according to modern ideas" is not a great age. People were still talking of her eternal youth, her inextinguishable vitality, her enduring charm. Her hair was white, but often one had the illusion that it was the blonde hair of a child. It still grew luxuriantly; and had a vitality which made the hair on younger heads one saw near hers, look dull and dead. The fine smooth texture of her skin, which like that of a youthful beauty, took a thin patina of "make-up" beautifully, was another contradiction of her age. Her features had gained in delicacy, without sharpening. Her figure had become slender, without withering. Her voice still had tone and volume. It had deepened, but without any loss of clarity and resonance. Her eyes on the rare occasions when she took off her spectacles were revealed as astonishingly beautiful; even the one the eye-smith had cut kept its lovely shape. On the stage Ellen Terry could still walk with the fluent grace of her youth. The very last time she appeared on one (at the Lyric Theatre, Hammersmith, in 1926) she floated across it as if she had indeed been the spirit-woman she was representing in Walter de la Mare's play. Elsewhere her movements were hesitating and uncertain. She disdained the aid of a stick, and, as she could not see very well, often stumbled; if there were no one by her side to catch hold of her arm, she fell. Fortunately her long experience of falling with relaxed muscles on the stage prevented these falls from having any serious consequences, until 1927 when she fell down a staircase in a friend's house, unfamiliar to her, and broke her arm. By that time she looked so fragile that the surgeon who attended her was astonished at her swift recovery from the shock of the accident. But from that blow dealt her by Time in 1921, she never recovered. It struck a mind and body consumed by the very abundance of vitality that had prolonged their youth, and this vitality proceeding from the unhurt spirit, made Ellen Terry's old age a problem which puzzled her, and every one who had the perspicacity to see that the common fate of man had overtaken a being so out of the common that there must be strife between them.

It was on April 26, 1921, that Ellen Terry wrote in her diary, "I am unhinged (*not* unhappy) and uncomfortable. I wonder where everything

310

Photograph by Alice Boughton

ELLEN TERRY IN 1911

is. Cannot remember new things. All is changed. Change at 73 puzzles the will. I live in puzzledom."

I HAD grown accustomed by this time to hearing Ellen Terry called an "old lady," but the description still gave me a shock, almost as great as on the day I first heard it applied to her. A dark-skinned turbaned waiter in an Indian restaurant informed me that "the old lady had gone." I had been lunching with Ellen Terry and her daughter, and had left them a minute to get my coat. Meanwhile they had gone downstairs. There was no doubt that the man was referring to Ellen Terry, and I could not have been more staggered if I had heard a skylark or an angel described as "an old lady." I reflected that he was an Oriental, to whom all women who are not girls are old, and still resented the description. It seemed to me disrespectful as well as ludicrously inappropriate. People ought not to employ a common term when speaking of a being so obviously unique. This feeling has persisted and is as strong now as when Ellen Terry was alive.

Clemence Dane, the distinguished novelist and dramatist, who first became personally acquainted with Ellen Terry in the year 1922, showed a rare sensitiveness in immediately apprehending that there was something exceptional in this exceptional woman's old age. She felt the tragic contrast, of which few of Ellen Terry's intimate friends were conscious, between the swift radiant spirit, and the dark confined cell into which Time had driven it. "Ariel in the tree," a mutual friend told me was Clemence Dane's impression of Ellen Terry at 74, when people of inferior vision saw only a dear old lady, rather deaf, rather blind, unable to concentrate her attention on any subject for long, yet able to talk on every subject brilliantly in disconnected fragments, an old lady who had been a famous actress, and was now a famous legend. "Ariel in the tree" was my illumination. I now understood perfectly why I could not identify the old lady with Ellen Terry. Time had dealt with her as the "damn'd witch Sycorax" dealt with Ariel:

> And for thou wast a spirit too delicate
> To act her earthly and abhorr'd commands,
> Refusing her grand hests, she did confine thee . . .
> Into a cloven pine; within which rift
> Imprison'd, thou didst painfully remain
> A dozen years.

Ellen Terry's imprisonment lasted only a little more than half that time, and it was by no means continuously painful. She could not get out of her tree. That irked her, and made her restless and impatient; even, on bad days, bitter and indignant. She had always hated to be ruled, although she had a passion for subjugating herself voluntarily to the wishes and interests of others, and now in this prison of old age she was compelled to accept its immutable restrictions and regulations. For a long time the compulsion chafed her. She tried to keep the control of her affairs in her own hands, heedless of the fact that in prison this was impossible. She realised the impossibility herself in that fateful year 1921 when she received her sentence. Accustomed to the idea that she could at any time earn a large sum of money by some profitable engagement, she had long been living beyond her means. She appeared not to be a spendthrift. Few actresses in her position can ever have dressed more economically; she was never tempted to squander money on personal luxuries. But she was not a good domestic manager. Her homes in London and the country, simple and unpretentious as they seemed, cost her more than they ought to have cost, and much more than she could afford, when she was not constantly in work. However, the real cause of the deplorable condition of her finances in 1921 was her reckless generosity. Besides being a regular subscriber to many well-known charitable institutions, she constantly sent a "trifle," and this trifle in her heyday as an actress, was often a cheque for £100, to more obscure ones in need. If her heart was moved by a begging letter, she would help the writer, feeling like Charles Lamb that even if the starving wife and children for whom he begged had no existence, she might "haply be relieving an indigent bachelor." Her income was further reduced by annual allowances to a troop of dependents, some of whom had no sort of claim on her. I have already told the reader, in a note to the fifth chapter of her Memoirs, that for years she contributed to the maintenance of the sisters of her second husband's first wife! By 1921 they were dead, but the dependents still alive were receiving allowances which made Ellen Terry poorer by £700 a year. As her income from investments and annuities amounted roughly to £380 a year, and she had an overdraft at her bank of about £1600, her situation would have become desperate if some one had not intervened. It was sufficiently grave already to call for immediate action.

At other periods of her life Ellen Terry had trusted businesslike friends to help her manage her affairs. They were all men. She was not a typical product of her age, but she had been imbued from childhood with the Victorian idea that in money matters men are generally very wise, and women generally very foolish. It may have been her fault that her male advisers (the last before the crash was her third husband) did not completely justify her high opinion of the businesslike ability of their sex. Not one of them seems to have been able to devise a plan for safeguarding the fortune she earned on the stage. Now, by a strange irony, when she had run through the fortune, a woman came to the rescue.

In the summer of 1916 Edith Craig and I had let two rooms in our flat in London to an artist. We were delighted to have this dear and talented friend as a tenant, and to Ellen Terry, who always got on well with painters, she was soon a *persona grata*. As our intimacy ripened, we all discovered that "Tony," as Clare Atwood was known in our family circle, had an aptitude for "business" which none of us possessed. It was to "Tony" that Ellen Terry turned in her perplexity about her finances. "Am I £1600 to the good, or to the bad, Tony?" Tony, investigating the passbook, was horrified. Her brushes lay idle for several weeks while she took counsel about what could be done to avert a catastrophe. Ellen Terry would soon have been insolvent, if Clare Atwood had not laid down her brushes, with a self-abnegation rare in the artist, and taken up the difficult problem of adjusting Ellen Terry's expenditure to her revenue. A very able and distinguished lawyer, Mr Gilbert Samuel (brother of Sir Herbert Samuel) volunteered his services, and the busy editor of *The Morning Post,* Mr H. A. Gwynne, also took an active part in the reform of Ellen Terry's finance. It was to him, as the husband of one of her oldest friends, that she entrusted a power of attorney. Her behaviour in the crisis was as calm and sensible as it had always been in the grave troubles of her life. She offered no opposition to the scheme proposed for balancing her budget. She was fully conscious that something had to be done, and that she must trust others to do it. The abolition of the allowances to dependents, the sale of her house in Chelsea and of some of her belongings, and the control of her personal expenditure, were the main features of the scheme. Its execution, and the augmentation of her capital by her film engagements in 1921 and 1922, sufficed to secure her a small income, and relieve her of anxiety about the future of her children (who despite their talents and their industry could earn money only fitfully), of Elena, and of those two beloved grandchildren in Italy. She made a will leaving the rehabilitated remnant of her fortune to these five descendants.

The economies which the rehabilitation involved, seemed absurd to her son, far away in Italy, and totally ignorant of the financial crisis. Besides the illusion that his mother was always as fit as a fiddle, he cherished another that she was always well-to-do. This illusion accounts for his doing scant justice in his biography to the friends who came to her rescue, and straightened out her tangled affairs. My collaborator, his sister, has asked me to refrain from any vindication of their action, to which she, who was on the spot, was convinced there was no alternative. But she wishes me to correct the inaccurate statement that among the possessions her mother sold at this time were presents from her son, rare copies of his illustrated journal "The Page," and drawings. There were sold only duplicates of the many complete sets of "The Page," and of bookplates Ellen Terry had bought in the past. None of Gordon Craig's drawings were put into this sale, and if any presented by him to his mother ever came into the market, we must attribute it to the lavishness with which she gave away books, pictures, and other treasures to her friends. This happy-go-lucky habit of offering, even to a casual visitor, anything singled out for admiration, increased in her old age, and there were few who were conscientious enough not to take advantage of it.

It seemed to some of Ellen Terry's more sentimental friends, as well as to her son, that the sale of her attractive Georgian house in Chelsea was a hardship she ought to have been spared. Perhaps they did not realise that the sale was an imperative necessity, but they ought to have known that Ellen Terry had been anxious for some time before the sale to leave the house, which had become a burden to her, and move into a small flat. She wanted to spend more time at her Elizabethan farm-house at Small-hythe (which not being of anything like the commercial value of the Chelsea house, had been spared) and less in London. The extravagance of keeping up a house, which she had found too large since the departure of her grandchildren, just for an occasional stay, had struck her before she realised it was an impossible extravagance. "Cant any one find me a nice little flat near the theatres?" was a constant cry of hers. Her chief joy in life, now that she could not act herself, was to watch others acting. A visit to the theatre also brought her the assurance, very precious to a woman of her warm temperament, that she was still loved by the public. Her appearance in the auditorium was often greeted with as much enthusiasm as her appearances on the stage had been. Her gift of getting *en rapport* with an audience could still be felt. Other actresses have had successes as great, perhaps greater than Ellen Terry's, but I doubt whether there has ever been one who engaged the sympathies of an audience to the same extent, or got such a hold on the affection of the public. The stipulation that the little flat must be "near the theatres," was inspired as much by a desire to keep in touch with that affection as by a keen interest in new plays and new players.

A friend lent her such a flat in St Martin's Lane, and after having stayed there a few weeks, she set her heart on living there. Immediately negotiations were started to secure it for her. It is of some importance to emphasise that she chose her new London home herself, as many have the impression that she was moved, against her will, into this rather cramped little flat, scornfully described by Gordon Craig as "most un-Terrylike." I recall that Tony and I worked hard for several weeks to make it more Terrylike, painting the walls in the colours Ellen Terry particularly liked. When the best pieces of her furniture had been adroitly placed by her daughter it looked charming enough. On the day Ellen Terry moved in, the first thing which attracted her attention was the inscription her decorators had painted over the arch in the hall in Roman capitals, which if not quite so perfect as those on Trajan's column were good examples of good lettering: "Parva Domus, magna quies." "Yes, I ought to have great peace in this dear little place," she said wistfully, but she could not keep tumult out of it, or out of her life. Rarely, rarely came the days when Ariel was tranquil in the tree. Her daughter, whom she once described in a letter to Shaw as "her greatest care and her greatest comfort," was now a near neighbour. That was one of the advantages of the little flat, which some of her friends who saw only its disadvantages did not appreciate. They were always urging her to leave it, and take a house, better suited to the dignity of the ex-queen of the English theatre. They liked the idea of an ex-queen presiding over a court of her old admirers, men and women of mark, such as had attended suppers in the Beefsteak Room at the Lyceum in Irving's palmy days. They saw her seated at the head of a beautifully-appointed dinner table, "candles in branched silver candelabra," and all that, entertaining artists, travellers and scientists, perhaps even those royal personages, who indeed maintained an affectionate interest in Ellen Terry until the end of her life. Fantastic vision! Apart from the fact that Ellen Terry could not afford the luxury of hospitality on this scale, and at no time had been tempted to indulge in it, she became confused now when more than two or three people were gathered together in her presence. Her unfitness for entertaining, or for being entertained, was definitely confirmed in 1924 by a high medical authority. He gave the opinion that "it is very important that she should lead a very quiet life. Indeed it is wiser for her not to see more than one or two persons at a time." Yet those who had earlier perceived the disorientation caused by her seeing many persons at a time, or even a few too frequently, and had sought to limit the number of her visitors, were accused of cutting her off from her friends. Her daughter in particular suffered from this misrepresentation. Never popular with the majority of these friends, who were curiously jealous of the place she occupied in her mother's heart, Edy now became the victim of every sort of spiteful calumny. "She doesn't spoil me," Ellen Terry wrote of Edy to Shaw in 1896. "But let any one try to hurt me! Murder then, if it would save me." Now there were many injudicious people who were unconsciously trying to hurt Ellen Terry in these days by not allowing her to lead a quiet and retired life, and if Edy stopped short of murdering them, it was because she hoped to be able to save her mother in a more sensible way. It mattered little to her that her efforts made her enemies. To protect her mother from being hurt, physically or mentally, she was quite willing to be stabbed by idle tongues. She did not say, yet she might have said, "*Et tu, Brute,*" when after her mother's death she read the last chapters of "Ellen Terry and Her Secret Self." Gordon Craig's jibes there at the "loving guardians" of Ellen Terry in her old age are the more unworthy, because he could have done much to make it happier. "My son who has all along been my sun. Without the warmth of him many a time I would have died and died, I know." How seldom was Ellen Terry warmed by that sun during her years in the "cloven pine"! She laid plans for going to Italy to bask in it only two years before she died, but they were defeated by her physical weakness. Apart from that, it was feared by her doctor that the excitement of new scenes and a different routine would have a very bad result mentally. She often expressed a desire to see Elena and the beloved grandchildren. I am quite unable to understand why it was not gratified. It is certain that if they had been anxious to come, the "loving guardians" of Ellen Terry who knew how she pined for the children would not have let the expense of the journey stand in the way. She had looked after them for years. Now an opportunity had come for them to repay her loving care by looking after her. The girl's companionship was exactly what she needed. It would have solved the problem, which worried Edy, of finding any stranger who could look after her mother with a sympathetic comprehension of her temperament. She herself was bound to go on working. At the time of the retrenchment scheme, she had voluntarily renounced her allowance, and there was more urgent need than in other days for her to earn money. As she could find no opening in London for her talents as a play-producer, she had to accept any engagement she could get in the provinces. Her niece, Nellie Craig, was old enough now to be her deputy at her mother's side when she was away. Nellie had no occupation in Italy to make this a waste of her youth. "The saddest word is 'might have been'," and perhaps it is also the idlest. Nellie might have been not only useful, but a source of joy, to Ariel in the tree, and again she might not. As her father did not let her come to England, she was not put to the test.

Ellen Terry needed some one at her side. She needed some one's eyes to read to her, to write for her, and some one's arm, though she was loth to lean on it, to guide her. She was not blind, as has been stated, but anything that disorientated her affected her eyesight. There were days when she could do more than tell a hawk from a hernshaw. She could, from the other side of the room, detect the presence of sorrel in a mixed green salad. Her eyes remained sensitive to beauty wherever they encountered it. Clare Atwood, who knew her only late in life, when she was supposed not to see well, was often astonished at Ellen Terry's swift appreciation of some subtle change in the light on some object in a room. "Look at it now!" she would exclaim as the colour of a bunch of flowers changed with the light. "It is twice as beautiful." It was Clare Atwood who said after Ellen Terry's death that her memory of her would for ever be associated with the perception of beauty in the commonest things. Nevertheless, in old age Ellen Terry could neither read, nor write, without pain and discomfort.

She needed some one at her side for other reasons than this. She had to be restrained from over-taxing her strength; restrained from wearing thin garments on a cold day; restrained from giving away valuable possessions; restrained from going out into the streets of London, unattended, and risking her life in the traffic. With her Ariel spirit she had a great desire for freedom, and any one who tried to restrain her, daughter or friend or bodymaid, had a difficult task. In five years twenty-seven bodymaids came and went. They seemed hopelessly inefficient to us, but to serve Ellen Terry efficiently in these days required an amount of patience, devotion and quick intelligence, rare in the best-trained bodymaids. The amateurs were rather more successful than the professionals. I remember that Marguerite Steen, now a distinguished novelist, then a young stage aspirant, proved a very capable personal attendant to Ellen Terry in an emergency. At a later date a sensible, good-humoured Yorkshire woman who could keep her head and her temper in the most trying circumstances, entered Ellen Terry's service. She could turn her hand to anything, which was lucky, as circumstances made it necessary for her to be housekeeper, cook, maid, secretary, companion and nurse at one time or another. "Barney," as Ellen Terry called personal attendant, Number 28, was obstinately faithful. She was not popular with the faction of friends and relations who thought that Ellen Terry ought to have her way, to be allowed to walk into a pond, or burn herself to death, if she liked. They resented, as an inexcusable presumption, Barney's vigilant care of her precious charge. In the winter of 1927, during Barney's absence on a brief holiday, Ellen Terry had a serious attack of bronchial pneumonia. Barney hurried back to nurse her. It was during this illness that the "Let-her-do-as-she-likes" faction invaded her flat, and were extremely annoyed at not being immediately admitted to her bedroom. She had a bad patch on her lung at the time, and although she had rallied, and was out of danger, she was still breathing with difficulty. A trained nurse was in attendance as well as the presumptuous Barney. Yet one of the faction, who could never be persuaded that Ellen Terry's maladies were anything more serious than the vapours, was annoyed at being asked by Barney to go away quietly, when he called late at night, rather noisily jovial after a good dinner, to cheer up the invalid. The faction worked hard to get this faithful watchdog whose bark offended them, dismissed, but were defeated by Ellen Terry's real affection for her, and Edy's appreciation of her loyalty and efficiency. Barney remained in Ellen Terry's service until her death.

§ 3

THE nature of my allusions to "the friends of Ellen Terry" in the narrative of the difficulties and afflictions of her old age may have led the reader to think that she had reason to say, like the ancient cynic: "My friends, show me my friend." The possibility makes me anxious to introduce the friends to whom an injustice would have been done by that satirical appeal. Ellen Terry once had the pretty conceit of making a collection of "friendship beads." It was a great privilege to be asked to send her a bead. The invitation conferred a title, admitted to an order, the insignia of which were, against all precedent, provided by the decorated and handed over to the decorator. The collection of beads, which is still in existence, shows that there were seventy members of the most noble order of the Friends of Ellen Terry. The habit does not make the monk, and when I look at these beads I am forced to the conclusion that the title of friend does not make the friend. "Love is not love which alters when it alteration finds." It was when Ellen Terry's friends found her altered by age that they were subjected to the true test of their worthiness of the distinction represented by the bead.

Of the host of girls who had worshipped her in her heyday both in England and America, only a few became intimate friends. One of them, "Laurence" (Miss Laurence Alma-Tadema), through the good fortune which made her Ellen Terry's neighbour at Smallhythe, had frequent opportunities for seeing her in the last years. Ellen Terry, old, was as dear to Laurence as Ellen Terry young. Laurence with her swift intelligence, could avoid the broken strings, and from the others produce the old music. Never a sign of heart or brain being jangled and out of tune during Laurence's visits.

Still she was but a visitor. Ellen Terry was only an incident in her life. In the life of E. D. G. (a schoolfellow of Edy's) Ellen Terry was an institution, and one of which this kind-hearted but rather despotic friend wished to have complete control. "I wont capitulate," Ellen Terry wrote in her diary after a tussle with E. D. G. in 1921. But E. D. G.'s attempts "to rule her" caused her more amusement than annoyance, and she was sensible of the genuine love that inspired them. In those distressing times when Ellen Terry could not manage her home, and yet was unwilling to resign from management, she fled from her discomfort to E. D. G.'s comfortable house in the country, and was always received with open arms.

Another refuge was Graham Robertson's home at Witley. Graham Robertson was one of the few men whose friendship never failed Ellen Terry. From the day, when a boy of thirteen he had seen her in "The Merchant of Venice," and had identified her with the "Impossible She" of his dreams, her name had been graven on his heart. It mattered little to him when the external radiance of that golden Portia dimmed with age, for she had become one of his closest and dearest friends, and he could see the inward radiance of her heart. A similar catholicity of taste, a Blake drawing for joy one moment, a racy joke the next, bound them together intellectually. Ariel was never less conscious of the prison walls of age than at Sandhills. Writing to Edy from there on her 78th birthday, she says: "This is one of the most perfectly lovely days I have ever lived in... What lovely days are around us now! I wish you could see the flowers here... Alix and Graham and the doggies are all most harmonious."

"Alix," (Lady Alix Egerton) had in youth, like Graham Robertson, imaged Ellen Terry as a Fairy Princess, and an atmosphere of fairy-tales, ballads and romances still pervaded this friendship in later years. "Alix" was a poet, and Ellen Terry inspired her to pour out her heart in verse. That chameleon faculty in Ellen Terry, which made it easy for her to take the form and colour of any image of herself she saw in another's mind, was affected by age. Those who had idolised their own image of her, were perhaps never fully conscious that the disparity between it and the old Ellen Terry, which distressed, or annoyed, or alienated them, according to their temperament, was due to the fact that she had lost the power, and perhaps also the desire, to identify herself with the image. "Alix" was one of the few imagists among Ellen Terry's friends, who were unselfish enough not to abandon her when she withdrew from all images into herself.

Let the galled jade wince. The withers of those who now thought more of what they could do for Ellen Terry than of what she could do for them are unwrung. The friends who were in closest touch with that inner life of contemplation in which her spirit, uninjured by age, was enclosed, could do most for her. There was one, who by reason of a vein of mysticism in a character which in the common ways of life struck the casual observer as merely eccentric, was at home in this enclosure, and Ellen Terry, who had always had an affection for her, was now more conscious of an affinity between them. G. P. (Miss Gwenllian Palgrave, a daughter of F. T. Palgrave of "Golden Treasury" fame) could have given Gordon Craig some valuable information about that "secret self" of Ellen Terry's he made the chief theme of his biography, and yet failed to reveal. Ellen Terry's letters to G. P. and to M. P., her sister, who for many years acted as Ellen Terry's secretary, at any rate give us glimpses of her only secret life, the one in which she walked with God. M. P. is now dead. She gave a last proof of her devotion to Ellen Terry by leaving her a legacy, which, knowing her free-handed generosity to others, she stipulated should be spent only on herself. But G. P. sent Edy some of the letters written by Ellen Terry to M. P., as well as those to her, at the time we thought of publishing a volume of letters to various correspondents, a project put on one side, when the publication of the whole Shaw-Terry correspondence was proposed. It is in one of the letters to M. P. that I have found something which throws light on the bond between Ellen Terry and both sisters. Referring to some scandalous report, Ellen Terry writes:

M. dear, it's nought but the idle tongue that says those silly things.—— is far from vicious or malign. I know your, and G.'s dear hearts are generously wounded for me, and because you love, you grieve and take to heart. But God forbid that I show any difference to ——. So much of the wisdom and true Christianity of Shakespeare was derived from his Maker. "Use every man after his deserts," which comes to this: Did God treat us as we deserved, we should hardly escape hell! *But,* God so loved the world! And then dear Tommy Kempy amplifies: "Thou ought'st not to take to heart if some think ill of thee." You mustnt, either of you, talk of my being forgiving. Oftentimes I have said, dear M., we should not withhold our love. Call it forgiveness if you will, but I prefer not to. Forgiveness seems to imply *we* are in the right, and as often as not, we are the stumbling blocks ourselves, only we dont know it! Oh do let's try, like the dear Saviour, to be *dumb* when we fancy we are injured, you and I and G. That's the way to love Him who loved us.

Talking of Tommy à K. I want those dear nuns at Stanbrook to tell me if I could learn much from another Tommy, Thomas Aquinas. I believe he is immensely learned, but very interesting. Dame Laurentia would know. You're a bit of a theologian, M. You might read with me, or better still *to* me, Aquinas. There's a thought!"

Dame Laurentia McLachlan, referred to in this letter, was then Prioress of the Benedictine Community at Stanbrook Abbey, Worcester. She has since been elected Abbess. Ellen Terry, while on a visit to Mary Anderson (Madame de Navarro) at Broadway in 1916, visited Stanbrook, and for years afterwards she talked of Dame Laurentia, and her predecessor as Abbess, Dame Cecilia Heywood, with loving enthusiasm. Both nuns told me, shortly after Ellen Terry's visit, that she had impressed them as one of the most spiritual women they had ever met. She was remembered in the prayers of the community in all her afflictions while she was alive, and now they pray for her soul. There is another nun at Stanbrook, besides the brilliant and lovable Abbess, to whom Ellen Terry was known personally. I. C. D., an intimate friend of Edy's, entered the convent in 1920.

To go back to the Order of the Beads. There was no more active member than "Bertie" or "The Bart," (Sir Albert Seymour). He and Graham Robertson, and "old Tom" (Tom Heslewood, actor and costume-designer) saved Ellen Terry from being obliged to put up with an almost exclusively feminine society during her last years. "Bertie has a heart of gold" was Ellen Terry's favourite tribute, and I never heard any one question that it was deserved. He understood her much better than many people who appeared to be nearer her intellectual level. Shrewd, rather than clever, he knew how to entertain her, and his quickness in seizing her mood astonished one in a person, who apart from her, seemed slow. I think "Bertie" studied Ellen Terry with the same diligence that others apply to their special subject, philosophy or art, or mathematics. He was really learned in Ellen Terry. This prevented him from forming some definite conception of her, which when she was old it would have fatigued her to try and satisfy. He was untiring in devising little pleasures for her, from a dinner at Claridge's, when she was in the mood to go out, to a present of fish or asparagus for her table when she was in the mood to stay at home. He fought gallantly by her side, when she was resisting Time, cossetting her with flatteries about her youthfulness. And when the war was over, even to those last days of her life when there was no past for her, and no future, only the present moment to be lived through, "Bertie" did not fail her.

Owing to my friendship with Edy, I saw a great deal of Ellen Terry after I had ceased to be associated with her as literary henchman, and had opportunities for observing how the Knights and Ladies of the Order of the Beads, whose cherished insignia had been strung into a necklace, behaved when their loyalty was tested. There were some who were not even conscious of a test. They found the singular fascination of Ellen Terry undiminished, and indeed it was as little affected by time as that spiritual flame which some could still see burning brightly in the mist which had gathered over her mind. There were others who were disconcerted by her inability to play her old part in their lives, and of these, few had the patience or unselfishness to adapt themselves to the change. The list of the faithful had grown tragically short by the year 1928 when Ellen Terry died, yet still it is too long for me to pay an adequate tribute to each one individually. I hear a voice once compared to "a bunch of red roses," the voice of Ellen Terry, which I have often heard prompting me during this narrative of her later years, protesting that I must at least mention the "Casella girls." So Ellen Terry still called two friends of her youth, clever artists both, when they were elderly women. In their house she often found peace and joy in her restless old age. They, like "Bertie," were "learned in Ellen Terry," and had no difficulty in following her in the days when she wandered from one distant recollection to another. "And Lindsay, dear Lindsay! And little Pipkin!", Ellen Terry prompts again, and I remember how faithfully L. J. (Miss Lindsay Jardine) supplied her with books for over twenty years, how faithfully she served her in other ways "all for love and nothing for reward," never preying on her time and strength like less judicious and more self-seeking friends. I knew L. J. myself. I did not know "Pipkin" (Mrs Irving Albery, younger daughter of Henry Arthur Jones), but no one who was much in Ellen Terry's company between 1920 and 1928 could be unaware of her affection for Pipkin. How often she spoke with enthusiasm of Pipkin's lovely old house in the country, where she stayed weeks at a time, an honoured and tenderly cared-for guest. It was fitting that her last journey to London after her death should have been broken at that house. The poignantly gay funeral procession, hearse hidden by bright flowers, coffin veiled by a pall of gold, halted outside the place where Ariel had been least conscious of the imprisoning tree.

"I have known many people, yet how few I have ever had time to know well," was one of Ellen Terry's wise sayings, when she was still on the stage. It throws light on the curious fact that she had few friends among members of her own profession. They were debarred, like her, from the leisure required for friendship. The only old actor who was really a friend of Ellen Terry's in her old age was Norman Forbes-Robertson; the only young one, Harcourt Williams. Both were helped to maintain the friendship by the fact that they had houses near Smallhythe, where she spent much of her time. Actresses were represented in the Order of the Beads only by Violet Vanbrugh, her sister Irene, Viola Tree, Pauline Chase and Jean Sterling Mackinlay, Harcourt Williams's gifted wife. Ellen Terry had a profound admiration for Jean's talent as an actress-singer, and there was a great personal sympathy between them. In the winter of 1927 when Ellen Terry's strength had become labour and sorrow, and the days when she could regain her delight in living and loving, were becoming rarer, she insisted on going out on a cold stormy day to attend the first performance of Jean Mackinlay's Christmas entertainment for children. It was her last entertainment. Jean had the privilege of being the last artist of the theatre who made Ellen Terry laugh and weep, and say in a loud clear voice: "What a genius!"

Ellen Terry loved her own kith and kin, although she had no conventional family sentiment. She could criticise the performances of a Terry on the stage without prejudice. If they were good performances, she was enthusiastic. If they were not, or at any rate not good enough to please her, she could not be induced by any nonsense about blood being thicker than water to flatter them against her convictions. She believed in the great talent of her niece Phyllis Neilson-Terry from the day when as a girl of seventeen she played Viola, yet, while this belief was never shaken, it did not make her blind to "Phyl's" faults. While in New York in 1915 Ellen Terry wrote in her diary after seeing "Phyl" as Trilby that her performance "lacks shape." A professional dramatic critic once said that Ellen Terry's critical faculties "have always remained singularly undeveloped," which showed only that his own critical faculties were singularly undeveloped. I have never known a better critic of acting than Ellen Terry; her autobiography is rich in illuminating criticisms. It was after reading it that Henry W. Lucy wrote: "If you had not been a supreme actress you would have been a superlative dramatic critic."

So when "Phyl" roused Ellen Terry's enthusiasm as Viola, as Desdemona and as Juliet, she had reason to be proud, and probably was, as she was proud of her famous aunt. Speaking of her once in an interview with an American newspaper man, "Phyl" said:

I looked proudly at my father, because he had so splendid a sister. That performance of my aunt's in "The Merry Wives of Windsor," I remember as one of the perfect things of this world. If I were to attempt to analyse her performances, I should say that there are three qualities never absent from any of them. They are beauty, inspiration and buoyancy.

They met seldom in Ellen Terry's last years. A pity.

Ellen Terry's meetings with her sister Marion were also infrequent owing to Marion's ill-health. The elder sister Kate died in 1924. Her daughters, one of whom was on the stage, were devoted to "Aunt Nell," and on terms of great intimacy with her. They were very attentive in these times, and watched her interests on behalf of the family with a zeal which sometimes outran discretion.

It will be remembered that Ellen Terry had another sister, Florence, who was more like Ellen in temperament than either Kate or Marion. The love that Ellen had for Floss, fascinating, mischievous, buoyant Floss, whose career on the stage ended at her marriage in 1882, was inherited after her death by Floss's children. Her daughter Olive had the bigger share of the fortune. She and her brother Jack, and Ellen Terry's brother

Charlie, were the relatives who were most often in the company of Ellen Terry in her old age, and most helpful to Edy in the difficult situation created by her brother's absence.

§ 4

ELLEN TERRY had in her great days been thrown with the great. This wise, witty, beautiful and fascinating creature could, if she had chosen, made friends of scores of admirers, distinguished in some way, men of great intellectual attainments, women eminent in the fashionable world. But she never took much trouble to draw them into her intimacy. She preferred to consort with the little ones of the earth. Often I heard it said: "What *can* Ellen Terry have in common with A. or B.?" It was indeed strange to watch her apparently wasting her love on a queer crew of people in whom one could not detect any ability or charm or outstanding originality. The vision of Ellen Terry in her old age, surrounded by the halt and the blind, the shabby and the eccentric, the despised and the rejected, is not nearly as fantastic as the one of her presiding over a court of the rich and famous.

§ 5

THE voice of Ellen Terry, who was of a sunny disposition although she loved the moon more than the sun, now prompts me not to make so many melancholy references to her old age. "Tell them about the good times."

In 1922 Miss Geneviève Ward was made a Dame of the Most Excellent Order of the British Empire. Now although Miss Ward had a considerable reputation in the English theatre as a tragic actress, which Shaw attributes less to her actual achievements than to her association with Ristori, it was felt that this official recognition of her services to the stage was rather strange in view of the fact that Ellen Terry's name had never appeared in an Honours List. It had often been rumoured that she was going to receive some high honour. I remember that an eminent dramatic critic once hinted that it would not be long before she would be entitled to write O.M. after her name, adding that it would be a great misfortune if she had to wait until, like Florence Nightingale, the only woman ever admitted to the Order of Merit, she was too old to appreciate the honour conferred on her. There appears to have been no foundation at all for this report of a project to single out Ellen Terry for this rare distinction. Its only unfortunate result was that Ellen Terry for a time believed it. She had a very vague idea of what constituted eligibility for the O.M., but she knew it was the kind of recognition which would be agreeable to her because it did not involve the assumption of a title. "If they ever do anything for me, I hope it will be that," she said to me once with touching simplicity. I had not the heart to tell her that I had been informed by an authority on honours that "they" did not think her eligible for the O.M. and that the award had never even been discussed.

The agitation for some honour for Ellen Terry appears to have struck Sir James Barrie as quite reasonable. As Lord Rector of St Andrew's University, he recommended that there should be conferred on her the honorary degree of LL.D., and on May 5, 1922, she received it, in the distinguished company of Earl Haig, John Galsworthy, Colonel Freyburg V.C., E. V. Lucas, Sir Squire Bancroft and Sir James Guthrie. In the course of Sir James Barrie's characteristically whimsical speech about the recipients he referred to a form of proposal of marriage common in the 'eighties and 'nineties. "As there's no chance of Ellen Terry marrying me, will you?"

She made several public appearances this year, some of them on the stage at charity matinées. In October she unveiled a memorial tablet to Sarah Siddons at Bath. The deterioration in her handwriting in her diary suggests that her eyesight was becoming worse, but there are no signs of "disorientation" in the contents. It was extremely difficult for some of us at this time to "suffer fools gladly," when they spread reports that "poor Ellen Terry is quite dotty now," for they, in the prime of life, had a far weaker mental grasp of things than she in her old age, and had never experienced the joy of intimacy with Shakespeare's mind, with field and hedge and flower, and changing skies, which still was hers. In August, 1922, she wrote in her diary: "As the twig is bent, the tree is inclined. At school nowadays children are taught to write a fair hand, and tots of 4 and 5 are masters of an astonishingly good script." This particular entry is written in a beautiful hand. Here is another:

I want no appreciation or thanks for anything I have done in life. No. Let them thank me, if they must, by employing the outstanding talents of my children, who rather "lack advancement." They could give me help then, should I ever be needing help, other than that they give me now in love and friendship.

This was written after a visit to the Little Theatre, where Ellen Terry had been struck by the proof of Edith Craig's "outstanding talent," which her lovely production of a play by a Japanese poet, "The Toils of Yoshi-tomo," had afforded.

"Keep clear," "Keep up," are frequently written in her diary for 1923. "Lindsay has sent me such a lovely book, D. H. Lawrence's 'The Lady

Bird.' L. always sends me captivating books." Next I come to a reference to a performance of "Twelfth Night" by the boys of the All Saints, Margaret Street, Choir School. Ellen Terry's first experience of these productions of Shakespeare at the school, which, judged by the highest standard, were remarkable, had been in 1921 when she saw "Julius Cæsar." I remember she spotted a future winner in the small boy who played Brutus. "Already a great actor," she said. The following year she notes in her diary that the "wonderful little Brutus" played Katharine in "The Taming of the Shrew," and that she had never seen the part played as well by any woman, except Ada Rehan. "This gives us an idea of what the boy-actors in Shakespeare's time were like, yet people assume they were clumsy hobbledehoys!" Laurence Olivier, whose talent Ellen Terry recognised when he was a schoolboy, has since established his reputation as an actor by many fine performances both on the stage and on the screen.

In 1923 Sarah Bernhardt died. It was in Sarah's dressing-room at the Prince's Theatre after a performance of "Daniel," the last play in which she appeared in London, that the two gallant comrades, diverse in temperament and talent, but alike in their unquenchable love of life and in their gay courage, met for the last time, Ellen blazing with enthusiasm over Sarah's tour de force (in "Daniel" she impersonated a young man, who like her was a cripple and could not move from an invalid's chair), Sarah shining with a paler flame, but much gratified by Ellen's homage. After Sarah's death in Paris, there was a solemn Requiem mass at Westminster Cathedral. I was in the organ loft, and had a good view of the congregation, composed mainly of English members of Sarah's profession. Ellen Terry alone seemed conscious that this was a ceremony, and that in honour of Sarah, an actress must play her part in it with dignity. She straightened her back, bowed by age, held up her still lovely head, and moved up the aisle to her seat near the catafalque with the stately grace of her more stately performances in the theatre.

Sarah Bernhardt had made her exit from the world's stage. Eleonora Duse was to make hers in the following year (1924). In the interval Duse came to London. She had recently come out of her retirement, and given performances in Italy in Ibsen's "Ghosts" and "The Lady from the Sea" and in two new plays, "Cosi Sia," and "La Porta Chiusa," which had stirred her compatriots to a frenzy of enthusiasm. Mr C. B. Cochran, who had been the live wire in the London theatre since the war, a showman genuinely anxious to show beautiful things in every branch of theatre art, determined to show the great Italian actress to London audiences once again. She was now past sixty, and older than her years. Her acute sensitiveness to suffering, and she had suffered much physically and mentally during her life, had aged her. Mussolini had offered her an "appanage" so that she would never have to work again, but in spite of her exhaustion after a long illness in 1922, she had refused it. She would accept money from the Government only on her own terms, and made a proposition that a theatre in Rome should be subsidised where she could appear at intervals. Mussolini replied that if the proposition was in the interest of the Italian theatre it would be law for any government presided over by him. Perhaps it was the "if" which made Duse feel that she was being offered a stone when she was in urgent need of bread. Mr Cochran was offering her bread, and before he had even sent her a contract she telegraphed that she was leaving for England.

He went at once to Paris to meet her. The night she was to arrive at Victoria I went to the station as Ellen Terry's deputy to receive her. Edy would have been a more worthy one, but she was producing a play in Leeds, and I had to do my best in her absence. I bought a bunch of red roses, and through my fear of being late hung about the cold platform for hours. The train came in, but it was not until the other passengers had dispersed that Duse, who always shrank from crowds, emerged. She looked terribly fatigued and frail, and my first impulse, when I saw her dragging her weary body along, held up on one side by her ward, on the other by Mr Cochran, was to leave her alone. Then I remembered I was there on a mission, and ran straight to her, as I knew Ellen Terry would have run, heedless of Italian admirers pressing round me, and waving the red roses on high, said: "With Ellen Terry's love." At the sound of Ellen Terry's name, the tired white face became young and radiant. It was as if a volcanic region, harsh and touched with death, had suddenly become a smiling fertile land. Of all the tributes to Ellen Terry I can recall, that is the most precious. My mission over, I was going away, when I saw Duse beckon from the car. She wished to speak to Ellen Terry's deputy. She wished to send a message of love and gratitude. "Dites-lui qu'elle m'a donnée bonheur, quel bonheur! Belle, généreuse Ellen Terry!" And she invited the deputy to come and see her in the morning at Claridge's, to be thanked again when she was not so tired after an abominable journey.

Duse's matinées at the New Oxford Theatre attracted huge audiences, but always at her request a box was reserved for Ellen Terry. It was on June 7, 1923, that Duse made her first appearance in "The Lady from the Sea." "Oh! she was Perfection! There is none like her, none!" Ellen Terry writes in her diary, "I took her some flowers and she used them in the play. Afterwards I went round to see her. She seems even nobler now than when she was young. Was warmly affectionate to me and to my Edy." Another day in June. "'Ghosts.' A horrible play, but Duse superb."

Another day, farewell to Duse after her last performance in "Cosi Sia," a last farewell. Duse sailed for America in the autumn, and in the middle of her second tour of the States was seized with a mortal illness at Pittsburgh. One of her biographers states that she caught cold one evening through being kept waiting in an icy wind and a downpour of rain outside the theatre. The door at which her chauffeur had left her was closed. There was a sad significance in the placards on the building, announcing "La Porta Chiuso." This was on April 5, 1924. Pneumonia developed, and on April 21 she died.

Ellen Terry had said farewell to Bernhardt and Duse alike in an hour of triumph, only a few minutes after an audience crowding forward to the stage had been throwing flowers and shouting: "Come back soon." And in such an hour she said farewell to Isadora Duncan. On June 25, 1921, before her departure for Russia, Isadora appeared at Queen's Hall. In her programme was that amazing "Revolution" dance, the most magnificent conception of her later years, perhaps of her whole life. "I never saw *true* tragedy before," said Ellen Terry, and left it at that. Isadora made a characteristic speech at the end of the performance—it came naturally to her to wear her heart upon her sleeve—saying that there was one in the audience far greater than she. "Let us applaud her, let us rejoice in Ellen Terry," she cried, holding out her arms with one of those primal gestures which seemed to some almost indecent. "No, no!" said Ellen Terry, for she was genuinely humble, although her humility, like her simplicity, was often suspected of being a pose. And Isadora's audience, and Isadora's orchestra and conductor too, responded, and cheered Ellen Terry for several minutes. Then she went round to the artist's room. Farewell to Isadora.

"Are these what you meant by 'good times,' Ellen?" No answer. Perhaps I am wrong in having included among them last meetings on earth with creators of transient forms of beauty. Yet did not Ellen Terry, living, reckon among her "golden days" Irving's funeral in Westminster Abbey?

A word about her seventy-fifth birthday. She had overcome her dislike to the cinema by this time, one manifestation of her flexibility. Times had changed. New pleasures had come along, motoring, for example, and she who, young, had enjoyed jogging along behind a horse, now could enjoy being whizzed along in a car. I never heard her talk regretfully of the good old times. She was not an alien in this brave new world. She saw some bad films, among which I regret to say were those in which she had appeared herself, and they created a prejudice. She judged it impossible for any one to act well in this medium. Then one day I persuaded her to see "Blood and Sand," and Rudolph Valentino's romantic performance charmed her so much that she said: "If I were going to play Romeo, I should come here every night and study that man. *That's* the way to stand under the balcony!" She was also greatly impressed by Conrad Veidt as the somnambulist in "Dr Caligari's Cabinet," wishing then that Henry Irving were alive to create the same kind of uncanny effect on the screen. So she chose as her birthday treat on February 27, 1924, a visit to the cinema, and we went to the Tivoli to see Charlie Chaplin's film "A Woman of Paris." The management gave her a royal welcome, not wholly disinterested, no doubt, for the visit was a splendid advertisement, Ellen Terry's birthdays always being in the news, but it gave Ellen Terry no less pleasure on that account. She liked these occasional basks in the limelight. She had been a Chaplin enthusiast since she had seen "The Kid" in 1921, which she describes in her diary as a "most moving movie. C. C. and the little chap (Jackie Coogan) splendid. The idea of heaven, splendid. All of them good." Now she recognised Chaplin's cleverness as a producer in "A Woman of Paris," saying, I remember, to the Tivoli manager that she had enjoyed it so much that she had not been disappointed that it was "Chaplin, with the part of Chaplin left out." (Chaplin appeared only for a minute in the film, and anonymously, as a railway porter.)

Another "good time" in 1924 was due to Bernard Shaw. Where was he, by the way, when the friend with whom he had corresponded for a period of twenty-five years, was an old woman? They met occasionally at the Shakespeare Festivals at Stratford-on-Avon. I can trace no other meetings, and no letters passed between them after that last one Ellen Terry wrote in 1922 to tell him about her LL.D. Shaw, whatever he is, is no masochist. Why should he enter Ellen Terry's second childhood? Yet it was as beautiful, and much wiser than her first. He had no more devout admirer of "Back to Methuselah" than the old love of his letters. Ellen Terry went to every performance of the first production of Shaw's "Pentateuch" at the Court Theatre in February, 1924. She was indignant with the Polonius critics who said: "This is too long."

In 1925 the name of Ellen Terry appeared in the New Year's Honours List. She had long ago forgotten the dream of the O. M. and the reality, the distinction of being created a Dame Grand Cross of the Most Excellent Order of the British Empire, gave her great pleasure. She was not perturbed, as I immediately was, at the change in her name the honour involved. "Ellen Terry is the most beautiful name in the world," Shaw wrote to her in 1896. "It rings like a chime through the last quarter of the 19th century. It has a lovely rhythm in it." Custom never reconciled me to the alteration in the rhythm produced by the addition of "Dame." Whether it was "Dame Ellen," or "Dame Ellen Terry" that the public called her, I felt something was wrong. To me "Ellen Terry" could never be old, but "Dame Ellen" could; and it gave me no shock to hear "Dame Ellen" called an old lady. She herself, I believe, never really liked being "damed," although she had liked being honoured.

When the reporters came buzzing in, like flies to a honeypot, to know what she thought about her Grand Cross, she had a little speech ready: "I am delighted. It is an honour to my profession, an honour to women, and very pleasant for me." That was the exact truth.

In February she was summoned to Buckingham Palace to be invested with the Grand Cross by the King. Ellen Terry had always been, not in name merely, but in deed and in truth, a "loving subject" of the Royal house. Her devotion to Queen Alexandra, with whom she had an affinity arising from the generous desire of both women to help the poor and afflicted, was as warm as it was disinterested. Only Ellen Terry's intimate friends knew anything about Queen Alexandra's affectionate response to this devotion. She never forgot her "dear Ellen Terry's" birthday, as a sheaf of telegrams carefully cherished by Ellen Terry now testify. We may assume that the kindly consideration shown by the King on the day of Ellen Terry's investiture was as much for one dear to his mother as for one dear to his subjects. "A lovely time," Ellen Terry writes in her diary. "Gracious folk all around." Others, who were invested that day, went to the Throne Room, but to spare Ellen Terry, who was now seventy-seven, as much fatigue as possible, the King invested her privately. Edy, who had been allowed to accompany her, and walked by the wheeled chair in which her mother was conveyed through long corridors to the door of the room where the King received her, says that "Mother made a most wonderful curtsey on entering—slow, stately, very expressive." The door was then closed. When after a few minutes it opened again, Edy saw her mother, now decorated with the Cross, groping for the door, assisted by an equerry. When she reached it, she became conscious of something amiss with her exit. "Oh dear! I quite forgot to walk out backwards!" The King, who was just behind her, could not help laughing. It was a genial, delightful laugh which brought the Investiture to a merry end.

Queen Mary had expressed a wish to see Ellen Terry before she left, and they had a charmingly informal talk about the old Lyceum days when the Queen was Princess May, and paid many visits to the theatre with her mother and father, including that famous one on her twentieth birthday, recorded in Ellen Terry's memoirs. At the conclusion of the interview the Queen herself helped Ellen Terry into the chair, and tucked in her cloak, for fear it should catch on the wheel. "Gracious folk all around" indeed. And now that that Grand Cross was associated in

Ellen Terry's mind with these gracious folk, it had acquired a new significance.

It is fortunate that Ellen Terry kept a diary up to the end of the year 1926. There is the evidence of the many good times she had in spite of the limits age imposed on her freedom. How blessed are the survivors among her friends who helped her to forget these limits. With their names the words "I have had a most happy time" are frequently coupled in her later diaries. To "P" (Pauline Chase, the Peter Pan of other days, now Mrs Drummond), Ellen Terry frequently refers as a source of joy in 1926, which came very near to being her last year on earth. She had a serious illness in January, 1927, and her son was summoned from Italy. He came, and found her "pretending to be far more ill than she would in secret allow." This contradicts the opinion of the doctors that she was far more ill than she would, to cheerily optimistic visitors like her son, allow herself to appear. However, even this illness must be reckoned one of the good times, since it brought home for a few hours the beloved son whom she had not seen for three years.

After her death, when Edy was considering the publication of some of her letters and made an appeal in *The Times* to her correspondents to send any they had preserved, it became clear from the response that she had written fewer letters between 1921 and 1928 than at any period in her life. But there were interesting proofs that now and again she had followed her old custom of pouring out the largesse of her sympathy in this way, often on people whom she did not know personally. Lord Dunsany gave one of the proofs:

I have just read of your appeal for any letters from your much regretted mother. I have a very brief one indeed, but it always loomed large to me on account of the sympathy and kindness with which the scrap of paper was filled.

I was going to give a lecture on poetry in the autumn of 1921, and a journalist wrote under the heading of "The Muse Bemused," the following piece of journalism:

"Lord Dunsany is about to stump the country on behalf of the Poetry Society. His lecture bears the pretty title, 'What is the darned use of poetry?' He thinks there would be more suicides, were there no poets."

I received this, torn out of a newspaper with the last sentence underlined, and under it, written in ink: "I am *sure* so. E.T." and at the foot of the scrap was the signature in full, "Ellen Terry." I have kept it to this day. The postmark of the letter is November 21, 1921, but it may have been posted some while sooner than that, for the address, in a beautiful handwriting, was no more sufficient than "Lord Dunsany, London."

This little note outweighed in my mind all the usual sneers I have ever heard against poetry.

331

On Christmas Day, 1925, we had a merry little gathering at Edy's flat in Bedford Street. "Ask some lonely people who wouldn't otherwise see a turkey or a pudding," said Ellen, who had come to stay with us, bringing with her an immense turkey, an annual present from Graham Robertson. One of the lonely guests was a young writer, Velona Pilcher. She afterwards recorded an incident at the Christmas party in an article on Ellen Terry in *The Theatre Arts Monthly*.

Her health drunk, the jokes failing, the last Christmas crackers popped, she at last said good-night and went to bed. A little later the guests began a gramophone dance round the deserted dinner-table to a tune from Whiteman's Band. Around and around they went, absurdly, not very gracefully, the paper caps wilting foolishly on their heads ... when suddenly in the doorway swayed a silver figure, wrapped in a long loose cloak of snow-white fur. The head was high, flung back defiantly from the bent body; the white hair haloed it, and waved, as it moved, to the rhythm of the record. One poised hand beat the beat, posed like an Angel Gabriel, making the sign annunciate, and as the little group of earthly dancers fell back in a sort of fear from this dream whose sleep had been disturbed, and stood struck still before this pre-Raphaelite figure, drawn back into life by music and mirth, Ellen Terry began to dance. Silently once around the table, she danced— slowly, stately, delicately, pouring beauty from her bones, bearing her years like a burden of long-stemmed lilies, moving like a blossom of snow blown down to its rest on the ground—and then silently passed again out at the door.

CHAPTER IV

DEATH: ARIEL SET FREE

(1928)

§ 1

ON Christmas Day, 1925, Ellen Terry danced. On Christmas Day, 1926, Ellen Terry could not dance. She had caught cold in the absence of the vigilant "Barney," who was snatching one of her brief holidays from work more onerous than any one who has not ministered to an imprisoned Ariel can conceive, and sat at the head of her table in the despised little flat, shivering and coughing. Those who always suspected her of play-acting when she said: "I feel so ill," and she had given excellent performances of a sick woman in other days when she was in more robust health, might not have been alarmed, but Edy, who could always tell the difference between what was real and what was feigned in "I feel so ill," was anxious, and persuaded her mother to go to bed before we had come to the crackers. This time there was no mirth, nor music, to draw Ellen Terry back to the Christmas board. The little company dispersed silently at the news of a temperature, and other disquieting symptoms. The sequel to that Christmas dinner has already been described. Ellen Terry nearly made her final exit, then rallied, thanks to a superb constitution and immense vitality, and returned for another scene, a tragic scene, perhaps the most tragic in the whole drama. Four years and more have passed since it was acted, yet the recollection of it still appalls me. I could not re-create it in words without taking part in it, dealing blows right and left. There was a horrid scuffle in the dark in the year 1928 to win those three serene, sunlit months at Smallhythe before Ellen Terry's death.

On Christmas Day, 1927, Ellen Terry could not dance. She was far too weak. We had no lift to our flat in those days, but she had set her heart on spending Christmas with Edy, and Edy got four ambulance men from a hospital near by to carry her up the three long flights of steps. Our party of the lonely ones was much smaller than in 1925 or 1926, but Graham Robertson's turkey was as big as ever. Ellen Terry was gay, but more restless than I had ever seen her. I had heard of the therapeutic effects of Bach's music, and believed in them when she stopped trying to follow up some forgotten spring of action to listen serenely to a gramophone record of the slow movement of the Concerto for two violins in D minor. She wrote my name in the volume of the new edition of Grove's Dictionary of Music she had given me as a Christmas present in a beautifully clear hand; the inscription, however, cost her an effort. She could not concentrate on anything now, not even on a simple task like this, for any length of time. As want of concentration, and physical restlessness had always been characteristic of her, we who knew her well had not hitherto been alarmed at their having been aggravated by age. Yet when she left us for a visit to her old friends "the Casella girls," I had a foreboding of disaster.

The little flat which had been her home in London since 1921 had been given up. Her country home at Smallhythe, where she was always happy, was, owing to its being on marshland, very cold and damp in mid-winter. This disadvantage had been remedied to a certain extent by the installation of central heating, and other alterations which had made the old house more comfortable. If something had not gone wrong with that heating, which, owing to the dilatory methods any work connected with water pipes seems to involve, took an unconscionably long time to put right, Ellen Terry could have gone back to Smallhythe after her Christmas in London with us and the "Casella girls," and been spared the tragic episode to which I have alluded. No one could have foreseen it. It did not seem possible that she could come to any harm in the comfortable house near Maidstone, which she was to share with a friend until those refractory pipes at Smallhythe had been made to function again. The house was near enough to London for Edy to get away from her work and visit her mother constantly. It had many other advantages. Yet the darkness descended. For the first time Ellen Terry lived without taking any personal part in life. It will be remembered that she had suffered greatly in New York, before the operation to her eye, from the terror that she might become blind. Now she was a prey to the terror that she might go mad. She feared already, like Lear, that she was not in her perfect mind. This fear grew because she was surrounded by people who, being convinced that she was not, made no effort to lighten her darkness. Well-meaning, but ill-advised, they adopted a treatment which would soon have made Ellen Terry a complete wreck, if her daughter had not intervened, and, supported by doctors more familiar with her mother's case than the one who attended her at the house of darkness, succeeded at last after a weary struggle in getting her to Smallhythe where those darned pipes had long since been made to behave. This was in March, 1928. Ellen Terry, quite conscious that she was "going home," and the de-

334

sire to "go home" had been the only one she had expressed in her darkness during January and February, stood the journey by car remarkably well, although she had been physically enfeebled by an attack of bronchitis in February. After she had been wheeled up the path into the old familiar living-room, shining bright with the pewter she had collected in the past, and was seated at the old familiar table, she exclaimed proudly to the doctor who had accompanied her on the journey: "This is my own house, doctor, bought with my own money." In this dear house, under the care of Barney, who had not been allowed to care for her in the house of darkness, and two nurses (for she needed attention day and night), cheered by the companionship of Edy, the only person in the world of whose identity she was now sure, she recovered her lost happiness. Her spirit was no longer tortured by the consciousness of physical and mental decay. When I met her again at Easter, the serenity of her face, which by some miracle had become young and lovely, made me think of her eightieth birthday in the house of darkness as a hideous nightmare.

There was the usual birthday limelight, an extra strong flood of it, because she had passed the four-score limit, and was still reputed vigorous. Ellen Terry would have loved to bask in it, but it could not penetrate her darkness. The B. B. C. had arranged a special Ellen Terry programme on the evening of her eightieth birthday, and in the hope that her "slight attack of bronchitis" would not prevent her from broadcasting a message to her loving public, a microphone had been installed in a sitting-room in the house where she was staying. One of the latest "portables" had also been brought down in order that she might listen to the programme, in which many members of the Terry family were taking part. I recall as the most poignant moment in my life hearing the mad scene from "Hamlet," with Fay Compton as Ophelia, downstairs, while upstairs the fair Ophelia of 1878, now a distraught old woman, "bound upon a wheel of fire, that mine own tears do scald like molten lead," was playing Lear.

The loving public! Wretched as Edy was, she thought of that public on her mother's behalf. I had been put to work at my old "literary henchman's" job the day before, and had composed "a message." Years of experience had made me familiar with the kind of thing Ellen Terry liked to say on such occasions, and the message came to me automatically, in spite of the unfamiliarity of the situation. Now I could not go to Ellen Terry with my draft, hear her read it, and vivify it with spontaneous revisions as she read. I give the message here, as well as its history, for fear that at some future time it should be included among Ellen Terry's authentic utterances. It was a reply to a salutation, in verse, spoken by her old friend and stage comrade, Sir Johnston Forbes-Robertson.

I am very grateful for this lovely posy of words you have sent me for my birthday. I am very grateful to every one who has thought of me today. It seems to me very wonderful that I should still be remembered, and that all this delightful fuss should have been made simply because I am eighty. *I know I have to thank Shakespeare for it.* It is because I am associated with him in people's minds, because the parts of his I played are more enduring than "marble or the gilded monument" that I am not forgotten.

This tribute to me is a tribute to Shakespeare, and so, to England, for is he not the chief glory of England? This celebration of my birthday has bereft me of words. Only "my blood speaks to you in my veins."

But I am forgetting the instruction I heard just now: "Be merry." It is easy for me to obey it even at my age. *I was always more proud of making an audience laugh, than of making it weep.*

This is rather a solemn occasion, perhaps, who knows, a real farewell performance. Let the curtain come down on a smile. On four-score smiles, one for every year which has been made happy by the devotion of family and friends, known and unknown. Good-night. My love to every one.

I have italicised the words in the message which I had heard Ellen Terry say dozens of times, and every time with perfect sincerity.

Edy, who was greatly moved by her mother's inability to act her part in this last public scene, had some difficulty in reading the message in a steady voice, but she understudied Ellen Terry so well that many listeners wrote to tell her they could hardly believe that it was not Ellen Terry herself speaking.

§ 2

THE best evidence I can give of the great improvement in Ellen Terry's condition after her return to Smallhythe is to quote some notes, made at the time, of conversations with her in April, 1928. She now could talk of her failing memory with all her old humour. "There are times," she said, "when I feel rather like Bottom. 'Methought I was—there is no man can tell what. Methought I was, and methought I had—but man is but a patched fool if he will offer to say what.' *I cant say what! I forget.*"

I offered once to read to her, for all this talking, entertaining as I found it, must, I thought, be exhausting to her. "No, thank you! I've got used to hearing people read badly. Good reading would be so odd! I couldnt stand the shock."

We were in the middle of an argument about "Macbeth." She could remember and quote far more lines to support her case than I could to support mine. Barney came in with some tea. "Now you'll hear my new name!" said Ellen Terry mischievously. "Darling, here's your tea," said Barney, who had not heard this "aside." "There! What did I tell you?

336

From a photograph by E. O. Hoppé

EDITH CRAIG

Darling! Every one calls me that nowadays." I gathered from this that Ellen Terry had not lost her old objection to gush. She had had experience recently of the conventionally affectionate terminology of nurses, who have a habit of addressing their patients as "dear" or "darling" in the hardest of voices. Now, seeing Barney's perplexed expression, she seized her hand, and said: "*She* can darling me as much as she likes. She's a dear, good thing, the salt of the earth."

Sooner or later the conversation would turn to Shakespeare, or the art of acting. Ellen Terry told me how she learned to cry on the stage. "I learned so well that it came too naturally to me. Then my difficulty was to stop my tears. No, I dont mean 'stop.' What is the word, the exact word, the *mot juste?*" I suggested "control," and it was approved.

April 12. E. T. very much interested to hear that there are only about 380,000 words in the English lauguage. This was in reference to her readiness to bet that Shakespeare had the biggest vocabulary of any English writer.

April 13. "I am glad you think my Ted (Gordon Craig) writes so well. But you never saw him act! He acts far better than he writes."

"When we act, we must *feel,* not necessarily with our own personal feelings. Your voice, your movement, your whole body, are only an instrument for this *feeling.* However perfect you make the instrument, it wont resound, unless you can feel."

Once, only once that Easter-time, she cried, and said: "I hate being old. Yes, I just hate it. People are very kind, but that makes it worse. However, it's absurd to cry over spilt milk. I intend to go into my grave smiling." That was the day she spoke of mouths. We were talking about a certain actress, who, admired by many, was never admired by Ellen Terry. "I dont think she can be very good, because I cant remember her face. Describe it." I tried, admitting that the mouth was the weak point. "But the mouth is nearly every one's weak point. Look at mine! Much too large!"

When I got up to leave her one evening (I was staying at Edy's cottage, about a hundred yards from her house), she said it was unkind of me to go. She acted "being hurt" so well that I was completely taken in, and although I had strict instructions not to stay longer than an hour, and the time was up, sat down again. "You actually thought I meant it! Hurray! I still can act! I have to act sometimes to find out if I can."

Then she referred to the possibility of a farewell appearance. "I believe, old as I am, people would still like to see me.

"I am talking much too loud. That was a fault of mine on the stage. Henry used to stand at the side in old days, and drop a handkerchief when I shouted.

"I dream constantly of a beautiful fair woman, who kisses her hand to me." (At that point Ellen Terry changed before my eyes into Imogen and kissed her hand, exactly as she is kissing it in her favourite photograph of herself as Imogen.) "She looks very like me. Is it the old me, or my mother? More likely mother, as she is beautiful.

"My memory! Oh, what agony it has always been to me. I knew all about my parts long before I could get the words into my head. The pleasure of acting was spoiled by the terror of forgetting."

I sent these notes to Edy, who was in London for a week, with the comment: "Is this what they call 'senile decay'? You know what Coleridge said about Kean's acting—that it was like 'reading Shakespeare by flashes of lightning.' That is how one can read Ellen Terry now. All is obscure. Then a flash, and if you are quick, you see her mind, quite unspoiled, her wise, witty, beautiful mind. Sometimes I think she may live in this obscurity, illumined by flashes, for years. On the whole a tragic prospect."

§ 3

ONE doctor, a woman who had attended Ellen Terry in London since 1924, said, after the release from the house of darkness in March, 1928, that she hoped she would have six weeks of happiness, at least, before the end. The local doctor, who saw her frequently, visiting Smallhythe several times a week, and keeping in touch with the nurses on the telephone, thought she might live until the winter. Neither of them was far out. Ellen Terry had a stroke at 10.15 on the morning of July 17, and died at 8.30 on the morning of the 21st.

June left it to July to flame that year. Ellen Terry's garden was gay with flowers. Her marshland glittered in the dazzling sunlight. She was not content to watch this beauty from the window of her bedroom upstairs; she wanted to go out into it, and constantly said: "What about a drive?" Drives were out of the question, the doctor knew, and indeed we all knew that Ellen Terry's driving days, whether in car or carriage, were over. But early in July, Edy, with the doctor's approval, moved her mother downstairs, into a room on the ground-floor, leading into the garden, so that she could go out, without fatigue, in a wheeled chair. This spacious, cool room became her bedroom. It was there that she was stricken.

The possibility that Nature would deal Ellen Terry this knock-out blow may have been known to the doctor,[1] but he was so far from

---

[1] Ellen Terry's woman doctor, a heart specialist, did know it. As Gordon Craig, in his biography, has implied that the stroke could have been averted, I think it necessary to state, on this high authority, that it might have occurred at any time after 1924. It could

expecting it on July 16 that he assured Edy that her mother's state of health was so good that there was no need for her to cancel an engagement in London to adjudicate at the annual examination of the pupils of Miss Elsie Fogerty's dramatic school. Edy left in the afternoon, cheered by this assurance, and also by the improvement she herself had noticed since her mother had been able to go out. She had intended, in any case, to return the following evening.

I had come down from London to the cottage for my summer holiday on the 16th. I arrived too late to see Ellen Terry. One of the nurses told me she was very well, and sleeping like a child. She had been taken out in her chair in the afternoon, and, at her own request, out beyond the garden and orchard for the first time since her return to Smallhythe. "On this lovely day we ought to go *really* out," she said, and Barney and the nurse wheeled the chair through the toll-gate, over the little bridge spanning that narrow stream, all that is left of the creek of the sea, on which old Smallhythe stood. The busy wharf is now green pasture, the ferry over the creek to the slopes of Oxney Island is now a road running through marshland. It was along this road that Ellen Terry went on her last drive. The toll-gate was kept in those days by a poor cripple from whom many strangers passing through in cars turned away their eyes, distressed by the sight of one who could not lift his chin from his chest, nor his gaze from the ground. But he was one of Ellen Terry's friends. There were none dearer to her in Smallhythe than he and his handsome gipsy wife. I was told that on this last day of consciousness of the visible world, she leaned out of her chair and kissed his hand. Barney and the nurse, a little fatigued by pushing the chair so far, halted in a grassy space by the roadside, and left Ellen Terry to contemplate the river-like road, fringed with wild yellow iris, the sheep-dotted marshland, and the immense blue dome of the still, cloudless heavens, while they gossipped at a gate into a field near by. Soon Ellen Terry, who never liked to be out of things, grew restive at this murmur of conversation in which she was not included, and called her attendants. They took no notice, for which they are not to be blamed, as in these days Ellen Terry exhausted herself by talking, and spells of quiet had somehow to be secured. Then Ellen, with a touch of her old martinettishness with those in her service, took off her shoes and threw them into the road. The noise brought both women running from the gate, to find Ellen in fits of laughter at the success of her ruse.

Her gardener was waiting at the gate of the farm as usual when they

be, and was, postponed by regulating her life, but it could not be prevented indefinitely. The walls of the cerebral arteries were rapidly thinning and weakening. Finally and inevitably one gave way and caused a fatal hæmorrhage.

reached home, to help her out of her chair. He is still in her daughter's service, one of his duties now being to show visitors the memorial museum into which her house has been converted. He often recalls Ellen Terry's last words to him. They touched him to the heart. "Do you like being in my service?" "Oh, yes, Dame Ellen." "I am glad to hear that. I like people to like serving me. Please go into the kitchen and tell them to give you some beer."

The morning of July 17 was magically beautiful. "Tony" Atwood, who was at the cottage with me, went down early through the orchard, dividing us from Ellen Terry's farm, along the grass path, snow-white now with the petals of the syringas, nodding over it, richly perfuming the hot air, to ask how she was. Tony came back with the news of a very good night. Ellen had slept nearly eight hours, a record, "but," Tony added, "they tell me she refused to have any breakfast. I dont like that." We began talking of the future. I said optimistically, remembering the lovely young face I had seen last in April, the vitality of the voice that had said so many lovely things to me: "She may live a long time yet," and the sweetness and warmth of the July morning in this haunt of peace made the gift of life even in great age seem a precious thing. "I dont think she will," said Tony. "I have an idea she will have a stroke." This was at 9.54. At 10.20 Barney came rushing through the orchard, her face as white as the syringa-strewn path, to tell us what had happened. "I have sent for the doctor. The nurses say there is no hope. Telephone to Edy." Her manner was very calm and business-like. Only her face showed that she was appalled. It must have been a consolation to this staunch little woman, who had stuck to her post, in spite of the intrigues to dislodge her, and made light of accusations of harshness in the performance of her duties, that, as Ellen Terry reeled under the knock-out blow, she called out "Barney!" Then her eyes closed, never to open again. She lay on her bed sightless, paralysed—unconscious, and dumb, except at brief intervals—for four days.

Edy was not in her flat in London when Tony, a few minutes after Barney's rush through the orchard, telephoned a message there. She first heard of her mother's mortal illness early in the afternoon when she went to the Arts Theatre for the Fogerty Pupils' Performance. As she drove up to the door in a taxi, she was met by Miss Fogerty with whom we had been able to communicate. "Dont get out. Your mother is very ill. They want you to go home at once. It's a stroke." I asked Edy at a later time how she reacted to this shock. "I felt nothing, except that I must act swiftly. I must get home." She remembered that her brother was in London, however. He had come over from Italy a few weeks before to attend his exhibition of designs for "The Pretenders," but had not found

340

time to go down to Smallhythe to see his mother. It was difficult to make him realize her serious condition.

His sister had to take him by the scruff of his neck (so to speak), and put him, dazed, and protesting that he had an important meeting with representatives of the press, into Olive Terry's car. With Olive, a driver of Brooklands calibre, at the wheel, the car reached Smallhythe in record time.

Edy's first action on arrival was very characteristic of her. She put on the smock she always wore at Smallhythe so that her mother would see something familiar, if she rallied and recognised her. Ellen Terry was past recognition of either of her children through the eye, but I had a proof the day after their arrival that she was not past finding consolation in their presence in the room. Her right arm twitched incessantly, and I, who am credited with the gift of a healing hand, sat by her bed, gently stroking that poor arm, thinking sadly that never again should I see it spring up with that wonderful gesture of love, and encircle the neck of some one dear to her, a familiar action of hers. Her hand gripped mine; it was searching for something. I knew for what, when it reached my thumb. Edy has a peculiar square thumb. "The murderer's thumb" it has been called in jest. It was by the thumb, Ellen Terry knew she could tell whether the hand on hers was Edy's. Edy was the one she wanted to give her a hand in her extremity, and with a strong powerful gesture of disappointment, she pushed my hand away.

"Could ye not watch with me one hour?" Ellen Terry had written in her last diary. I remembered those words while she lay dying. Who would watch with Ellen Terry in this hour, who would turn a deaf ear to the voice of the tempter, saying: "There is nothing to be done. You can be of no use. Go about your business, or go to sleep." All indeed that can be *done* for the dying, whose senses are shut, is done best by experts. Ellen Terry had efficient careful nurses who, after she was stricken, did their duty tenderly as well as capably. She had a shrewd, intelligent doctor, who was moreover a kind and sympathetic man with a real affection for her. When he knew that she was doomed, he devoted all his skill to allaying the restlessness which was the one distressing symptom during her passage from life to death. This good physician, tired after a long day's work, thought nothing of getting out his car in the middle of the night, and driving down to Smallhythe with an anodyne, when a nurse telephoned that Ellen Terry could not rest. Then there was Barney, well trained in apprehending, through some channel of communication unknown to others, what Ellen Terry wanted. "She wants something cool on her forehead." "She wants to be moved." "She

341

wants Edy." Barney watched with pathetic vigilance for signs of these wants.

Yet I am certain that Ellen Terry would have known great desolation of spirit, if others, more closely bound to her than her professional attendants, those others who could not do anything for her any more, had allowed any considerations of their uselessness to hinder them from withdrawing themselves from the world awhile to watch with her. These were perhaps the most important moments in her secret life. I never entered that cool, spacious room without feeling that great events were taking place, that Ellen Terry's spirit had never been more active.

What faces did I see there? The face of Edy day and night. Once, tiptoeing to the door, Tony and I heard what sounded almost like the old Terry laugh. Edy was sitting by her mother's bed, and prompting her in a nursery rhyme:

> One, two; buckle my shoe.
> Three, four; open the door.
> Five, six; pick up sticks.
> Seven, eight; lay them straight.
> Nine, ten; a good, fat hen ...

Ellen Terry's voice had been stricken. She could speak only in a strange, indistinct growl. Yet I said to Tony: "This is more beautiful than any prayer."

I saw too the anxious wan face of Ellen Terry's brother Charlie, a Pre-Raphaelite face grown old. And there was Olive, with all her dead mother's love for Nell looking out of her eyes. Into the rays of warm, yellow sunshine which shot through the curtains (so like the gas limes at the old Lyceum) there stepped one day Nell's brother, Fred, and Nell's sister Marion, with the tearful look which becomes the Terry face so well. Nell's brow knitted as they came near the bed to say goodbye. She almost said: "Now dont let's have any crying. We all cry far too much." They went back to London, and were soon followed by her son, who had important business there. Poor Marion was indeed too sick and infirm to be a watcher.

This was the 18th of July. On the evening of the 20th Edy had gone across the road to the gardener's cottage, immediately opposite Ellen Terry's house, to telephone to her brother. The news that Ellen Terry was sinking had spread all over England; that cottage room had become a news bureau. Messages came and went over the telephone day and night. The King and Queen were among the first to express their concern. I think it was a shock to every one, familiar with the legend of an eternally youthful Ellen Terry, to hear that she was sick unto death.

There can be no privacy for a public personage in the last hours of life, as Edy soon discovered. She had a staff of willing helpers in the news bureau, but her presence there was at times imperative. I left her at the telephone at about ten o'clock that evening and crossed the road again to the farm. As I walked up the brick path to the door, I heard from the room on the right where Ellen Terry lay, a loud clear voice, the voice I had never expected to hear again, call out: "Edy!" Now, lest any one should think I heard it only with the mind's ear, I must add that Barney, who was in her bedroom upstairs, heard it too, and came to the window, amazed at the miracle. I hurried back to the cottage to tell Edy to come at once. "She is calling for you." Then Edy went into her mother's room again, and never left it until 8.30 the next morning when Ariel was roused from her earthly sleep in the prison, and set free.

During those hours, Edy sat by the bed constantly, holding that beautiful, still expressive right hand. The left one was powerless, motionless. The face had not been much changed by that cruel blow from Nature. But the breath of life was changed. It came more and more painfully as the dawn approached. The hand, gripping Edy's, moved from finger to finger, and with a last effort the voice, not miraculously clear and loud now, but thick and indistinct, spelt out on those fingers the word "Happy," "H-a-p-p-y" over and over again.

Ellen Terry's long-haired, brindled cat, Boo-boo, the cherished pet of her last years, had not been seen for days. This rather callous beauty had never had much use for Ellen Terry since she had grown too tired with age to make a fuss of her. Boo-boo was essentially a fair-weather friend, and she hid, panic-stricken, when the dread bolt descended. But Edy's less beautiful black cat, Snuffbox, did not hide. On this last night of Ellen Terry's life she left her comfortable home at our cottage, and came down through the orchard to join the watchers.

I was one of the disciples whose spirit was willing, out whose flesh was weak. At about midnight I threw myself on a hard garden-seat in the old cow-shed, Ellen Terry's garden-house, just outside the room where she lay, and fell asleep to the sound of her rattling breath. I woke up at the moment it ceased. I came into the room, and heard Edy cry out: "Light! More light!" and someone drew back the curtains. The glorious July sun was now high in the heavens. There was an atmosphere of exaltation in that death-chamber. "She cant be dead!" said her niece, Olive. "She cant be dead!" And indeed the prison had vanished directly Ariel had flown into the light. A young, beautiful woman lay on the bed, like Juliet on her bier. I knelt by the bier and said, "Hail Mary." "Flowers," said Edy, and then we went through the syringa-scented orchard, like acolytes, in our white smocks, to gather flowers. The feathered sons of the morning were shouting for joy, yet not all. At our cottage, we found a dead thrush on the couch by the window. On the marsh at the same hour a shepherd found a dead heron.

§ 4

THERE was on Edy's little staff of helpers in the gardener's cottage that same young writer, Velona Pilcher, who had seen Ellen Terry dance on Christmas Day 1925. She had arrived at Smallhythe by chance on July 19th, and stayed to do errands in her car, sit by the insistent telephone, and lend a hand in any way she could. She appeared to be all mazed and dazed, yet she was observing with extraordinary accuracy all those incidents which made Ellen Terry's death as wonderful as her life, and was able to record them faithfully later on. Her chronicle, to which she gave the title, "The Marvellous Death of Ellen Terry," may never be published, I fear, for the reason that it abounds in allusions meaningless to a reader unacquainted with what took place at Smallhythe in these days. It is a precious record to us who were there. We recognise its truth, overgrown as the truth is by the lush imagery of Velona Pilcher's curious literary style. Given the clue that we were pestered by journalists at Smallhythe from the day Ellen Terry was stricken to the day she died, that they were not content with the official bulletins Edy issued through her press representative, but went to outrageous lengths to secure "exclusive information," the following passage from "The Marvellous Death of Ellen Terry," ought to be perfectly intelligible:

But the night was ugly. (July 20, 1928.) The night was a nightmare, for down at the toll-gate four big black beasts of prey were crouching, cutting the gardens into gashes with their greedy eyes. Four murderous motors, their livid headlamps levelled on the farmhouse, cottages and roadway, were waiting in the dark with reporters sent by the morning papers to be in at the death, or die. Last night, one had crawled through the hedge, and tried to spy in at that curtained window. Tonight the town of Tenterden had sent police to guard the house. But no one could slip out of the sick-room to take courage from a star, or strength from the fresh air, without staring strangers making a note of it; or cross the road with a message without being cut to the quick by those bestial beams. To use the telephone meant first making sure that no eavesdroppers were crouching outside the cottage window to make a scoop of sorrow.

It is dawn. The sun is rising. The burning ball of the sun is rising, rolling up the sky like an eyeball rolling in anger, and under that look of indignation, with frustrated faces, the black beasts are filing off, driven off by the advance of the avenging day. She has waited! Five o'clock. The earth smells good again. Papers have gone to press.

344

THE gipsy woman at the toll-gate, one of Ellen Terry's affinities, had with deft, loving hands, laid out the fair body of Juliet on her bier. Edy had put a sprig of jasmine between the quiet folded hands. The room was brilliant with flowers. In Ellen Terry's old bedroom upstairs Barney had found her shabby little copy of "The Imitation of Christ." "Look at this!" And Edy read on the fly-leaf:

> No funeral gloom, my dears, when I am gone;
> Corpse-gazings, tears, black raiment, graveyard grimness.
> Think of me as withdrawn into the dimness,
> Yours still, you mine. Remember all the best
> Of our past moments, and forget the rest.
> And so, to where I wait, come gently on.

Under these lines by William Allingham was written: "I should wish my children, relatives and friends to observe this when I die. E. T."

Here was a definite direction of great value to Edy in this hour. The news bureau had now become a stage-manager's office, in which arrangements were being made for a series of ceremonies. Edy now knew from her mother how they were to be conducted, and what was to be their character. Her brother, who had returned at the news of his mother's death, undertook to carry out the plans in London. A few intimate friends, and a few villagers alone were allowed to gaze at Juliet on the bier. I was instructed by Edy to copy the inscription in "The Imitation of Christ" and affix it to the gate that all who passed by might know that there was to be no funeral gloom in their grief at Ellen Terry's death. A friend in Tenterden had the happy idea of having it printed, and displayed elsewhere, so that those last wishes might become more widely known. In the big living-room of the farm, Olive and a band of helpers set to work to transform a piece of shimmering gold material that a young actor had brought back from India for a dress for Ellen Terry, years ago, into a pall. We began picking rosemary and other sweet herbs of grace to carpet the floor of Smallhythe church where the first ceremony was to take place. These obsequies were to shine with the radiance of Ellen Terry. Candles and candlesticks were collected. Let there be light and colour everywhere.

I sat some time meditating over that little copy of "Tommy Kempy," as I did not know then that Ellen Terry affectionately called him. The lines scored were a revelation to me, such a revelation as people had in other times when, after the death of some fine gallant or beautiful lady, they discovered that underneath their finery they had always worn a hair shirt.

Before the sun went down that evening, Miss Margaret Winser, a talented sculptor, living in the neighbourhood, came down to Smallhythe with an assistant, and took a cast of the beautiful hands and the beautiful face. Then we took farewell of the temple, stammering out incoherent words of love and gratitude and grief. We left Edy to take her farewell alone, and in the hall outside I heard her crying like a child. She had become the tiny tot of Harpenden days again, bringing the darling mother little bunches of flowers from the garden with the assurance: "There's lots more."

The next time I went into the cool, spacious room, the bier was empty. Juliet, with the jasmine between her fingers, which death, like some medieval sculptor, had touched with beauty, was in her coffin, "slender as a canoe, and carpentered as carefully, its ends delicately pointed, with one that arched like a prow, more proudly than the other." So it looked to the observant eyes of Velona Pilcher, who adds that this shapely vessel was designed by Ellen Terry's son. But I noted only that the room looked like a *chapelle ardente,* with the guardian candle-flames burning bright round the coffin, and the flowers shining out of dim corners. Later I saw the lustrous pall in place, and remember taking "Pax" out of my missal and pinning it to the pall beneath Ellen Terry's crucifix which Edy had laid there. Those three burnished gold letters on a scrap of parchment were like the peace one desired for Ellen Terry, the peace of eternal light. We were all watchers still. From the night of July the 22nd to the morning of July 24th when the coffin was carried up the road into Smallhythe church, we watched. The candle-flames flickered during one midnight watch on the fair head of "little Teddy," one of the beloved grandchildren, as well as on the now white head of his father, the "little Teddy" of a remote past.

The first funeral wreath was brought from Tenterden by a chauffeur who had often driven the car Ellen Terry hired. "We all hope it's gay enough," he said, looking proudly at the variegated flowers. And soon that bright wreath was joined by others. From North and South, from East and West they came, until all the gardens of England seemed to be massed on the lawn outside Ellen Terry's house.

That was not the only strange sight in Smallhythe on July the 24th, 1928, the day of Ellen Terry's funeral. The road for miles was packed with cars, moving as slowly as in a busy street in a great city. On the grass bank skirting the hundred yards of road between the house and the church were clustered groups of photographers. The green pastures were not separated from the road by the familiar hedges and oak palings, but by an unfamiliar wall of men and women, the men in summer flannels with coloured ties, the women in gay summer dresses. "No

346

funeral gloom, my dears, when I am gone." The spectators had remembered that as well as the mourners who followed in the wake of the coffin in its shimmering gold veil.

Another strange sight, exquisitely strange, was to be seen as the coffin was borne up the steps into the church. There, outside the porch was a guard of honour fit for one who had been simple in her life, and loved beauty in her ways. The men from the fields had left their work for an hour, and had come to the church with their tools—haymakers with their rakes and pitchforks, shepherds with their crooks and sheep-dogs—and were standing there, in the attitudes of good and faithful toilers of the earth, resting from their labours.

Inside the church, no dirge, but hymns of praise, hymns Ellen Terry had loved, and from the little choir rose a voice that she had loved, the voice of her friend and neighbour, Lady Maud Warrender, who opened each verse of the old song of praise, "Ye watchers and ye holy ones," with an exaltation inspiring us to think of resurrection, not of death. The reader of the lesson exalted us too with the praise of famous men:

> Such as found out musical tunes,
> And recited verses in writing.

"All things bright and beautiful." The feeling that Ellen Terry was inspiring every one to substitute these things for funeral gloom persisted. The town of Tenterden was beautiful, if not bright, as we strange mourners in our festal clothes drove through it in cars, following Ellen Terry on her last journey to London, the journey that, living, she had taken so many times. Quiet was the beauty here. All business had been abandoned. The shops were closed; the sun shone on houses darkened by drawn blinds. The people stood silent and motionless in the High Street, as if they were observing the Two Minutes Remembrance on Armistice Day. Not a sound except the muffled peal of the big church bells.

Our destination was Golders Green. A great crowd had collected outside the crematorium, a crowd not of curious sightseers, but of sympathetic friends. They were of all classes and all ages, but the majority were poor and old.

The songs of praise rose again in this burning temple. The clear blackbird voices of boy choristers piped out, "All Things Bright and Beautiful," just before all that was left of that bright and beautiful thing, Ellen Terry, was committed to the flames.

Late that night, the slender boat-shaped coffin was taken to St Paul's Church, Covent Garden, and now it was very light, for within was only a silver casket, containing some silvery dust.

347

Smallhythe, big in the news of the world for a day, is very small again, deserted and obscure. St Paul's, Covent Garden, the barn-like church that Inigo Jones built, and lesser men rebuilt after the fire, is now the place where men and women have gathered to mourn Ellen Terry without funeral gloom. The work in that humble stage-manager's office at Smallhythe is bearing fruit. This last ceremony is beautifully "produced." It does the Craigs credit, the audience of actors and actresses and playgoers agree. As in Smallhythe Church the floor is carpeted with sweet-smelling herbs. A dramatist comes in with boxes of carnations and roses, and patterns the greenish-gray carpet with red and white and yellow. Distinguished actors are showing distinguished actresses into their seats. The light from the six tall candles in their tall candlesticks, transported from Smallhythe, flickers again on the gold veil. But there is nothing here of such rare beauty as that guard of honour from the fields.

The players stream out into the sunlight. The photographers snap the ones with famous names. Of one celebrity, in full Ascot rig, it was said that she "had exceeded Ellen Terry's instructions."

How Ellen Terry would have enjoyed it all!

It comes naturally to most of us to make such assumptions about a dead friend or relative. Very often they are coloured by our own conception of the dead person's character, temperament and tastes. Very often they are stultified by our failure to recognise that what the living are known to have liked or disliked throws no light at all on what might be their attitude, if dead, they could communicate with us and express their desires. After the publication of the Shaw-Terry correspondence, some friends and relatives of Ellen Terry's said, with a great show of confidence that they were able to judge: "How she would have abhorred this!" I have already produced a considerable amount of evidence that Ellen Terry was quite aware that death makes a difference. She could conceive that what is undesirable, and even offensive in life, may not be so after death, and with great wisdom refrained from the destruction of letters and documents of intrinsic value. My conviction that, anyhow, assumptions about what "Ellen Terry would have wished" are as arrogant as they are unsafe, ought perhaps to deter me even from this harmless little assumption that she would have delighted in her funeral ceremonies. But here is a letter she wrote after Henry Irving's funeral which justifies me to some extent:

My thoughts and remembrance. Thank you. It is just as you say. *Such* a passing! He hated illness and weakness. Finished his work and then went quietly away—with *distinction* to the last. The hubbub is glorious to me. He would have loved it! And I do for him. E.T.

So perhaps we were not wrong in loving, for Ellen Terry, the hubbub after her death.

When it had subsided, after that final ceremony at St Paul's, Covent Garden, her son and daughter brought the silver casket, the work of Paul Cooper, great silversmith, good friend, a friend dear to mother and children alike, from the deserted church to Edy's flat which overlooks the churchyard. We had converted a small room there into an oratory, had it blessed, and erected an altar on which the casket stood for over a year, a sanctuary lamp burning night and day. It was not until August 1929 that the negotiations for obtaining a "faculty" for placing the ashes in St Paul's, Covent Garden, and erecting a memorial tablet, were concluded. Such are the law's delays, ecclesiastical as well as civil.

During that year, while Ellen Terry was kept waiting, her husband James Carew, showed his devotion to her by sending flowers for the oratory every week.

Sir John Martin Harvey unveiled the tablet in August 1929. Like the casket, its setting was the work of Paul Cooper. The niche in which the casket stands is enclosed by a plain bronze grille of beautiful workmanship. The canopy and base of the monument are in dark green marble. On the base is the concise epitaph, graved in austere Roman capitals: "Ellen Terry. Actress. Born 1848. Died 1928." When the design was submitted to the ecclesiastical authorities, they made the characteristically Protestant stipulation that the base must be constructed in such a way that it would be impossible to place flowers on it. Perhaps it was feared that Ellen Terry's dust would be venerated like that of a saint. And indeed Ellen Terry was a saint, although her sanctity was not of the orthodox kind. She worked miracles in her lifetime by her kindness, constantly turning hearts of stone into hearts of flesh. Among the hundreds of letters Edy received after her death there are few in which some kind word or deed which had a lasting influence is not recorded. A young actor who had been in the cast of "Romeo and Juliet" when Ellen Terry played the Nurse wrote that her "kindness was as real and impartial and personal as the sunlight, but it was a human sun that seemed only to see the things one wanted seen. The rest werent there, or it didnt matter in the least if they were. If that is not theological charity, what is? It is the greatest virtue, and only saints and very great artists can possess it. It makes life possible."

Another letter from one who had known her from childhood, one of the "Casella girls," who were on terms of the closest intimacy with her, speaks of Ellen Terry as "the most generally beloved being of her time. No wonder either, for she was endowed by Nature with the most precious gifts that she has to bestow: genius, beauty, grace, charm, *goodness* in the true sense of the word, nobility of character without a trace of jealousy in her disposition, sympathy with all, always denying herself to help others. I could go on enumerating her virtues for ever, and withal the sunniest and most charming disposition that can be imagined."

"It is like a light going out," wrote Granville-Barker, when he heard the news of her death. "It had burned long and brightly, and had given everything it came near brightness, and some of its beauty."

"Whenever I had the honour of meeting her, I used to think: 'Merrie England is here, is actual, not a mere fable! Here it is, visible and audible!' She was indeed a wondrous creature. And how she would laugh at me for trying to describe her to you, her daughter!" (Max Beerbohm.)

"She seemed to me the embodiment of all the loveliest and highest qualities of humanity," wrote one of her oldest friends who had known her in all the vicissitudes of her life, and seen her stand the tests of joy and success, sorrow and failure alike. "She had beauty, grace and genius, but more wonderful still was her heart! It was because she was all glorious *within* that she radiated happiness wherever she went."

Another friend recalled that when her mother, her constant companion, whom she tenderly loved, died, and she was plunged into great darkness and bitterness of spirit, Ellen Terry had brought her light and sweetness, with the simple words: "Think of your mother as if she were in the next room to you, only with the door shut."

Many people thought that Ellen Terry's ashes ought to have found a resting place in Westminster Abbey. A petition was in fact drawn up, and supported by eminent members of Ellen Terry's profession and other men and women of mark. When they discovered that the petition was not likely to be granted, they, perhaps wisely, dropped it. An allusion in the press to official opposition to Ellen Terry's burial in the Abbey inspired the following letter which may be deemed an index of popular feeling on the subject. It was written to Ellen Terry's daughter by a playgoer, who was an absolute stranger to her:

I must write a line to express my sympathy and indignation at the incident reported in today's *Express*. I have a large acquaintance at Bournemouth among the most intellectual here, and we all expected that your mother would have been buried in Westminster Abbey—the greatest actress who ever lived at any time in this, or any other country. My brother, who was M.P. for Cambridge for 25 years, saw her in every part she played, and his opinion is the same as mine. We all thought she would have a public funeral worthy of her supreme position in the supreme ranks of genius. Every charlatan of a politician, financier, and profiteer is buried in Westminster Abbey. Is not Darwin there? Whereas the proper Valhalla for him was the monkey-house at the Zoo.

And now the greatest actress and artist, and probably the greatest woman, taken all round, who ever lived is excluded!

Every one who ever saw her act, is seething with indignation that the honour she so much more than deserved has not been bestowed on her.

I have many French and Italian friends, and they share the universal amazement and indignation.

CHAPTER V

IN MEMORIAM

(1928-1932)

§ 1

THERE had been so many signs at Ellen Terry's death of the veneration in which she was held, that when a memorial to her was initiated, it was natural to expect that it would be enthusiastically supported. It was true that only a small remnant of the public who had seen her act in her great days survived, and that the beauty she had created nightly on the stage for a long period had become a dim memory. But it was imagined that the legend of her greatness in the English theatre, of the love she had inspired, of the dignity of her public life, of her generosity, courage, and sincerity, of all those things which made her a remarkable woman, apart from her services to the stage, would suffice to inspire the English people to do their duty by her after her death. It is generally agreed, I believe, that it is a duty to honour the great dead, to commemorate their lives and their achievements in such a way that they shall not be totally forgotten. "Imperfectly, not perfectly done, this duty must always be. But not done at all, not remembered as a thing that God and Nature and the Eternal Voices do require to be done—alas, we see too well what kind of world that ultimately makes for us."

So a memorial to Ellen Terry was initiated in a spirit of optimism which was very quickly damped by the poor response to an appeal for contributions to a memorial fund. As a member of the Executive Committee appointed to collect the sum required, I had proofs that even among those who had professed great admiration for Ellen Terry in her lifetime (her archives at Smallhythe contain many written professions of such admiration, and also of gratitude for acts of generous kindness), there was a strange indifference to her now that she had left the world's stage.

Ellen Terry had made Smallhythe famous for a week or two by dying there. This may account for the suggestion, made first, publicly, by *The Daily Mail*, that her house, which had been revealed by the many pictures of it in the press at the time it was in the limelight, as a very fine old timbered farmhouse of the Tudor period, should be acquired as a national possession, and preserved as a memorial to her. The suggestion was adopted by a preliminary committee, formed to consider various plans for giving some permanent expression to England's gratitude for her work and her life. A prospectus was drawn up, outlining a scheme for a memorial at Smallhythe, and sent to eminent men and women in Great Britain and the United States, with an invitation to join a General Committee to be appointed for the purpose of appealing to the public for funds. The response to this invitation was encouraging. Many people with famous names joined the General Committee. But apparently some of them had not read the prospectus and were not in the least interested in the scheme. A few even criticised it later on as impracticable. There was nothing abnormal in this; there are defeatists on all general committees. Still I think that the Ellen Terry Memorial general committee had an unusually large number.

Its first meeing was held at the Globe Theatre in December 1928. The few of the famous members who attended offered no criticism of the scheme in its general outlines, and no alternative scheme was suggested. No alternative scheme was suggested either by people outside the committee, who excused themselves from supporting the memorial at Smallhythe on the ground that it did not appeal to them. They were in favour of honouring dear Ellen Terry of course, but not in this way. "And what an absurdly large sum you are trying to raise! As if you could hope to get anything like £15,000!" I remembered the "trifles" of £100 generous Ellen Terry had so frequently contributed to any charity in need. Now people, far more wealthy than she ever was, were talking in this niggardly way about her memorial.

The Executive Committee, appointed by the ornamental General Committee, got to work (at least about two or three of them did, which I believe is also not abnormal) and drew up a prospectus, more definite than the brief one, privately circulated among eminent folk, on which to issue the appeal for contributions. The main objects of the memorial scheme were to acquire Ellen Terry's house, and endow it with an income sufficient to keep it in repair and pay the salary of a custodian; to adapt the rooms to the purpose of a memorial museum and library, with the exception of Ellen Terry's bedroom which was to be kept as it was in her life-time; and to adapt the barn adjacent to the house to the purpose of a theatre, where it would be possible to commemorate the anniversary of Ellen Terry's death at Smallhythe by a dramatic performance every year. The cost of carrying out the scheme adequately was carefully gone into by expert advisers, and £15,000 was rather below than above their estimate.

Then the defeatist party went about saying that £15,000 was a fantastic sum to pay for a farmhouse even if it was a 16th century farmhouse. There was the prospectus, stating clearly that the bulk of the sum was to be devoted to an adequate Endowment Fund, that the heirs of Ellen Terry had no wish to profit by the Memorial, and were willing to sell the house for its purpose, at the lowest market price, but apparently, like the preliminary prospectus, the one issued with the appeal was never read.

During the first months of 1929 when subscriptions were dribbling in, chiefly from obscure people, who gave generously according to their means, Edith Craig, to whom the house had been left, perhaps because Ellen Terry had a prescience of its destiny, began building up the memorial alone. She had a cottage of her own, which her mother had given her in her life-time, to keep up, and part of the flat she shared with two friends in London. By the terms of the will, she had inherited part of her mother's small fortune, but less than the other beneficiaries, Gordon Craig, Elena, and their children. The value of the house at Smallhythe was no doubt reckoned as equivalent to the difference in the shares. Ellen Terry's will, by the way, was well-considered, and very shrewd. Edy would not have been so badly off if she had sold the house. But she had no intention of selling it except for the purpose of the Memorial, and determined to keep it up at her own expense until the promoters of the Memorial scheme could buy it.

The revolution in her life, caused by her mother's death, and the strain of her arduous work as one of the executors of the will, had affected Edy's health. She was neither young nor robust when she began work on her mother's shrine. But she had inherited some of her mother's immense vitality, and gay optimism. In these days I was often reminded of a passage in *A La Recherche du Temps Perdu* in which Marcel Proust describes the change in his mother after his grandmother died:

... Ce n'etait plus ma mère que j'avais sous les yeux, mais ma grand'-mère. Comme dans les familles royales et ducales, à la mort du chef, le fils prend son titre, et le duc D'Orleans, le prince de Tarente, ou le prince de Laumes, devient roi de France, duc de la Tremoille, duc de Guermantes, ainsi souvent, par un avènement d'un autre ordre, et de plus profonde origine, le mort saisit le vif qui devient son successeur, ressemblant le continuateur de sa vie interrompue.

Peut-être le grand chagrin qui suit chez une fille, telle qu' était maman, la mort de sa mère, ne fait-il que briser plus tôt la chrysalide, hâter la métamorphose et l'apparition d'un être qu'on porte en soi, et qui, sans cette crise qui fait brûler les étapes, et sauter d'un seul coup les périodes, ne fait survenu que plus lentement.

Peut-être dans le regret de celle qui n'est plus, y-a-t-il une espèce de suggestion qui finit par amener sur nos traits des similitudes que nous avons d'ailleurs en puissance, et y-a-t-il surtout arrêt de notre activité plus particulièrement individuelle.... que nous craignions pas, tant que vivait l'être bien-aimé, d'exercer, fût-ce à ses depens, et qui contrebalançait le caractère que nous tenions exclusivement de lui.

Une fois qu'elle est morte, nous aurions scrupule à être autre, nous n'admirons plus que ce qu'elle était, ce que nous étions déjà, mais mêlé à autre chose, et ce que nous allons être désormais uniquement....

Enfin dans ce culte de regret pour nos morts, nous vouons une idolâtrie à ce qu'ils ont aimé.

There you have the explanation of the measure of success the Ellen Terry memorial has achieved during the four years which have passed since her death.

While the Memorial Committee, disappointed at the result of the appeal, which brought in only a little over £1,000 during 1929, accepted the situation, and with the exception of the Honorary Treasurer, Lady Maud Warrender, whose zeal never flagged, made no effort to devise some other means of raising money, Edy began carrying out the objects of the scheme in the only way she could, a makeshift way, imposed on her by her slender financial resources. By the summer of 1929, she had transformed the house into a memorial museum, displaying in two rooms the interesting theatre relics in Ellen Terry's collection, with additions from her own, and had arranged for the admission of visitors. The Barn, which one croaker on the Memorial Committee had come to see (for that he deserves an honourable mention, since some of his colleagues have never visited Smallhythe to this day), and pronounced impossible for the purposes of a theatre until at least £1,000 had been spent on its restoration and conversion, was ready for a performance on the first anniversary of Ellen Terry's death. There were holes in the thatched roof, gaps in the timbered walls; the audience, invited to take part in the commemoration of a great actress, sat on rough benches on a beaten earth floor. But the improvised stage, because it was improvised by a Craig, did not look like a makeshift. The programme had been hastily arranged, but it was of rare quality. Jean Sterling Mackinlay sang and Rae Robertson played with inspiration to the glorious memory of Ellen Terry. Edy's gallantry and devotion produced results. Visitors to Ellen Terry's humble shrine were deeply moved, and went away to talk of it to their friends. There has been a steady increase in the number of pilgrims every year. The Barn theatre has been improved by the addition of chairs presented by people to whom this part of the Memorial scheme particularly appealed. The roof has been re-thatched. The gaping walls have been patched up. Every July, since that first anniversary per-formance in 1929, members of Ellen Terry's profession, sensible of the lustre her career shed on their calling, have come to Smallhythe to take part in a programme of scenes from Shakespeare. On a modest scale the Ellen Terry memorial scheme is working, but until this year (1932) it was working entirely at Edith Craig's expense.

In this situation, the Memorial Committee came to the conclusion that they ought not to conserve the fund raised by public subscription, and continue the appeal as before for an indefinite period. The fund had not yet reached a figure making the purchase and endowment of Ellen Terry's house possible. It was decided to enter into an agreement with Edith Craig, whereby she would give the Memorial Trustees, recently appointed, an option to purchase the house of Smallhythe within the next ten years; and further, undertake to maintain it, and conduct it for the benefit of visitors, as before, but now, assisted by a yearly contribution from the income of the fund. This cheese-paring scheme was perhaps the only one that could be adopted, but while it has eased Edith Craig's problems, I am anxious to make clear that it has not solved them. The Memorial as it exists today is still more or less a makeshift for that national memorial we had such high hopes in 1928 of erecting on a firm and permanent basis. We are still honouring Ellen Terry on the cheap.

§ 2

MEANWHILE another monument to Ellen Terry, of a different kind, has come into being, and this also owes it existence to her daughter. Aware that her mother, because her genius was a quality of the mind, still lived in her letters, although as an actress she was dead, except in the memory of a diminishing band of elderly people, Edy planned the publication of a volume of letters to various correspondents. She knew that this was the best way to prove that Ellen Terry, the artist, had amounted to something, because Ellen Terry, the woman, had amounted to something. The nature of what she had amounted to had been mis-represented in the trifling biographies written in her life-time, in criti-cisms of her performances on the stage, in many pretty and romantic legends. Even her own autobiography had not sufficed to blow away the notion that she was a charming scatter-brain, who had lived, as she had acted, without much wisdom. The affectionate, but rather patronising label, "A great dear," had stuck; it seemed likely that if she were remem-bered at all, it would be on account of her lovableness. And indeed she was lovable, but for deeper reasons than was generally supposed. Why she should be loved and praised from age to age, Edy thought that her letters

356

would show. She guessed from the large number of letters from Bernard Shaw, found in her mother's archives after her death, that he might be able to contribute some of the letters that had inspired his, to her collection, and wrote, telling him of the volume she was planning. She threw out the suggestion that as a friend of her mother's, and as her most distinguished living correspondent, he was the man to write the preface. Bernard Shaw replied, on a postcard, that he had hundreds of letters from Ellen Terry, and that when he had looked them out he would bring them. He called at our flat shortly afterwards with his collection, neatly arranged in chronological order, and docketed. It was then that the possibility of publishing the complete Shaw-Terry correspondence was first discussed.

The plan appealed to Edy. She could not help seeing that her mother's letters would gain a great deal from being illuminated by Shaw's. Nor, being a practical person, was she indifferent to the fact that their addition, constituting a correspondence with very few parallels in literature, would mean the production of a book likely to have a far bigger circulation than the one she had contemplated. She had formed the opinion from reading Shaw's letters, which was confirmed when she read Ellen Terry's letters to him, that the correspondence was not one revealing those intimate secrets of the emotional life which ought to be protected from the public gaze. She knew that the only objection her mother had raised, when writing her autobiography, to the inclusion of other letters from Shaw than the one she selected for publication, was that there were references in them to Henry Irving, "which ought not to be published so soon after his death." Twenty-four years had now passed since Irving's death. Edy, who had loved and admired him, "this side idolatry," as much as anyone, was convinced moreover that, while individual letters from Shaw might contain severe criticism of Irving, the whole correspondence was a vindication of his character and genius, and a fresh confirmation of her mother's loyalty to him.

Edy would not however enter into negotiations for the publication of the correspondence without consulting her brother. The impression, created by Gordon Craig in his biography, that she was antagonistic to him, is very far from the truth. He had no more honest champion of his great talents, and she had always taken with great good humour his masculine contempt for her own. The copyright of her mother's letters was her property. She was not under the necessity of obtaining her brother's consent to the publication of the letters to Shaw, or of any others. But she desired his consent, for many reasons. One was that she did not want this literary monument to her mother to be the occasion of any undignified controversy. Her brother's notorious animosity to Shaw, who was a sort of "King Charles's Head" to him—he could not write on any subject without introducing the head—made her resolute that the correspondence should not be published under conditions which would provoke a fresh outburst of this animosity.

Gordon Craig at his sister's request read his mother's letters to Shaw, and was not impressed by them. He did not think that they were worth publishing on their merits. Moreover, he had a touching belief that no one by writing, least of all herself, could add to her fame, although all fame depends ultimately on the written word. The fame of deeds is more insubstantial and transitory than the fame of records of them, and Iliads are more enduring monuments than Parthenons. He raised other objections to the publication of the whole correspondence; but, largely I believe owing to his respect for the opinion of Max Beerbohm, who advised him to reconsider them, he came round. At any rate he discussed the publication quite complaisantly, speculating whether the letters would not be more commercially valuable after Shaw's death, and wrote to his sister asking that a letter from Shaw criticising his production of "The Vikings" should be suppressed. Apparently he had forgotten that his mother had already made public the substance of that letter in her autobiography. But Edy excluded the letter all the same.

Shaw, once convinced of the advisability of the publication of the complete correspondence, and he was not immediately convinced, as we shall see, took the same line as Edy. He insisted on Gordon Craig's consent, which was given at last formally, if grudgingly, in a letter to Shaw in October 1930. Within Shaw's history of the battle over the book, given below, is a history of the Craigs and of their relations with their mother, which is of great psychological interest. I am very grateful to Shaw for allowing me to reproduce it here. It was first printed in *The Observer* on November 8, 1931. Gordon Craig's position as the chivalrous son who had fought in vain to prevent this outrage, the publication of a correspondence which threw new light on the beauty, goodness and wisdom of his mother, was by that time so firmly established that even this masterly assault failed to smash it. Its repetition here will, I hope, administer the *coup de grâce*.

Shaw had been accused, in Gordon Craig's preface to his biography of Ellen Terry, of blind vanity and jealousy, and of insulting the dead. His method of dealing with the accusation was to probe to the hidden roots from which it had sprung:

Craig flew away from the nest the moment his wings were fully fledged; and he saw very little of his mother afterwards. And he was perfectly right. He had to save his soul alive. Make no mistake about it: Ellen Terry, with all her charm and essential amiability, was an impetuous, overwhelming, absorbing personality. She could sweep a thousand people away in a big theatre; so you can imagine what she could do with a sensitive boy in a small house. It was not until he had put the seas between them that he himself developed an impetuous and charming personality. What makes this book so tragically moving—for if you disregard the rubbish about me, which is neither here nor there, it is a poignant human document—is his desperate denial of the big woman he ran away from, and his assertion of the "little mother" he loved. He still resents the great Ellen Terry, the woman who would have swallowed him up if he had stayed within her magnetic hold, so intensely that he is furious with me because I did not tear up her letters and stamp them and her into the earth, so that the world would never have known her.

In letting that correspondence of mine with Ellen Terry be published, I made a revelation of that side of her character he suffered from; and for that he will never forgive me. There is also the complication that I am the ally of his sister, Edith Craig, the Edy of the correspondence. Now if you read the account of Edy's childhood which Ellen Terry wrote to me, and compare it with what Craig says in his book, you will see that Edy was unsympathetic to her mother in her early years because she was developing her powers of resistance to this domestic tornado. Edy finally got the upper hand, and so lost her fear of her mother, and with it her hatred of her. The word is a hard one, but children do really hate their parents in their struggle for independence. She became the champion of the great Ellen Terry, and had no patience with "Nelly." That is why the brother and sister are at loggerheads over the publication of the correspondence, and why I, caught between the fell incensed points of these mighty opposites, am getting more kicks than ha'pence from the man's side. Edy wont let me hit back. Everything that could possibly hurt Teddy is taken from my hand, although his most furious blows hit her, and hurt her, as they cannot hurt me.

To many people I am a repellent person with an odious character. One of my professions is the profession of critic, a sort of literary gangster whose business it is to put my victims on the spot; and the more skilfully and accurately I do it, the less they like it. Craig is under no obligation to like me. His mother did not like me at first: quite the contrary. And then, consider Craig's very odd profession. He has presented himself to the world, and to some extent conquered it, in the capacity of a Thwarted Genius.

All geniuses are thwarted in this world of commonplace. Craig was no more thwarted than Charles Ricketts, who died the other day: the noble and generous Ricketts, who always dealt *en grand seigneur,* a natural aristocrat as well as a genuine and devoted artist. Some of the work Ricketts did for me would have made a great reputation for a German artist. He got neither praise nor pence for it here. Look at the other men whose work in the theatre has been associated with mine: Paul Shelving, Norman Wilkinson, Albert Rutherston, Granville-Barker. Look at Edith Craig herself, who under conditions that would thwart any genius, if it were thwartable, has not only produced many interesting plays, but decorated them with her own scene-designs and costumes as well.

There was nothing to prevent Gordon Craig from doing what they did, except that if he had, he would no longer have been a Thwarted Genius. But do not conclude that Craig has been of no use. The people who do the jobs, who are dexterous enough to adapt themselves to circumstances, however desperate, and yet can produce a presentable result—people like myself, for instance—are the curse of the theatre, because they accept its poverty and insecurity and subjection to commercial considerations, instead of going on permanent strike, like Craig. To him they are artistic blacklegs. I am very well pleased that he should keep on reminding people that such a thing as a model performance of a play today is quite impossible.

Craig was buried at the old Lyceum for years, with the personality of Irving absorbing anything that his mother had left; and when he ran away from Irving too, he was left floundering in the nineteenth century instead of looking forward to the twentieth. That is why he is known now mainly as a theatrical antiquary who writes very charmingly about his hobby. But he learnt one lesson from me, and one only. I had pointed out that all progress depends on the man who will not listen to reason. Craig has never listened to reason, and I dont want him to begin, as he does very good work outside the theatre, and is a useful agitator for better conditions in it.

I have been asked whether the statements about me, tucked into the folder of Craig's book, are true. Technically and literally they are not. They are a string of flat whoppers. I have his written consent to the publication of the letters. He not only consents to the publication, but explicitly gives his word not to do what he has done in his book. But do not get virtuously indignant. His consent was extorted by circumstances, and his heart was not in his promise. I did not blame him, for I knew my man; and my object in refusing to allow my letters to be published without his assent was to make it impossible for him to attack his sister, and denounce the publication as an outrage. I guessed that he would be unable to resist attempting it, and I guessed right. But I shall not pretend to mount the moral high horse at his expense; for he was not on the spot, and does not know what really happened. There was a change of attitude on my part which no doubt misled him.

When Ellen Terry died, Edith Craig thought that a volume of her letters might be compiled for publication; and she wrote to me, as to other friends, to ask if I had any letters. I replied that I had hundreds. I had never read the correspondence as a whole; and I recollected it at a distance of thirty years. But after I had sent her my letters from Ellen Terry, Edith did read it as a whole, and at once formed the opinion, which has received such overwhelming confirmation from the reviewers of the book, that it brought her mother to life in her real character, and in all her strength, with a force and vividness which made it a duty to her memory to publish the correspondence in full.

At first I was almost as stupid as Craig. I remembered only the very intimate and affectionate character of the letters, and declared their immediate publication impossible. But as it was clear that some day or other they would be published, and I had better leave a document to explain them, I wrote an explanation for posterity. This was entitled: "Preface to be attached to the Correspondence of Ellen Terry and Bernard Shaw, should it ever be published," and was marked "Very Private." I sent a proof of it to Gordon Craig and another to Edith Craig. It is now before the public as the preface to the correspondence. Gordon Craig and his family are none the worse for it; and I will give a penny to any one who can discover in it the faintest disparagement of his father, Edward Godwin, whom I never met, and whose production of a Greek play at the old Circus in Argyll Street many years ago, pleased me very much.

The effect on Edith Craig was that she made up her mind that the preface should be published as well as the letters. I was perplexed, and showed the proofs to a small court of honor, consisting of two persons, one of them a famous soldier, and the other a lady, the head of a religious house, much respected by both of us. Without the letters, the preface suggested to them only a correspondence that should not be published. I accepted their verdict; but Edith Craig remained unshaken. Presently legal questions arose. Ellen Terry's executors had to realize her estate for the benefit of Edith Craig, Gordon Craig and his children. My letters and Ellen Terry's copyrights were sold; and the assignee of the copyrights announced his intention of publishing Ellen Terry's letters by themselves if he could not induce me to consent to the publication of mine with them.

Under this pressure I consented to the publication of a limited edition at a high price, for the benefit of the Ellen Terry Memorial Institute which Edith Craig and Lady Maud Warrender were establishing at Smallhythe in Kent, and which could be financed by no other means. It was the preparation of this edition which led to my reading the correspondence as a whole for the first time; and it converted me at once to Edith Craig's opinion. I saw that she had been right all through, and that Gordon Craig's notion that the letters should have been destroyed appeared very much as if he had reproached King George for allowing his grandmother's letters to be given to the world.

When I make up my mind, I do not make it up by halves, and I agreed that my hesitations had been absurd, and that the limited edition should be followed by an ordinary unlimited trade edition at ordinary prices. But I made it a condition that Craig should be consulted, and he, swearing he would ne'er consent, consented, as has been seen. I proposed that he should write a preface; and he entertained this until he learnt that the proposal was suggested by me, whereupon he repudiated it with vehemence, declaring that it was a trap for him. He was treated by me throughout with inhumanly scrupulous correctness, and by his sister with anxious consideration; for she made me omit everything written by me that could possibly wound him.

To sum it all up, I dont think the public will be misled by Craig's grouch against me. After all, I wounded that sacred thing, a boy's idolatry of the first great actor he ever saw. And his psychopathic hatred of 'the great

361

Ellen Terry' will be forgiven for the sake of his romance about 'little mother Nelly.' "

The letter from Gordon Craig to which Shaw refers in this history, unimpeachably accurate in its facts, contained, besides a formal assent to the publication of the letters, an assurance that when they were published, Shaw could rely on Craig's not writing about it in the papers nor giving interviews. Nevertheless Craig gave an interview to a representative of the British United Press in Paris shortly after the appearance of the limited edition, in which he spoke with pious indignation of the man who could sink so low as to publish a woman's private letters. The genuineness of the indignation can be judged from the fact that Gordon Craig in his own book about Ellen Terry had published extracts from her private letters to him, and to her friend Graham Robertson. But I must follow Shaw's example, and refrain from mounting the high moral horse at Craig's expense. After all, he did no harm. His mother's monument stands; and I, who edited the correspondence had a small share in erecting it, feel that this is all that matters. We have in this monument, and in those other literary monuments, Ellen Terry's autobiography, and her lectures on Shakespeare, as well as in her shrine at Smallhythe, something to inspire those who come after us with the same devotion to her memory.

§ 3

Let us now praise famous men
And our fathers that begat us.
The Lord hath wrought great glory by them
Through His great power from the beginning.
Such as did bear rule in their Kingdoms,
Men renowned for their power,
Giving counsel by their understanding,
And declaring prophecies:
Leaders of the people by their counsels,
And by their knowledge of learning meet for the people.
Wise and eloquent in their instructions;
Such as found out musical tunes,
And recited verses in writing. . . .

Let us now praise Ellen Terry, simple and loving in her private life, noble and beautiful in her public ways.

SMALLHYTHE PLACE,
April 17—June 17, 1932.

INDEX

*(The plays in which Ellen Terry appeared are listed chronologically in the final note
at the end of each chapter.)*

363